Focus on Grammar 2

Irene E. Schoenberg

Focus on Grammar 2: An Integrated Skills Approach, Fifth Edition

Pearson Education, 221 River Street, Hoboken, NJ 07030

Staff credits: The people who made up the *Focus on Grammar 2, Fifth Edition* team, representing content creation, design, manufacturing, marketing, multimedia, project management, publishing, rights management, and testing, are Pietro Alongi, Rhea Banker, Elizabeth Barker, Stephanie Bullard, Jennifer Castro, Tracey Cataldo, Aerin Csigay, Mindy DePalma, Dave Dickey, Warren Fischbach, Pam Fishman, Nancy Flaggman, Lester Holmes, Gosia Jaros-White, Leslie Johnson, Barry Katzen, Amy McCormick, Julie Molnar, Brian Panker, Stuart Radcliffe, Jennifer Raspiller, Lindsay Richman, Robert Ruvo, Alexandra Suarez, Paula Van Ells, and Joseph Vella.

Text design and layout: Don Williams
Composition: Page Designs International
Project supervision: Bernard Seal
Contributing editors: Julie Schmidt and Bernard Seal

Cover image: Andy Roberts / Getty Images

Library of Congress Cataloging-in-Publication Data

A catalog record for the print edition is available from the Library of Congress.

Printed in the United States of America

ISBN 10: 0-13-411998-3
ISBN 13: 978-0-13-411998-4

25 2024

Contents

Contents (continued)

WELCOME TO
FOCUS ON GRAMMAR
FIFTH EDITION

BUILDING ON THE SUCCESS of previous editions, *Focus on Grammar* continues to provide an integrated-skills approach to engage students and help them understand, practice, and use English grammar. Centered on thematic instruction, *Focus on Grammar* combines comprehensive grammar coverage with abundant practice, critical thinking skills, and ongoing assessment, helping students accomplish their goals of communicating confidently, accurately, and fluently in everyday situations.

New in the Fifth Edition

New and Updated Content
Focus on Grammar continues to offer engaging and motivating content that appeals to learners from various cultural backgrounds. Many readings and activities have been replaced or updated to include topics that are of high interest to today's learners.

Updated Charts and Redesigned Notes
Clear, corpus-informed grammar presentations reflect real and natural language usage and allow students to grasp the most important aspects of the grammar. Clear signposting draws attention to common usage, the difference between written and spoken registers, and common errors.

Additional Communicative Activities
The new edition of *Focus on Grammar* has been expanded with additional communicative activities that encourage collaboration and the application of the target grammar in a variety of settings.

Expanded Writing Practice
Each unit in *Focus on Grammar* now ends with a structured "From Grammar to Writing" section. Supported by pre-writing and editing tasks, students engage in activities that allow them to apply the target grammar in writing.

New Assessment Program
The new edition of *Focus on Grammar* features a variety of new assessment tools, including course diagnostic tests, formative and summative assessments, and a flexible gradebook. The assessments are closely aligned with unit learning outcomes to inform instruction and measure student progress.

Revised MyEnglishLab
The updated MyEnglishLab offers students engaging practice and video grammar presentations anywhere, anytime. Immediate feedback and remediation tasks offer additional opportunities for successful mastery of content and help promote accuracy. Instructors receive instant access to digital content and diagnostic tools that allow them to customize the learning environment to meet the needs of their students.

The *Focus on Grammar* Approach

At the heart of the *Focus on Grammar* series is its unique and successful four-step approach that lets learners move from comprehension to communication within a clear and consistent structure. The books provide an abundance of scaffolded exercises to bridge the gap between identifying grammatical structures and using them with confidence and accuracy. The integration of the four skills allows students to learn grammar holistically, which in turn prepares them to understand and use English more effectively.

STEP 1: Grammar in Context integrates grammar and vocabulary in natural contexts such as articles, stories, dialogues, and blog posts. Students engage with the unit reading and theme and get exposure to grammar as it is used in real life.

STEP 2: Grammar Presentation presents the structures in clear and accessible grammar charts and notes with multiple examples of form and meaning. Corpus-informed explanations and examples reflect natural usage of the target forms, differentiate between written and conversational registers whenever appropriate, and highlight common errors to help students avoid typical pitfalls in both speaking and writing.

STEP 3: Focused Practice provides numerous and varied contextualized exercises for both the form and meaning of the new structures. Controlled practice ensures students' understanding of the target grammar and leads to mastery of form, meaning, and use.

STEP 4: Communication Practice provides practice with the structures in listening exercises as well as in communicative, open-ended speaking activities. These engaging activities provide ample opportunities for personalization and build students' confidence in using English. Students also develop their critical thinking skills through problem-solving activities and discussions.

Each unit now culminates with the **From Grammar to Writing** section. Engaging and motivating writing activities encourage students to apply grammar in writing through structured tasks from pre-writing that contain writing models to editing.

Recycling

Underpinning the scope and sequence of the *Focus on Grammar* series is practice that allows students to use target structures and vocabulary many times, in different contexts. New grammar and vocabulary are recycled throughout the book. Students have maximum exposure, leading them to become confident in using the language in speech and in writing.

Assessment

Extensive testing informs instruction and allows teachers and students to measure progress.

- **Unit Reviews** at the end of every unit assess students' understanding of the grammar and allow students to monitor their own progress.

- **Diagnostic Tests** provide teachers with a valid and reliable means to determine how well students know the material they are going to study and to target instruction based on students' needs.

- **Unit Review Tests, Mid- and End-of-Term Review Tests, and Final Exams** measure students' ability to demonstrate mastery of skills taught in the course.

- The **Placement Test** is designed to help teachers place students into one of the five levels of the *Focus on Grammar* course.

The Importance of Context

A key element of *Focus on Grammar* is presenting important grammatical structures in context. The contexts selected are most relevant to the grammatical forms being introduced. Contextualized grammar practice also plays a key role in improving fluent use of grammar in communicative contexts. It helps learners to develop consistent and correct usage of target structures during all productive practice.

The Role of Corpus

The most important goal of *Focus on Grammar* has always been to present grammar structures using natural language. To that end, *Focus on Grammar* has incorporated the findings of corpus linguistics,* while never losing sight of what is pedagogically sound and useful. By taking this approach, *Focus on Grammar* ensures that:

- the language presented reflects real, natural usage
- themes and topics provide a good fit with the grammar point and elicit the target grammar naturally
- findings of the corpus research are reflected in the syllabus, readings, charts, grammar notes, and practice activities
- examples illustrate differences between spoken and written registers, and formal and informal language
- students are exposed to common errors in usage and learn how to recognize and avoid errors in their own speech and writing

Focus on Grammar Efficacy

The fifth edition of *Focus on Grammar* reflects an important efficacy initiative for Pearson courses—to be able to demonstrate that all teaching materials have a positive impact on student learning. To support this, *Focus on Grammar* has been updated and aligned to the **Global Scale of English** and the **Common European Framework** (CEFR) to provide granular insight into the objectives of the course, the progression of learning, and the expected outcomes a learner will be able to demonstrate upon successful completion.

To learn more about the Global Scale of English, visit www.English.com.

Components

Student Books with Essential Online Resources include access codes to the course audio, video, and self-assessment.

Student Books with MyEnglishLab offer a blended approach with integration of print and online content.

Workbooks contain additional contextualized practice in print format.

Digital Teacher's Resources include printable teaching notes, GSE mapping documents, answer keys, audio scripts, and downloadable tests. Access to the digital copy of the student books allows teachers to project the pages for whole-class instruction.

FOG Go **app** allows users to access the student book audio on their mobile devices.

---

* A principal resource has been Douglas Biber et al, *Longman Grammar of Spoken and Written English*,
Harlow: Pearson Education Ltd., 1999.

The *Focus on Grammar* Unit

Focus on Grammar introduces grammar structures in the context of unified themes. All units follow a four-step approach, taking learners from grammar in context to communicative practice. Thematic units add a layer to learning so that by the end of the unit students will be able to discuss the content using the grammar points they have just studied.

STEP 1   GRAMMAR IN CONTEXT

Before You Read activities create interest and elicit students' knowledge about the topic.

Vocabulary exercises help students improve their command of English.

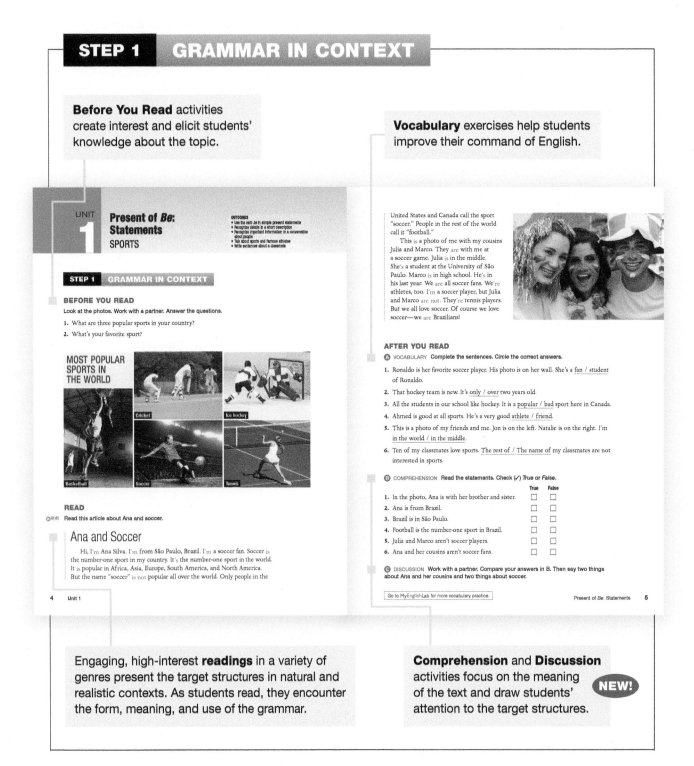

Engaging, high-interest **readings** in a variety of genres present the target structures in natural and realistic contexts. As students read, they encounter the form, meaning, and use of the grammar.

Comprehension and **Discussion** activities focus on the meaning of the text and draw students' attention to the target structures.

NEW!

STEP 2 GRAMMAR PRESENTATION

Grammar Charts present the structures in a clear, easy-to-read format.

STEP 2 GRAMMAR PRESENTATION

SIMPLE PRESENT: AFFIRMATIVE AND NEGATIVE STATEMENTS

Affirmative Statements			Negative Statements			
Subject	Verb		Subject	Do not/ Does not	Base Form of Verb	
I You* We They	eat like	noodles.	I You We They	do not don't	eat like have	noodles.
He She It	has		He She It	does not doesn't		

* *You* can be singular or plural.

ADVERBS AND EXPRESSIONS OF FREQUENCY

Adverbs of Frequency				Adverbs of Frequency with *Be*			
Subject	Adverb	Verb		Subject	Be	Adverb	
I You We They	usually almost never	cook	on holidays.	I	am	usually almost never	busy.
				You We They	are		
He She		cooks		He She	is		
It		rains.		It			

Adverbs of Frequency			Expressions of Frequency	
always	100%			every day.
almost always	↑			twice a week.
frequently			Emiko cooks	three times a month.
usually				several times a year.
often				once in a while.
sometimes	50%			
rarely / seldom				
almost never	↓			
never	0%			

88   Unit 8

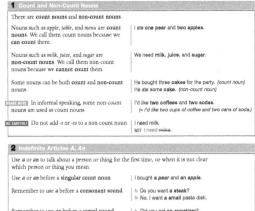

NEW! The newly designed **Grammar Notes** highlight the main point of each note, making navigation and review easier. Simple corpus-informed **explanations** and **examples** ensure students' understanding.

GRAMMAR NOTES

1 Count and Non-Count Nouns

There are **count** nouns and **non-count** nouns.

Nouns such as *apple*, *table*, and *menu* are **count** nouns. We call them count nouns because we **can** count them.	I ate **one pear** and **two apples**.
Nouns such as *milk*, *juice*, and *sugar* are **non-count** nouns. We call them non-count nouns because we **cannot** count them.	We need **milk, juice,** and **sugar**.
Some nouns can be both count and **non-count** nouns.	He bought **three cakes** for the party. *(count noun)* He ate some **cake**. *(non-count noun)*
USAGE NOTE In informal speaking, some non-count nouns are used as count nouns.	I'd like **two coffees** and **two sodas**. *(= I'd like two cups of coffee and two cans of soda.)*
BE CAREFUL! Do not add *-s* or *-es* to a non-count noun.	I need **milk**. NOT I need milks.

2 Indefinite Articles *A, An*

Use *a* or *an* to talk about a person or thing for the first time, or when it is not clear which person or thing you mean.

Use *a* or *an* before a **singular count** noun.	I bought **a pear** and **an apple**.
Remember to use *a* before a **consonant sound**.	A: Do you want **a steak**? B: No. I want **a small** pasta dish.
Remember to use *an* before a **vowel sound**.	A: Did you eat **an appetizer**? B: Yes. I had **an avocado** salad.
BE CAREFUL! Do not put *a, an*, or a number before a non-count noun.	I want **rice**. NOT I want a rice.

3 Definite Article *The*

Use *the* when it is clear which person or thing you mean.

You can use *the* before singular count nouns, plural nouns, and non-count nouns:

• singular count nouns	**The restaurant** is open. *(Both the speaker and listener know which restaurant.)*
• plural nouns	A: Do you have any napkins? B: Yes. **The napkins** are over there. *(the napkins that A asked about)*
• non-count nouns	**The soup** is delicious.

Articles with Count and Non-Count Nouns; *Some / Any*   311

NEW! **Clear signposting** provides corpus-informed notes about common usage, differences between spoken and written registers, and common errors.

PRONUNCIATION NOTE

 Regular Past Tense Endings

Regular simple past verbs end in three sounds: /d/, /t/, or /ɪd/.

• /d/	He **arrived** late.
• /t/	They **worked** at a hotel.
• /ɪd/	She **waited** for him at the airport.

Pronunciation Notes are now included with the grammar presentation to highlight relevant pronunciation aspects of the target structures and to help students understand authentic spoken English. **NEW!**

The *Focus on Grammar* Unit   **ix**

STEP 3 FOCUSED PRACTICE

Discover the Grammar activities develop students' recognition and understanding of the target structures before they are asked to produce them.

Controlled practice activities lead students to master form, meaning, and use of the target grammar.

STEP 3 FOCUSED PRACTICE

EXERCISE 1
DISCOVER THE GRAMMAR

A GRAMMAR NOTES 1, 3
A student is people watching in her psychology class. Underline all the uses of the present progressive.

I'm in my psychology class. This semester we're studying child psychology. Today's class is almost over. Julia and Maria are closing their books. Our teacher is returning a test. Bob has a smile on his face. He always gets a good grade. Ryan isn't smiling. Maybe his grade is low. Shoko is texting under the table. Jon isn't listening to the teacher. He's thinking about lunch. I can hear his stomach. It's making noises.

B Write the base form of the underlined words in A.

1. _study_   4. _____   7. _____
2. _____   5. _____   8. _____
3. _____   6. _____

EXERCISE 2 AFFIRMATIVE AND NEGATIVE STATEMENTS

GRAMMAR NOTES 1–3 Complete the sentences with the present progressive forms of the verbs in parentheses.

1. I'm tired of studying. I'm taking ___ a break and _____ around.
   (take)   (look)
2. Julie and Maria _____ games, and Bob _____ someone.
                    (play)   (text)
3. Shoko and Ryan _____ homework, and Jon _____ the paper.
                   (do)   (read)
4. It _____ outside now. People _____ umbrellas.
      (rain)   (use)
5. Some people _____ at the door. They _____ for the rain to stop.
               (stand)   (wait)
6. I _____ homework. I'm looking at the people in the library.
     (not / do)
7. It _____ now. It _____.
      (not / snow)   (rain)
8. They _____ at this moment. They _____.
         (not / study)   (relax)
9. This semester, Hugo _____ five courses. He _____ hard.
                        (take)   (work)
10. This week in psychology class, we _____ about the behavior of
                                       (learn)
    three-year-old children.

176 Unit 15

EXERCISE 2 ADVERBS OF MANNER

GRAMMAR NOTES 1–2 Complete each sentence. Change the adjectives in parentheses to adverbs.

1. The audience listened ___carefully___
                           (careful)
2. He spoke _____
             (quick)
3. Sally writes _____.
                (good)
4. They speak Spanish _____
                       (fluent)
5. He spoke _____
             (clear)
6. He drove _____
             (fast)
7. Did he drive _____?
                (dangerous)
8. Did they sing _____?
                  (bad)
9. The movie began _____
                    (slow)
10. It rained _____ last night.
              (hard)
11. She woke up _____
                 (early)
12. He stayed up _____
                  (late)

EXERCISE 3 LINKING VERBS

GRAMMAR NOTE 3 Match the beginnings of the sentences with the endings.

_c_ 1. She looks   a. awful. I hate heavy metal music.
___ 2. He looks   b. happy. I guess he gave a good talk.
___ 3. The soup tastes   c. sick. Does she have a fever?
___ 4. Her speech was   d. good. Are they baking cookies?
___ 5. This CD sounds   e. great. People clapped for a long time.
___ 6. Their home smells   f. terrible. Don't eat it.

EXERCISE 4 ADVERBS OF MANNER AND ADJECTIVES

GRAMMAR NOTES 1–3 Complete the conversations. Circle the correct answers.

1. A: How was the debate?
   B: Good. Both sides spoke good /(well).
2. A: How was the food at the reception after the debate?
   B: It tasted bad / badly.

Adverbs of Manner **395**

A variety of exercise types engage students and guide them from recognition and understanding to accurate production of the grammar structures.

Editing exercises allow students to identify and correct typical mistakes.

EXERCISE 6
EDITING

GRAMMAR NOTES 1–7
Correct the paragraph. There are eight mistakes. The first mistake is already corrected. Find and correct seven more.

                                     usually start
In the United States, people start usually the New Year holiday on New Year's Eve. Many people plans celebrations weeks in advance. My cousin always invite friends to a party. My parents usually goes to a restaurant with friends. Many people watch an event on TV just before midnight. On New Year's Day, people usually am relax from the night before. My brother watches football games on TV, and my sister is go to her friend's home. I sleeps all day long and not do anything.

Go to MyEnglishLab for more focused practice.

---

x The *Focus on Grammar* Unit

Listenings in a variety of genres allow students to hear the grammar in natural contexts.

EXERCISE 7 LISTENING

A Listen to a quiz show about animals. Read the questions. Choose the correct answers.

1. The first question asks, "Which land animal has the longest gestation period?" A gestation period is _____.
   a. the time the baby is inside its mother b. the time the baby learns to walk

2. The second question asks, "Which animal is _____?"
   a. the fattest b. the fastest

3. The third question asks, "Which animal is _____?"
   a. the loudest b. the proudest

4. The last question asks, "Which animal is _____?"
   a. the smallest b. the deadliest

B Listen again. What were the answers to the four questions in the quiz show? Choose from the words in the box.

| ant | cheetah | cow | horse | monkey | peacock |
| bear | cockroach | elephant | lion | mosquito | tiger |

Question 1: the Asian _____
Question 2: the _____
Question 3: the howler _____
Question 4: the _____

C Work with a partner. Say two statements about animals using the superlative. Your partner decides if they are true or false. Take turns.

EXAMPLE: A: The Asian elephant is the loudest land animal.
B: That's not true. The howler monkey is the loudest land animal.

The Superlative 423

Engaging **communicative activities** (conversations, discussions, presentations, surveys, and games) help students synthesize the grammar, develop fluency, and build their problem-solving skills.

EXERCISE 7 WHAT DO I REALLY MEAN?

ROLE PLAY How we speak gives a different meaning to a sentence. Work with a partner. Say the following sentences in the ways in the box or choose your own ways. Your partner guesses how you're talking.

| angrily | decisively | questioningly | sadly | sarcastically |

1. I love English grammar.
   EXAMPLE: A: I love English grammar.
   B: You're speaking sarcastically.
   A: You're right.

2. The speech was great.
3. The movie was wonderful.
4. I love to exercise.
5. It's mine, all mine.

EXERCISE 8 WHAT AM I DOING?

GAME Work in groups. Choose a verb and an adverb from the list. Act it out in front of your group. They say what you're doing.

Verbs		Adverbs	
dance	sing	badly	quietly
drive	speak	carefully	quickly
eat	walk	nervously	slowly
listen		noisily	

398 Unit 32

Go to MyEnglishLab for more communication practice.

In the **listening activities**, students practice a range of listening skills. A **new step** has been added in which partners complete an activity that relates to the listening and uses the target grammar.

NEW!

A **From Grammar to Writing** section, now in every unit, helps students to confidently apply the unit's grammar to their own writing. **NEW!**

A BEFORE YOU WRITE Read about a student's pet. Then complete the chart with information about your pet or a pet you know about. Work with a partner. Use the chart to tell your partner about the animal.

I have a beautiful parakeet. His feathers are bright green. His name is Chichi. He is two years old. He lives in a cage in my living room. Sometimes he flies around the room. Chichi can sing very beautifully. Chichi couldn't do anything when he was younger. But now he can sit on my finger and eat from my hand. He can't speak, but I'm happy about that. I tell him all my secrets, and he doesn't tell anyone. That's a wonderful quality. I love my Chichi.

	Student's Pet	My Pet
Kind of animal	bird / parakeet	
Description	green feathers	
Name	Chichi	
Age	two years old	
Home	cage	
Abilities	sit on finger / eat from hand	

B WRITE Write a paragraph about a pet. Use the paragraph in A and your chart. Use *can, can't, could,* or *couldn't.*

C CHECK YOUR WORK Read your paragraph in B. Underline *can, can't, could,* or *couldn't* and the verb that follows. Use the Editing Checklist to check your work.

Editing Checklist

Did you . . . ?
- [ ] follow *can, can't, could,* and *couldn't* with the base form of the verb
- [ ] use *can* for the present and *could* for the past
- [ ] check your spelling

D REVISE YOUR WORK Read your paragraph again. Can you improve your writing? Make changes if necessary.

158   Unit 13

Go to MyEnglishLab for more writing practice.

The **Before You Write** task helps students generate ideas for their writing assignment. They typically contain writing models for students to analyze and emulate.

In the **Write** task, students are given a writing assignment and guided to use the target grammar.

Check Your Work includes an Editing Checklist that allows students to proofread and edit their compositions.

In **Revise Your Work**, students are given a final opportunity to improve their writing.

UNIT **REVIEW**

Unit Reviews give students the opportunity to check their understanding of the target structures. Students can check their answers against the Answer Key at the end of the book. They can also complete the Review on MyEnglishLab.

UNIT 25 **REVIEW**

Test yourself on the grammar of the unit.

A Complete the sentences. Circle the correct answers.

1. Do you want to start / starting a business?
2. I hope to sell / selling my business next year.
3. She decided to return / returning to school.
4. She hopes to become / becoming a pilot.
5. She enjoys to fly / flying and to see / seeing the world.

B Complete the sentences with the correct forms of the verbs in parentheses.

1. She doesn't want _____ evenings.
   (work)
2. Her boss refuses _____ her hours.
   (change)
3. She's thinking about _____ her job and _____ back to school.
   (quit)   (go)
4. Her English keeps _____.
   (improve)

C Write sentences. Put the words in parentheses in the correct order.

1. _____
   (helping / people / she / enjoys)
2. _____
   (to / graduate / in June / expect / we)
3. _____
   (to / trying / study / are / they)
4. _____
   (avoids / and / he / eating / candy / ice cream)

D Correct the paragraph. There are six mistakes.

MyEnglishLab delivers rich online content to engage and motivate **students**.

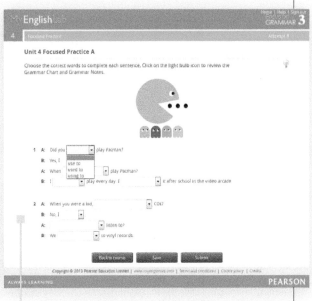

Grammar Coach videos give additional grammar presentations.

NEW!

MyEnglishLab delivers innovative teaching tools and useful resources to **teachers**.

MyEnglishLab provides students with:

- rich interactive practice in grammar, reading, listening, speaking, and writing
- immediate and meaningful feedback on wrong answers **NEW!**
- remediation activities
- grade reports that display performance and time on task

With **MyEnglishLab**, teachers can:

- view student scores by unit and activity
- monitor student progress on any activity or test
- analyze class data to determine steps for remediation and support

MyEnglishLab also provides teachers with:

- a digital copy of the student book for whole-class instruction
- downloadable assessments, including the placement test, that can be administered on MyEnglishLab or in print format
- printable resources including teaching notes, suggestions for teaching grammar, GSE mapping documents, answer keys, and audio scripts

Scope and Sequence

	UNIT	GRAMMAR	READING
PART 1 *Be*: **Present and Past**	**1** **Present of *Be*: Statements** Page 4 THEME Sports	■ Can use the verb *be* in simple present affirmative and negative statements ■ Can use contractions in speaking and writing	Personal Story: *Ana and Soccer* ■ Can determine the general meaning of a short, simple personal description with visual support
	2 **Present of *Be*: Questions** Page 15 THEME School	■ Can ask a range of *yes/no* and *wh-* questions with *be* in the simple present ■ Can construct short answers to questions in the simple present	Conversation Transcript: *Are We Late?* ■ Can understand details in a conversation in a classroom setting
	3 **Past of *Be*** Page 28 THEME A First Day	■ Can make simple past statements with *be* ■ Can ask simple past *yes/no* and *wh-* questions with *be* ■ Can use a range of common time markers for the past	Narrative: *Sarah's First Day* ■ Can identify specific information in a narrative article
PART 2 **Nouns, Adjectives, and Prepositions**	**4** **Count Nouns and Proper Nouns** Page 42 THEME Photographs and Photographers	■ Can use *a/an* with singular count nouns ■ Can use common regular and irregular nouns in the plural form ■ Can identify and use proper nouns PRONUNCIATION Plural Noun Endings	Biography: *A Photographer and a Photo* ■ Can identify specific information in a short biography
	5 **Descriptive Adjectives** Page 54 THEME Interesting and Unusual Places	■ Can place adjectives in the correct position before nouns ■ Can use the appropriate articles with adjectives that come before count nouns	Information Article: *Cappadocia, a Place of Mystery* ■ Can identify key details in an article about a location and its geographical features
	6 **Prepositions of Place** Page 63 THEME Locations	■ Can use a range of prepositions of place ■ Can use *on*, *at*, and *in* for specific addresses and locations	Magazine Article: *The American Museum of Natural History* ■ Can recognize important details in a descriptive passage

LISTENING	SPEAKING	WRITING	VOCABULARY
A conversation about athletes ■ Can identify key details about people in conversations that are conducted clearly and slowly	■ Can discuss likes and dislikes ■ Can describe something in a simple list of points	■ Can write personal information about a friend or colleague, using notes for guidance	athlete fan (n) in the middle only popular the rest of
A conversation about classmates ■ Can recognize and describe basic information about people in conversations that are conducted clearly and slowly	■ Can ask simple questions to find out more about someone ■ Can use brief, everyday expressions to ask for and give personal details	■ Can write a detailed list of questions about a familiar place	excuse me office on time right (adj) room (n)
A series of phone messages ■ Can extract key factual information from a recorded phone message	■ Can communicate in routine tasks that require simple, direct exchanges of information, such as descriptions of the weather and everyday activities	■ Can write a paragraph about a personal experience (first day of school)	afraid (of) difficult nervous principal (n) AWL surprise (n)
A lecture about art ■ Can identify important details in a brief lecture about a famous artist	■ Can give a brief presentation about people, places, or things	■ Can write short, basic descriptions of people, places, or things	all over occasion public (n) striking (adj) to be born
A telephone conversation ■ Can recognize details in a conversation about a vacation if delivered slowly and clearly	■ Can share information about known places ■ Can offer opinions and comment on statements provided by one's peers	■ Can write a detailed paragraph about a location that has personal significance	climate comfortable dry safe (adj) unusual
A recorded description ■ Can infer information about a location by recognizing important details in a recorded description	■ Can give directions to help one's peers find information on a map or brochure	■ Can write a short invitation to a party or event, including important details like time and location	app dinosaur huge interested locate AWL tour (n)

AWL = Academic Word List item

LISTENING	SPEAKING	WRITING	VOCABULARY
A product advertisement ■ Can follow the main points in a recorded advertisement	■ Can discuss what to do and where to go, and make arrangements to meet ■ Can give basic advice about everyday topics, using simple language	■ Can write an advertisement for a hotel, using a model for guidance	advice dead island nap (n) pray secret
A conversation about holidays ■ Can take detailed notes on a short conversation, listing both main ideas and supporting details	■ Can work with one's peers to prepare a short presentation about a holiday or custom ■ Can describe habits and routines	■ Can write a paragraph about a favorite holiday or tradition, using notes for support	at the stroke of culture AWL eve get together look ahead tradition AWL
A conversation about roommates ■ Can identify a speaker's likes and dislikes in a simple conversation	■ Can answer simple questions in a face-to-face survey ■ Can use a limited range of fixed expressions to describe objects, possessions, or products	■ Can write a simple email that provides personal information and asks routine questions	bother (v) easygoing messy outgoing private (adj) stay up
A conversation about dreams ■ Can identify key details in a conversation about dreams	■ Can give and elicit personal information about sleep habits, taking turns with a partner	■ Can ask for personal details in written form and use the material to write an interview	author (n) AWL guest nightmare remember unfortunately

LISTENING	SPEAKING	WRITING	VOCABULARY
A conversation about a place ■ Can provide directions to someone, based on information heard in a prior conversation	■ Can gather information about a place from a partner or group, summarize it, and present it to others	■ Can write a short description of a favorite place to shop	aquarium including (prep) indoor join luxury parking space
A conversation about possessions ■ Can identify ownership of possessions in a conversation that's delivered slowly and clearly	■ Can describe an everyday object in detail, also indicating who owns it ■ Can ask and answer questions about possessions	■ Can write a detailed paragraph that describes people in one's family	back (prep) composition excellent grade (n) AWL recognize

AWL = Academic Word List item

LISTENING	SPEAKING	WRITING	VOCABULARY
A conversation about dolphins ■ Can identify abilities of animals in a short conversation	■ Can offer one's opinions or beliefs about a common topic to a partner or group ■ Can exchange information on animals and their behavior	■ Can write a paragraph about a pet, using notes for guidance	genius intelligent AWL invent professor surprised (adj)
A conversation between a doctor and a patient ■ Can identify foods that a patient can or cannot have due to allergies or adverse reactions	■ Can tell a peer or medical professional what one can or cannot eat ■ Can communicate simple rules and regulations	■ Can write a note that describes the dietary restrictions of oneself or of others	dairy in common nutritious recipe substitute AWL

LISTENING	SPEAKING	WRITING	VOCABULARY
A telephone conversation between friends ■ Can use the information from a phone call to describe the location of people or objects	■ Can describe basic activities or events that are happening at the time of speaking	■ Can write a short narrative about what is currently happening in one's life or immediate environment	bored departure detective AWL psychologist AWL suit
A telephone conversation about family ■ Can identify a speaker's current location and describe what he or she is doing	■ Can rehearse a structured conversation with a partner, using prompts for guidance ■ Can discuss basic activities or events that are happening at the time of speaking	■ Can write a telephone conversation between friends about seeing a famous person	catch a cold cough fever scene still (adv)
A series of phone messages ■ Can identify a speaker's main purpose in a phone call or recorded message	■ Can express a variety of likes and dislikes to one's peers ■ Can collaborate with peers to prepare for and participate in a debate	■ Can write a short fictional story about everyday events, using an illustration as a prompt	connect constantly AWL feature (n) AWL improve waterproof

LISTENING	SPEAKING	WRITING	VOCABULARY
A conversation about a trip to Japan ■ Can confirm the length of time that someone did something in a conversation about travel	■ Can give a description of everyday topics, such as past habits, plans, and experiences ■ Can ask and answer simple questions about the past	■ Can write a detailed email about a vacation	cancel freeze land (v) miss (v) pick up

AWL = Academic Word List item

LISTENING	SPEAKING	WRITING	VOCABULARY
A story about the past ■ Can confirm important details from an oral story about past events	■ Can use time markers to tell a story that has a sequence of events	■ Can write a short descriptive story	appear border (v) fight (v) ride (v) run away unlucky
A conversation about a movie ■ Can take detailed notes during a conversation, using them to answer detailed *wh-* questions based on that information	■ Can take turns with a partner, asking questions about their favorite book, play, or movie ■ Can ask and answer questions about the life of a famous writer	■ Can write a series of questions and answers about the life of a famous person	exact jealousy mystery (n) play (n) pride (n)
A conversation about a quiz show ■ Can answer *wh-* questions based on information in a short conversation	■ Can take turns with a partner or group, asking questions about famous people and past events ■ Can discuss one's childhood in detail and prompt similar responses from others	■ Can write a short autobiographical passage, using a series of *wh-* questions for guidance	admire base on notice routine statue
A conversation about a building ■ Can follow a slow-paced conversation about a location or place and provide key details about it	■ Can describe future plans and intentions using a variety of time markers ■ Can discuss a life-changing event with a partner or small group	■ Can write a letter or email that expresses and defends an opinion on a controversial topic	against announce gain increase in my opinion tuition
A conversation between a TV news reporter and two people ■ Can identify who the main speaker is referring to in a conversation with multiple participants	■ Can make predictions about future events, providing an opinion or rationale for each prediction ■ Can offer suggestions or solutions to help others with everyday problems and complaints	■ Can write a paragraph that offers detailed predictions about future events	disappear majority memory robot spend time

AWL = Academic Word List item

UNIT	GRAMMAR	READING
▼ PART **8** CONTINUED		
24 **May or Might for Possibility** Page 285 THEME The Weather	■ Can use *might* and *may* to express likelihood in the present and the immediate future ■ Can use *will* and *won't* to express what is certain and what is impossible ■ Can use *be going to* to ask questions about future possibility	News Report: *The Weather Forecast* ■ Can identify detailed information in a weather report
25 **Gerunds and Infinitives** Page 295 THEME Careers	■ Can use gerunds and infinitives after certain verbs	Magazine Article: *The Right Career for You* ■ Can match people with their characteristics based on information in a magazine article
PART **9** Count / Non-Count Nouns; *Much / Many*; Quantifiers **26** **Articles with Count and Non-Count Nouns;** *Some / Any* Page 308 THEME Restaurants and Food	■ Can use indefinite articles to refer to general subjects and definite articles to refer to specific subjects ■ Can use *some* and *any* as quantifiers with count and non-count nouns PRONUNCIATION Indefinite Articles	Restaurant Review: *Kassandra's Food Reviews* ■ Can understand recommendations in restaurant reviews
27 **How much and How many; Quantifiers** Page 322 THEME Desserts	■ Can ask for information about quantity with *how much / many* ■ Can use *a lot, a few,* and *a little* to refer to quantities with nouns ■ Can describe quantities using *(not) any, a lot, much,* or *many*	Conversation Transcript: *International Desserts* ■ Can identify the quantities of things that were listed in a short conversation about food
28 **Too many and Too much; Enough + Noun** Page 335 THEME The Right Place to Live	■ Can express sufficiency and insufficiency with *enough* and *too* ■ Can use *too many* and *too few* with plural count nouns and *too much* and *too little* with non-count nouns	Blog Post: *Dream Locations* ■ Can identify important details about specific locations or cities

LISTENING	SPEAKING	WRITING	VOCABULARY
A conversation about a trip ■ Can distinguish what actions a speaker takes when he or she is debating among several possibilities	■ Can explain why certain objects or actions might be necessary in certain situations ■ Can explain reasons and possibilities for different situations and events ■ Can discuss possible or tentative plans with a partner or small group	■ Can write a weather report that makes predictions about the present and future	commute (n) flood (v) highway mild predict (v) storm (n)
A lecture about design ■ Can identify how a speaker feels about his or her job after listening to a short lecture	■ Can discuss career interests with a partner or in small groups ■ Can use a short questionnaire to elicit information from others and then communicate that information to one's peers	■ Can write a paragraph about future career goals and aspirations, detailing how these goals will be achieved	career chef compete deadline lawyer salary

LISTENING	SPEAKING	WRITING	VOCABULARY
A conversation about party preparations ■ Can recognize a great number of details in a conversation about everyday topics	■ Can use simple phrases to order a meal ■ Can offer recommendations to others about food and restaurants	■ Can write a review of a restaurant that includes information about its prices, food quality, atmosphere, and service	atmosphere delicious main course menu reservation service (n)
A conversation about a recipe ■ Can list the ingredients in a recipe that was discussed in a conversation about food	■ Can work with others to answer items on a quiz about desserts ■ Can research and discuss how much of an item is needed to make a specific kind of food	■ Can write a simple conversation between a shopper and a clerk, referring back to a list of items	ingredient in season neighborhood prepare pretty good taste
A conversation about real estate ■ Can recognize and recall specific details about apartments described in a conversation	■ Can describe the pros and cons of living in the city versus the suburbs ■ Can provide a list of criticisms about one's hometown or city	■ Can write a letter to a newspaper or blog that describes a major problem in one's hometown or city	cosmopolitan crime pollution traffic transportation AWL unemployment

AWL = Academic Word List item

LISTENING	SPEAKING	WRITING	VOCABULARY
A conversation about a business trip ■ Can recognize and recall specific details about someone else's travel or work plans	■ Can describe cultural and business customs in one's home country and around the world ■ Can explain the meaning of different body language in one's home country	■ Can write one or two paragraphs that provide someone with advice on how to do business in one's home country	confusion head for insult (v) reception timing (n)
A conversation about academics ■ Can identify what things a speaker must do in order to achieve his or her academic or career goals	■ Can describe rules and requirements at different schools ■ Can discuss and determine ways to solve common problems that occur in schools	■ Can write a paragraph about the different types of rules at a school	average (n) due (adj) fail midterm outline (n) pass (v)
A conversation about a city ■ Can identify what changes are happening in a speaker's hometown or current environment	■ Can describe the similarities and differences between popular locations ■ Can compare and contrast the transportation systems of two major cities	■ Can write a paragraph that compares and contrasts the different ways one can get around a major city	coast (n) diverse AWL personality population wonder (v)
A presentation about public speaking ■ Can identify and recall specific instructions in a talk or a lecture given at a slow, clear pace	■ Can use tone to communicate different levels of emotion, such as excitement or anger ■ Can describe the way someone is performing an action	■ Can write a paragraph about a talent, providing specific examples of the actions one does well	applause appreciate AWL audience fact joke (n) serious
A conversation about two employees ■ Can infer information about the characteristics of people who are being discussed in a conversation	■ Can offer criticisms of plans about things to do during one's free time ■ Can explain why something isn't sufficient or appropriate for a given situation	■ Can write a paragraph that contains complaints about a store	according to in her eyes point of view point out sincerely solution
A quiz show about animals ■ Can, after listening to a speaker, recall detailed information and distinguishing characteristics about animals	■ Can conduct a survey, reporting the results to one's peers ■ Can discuss the characteristics of different animals in detail	■ Can write a paragraph that provides a thorough description of animals encountered at a zoo or in one's local area	centimeter extinct inch kilogram pound (n) species

AWL = Academic Word List item

About the Author

Irene E. Schoenberg has taught ESL for more than two decades at Hunter College's International English Language Institute and at Columbia University's American Language Program. She holds a master's degree in TESOL from Columbia University. She has trained ESL and EFL teachers at Columbia University's Teachers College, the New School University, and Hunter College's English Language Institute. She has given workshops and academic presentations at conferences, English language schools, and universities in Brazil, Canada, Chile, Dubai, El Salvador, Guatemala, Japan, Mexico, Nicaragua, Peru, Taiwan, Thailand, Vietnam, and throughout the United States. She is the author of *Talk about Trivia*; *Talk about Values*; *Speaking of Values 1: Conversation and Listening*; *Topics from A to Z*, Books 1 and 2; and *Focus on Grammar 2* (editions 1–5). She is the co-author with Jay Maurer of the *True Colors* series and *Focus on Grammar 1* (editions 1–4) and is one of the authors of *Future 1: English for Results* and *Future 3: English for Results*.

Acknowledgments

I'd like to thank **Bernard Seal** for expertly overseeing the fifth edition of the *Focus on Grammar* series. He not only found very talented people for me to work with, but he tirelessly worked to ensure that the series is consistent, complete, and appealing to look at.

I want to thank **Julie Schmidt**, my development editor, for her insight, thoughtful comments, and devotion to the project. It amazed me at how quickly she was able to return material with perceptive suggestions and comments. My thanks to **Diane Piniaris** for her fine work on the initial units.

Many thanks are extended to **Don Williams** for his talent at designing the pages and choosing photographs so that the readings and the exercises are visually engaging. The book is beautiful!

Thanks to **Gosia Jaros-White**, Publisher at Pearson Education, for her role in managing the entire series.

I thank **Marjorie Fuchs** and **Jay Maurer** for offering helpful and honest suggestions whenever I asked.

As always, I thank **my students** at Hunter College's *International English Language Institute* whose desire to learn English teaches me so much about the challenge of language learning; and my colleagues, **Ruth French** and **Victor Wheeler**, for giving me great feedback on any questions I had about grammar or methodology.

I thank **Joanne Dresner** for her original vision and guidance of the *Focus on Grammar* series.

Finally, I'd like to thank my family for their love and support: **Harris**, **Dan**, **Dahlia**, **Jonathan**, **Laura**, **Olivia**, **Ella**, and **Drew**.

Reviewers

We are grateful to the following reviewers for their many helpful comments.

Susanna Aramyan, Glendale Community College, Glendale, CA; **Homeretta Ayala**, Baltimore Co. Schools, Baltimore, MD; **Barbara Barrett**, University of Miami, Miami, FL; **Rebecca Beck**, Irvine Valley College, Irvine, CA; **Crystal Bock Thiessen**, University of Nebraska-PIESL, Lincoln, NE; **Janna Brink**, Mt. San Antonio College, Walnut, CA; **Erin Butler**, University of California, Riverside, CA; **Joice Cain**, Fullerton College, Fullerton, CA; **Shannonine M. Caruana**, Hudson County Community College, Jersey City, NJ; **Tonya Cobb**, Cypress College, Cypress, CA; **David Cooke**, Mt. San Antonio College, Walnut, CA; **Lindsay Donigan**, Fullerton College, Fullerton, CA; **Mila Dragushanskya**, ASA College, New York, NY; **Jill Fox**, University of Nebraska, Lincoln, NE; **Katalin Gyurindak**, Mt. San Antonio College, Walnut, CA; **Karen Hamilton**, Glendale Community College, Glendale, CA; **Electra Jablons**, International English Language Institute, Hunter College, New York, NY; **Eva Kozlenko**, Hudson County Community College, Jersey City, NJ; **Esther Lee**, American Language Program, California State University, Fullerton, CA; **Yenlan Li**, American Language Program, California State University, Fullerton, CA; **Shirley Lundblade**, Mt. San Antonio College, Walnut, CA; **Thi Thi Ma**, Los Angeles City College, Los Angeles, CA; **Marilyn Martin**, Mt. San Antonio College, Walnut, CA; **Eve Mazereeuw**, University of Guelph English Language Programs, Guelph, Ontario, Canada; **Robert Mott**, Glendale Community College, Glendale, CA; **Wanda Murtha**, Glendale Community College, Glendale, CA; **Susan Niemeyer**, Los Angeles City College, Los Angeles, CA; **Wayne Pate**, Tarrant County College, Fort Worth, TX; **Genevieve Patthey-Chavez**, Los Angeles City College, Los Angeles, CA; **Robin Persiani**, Sierra College, Rocklin, CA; **Denise Phillips**, Hudson County Community College, Jersey City, NJ; **Anna Powell**, American Language Program, California State University, Fullerton, CA; **JoAnna Prado**, Sacramento City Community College, Sacramento, CA; **Mark Rau**, American River College, Sacramento, CA; **Madeleine Schamehorn**, University of California, Riverside, CA; **Richard Skinner**, Hudson County Community College, Jersey City, NJ; **Heather Snavely**, American Language Program, California State University, Fullerton, CA; **Gordana Sokic**, Douglas College, Westminster, British Columbia, Canada; **Lee Spencer**, International English Language Institute, Hunter College, New York, NY; **Heather Stern**, Irvine Valley College, Irvine, CA; **Susan Stern**, Irvine Valley College, Irvine, CA; **Andrea Sunnaa**, Mt. San Antonio College, Walnut, CA; **Margaret Teske**, Mt. San Antonio College, Walnut, CA; **Johanna Van Gendt**, Hudson County Community College, Jersey City, NJ; **Daniela C. Wagner-Loera**, University of Maryland, College Park, MD; **Tamara Williams**, University of Guelph, English Language Programs, Guelph, Ontario, Canada; **Saliha Yagoubi**, Hudson County Community College, Jersey City, NJ; **Pat Zayas**, Glendale Community College, Glendale, CA

Credits

Continued on page 463

Be: Present and Past

PART 1

OUTCOMES
- Use the verb *be* in simple present statements
- Recognize details in a short description
- Recognize important information in a conversation about people
- Talk about sports and famous athletes
- Write sentences about a classmate

OUTCOMES
- Ask and answer *yes/no* and *wh-* questions in the simple present
- Answer questions about details in a conversation
- Recognize main ideas and details in a conversation about two people
- Ask questions about a person and a place
- Write a list of questions about a place

OUTCOMES
- Use the verb *be* in the simple past
- Ask and answer questions about the past with *was/were*
- Correct false statements from an article
- Recognize detailed information in phone messages
- Talk about the weather
- Talk about the first day of school
- Write a paragraph about your first day of school

Present of *Be*:
Statements
SPORTS

OUTCOMES
- Use the verb *be* in simple present statements
- Recognize details in a short description
- Recognize important information in a conversation about people
- Talk about sports and famous athletes
- Write sentences about a classmate

STEP 1 GRAMMAR IN CONTEXT

BEFORE YOU READ

Look at the photos. Work with a partner. Answer the questions.

1. What are three popular sports in your country?

2. What's your favorite sport?

MOST POPULAR SPORTS IN THE WORLD

Basketball

Cricket

Ice hockey

Soccer

Tennis

READ

01|01 Read this article about Ana and soccer.

Ana and Soccer

Hi, I'm Ana Silva. I'm from São Paulo, Brazil. I'm a soccer fan. Soccer is the number-one sport in my country. It's the number-one sport in the world. It is popular in Africa, Asia, Europe, South America, and North America. But the name "soccer" is not popular all over the world. Only people in the

United States and Canada call the sport "soccer." People in the rest of the world call it "football."

This is a photo of me with my cousins Julia and Marco. They are with me at a soccer game. Julia is in the middle. She's a student at the University of São Paulo. Marco is in high school. He's in his last year. We are all soccer fans. We're athletes, too. I'm a soccer player, but Julia and Marco are not. They're tennis players. But we all love soccer. Of course we love soccer—we are Brazilians!

AFTER YOU READ

Ⓐ VOCABULARY **Complete the sentences. Circle the correct answers.**

1. Ronaldo is her favorite soccer player. His photo is on her wall. She's a <u>fan / student</u> of Ronaldo.

2. That hockey team is new. It's <u>only / over</u> two years old.

3. All the students in our school like hockey. It is a <u>popular / bad</u> sport here in Canada.

4. Ahmed is good at all sports. He's a very good <u>athlete / friend</u>.

5. This is a photo of my friends and me. Jon is on the left. Natalie is on the right. I'm <u>in the world / in the middle</u>.

6. Ten of my classmates love sports. <u>The rest of / The name of</u> my classmates are not interested in sports.

Ⓑ COMPREHENSION **Read the statements. Check (✓) *True* or *False*.**

	True	False
1. In the photo, Ana is with her brother and sister.	☐	☐
2. Ana is from Brazil.	☐	☐
3. Brazil is in São Paulo.	☐	☐
4. Football is the number-one sport in Brazil.	☐	☐
5. Julia and Marco aren't soccer players.	☐	☐
6. Ana and her cousins aren't soccer fans.	☐	☐

Ⓒ DISCUSSION **Work with a partner. Compare your answers in B. Then say two things about Ana and her cousins and two things about soccer.**

Go to MyEnglishLab for more grammar in context practice.

PRESENT OF *BE*: STATEMENTS

Affirmative Statements

Singular		
Subject	*Be*	
I	am	
You	are	
Mike He	is	a student.
Carrie She	is	
Hockey It		a sport.

Plural		
Subject	*Be*	
Marco and I We		
You and Julie You	are	cousins.
Ivona and Boris They		
Seoul and Tripoli They		cities.

Negative Statements

Singular		
Subject	*Be + not*	
I	am not	
You	are not	from Istanbul.
He	is not	
She	is not	
It	is not	new.

Plural		
Subject	*Be + not*	
We	are not	
You	are not	in Seoul.
They	are not	

Contractions

Affirmative Contractions		
I am	→	I'm
you are	→	you're
he is	→	he's
she is	→	she's
it is	→	it's

we are	→	we're
you are	→	you're
they are	→	they're

Negative Contractions			
I am not	→	I'm not	
you are not	→	you're not	you aren't
he is not	→	he's not	he isn't
she is not	→	she's not	she isn't
it is not	→	it's not	it isn't

we are not	→	we're not	we aren't
you are not	→	you're not	you aren't
they are not	→	they're not	they aren't

GRAMMAR NOTES

1 Present Forms of *Be*

The **present of** *be* has three forms: *am*, *is*, and *are*.

• *am*	I **am** a student.
• *is*	He **is** from São Paulo.
• *are*	They **are** athletes.

2 Negative Statements

Use *not* after a form of *be* to make a negative statement.

• *am not*	I **am not** from Turkey.
• *is not*	Seattle **is not** in Canada.
• *are not*	We **are not** hockey players.

3 Contractions

Use **contractions** (short forms) in speaking and informal writing.	I**'m** from Mexico. I**'m not** from Ecuador. She**'s** from Morocco. She **isn't** from Egypt. They**'re** from Brazil. They **aren't** from Argentina.
There are two negative contractions for *is not*.	It**'s not** difficult. It **isn't** difficult.
There are two negative contractions for *are not*.	We**'re not** single. We **aren't** single.
BE CAREFUL! There is only one negative contraction for *am not*.	I**'m not** from Ecuador. NOT I ~~amn't~~ from Ecuador.

4 Subjects and Verbs

All sentences have a **subject** and a **verb**.	**SUBJECT**	**VERB**	
	I	*am*	from São Paulo.
	Julia	*is*	a soccer fan.
	My cousin and I	*are*	soccer fans.

BE CAREFUL! You cannot make a sentence without a subject. You cannot make a sentence without a verb.	**Julia is** a soccer fan. NOT ~~Is a soccer fan.~~ *(No subject)* NOT ~~Julia a soccer fan.~~ *(No verb)*

5 Subjects, Nouns, and Subject Pronouns

The **subject** is a **noun** or a **pronoun**. Subject pronouns replace subject nouns.	SUBJECT NOUN **Marco Silva** is a student. SUBJECT PRONOUN **He** is from São Paulo.
BE CAREFUL! You cannot put a subject pronoun right after a subject noun.	**Marco is** from São Paulo. NOT Marco ~~he~~ is from São Paulo.

Go to MyEnglishLab to watch the grammar presentation.

EXERCISE 1   DISCOVER THE GRAMMAR

GRAMMAR NOTES 1–3   **Read the paragraph. Underline the forms of _be_.**

Mourad <u>is</u> from Casablanca. It's the largest city in Morocco. Mourad is a big soccer fan. He isn't a soccer player, but he loves the game. His sister and two brothers are soccer players. They're all excited about the World Cup.

EXERCISE 2   AFFIRMATIVE STATEMENTS

GRAMMAR NOTE 1   **Complete the sentences with _am_, _is_, or _are_.**

1. Soccer _____*is*_____ popular all over the world.

2. Football _____ popular in the United States and Canada.

3. Football and soccer _____ different sports.

4. Aaron Rodgers and Lionel Messi _____ great athletes.

5. Aaron Rodgers _____ a great football player.

6. Lionel Messi _____ a great soccer player.

7. I _____ a football fan. I love football.

8. My cousins and I _____ soccer fans. We love soccer.

EXERCISE 3 AFFIRMATIVE AND NEGATIVE STATEMENTS

GRAMMAR NOTES 1–3 Complete the paragraphs with affirmative or negative forms of *am*, *is*, or *are*. More than one answer is sometimes possible.

Parminder Nagra _____*is*_____ a talented actor.
                        1.

She and Keira Knightley _____ the stars of
                              2.

the 2002 movie *Bend It Like Beckham.* It _____
                                              3.

a comedy. In the movie, Parminder _____ a
                                        4.

young Indian girl in England. She _____ a
                                        5.

good soccer player, and she loves soccer. But her

parents _____ traditional. They
              6.

_____ happy. They do not want her to play
  7. (not)

soccer. They say, "Soccer _____ for girls.
                              8. (not)

Marriage _____ for girls. Look at your sister.
              9.

Your sister _____ a soccer player, and she
                10. (not)

_____ about to marry." Parminder says, "I
  11.

_____ my sister."
  12. (not)

EXERCISE 4 SUBJECT PRONOUNS AND AFFIRMATIVE CONTRACTIONS

GRAMMAR NOTES 3, 5 Change the underlined words to pronouns and contractions of *be*.

1. Cricket is popular in India. ~~Cricket is~~ *It's* the number-one sport there.

2. Mr. Patel is a cricket fan. <u>Mr. Patel is</u> a soccer fan, too.

3. Soccer is a great sport. <u>Soccer is</u> popular all over the world.

4. <u>My partner and I are</u> on a soccer team.

5. Ms. Cameron is an English teacher. <u>Ms. Cameron is</u> a basketball coach, too.

6. Basketball and baseball are great sports. <u>Basketball and baseball are</u> exciting games.

7. My favorite sport is basketball. <u>Basketball is</u> fun to watch.

8. My cousin and I are at a basketball game in this photo. <u>My cousin and I are</u> in the middle of the row.

EXERCISE 5 AFFIRMATIVE OR NEGATIVE STATEMENTS

GRAMMAR NOTES 1–4 Write true sentences with the correct simple present forms of *be*.

1. I <u>*'m or 'm not*</u> a tennis player.

2. My mother _____ a baseball fan.

3. My father _____ a soccer fan.

4. Soccer _____ popular in my country.

5. Soccer _____ popular all over the world.

6. My friends and I _____ cricket fans.

7. Tennis and ping-pong _____ my favorite sports.

8. I _____ a good tennis player.

9. I _____ a good cricket player.

10. My parents _____ good athletes.

EXERCISE 6 EDITING

GRAMMAR NOTES 1–5 Read the sentences about a soccer movie. There are seven mistakes. The first mistake is already corrected. Find and correct six more.

1. "The Beautiful Game" ^is^ a movie about soccer.

2. It a documentary.

3. Soccer players from all over Africa in the movie.

4. One boy he is good at soccer.

5. The boy goes to the United States. His parents is happy and unhappy.

6. His mother says, "I'm happy. His future good."

7. She says, "I unhappy. He isn't near us."

Go to MyEnglishLab for more focused practice.

EXERCISE 7 LISTENING

01|02 **A** Study the chart. Then listen to a conversation about athletes. Write the sport and country of origin for each of these famous athletes. Use the words in the boxes.

Sport:	baseball	basketball	golf	soccer	tennis

Country:	Argentina	Brazil	Japan	Portugal	Romania	United States

Name	LeBron James	Lionel Messi	Cristiano Ronaldo	Masahiro Tanaka
Sport	Basketball			
Country	United States			

Name	Michelle Wie	Alex Morgan	Marta Vieira da Silva	Simona Halep
Sport				
Country				

01|02 **B** Listen again and check your answers in A.

C Work in pairs. Use the information in the chart in A to talk about the athletes.

EXAMPLE: A: LeBron James is a basketball player from the United States.
B: Lionel Messi is . . .

EXERCISE 8   TRUE OR FALSE?

Ⓐ GAME   **Prepare for the game in B. Complete the sentences. Write three true sentences and one false sentence.**

1. **a.** My favorite athlete is _____ .

   b. He/She is _____ .

2. **a.** My cousin and I are _____ .

   b. We are _____ .

Ⓑ **Work in a group. Read your sentences to the group. The group guesses the false sentence. Take turns.**

EXAMPLE: A: My favorite athlete is Serena Williams. She's from South Africa. My cousin
        and I are tennis players. We are tennis fans, too.
      B: Serena Williams isn't from South Africa.
      A: That's right. She's from the United States.

EXERCISE 9   PING-PONG IS BORING!

Ⓐ DISCUSSION   **Prepare for the discussion in B. Complete the chart with one or more words about each sport. Use the words in the box or your own ideas.**

| boring | dangerous | exciting | fun | interesting | popular in my country | relaxing |

ping-pong	**volleyball**	**running**	**swimming**	**skateboarding**	**snowboarding**
Fun					

Ⓑ **Work in a group. Talk about each sport in A.**

EXAMPLE: A: Ping-pong is fun.
      B: I agree. It's exciting, too.
      C: I'm not a big ping-pong fan. I think it's boring.
      A: OK. Volleyball is next. So, what do you think?

Ⓒ **Tell the class three things you agree on.**

EXAMPLE: We agree on three things. First, . . . Second, we think that . . . Third, . . .

Go to MyEnglishLab for more communication practice.

A BEFORE YOU WRITE Look at the chart. Complete the "You" column. Then work with a partner. Talk about yourself. Then listen and take notes about your partner.

	Example	You	Your Partner
Name	Tom Cummins Nickname: Tommy		
City, Country	Toronto, Canada		
A sport in your country	Hockey: very popular in Canada		
Your family and this sport	My two brothers: hockey players and hockey fans		
You and sports	Not a hockey player, not a big hockey fan My favorite sport: snowboarding		

B WRITE Write eight sentences about your partner. Use your notes in A. Use the verb *be* in every sentence.

EXAMPLE: My partner's name is Tom Cummins.
His nickname is Tommy. . . .

C CHECK YOUR WORK Read your sentences in B. Underline all examples of the verb *be*. Use the Editing Checklist to check your work.

Editing Checklist

Did you . . . ?
- [ ] use *am* with *I*, *is* with *he/she/it*, and *are* with *you/we/they*
- [ ] a subject and verb in every statement

D REVISE YOUR WORK Read your sentences again. Can you improve your writing? Make changes if necessary.

UNIT 1 **REVIEW**

Test yourself on the grammar of the unit.

A Complete the sentences with *am*, *is*, or *are*.

1. My brother and I _____ baseball fans.

2. Our favorite sport _____ baseball.

3. I _____ a good baseball player.

4. My brother _____ a good baseball player, too.

5. We _____ athletes.

B Complete the sentences with *'m*, *'s*, or *'re*.

1. I_____ from Korea.

2. She_____ from Brazil.

3. We_____ basketball fans.

4. He_____ a good basketball player.

5. We_____ from Ohio, and LeBron James is from Ohio, too.

C Rewrite the sentences. Change the underlined words to pronouns and contractions of *be*.

1. <u>Lionel Messi</u> is not in Argentina now.   _____

2. <u>Soccer and baseball</u> are exciting sports.   _____

3. <u>My partner and I</u> are not baseball fans.   _____

4. <u>Ms. Nagra</u> is the star of a movie.   _____

D Correct the paragraph. There are six mistakes.

My father and mother are from India, but they're in Canada now. My parents are

doctors. My father a sports doctor, and my mother she is a family doctor. My parents

and I love sports. My father are a soccer fan, and my mother a baseball fan. I'm a soccer

fan. My father and I am fans of Lionel Messi and Nuno Gomes. My sister no is good at

sports. She's not a sports fan. She loves movies.

Now check your answers on page 445.

Go to MyEnglishLab to complete the review online.

Present of *Be*: Questions
SCHOOL

OUTCOMES
- Ask and answer *yes*/*no* and *wh-* questions in the simple present
- Answer questions about details in a conversation
- Recognize main ideas and details in a conversation about two people
- Ask questions about a person and a place
- Write a list of questions about a place

STEP 1   GRAMMAR IN CONTEXT

BEFORE YOU READ

Work with a partner. Answer the questions.

1. Are you usually on time for school? For work? For parties? For family dinners?

2. Who in your family is often late?

READ

▶02|01 Read this conversation about the first day of an English class.

Are We Late?

AVA: Excuse me. Where's room 2?

AL: It's right here, next to the office.

AVA: Thanks. Are we late for class?

AL: No, we're right on time.

AVA: Whew! That's good. I hate to be late on the first day. Is the teacher here?

AL: Yes, he is.

AVA: How is he? Is he a good teacher?

AL: I think so. I'm Al. What's your name?

AVA: Ava.

AL: Nice to meet you. Are you new here?

AVA: Yes, I am.

AL: Where are you from? Are you from Latin America?

AVA: No, I'm from Spain. Hey, your English is so good!... Where are *you* from?

AL: I'm from Michigan.

AVA: Michigan? But that's in the United States. Are you in the right class?

AL: Yes, I am.

AVA: Why are you here? Who are you?

AL: I'm not a new student. I'm a new *teacher*. I'm *your* new teacher.

AVA: Oh . . . !

AFTER YOU READ

Ⓐ VOCABULARY Complete the sentences with the words from the box. Use a capital letter when necessary.

excuse me	office	on time	right	room

1. A: _____ , where's the elevator? B: It's around the corner.

2. A: Your class is in _____ 102, next to the stairs. B: Thanks.

3. A: Room 202 is _____ over there, near the elevator. B: Oh, I see it. Thanks.

4. A: We're _____ . We're not late or early. B: Good.

5. A: Where's the director's _____? B: It's on the second floor.

Ⓑ COMPREHENSION Read the questions. Choose the correct answers.

1. Are Ava and Al on time for class?
   a. Yes, they are.　　　b. No, they're late.　　　c. No, they're early.

2. Where is Ava from?
   a. Argentina　　　b. Michigan　　　c. Spain

3. Where is Michigan?
   a. in the United States　　　b. in Argentina　　　c. in Spain

4. Are Ava and Al students?
   a. She isn't a student, but he is.　　　b. She's a student, but he isn't.　　　c. Yes, they are.

5. What is true?
   a. Al is in the wrong class.　　　b. Al isn't a good teacher.　　　c. Al is Ava's teacher.

Ⓒ DISCUSSION Work with a partner. Compare your answers in B. Why do you think your answers are correct?

Go to MyEnglishLab for more grammar in context practice.

PRESENT OF *BE*: QUESTIONS

Yes/No Questions: Singular

Be	Subject	
Am	I	
Are	you	
	he	in room 2?
Is	she	
	it	

Short Answers: Singular

Yes		No	
	you **are**.		you're **not**. you **aren't**.
	I **am**.		I'm **not**.
Yes,	he **is**.	No,	he's **not**. he **isn't**.
	she **is**.		she's **not**. she **isn't**.
	it **is**.		it's **not**. it **isn't**.

Yes/No Questions: Plural

Be	Subject	
	we	
Are	you	on time?
	they	

Short Answers: Plural

Yes		No	
	you **are**.		you're **not**. you **aren't**.
Yes,	we **are**.	No,	we're **not**. we **aren't**.
	they **are**.		they're **not**. they **aren't**.

Wh- Questions

Wh- Word	Be	Subject	
Where	are	you	from?
Why			here?
What		your	name?
How	is	he?	
Who		she?	
When	am	I	in class?

Short Answers

Michigan.
I'm the teacher.
Al.
Good.
A student.
From 8:00 to 11:00.

Long Answers

I'm from Michigan.
I'm here because I'm the teacher.
My name is Al.
He's a good teacher.
She's a student.
You're in class from 8:00 to 11:00.

GRAMMAR NOTES

1 *Yes/No* and *Wh-* Questions

Yes/no **questions** usually have a *yes* or *no* answer.	A: Is he a student? B: **Yes**, he is. **or No**, he isn't.
Wh- **questions** ask for information.	A: **Who** is he? B: He's the teacher.

2 Yes/No Questions: Form

Use *am*, *is*, or *are* before the subject in *yes/no* questions.	**BE** **SUBJECT** **Am** I in English 2? **Is** she a student? **Are** we late?

3 Yes/No Questions and Answers

We usually give **short answers** to *yes/no* questions, but we can also give **long answers**.	A: Are you a new student? B: **Yes.** or **Yes, I am.** A: Are you a new student? B: **Yes, I'm new.** or **Yes, I'm a new student.**
BE CAREFUL! Do not use contractions in short answers with *yes*.	Yes, I am. NOT Yes, ~~I'm.~~ Yes, he is. NOT Yes, ~~he's.~~
USAGE NOTE When we do not know the answer to a question, we say, "I don't know."	A: Is he a new student? B: **I don't know.**
USAGE NOTE When someone asks a *yes/no* question that we think is true, we can say, "Yes, I think so."	A: Is he a new student? B: **Yes, I think so.**
USAGE NOTE If we think an answer is not true, we can say, "No, I don't think so."	A: Is he a new student? B: **No, I don't think so.**

4 Wh- Question Words

Wh- question words ask about the following: • *Who* → people • *What* → things • *Where* → places • *When* → time • *How* → in what way • *Why* → reason	**QUESTIONS** **Who** are they? **What** is in your bag? **Where** is our classroom? **When** is lunch? **How** is school? **Why** are you late?	**SHORT ANSWERS** **My classmates.** **My phone.** **In room 2.** **At noon.** **Good.** **My bus was late.**
In **long answers** to questions that start with *why*, use *because* before the reason.	A: **Why** are you late? B: I'm late **because** my bus was late.	

5 Wh- Questions: Form

Use a **wh- word** before *is* or *are* in *wh-* questions.	**WH- WORD** **BE** **What** **is** your name? **Where** **are** the books?
USAGE NOTE We often use **contractions** (short forms) with *wh-* words + *is* in speaking and informal writing. We don't usually write contractions with *wh-* words + *are*.	**What's** your name? **How's** your class?

6 Wh- Questions and Answers

We usually give **short answers** to *wh-* questions, but we can also give long answers.	A: Where are you from? B: **Mexico.** *(short answer)* A: Where are you from? B: **I'm from Mexico.** *(long answer)*
USAGE NOTE When we don't know the answer to a *wh-* question, we say, "I don't know."	A: Where is he from? B: **I don't know.**

Go to MyEnglishLab to watch the grammar presentation.

STEP 3 FOCUSED PRACTICE

EXERCISE 1 DISCOVER THE GRAMMAR

GRAMMAR NOTES 1–6 **Look at the picture. Circle the correct answers.**

1. Are the students hungry?

   a. Yes, it is.   **b.** Yes, she is.   **c.** I don't know.

2. What time is it?

   a. It's September.   **b.** It's ten o'clock.   **c.** It's late.

3. Is the teacher a man?

   a. Yes, he is.   **b.** No, he's not.   **c.** Yes, she is.

4. Is the door open?

   a. Yes, she is.   **b.** No, it isn't.   **c.** Yes, it is.

5. Is the student at the door early?

    a. Yes, she's early.   **b.** No, she's late.   **c.** Yes, he is.

6. Is the student at the door unhappy?

    a. No, they aren't.   **b.** I think so.   **c.** Yes, he is.

7. Where is the teacher?

    a. Near the board.   **b.** At the door.   **c.** In September.

8. What month is it?

    a. It's September.   **b.** Yes, it is.   **c.** It's late.

EXERCISE 2 *YES/NO* QUESTIONS

GRAMMAR NOTE 2 Write *yes/no* questions about the statements in parentheses.

1. (The office is on this floor.)   *Is the office on this floor?*

2. (We are in the right building.)

3. (You are a new student.)

4. (Our teacher is from Canada.)

5. (It's ten o'clock.)

6. (Your classmates are friendly.)

7. (Two students are absent today.)

8. (I'm in the right room.)

9. (This exercise is easy.)

EXERCISE 3 *YES/NO* QUESTIONS AND SHORT ANSWERS

GRAMMAR NOTES 2–3 Write *yes/no* questions. Put the words in parentheses in the correct order. Then write true short answers with *yes, no, I don't know, I think so,* or *I don't think so.* Use contractions when possible.

1. (you / Are / usually early)

    A: *Are you usually early?*

    B: *Yes, I am.* **or** *No, I'm not.*

2. (your watch / fast / Is)

    A:

    B:

3. (from Italy / your jacket / Is)

A: _____

B: _____

4. (on this floor / the restroom / Is)

A: _____

B: _____

5. (your name / Is / easy to pronounce)

A: _____

B: _____

6. (different cities / Are / from / you and your classmates)

A: _____

B: _____

7. (busy / Are / your classmates / now)

A: _____

B: _____

EXERCISE 4 *WH-* QUESTIONS

GRAMMAR NOTES 4–5 **Read the answers. Then write *wh-* questions with the words in parentheses.**

1. A: (Who) *Who's Al Brown? or Who is Al Brown?* _____

B: Al Brown is the teacher.

2. A: (Where) _____

B: The computers are in room 304.

3. A: (What) _____

B: Today's date is September 3.

4. A: (Why) _____

B: We're late because we were in the wrong classroom.

5. A: (Why) _____

B: Diane is the teacher today because Al isn't here.

6. A: (How) _____

B: My computer class is great.

EXERCISE 5
YES/NO AND WH- QUESTIONS AND ANSWERS

GRAMMAR NOTES 1–6
Read this paragraph about Hao. Then complete the questions and answers.

Hao is a student in level 2. He's in his grammar class now. His grammar class is in room 201. His teacher is Diane. She's a wonderful teacher. The classroom is small, but comfortable. The students are great. They're from six different countries: China, Korea, Japan, Saudi Arabia, Argentina, and Italy.

1. A: _Is_ _____ Hao in level 2?

   B: _Yes, he is_ _____ .

2. A: _____ Hao's grammar class?

   B: It's in _____ .

3. A: _____ ?

   B: Diane.

4. A: _____ ?

   B: It's small, but _____ .

5. A: _____ ?

   B: _____ great.

6. A: _____ six different countries?

   B: Yes, _____ .

7. A: Where _____ ?

   B: China, Korea, Japan, Saudi Arabia, _____ , and _____ .

EXERCISE 6 QUESTIONS AND ANSWERS

(A) GRAMMAR NOTES 1–6 Read Alejandra's post on SmartGirl's blog. Write simple present questions with the words in parentheses. Then write short answers.

smart girl .com

Alejandra Suarez

Hey SmartGirl,

I have a great boyfriend, Oscar. He's fun and intelligent. We're a good match. But there's one problem. He's always late. He's late to school. He's late to work. He's late for me. Always.

Why?

Alejandra

1. (Oscar / fun)

   A: _Is Oscar fun?_

   B: _Yes, he is._

2. (Oscar / smart)

   A: _____

   B: _____

3. (Alejandra and Oscar / a good pair)

   A: _____

   B: _____

4. (Who / always late)

   A: _____

   B: _____

B Read SmartGirl's answer. Write simple present *yes/no* questions with the words in parentheses. Answer the questions with "*Yes, I think so,*" "*No, I don't think so,*" or "*I don't know.*"

SmartGirl

Hey Alejandra,

OK, so your guy is great, but late. And you hate to wait. Why is he always late? Maybe he thinks, "I'm late. That means I'm important." Maybe he doesn't know it's a problem for you. He thinks it's no big deal. Tell him it is a big deal to you. Maybe he's just bad at planning his time. Try to help him.

Good luck.

SmartGirl

1. (Oscar / great)

   A: *Is Oscar great?*

   B: *No, I don't think so.* or *Yes, I think so.*

2. (Oscar / a bad boyfriend)

   A: _____

   B: _____

3. (Oscar / bad at planning time)

   A: _____

   B: _____

4. (SmartGirl's answer / good)

   A: _____

   B: _____

EXERCISE 7 EDITING

GRAMMAR NOTES 1–6 Read the conversations. There are ten mistakes. The first mistake is already corrected. Find and correct nine more.

1. A: Are you in the office?
   B: Yes, ~~I'm.~~ *I am*

2. A: Is easy?
   B: No, it's hard.

3. A: He Korean?
   B: No, he's isn't.

4. A: Excuse me. Where's the office?
   B: Yes, it's in room 305.

5. A: Is this English 3?
   B: Yes, I think.

6. A: Is they in room 102?
   B: I don't know.

7. A: Where you from?
   B: I'm from Peru.

8. A: How your class is?
   B: It's very good.

9. A: What your nickname?
   B: Susie.

Go to MyEnglishLab for more focused practice.

EXERCISE 8 LISTENING

▶02|02 **A** Listen to a conversation between Elena and Hugo. Check (✓) the people and countries that they talk about.

People

☐ Elena

☐ Elena's classmates

☐ Hao

☐ Hugo's classmates

☐ Hugo's cousins

☐ Hugo's teacher

☐ school director

Countries

☐ Canada

☐ Chile

☐ England

☐ Korea

☐ Portugal

☐ Saudi Arabia

☐ South Korea

▶02|02 **B** Listen again and answer the questions.

1. Is Hugo happy with school? _____

2. How's Hugo's teacher? _____

3. Where are his classmates from? _____

4. What are Hugo and Elena good at? _____

5. What is Hao good at? _____

C Work with a partner. Change the questions in B to questions about your partner, your teacher, and your classmates.

EXAMPLE: A: Are you happy with school?
          B: Yes, I am, but English isn't easy. How about you?
          A: I'm . . .

EXERCISE 9 ARE THE ANSWERS AT THE BACK?

A Q & A Work with a partner. Answer these questions about your textbook.

1. Where is a world map?

    EXAMPLE: It's on page 430.

2. Where is a map of the United States and Canada?

3. Are the answers to all the questions at the back of the book?

4. Where is the Glossary of Grammar Terms?

5. What's on page 42?

6. Is the Unit 1 Review on page 50?

7. What's the title of your book?

8. Is the cover of the book red?

B Write five new questions with your partner.

Is the cover interesting?
Is the photo on page…?

C Work in groups. Take turns. Ask and discuss the questions in B.

EXAMPLE: A: Is the cover interesting?
B: No, I don't think so.
C: I disagree. The colors are nice.

EXERCISE 10 HI, I'M …

ROLE PLAY Work in pairs. Imagine you and your partner are at a school party. Give yourself a new name, a new country, and a new occupation. Introduce yourself to your partner.

EXAMPLE: A: Hi, I'm Prince Harry.
B: Nice to meet you. I'm Princess Elsa. Are you from around here?
A: No, I'm from England. What about you?

EXERCISE 11 WHAT IS ULS?

A Q & A Work with a partner. Read the ad for University Language School. Write five *wh-* questions and five *yes/no* questions.

What's ULS?
Where is ULS?

B Work with another pair of partners. Read the ad again, and close your books. Ask and answer your questions from A. Take turns.

EXAMPLE: A: Where is ULS?
C: It's in New York.
B: What can you learn at ULS?
D: English.

LEARN
ENGLISH
AT ULS!

Register *now*
for English classes at
University Language School

PLACEMENT TEST:
September 1 in Room 203

Classes begin September 8

DIRECTOR:
Jim Reilly

PHONE:
989-870-3456

EMAIL:
ULS@GreatSchools.com

University Language School, 650 Elm Street, Long Beach, New York

A BEFORE YOU WRITE Work with a partner. Ask and answer questions about your school. Use the ideas below or your own ideas. Take turns.

School Calendar
- the next school holiday
- the winter break
- the last day of class

School Staff
- your teacher
- the school director
- office assistant

Places in the School
- the school library
- the computer room
- the registration office
- the cafeteria
- the rest rooms
- the staircase

EXAMPLE: A: Is May 23 the last day of class?
B: Yes, it is. Who's the school director?
A: I don't know. Where's the . . . ?

B WRITE Write simple present questions with the verb *be* about your school. Use your ideas from A.

C CHECK YOUR WORK Read your questions in B. Underline the verb *be* in your questions. Use the Editing Checklist to check your work.

Editing Checklist
Did you . . . ?
☐ use *is* with *he/she/it* and *are* with *you/we/they*
☐ put *am, is,* or *are* before the subject in *yes/no* questions
☐ use a *wh-* word before *is* or *are* in *wh-* questions

D REVISE Read your questions again. Can you improve your writing? Make changes if necessary.

Go to MyEnglishLab for more writing practice.

UNIT 2 **REVIEW**

Test yourself on the grammar of the unit.

Ⓐ Complete A's questions. Circle the correct words.

1. A: Where's / What's the library?   B: In room 3.

2. A: Who's / How's your class?   B: It's great.

3. A: What's / How's your name?   B: Jin-Hee Lee.

4. A: Is / Are you from Seoul?   B: Yes, I am.

5. A: Is / Are it cold in Seoul now?   B: No, it isn't.

Ⓑ Complete the short answers.

1. A: Are you home?   B: Yes, _____ .

2. A: Is your nickname JD?   B: No, _____ .

3. A: Are they late?   B: No, _____ .

4. A: Are we in the right room?   B: Yes, _____ .

5. A: Am I late?   B: No, _____ .

Ⓒ Write questions. Use the words in parentheses and the simple present of *be*.

1. (What / today's date)   _____

2. (Where / the men's room)   _____

3. (Why / he / absent)   _____

4. (When / your first class)   _____

5. (Who / your teacher)   _____

Ⓓ Correct the questions. There are five mistakes.

1. She your teacher?

2. What your name?

3. Where your class?

4. Is Bob and Molly good friends?

5. Why you late?

Now check your answers on page 445.

Now check your answers on page 445.

Go to MyEnglishLab to complete the review online.

OUTCOMES
- Use the verb *be* in the simple past
- Ask and answer questions about the past with *was / were*
- Correct false statements from an article
- Recognize detailed information in phone messages
- Talk about the weather
- Talk about the first day of school
- Write a paragraph about your first day of school

STEP 1   GRAMMAR IN CONTEXT

BEFORE YOU READ

Work with a partner. Answer the questions.

1. How was your first day at school?
2. Were you happy? Were you nervous? Were you excited?

READ

○ 03|01   Read this article about Sarah's first day at a new school.

Sarah's First Day

The first day at a new place is sometimes difficult and sometimes scary. We're often afraid of new people and places. Sometimes we're nervous and excited at the same time. How was your first day at a new school? Do you remember it? Was it good? Were you nervous? Was it difficult? Were your classmates friendly?

    There is a wonderful children's book called *First Day Jitters*[1] by Julie

---

1 *jitters:* a nervous, uneasy feeling

Danneberg. It's about Sarah Jane Hartwell's first day at a new school. Sarah was frightened. She was nervous. Mr. Hartwell said, "Sarah. Wake up. It's time for school."

Sarah said, "I'm sick. My hands are cold. I don't want to go to a new school."

Mr. Hartwell was kind and patient.² He drove Sarah to school. The school principal took Sarah to the classroom. The children were all there. They weren't nervous. They were happy. Sarah was not happy, but the principal smiled and said, "Don't worry, Sarah."

Then the principal turned to the class and said, "Class, I want you to meet your new teacher, Mrs. Sarah Jane Hartwell."

Young children like the story. They like the surprise ending. They also like to learn that sometimes teachers are nervous, too.

2 *patient:* calm, slow to get angry

AFTER YOU READ

Ⓐ VOCABULARY **Complete the paragraph with the words from the box.**

afraid of	difficult	nervous	principal	surprise

1. Last year, Ms. Rogers was the _____.

2. She was never in her office. It was _____ to find her.

3. She wasn't kind to the students or the teachers. Many teachers and children were _____ her.

4. She complained a lot. Children were _____ when they were in her office.

5. One day, she was gone. It was a _____, but no one was sad. In fact, it was a very good thing since our new principal is great.

Ⓑ COMPREHENSION **All the statements are false. Correct them. There is more than one correct answer.**

1. People are never afraid of new places and new things.

2. *First Day Jitters* is a book for teenagers.

3. Sarah was in school before the children.

4. Sarah was a new student.

5. Teachers are never nervous.

Ⓒ DISCUSSION **Work with a partner. Compare your answers in B. Then discuss: Was the ending of the story a surprise to you?**

Go to MyEnglishLab for more grammar in context practice.

PAST OF *BE*: AFFIRMATIVE STATEMENTS

Singular			
Subject	*Be*		Time Marker
I	was	a student	last year.
You	were		
He She	was		
It		in Asia	

Plural			
Subject	*Be*		Time Marker
We You They	were	in New York	two weeks ago.

PAST OF *BE*: NEGATIVE STATEMENTS

Singular			
Subject	*Be* + *not*		Time Marker
I	was not wasn't	at school	last night.
You	were not weren't		
He She It	was not wasn't		

Plural			
Subject	*Be* + *not*		Time Marker
We You They	were not weren't	at work	last week.

PAST OF *BE*: *YES* / *NO* QUESTIONS

Singular			
Be	Subject		Time Marker
Was	I	in class	yesterday?
Were	you		
Was	he she it		

Plural			
Be	Subject		Time Marker
Were	we you they	in class	last week?

SHORT ANSWERS

Singular						
Yes	Subject	*Be*		*No*	Subject	*Be* + not
Yes,	you	were.		No,	you	weren't.
	I he she it	was.			I he she it	wasn't.

Plural						
Yes	Subject	*Be*		*No*	Subject	*Be* + not
Yes,	you we they	were.		No,	you we they	weren't.

PAST OF *BE*: *WH-* QUESTIONS

Wh- questions			Long Answers
Wh- Word	*Be*		
What	**was**	your first job?	I was a server.
Where		the restaurant?	It was in New York.
When		that?	It was in 2005.
How		the job?	It was fun.
Who	**were**	the other servers?	They were my brothers and my cousin.
Why		you in New York?	My parents were there.

GRAMMAR NOTES

1 Past Forms of *Be*

The past of *be* has two forms: ***was*** and ***were***.

• *was*	I **was** excited.
• *were*	They **were** happy.

2 Negative Statements

Use ***not*** after a form of ***was*** or ***were*** to make a negative statement.

• *was not*	I **was not** in school.
• *were not*	We **were not** late.

3 Contractions

In informal writing and speaking, use the contractions ***wasn't*** and ***weren't*** in negative statements and negative short answers.

• *wasn't*	He **wasn't** at the interview. No, he **wasn't**.
• *weren't*	They **weren't** in class. No, they **weren't**.

4 Yes/No Questions

To ask a *yes/no* question, put ***was*** or ***were*** before the subject.	**Was**	**he**	a student?
	Were	**they**	nervous?

5 Wh- Questions

Use a **wh- question word** before *was* or *were* in *wh-* questions.	**When was** he a salesman? **Where were** they students? **How was** your first day at school?
USAGE NOTE The answer to *Who was . . . ?* can be singular or plural.	Who **was** absent yesterday? Suna **was**. Who **was** absent on Monday? Suna and Paul **were**.

6 Time Markers

Time markers say when something happened. Examples of past time markers are: *yesterday, last week, two years ago,* and *in the past.*	
Time markers are often at the **end of statements**.	We were in class **yesterday**. John wasn't in class **last week**.
Time markers are sometimes at the **beginning of statements**.	**Yesterday**, we were in class. **Last week**, he wasn't in class.
Time markers are at the **end of a question**.	Were you in high school **two years ago**? Were they servers **in the past**?
BE CAREFUL! Do not put a time marker in the middle of a statement or question.	We were in class **yesterday**. NOT We were ~~yesterday~~ in class. Were they servers **in the past**? NOT Were they ~~in the past~~ servers?
BE CAREFUL! Use *ago* after a time period in the past. Do not use *before* + a time period.	Were you in high school **two years ago**? NOT Were you in high school ~~before two years~~?

Go to MyEnglishLab to watch the grammar presentation.

EXERCISE 1 DISCOVER THE GRAMMAR

A GRAMMAR NOTES 1–6 Read this article about the first jobs of famous people.
Underline *was*, *wasn't*, *were*, and *weren't*.

A first job is very exciting. A first boss and a first paycheck are hard to forget.
But a first job is not always the job of your dreams. Here are the first jobs
of some famous people.

- In the past, Chris Rock, the comedian, was a busser at a restaurant.

- George Clooney was a shoe salesman.

- Lady Gaga and Madonna weren't always singers. Many years before they were
  famous, they worked in restaurants: Madonna was a server and Lady Gaga
  was a busser.

- Patrick Dempsey, the actor, was a juggler.

So maybe you're not happy with your job today. Maybe it isn't the job you really
want. Don't feel bad. Just keep looking.

B Look at the article in A again. Answer the questions. Circle the correct answers.

1. Were Chris Rock and Lady Gaga jugglers?
   a. Yes, they were.   **(b.)** No, they weren't.

2. Was George Clooney a busser?
   a. Yes, he was.   **b.** No, he wasn't.

3. Who was a server?
   a. Madonna was.   **b.** Lady Gaga was.

4. Who was a shoe salesman?
   a. Patrick Dempsey was.   **b.** George Clooney was.

EXERCISE 2 WAS AND WERE

GRAMMAR NOTE 1 Complete the sentences with *was* or *were*.

1. My first day at school _____was_____ fun. The students _____ friendly, and the teacher _____ great.

2. Pablo and Maria _____ absent on the first day of school. They _____ in a different class.

3. Our first test _____ difficult, and it _____ long.

4. My first-grade teacher _____ a young, new teacher. She _____ tough, and my classmates and I _____ afraid of her.

5. My first job _____ in a restaurant. I _____ a server. The other servers _____ helpful. The job _____ great. I'm a doctor now. My first days at work in the hospital _____ scary. I _____ nervous and unsure of everything.

EXERCISE 3 AFFIRMATIVE AND NEGATIVE FORMS

GRAMMAR NOTES 1–3 Complete the sentences with *was*, *wasn't*, *were*, or *weren't*. Use contractions.

1. My first day at school was great. The students _____were_____ helpful and kind.

2. My first day at work _____ good. My boss was angry and my co-workers weren't helpful.

3. My two interviews _____ long. They were over two hours.

4. His interview _____ long. It was only fifteen minutes.

5. My first month at work was very easy. There was very little work. I _____ busy, and the work _____ hard.

6. *First Day Jitters* was Julie Danneberg's first book. It _____ a big success, and it's still popular today.

7. The weather was terrible on my first day of school. It _____ cold and windy.

8. In July, the classroom _____ hot. The air conditioner was broken.

9. Yesterday the classroom _____ hot. The air conditioner was good.

10. My first months in college _____ very difficult. I was up until 1 a.m. every night.

EXERCISE 4 WORD ORDER OF QUESTIONS AND ANSWERS

A GRAMMAR NOTES 1–3, 5–6 Complete the conversation. Put the words in parentheses in the correct order. Use a capital letter when necessary.

ANA: Hey, look at this. It's a photo of me on my first day at work at Lacey's.

CHAD: _____ *When were you there* _____?
1. (when / you / there / were)

ANA: _____.
2. (was / it / five years ago)

CHAD: So, _____? Do you remember it?
3. (your first day / how / was / at work)

ANA: Uh-huh. _____. I was nervous,
4. (it / hard / was)

_____, and _____.
5. (busy / were / my co-workers)   **6.** (afraid of / was / my boss / I)

_____.
7. (wasn't / sure of anything / I)

CHAD: And now?

ANA: I like my job. What about you? _____?
8. (your first day / was / how / at work)

CHAD: Great! _____. My boss was
9. (I / relaxed / was / and happy)

wonderful. But _____.
10. (wasn't / my second month / good)

ANA: Why?

CHAD: My boss and a co-worker were let go. _____.
11. (my new boss and new co-worker / helpful / weren't)

_____, but now it's OK.
12. (was / for a few weeks / hard / it)

03|02 **B** LISTEN AND CHECK Listen to the conversation and check your answers in A.

EXERCISE 5 PRESENT AND PAST OF *BE*

GRAMMAR NOTE 1 Complete the sentences with *is*, *are*, *was*, or *were*.

1. The weather ___*was*___ terrible on the first day of our vacation. Now the weather

   ___*is*___ great.

2. My father _____ the CEO of his company today. He _____ an assistant in 2001.

3. Bob and Steve _____ absent yesterday, but they _____ in class now.

4. The class _____ easy at first. Now it _____ very hard.

5. She _____ a great manager now, but she _____ terrible the first month

   on the job.

6. We _____ nervous on our first plane trip, but now we _____ relaxed.

EXERCISE 6 EDITING

GRAMMAR NOTES 1–6

Read the email. There are six mistakes. The first mistake is already corrected. Find and correct five more.

Hi Victor,

                  was
How your weekend ~~was~~? You were busy?
       ^

I was yesterday at a job interview. It was for a sales job at a drugstore. The interviewer be friendly. The questions no were easy, but I think my answers was good. I hope I get the job. It's not my dream job, but it's a job with a paycheck.

Write soon.
Ella

STEP 4   COMMUNICATION PRACTICE

EXERCISE 7 LISTENING

03|03 **A** Listen to five phone messages. Who is each message from? Check (✓) the correct column.

	Friend	Family Member	Business Contact			Friend	Family Member	Business Contact
1.	☐	☐	☐		4.	☐	☐	☐
2.	☐	☐	☐		5.	☐	☐	☐
3.	☐	☐	☐					

03|03 **B** Listen again. Discuss each statement. Then check (✓) *True*, *False*, or *No Information*.

		True	False	No Information
1.	Ella's interview was at a drugstore.	☑	☐	☐
2.	Emiko was at a party with Ella.	☐	☐	☐
3.	Ella and Emiko are classmates.	☐	☐	☐
4.	Mr. Hess is Ella's friend.	☐	☐	☐
5.	Ella's parents were out with Aunt Mona.	☐	☐	☐
6.	Dave was in Ottawa on a vacation.	☐	☐	☐
7.	Dave was stuck in Ottawa.	☐	☐	☐
8.	Dave wasn't at the party for Emiko.	☐	☐	☐

C Work with a partner. Make guesses about the people in the messages in A.

EXAMPLE: I think Ella and Dave are close friends because . . .
I think Ella's interview was good because . . .

EXERCISE 8 HOW'S THE WEATHER?

A GUIDED CONVERSATION Prepare for the conversation in B. Study the weather words.

hot	warm	cool	cold	sunny	windy	rainy	cloudy

B Imagine it is the second day of your vacation in a new city. A friend calls you. Use the chart below to have a conversation about the weather.

EXAMPLE: A: Hi, Maria. How's Bangkok?
B: It's great.
A: How's the weather?
B: Well, it's cloudy today, but yesterday it was sunny and warm.

City	Yesterday		Today	City	Yesterday		Today
Bangkok	☀	🌡	☁	Rio de Janeiro	☀	🌡	☁
Beijing	☁	🌡	☀	Seoul	🌧	🌡	☁
Budapest	☁	🌡	☀	Vancouver	🌬	🌡	☁
Istanbul	☀	🌡	🌧	Washington	☀	🌡	🌬

EXERCISE 9 ON THE FIRST DAY OF CLASS . . .

GAME Work in groups. Say one true thing and one false thing about the first day of class. The next person repeats the true statement and corrects the false statement. Use *was*, *wasn't*, *were*, and *weren't* in your sentences. Take turns.

EXAMPLE: A: On the first day of class, Boris was late and it was warm and sunny.
B: Boris was late, but it wasn't warm and sunny. It was cool and cloudy.
A: Right! Your turn.
B: Ali and Iota were absent, and the classroom was dirty.
C: . . .

Go to MyEnglishLab for more communication practice.

A BEFORE YOU WRITE Read about Mario's first day at a school. Then work with a partner. Think about a first day at one of your schools. Your partner asks you five questions about your first day. Write notes on your answers in the chart.

Mario's First Day

My first day at high school was ten years ago. It was a bad day for me. The weather was awful. It was rainy, and my bus was late. My umbrella was broken. I'm usually early, but I was late that day. All the students were there. My clothes and books were wet. My hair and shoes were wet. I was very unhappy. My teacher was unhappy, too. I wasn't late again.

	Mario's First Day at School	Your First Day at School
What school was it?	High school	
When was it?	10 years ago	
How was the weather?	Awful	
How was your day?	Bad day!	
Why?	Umbrella broken, late, wet, teacher unhappy	

B WRITE Write a paragraph about your first day at a school. Use the paragraph in A and your chart. Use *was*, *were*, *wasn't*, or *weren't*.

C CHECK YOUR WORK Read your paragraph in B. Underline examples of the past of *be*. Use the Editing Checklist to check your work.

Editing Checklist
Did you . . . ? ☐ use *was* with *I/he/she/it* and *were* with *you/we/they* ☐ use past time markers at the beginning or end of sentences ☐ use *ago* after time periods

D REVISE YOUR WORK Read your paragraph again. Can you improve your writing? Make changes if necessary.

Go to MyEnglishLab for more writing practice.

UNIT 3 REVIEW

Test yourself on the grammar of the unit.

Ⓐ Complete the questions. Use *was* or *were*.

1. When _____ your interview?

2. Where _____ your interview?

3. _____ you nervous?

4. How _____ the questions?

5. _____ she at a job interview, too?

Ⓑ Match the questions and answers.

_____ 1. How was the weather?   a. Yes, I was.

_____ 2. Who was there?   b. Jon and Sri.

_____ 3. Were they home all evening?   c. Warm and sunny.

_____ 4. Were you late last week?   d. No, they weren't.

Ⓒ Complete the conversation with *was*, *wasn't*, *were*, or *weren't*.

A: How _____ your weekend?
          1.

B: Great. I _____ at the park all day Saturday.
              2.

A: _____ you with Ali?
      3.

B: Yes, I _____. We _____ together all day Saturday and Sunday.
            4.   5.

A: Ali _____ in class this morning. Where _____ he?
        6.   7.

B: I don't know.

Ⓓ Correct the paragraph. There are four mistakes.

John is at a job interview yesterday. It were for a job at a bank. The questions no were easy, but John's answers were good. He was happy. It a good day for John.

Now check your answers on page 445.

Go to MyEnglishLab to complete the review online.

Nouns, Adjectives, and Prepositions

PART 2

OUTCOMES

- Use count nouns, proper nouns, and common irregular nouns
- Recognize details in a short biography
- Recognize main ideas and details in a short lecture
- Talk about favorite people, places, and things
- Write a paragraph about a family member

OUTCOMES

- Use adjectives to describe nouns
- Recognize details in an article about a place
- Recognize details in a conversation about an interesting place
- Talk about interesting places, using adjectives
- Write a paragraph about an interesting place

OUTCOMES

- Describe locations with prepositions of place
- Recognize important details in a short article
- Locate places on a map from recorded descriptions
- Give directions to help others find places
- Write a short invitation to a party or an event

Count Nouns and Proper Nouns

PHOTOGRAPHS AND PHOTOGRAPHERS

OUTCOMES
- Use count nouns, proper nouns, and common irregular nouns
- Recognize details in a short biography
- Recognize main ideas and details in a short lecture
- Talk about favorite people, places, and things
- Write a paragraph about a family member

STEP 1   GRAMMAR IN CONTEXT

BEFORE YOU READ

Look at the black and white photo. Work with a partner. Answer the questions. Make guesses and give your opinion.

1. Who are the people?
    Where are they?

2. What year was it?

READ

04|01   Read this article about Henri Cartier-Bresson and one of his photographs.

A Photographer and a Photo

Henri Cartier-Bresson was a photographer and an artist. He was born in France in 1908 and died in 2004. At that time, he was almost ninety-six years old. Cartier-Bresson

traveled the world. He was in West Africa, the United States, India, China, Egypt, and Russia. His photos are from all over the world.

Cartier-Bresson is famous for "street" photography. Street photographs are about people in the street or other public places such as parks and beaches. They are sometimes about a special moment in time.

Look at this photo by Cartier-Bresson. It's a photo of a woman and a man on a special occasion. They are both wearing fine clothes. The woman is wearing a big hat with many flowers. The man is wearing a suit. The man is looking at the woman. They are in Harlem, in New York City. It's 1947. People say photos by Cartier-Bresson are striking. What do you think? Is this a striking photo?

AFTER YOU READ

A VOCABULARY Match the words in **bold** with their meanings.

1. Henri Cartier-Bresson **was born** in France.
   a. came into the world   **b.** lived

2. His photos are from **all over** the world.
   a. some parts of   **b.** everywhere in

3. It's open to **the public**.
   a. everyone   **b.** only some people

4. His photos are **striking**.
   a. dangerous and hurtful   **b.** unusual and attractive

5. It's a big **occasion**.
   a. special day   **b.** usual day

B COMPREHENSION Read the statements. Check (✓) *True* or *False*.

	True	False
1. Henri Cartier-Bresson was almost 69 years old when he died.	☐	☐
2. Almost all of Cartier-Bresson's photos were of Europe.	☐	☐
3. Cartier-Bresson was in many countries during his life.	☐	☐
4. Cartier-Bresson is famous for "holiday" photography.	☐	☐
5. Street photography shows people in places like parks or beaches.	☐	☐
6. Harlem is not in New York.	☐	☐

C DISCUSSION Work with a partner. Compare your answers in B. Change the false statements to true ones. Then look at the black and white photo on page 42 again. Do you like it? Why or why not?

Go to MyEnglishLab for more grammar in context practice.

COUNT NOUNS AND PROPER NOUNS

Singular Nouns
He is **a photographer**.
He is **an artist**.

Plural Nouns
They are **photographers**.
They are **artists**.

Irregular Plural Nouns

Singular	Plural
a man	men
a woman	women
a child	children
a foot	feet
a tooth	teeth
a person	people

Proper Nouns

Harlem is in **New York City**.
The singer **Harry Belafonte** was born in **Harlem**.

GRAMMAR NOTES

1 Nouns

Nouns are the names of:	
• people	**Cartier-Bresson** was a photographer.
• places	He was born in **France**.
• animals	A **bird** is in the photo.
• things	His **camera** is in his hands.

2 Singular Count Nouns

Count nouns are nouns that **you can count**: *one photo, two photos, three photos.*

Use *a* before **singular count nouns** that begin with a **consonant sound** like /**n**/, /**b**/, or /**h**/.	She's **a n**urse. He's **a b**aker. It's **a h**ouse.
Use *an* before singular count nouns that begin with a **vowel sound**.	She's **an a**rtist. He's **an e**ngineer. It's **an u**mbrella.
BE CAREFUL! Use *a* before a *u* that sounds like *yew*.	This is **a u**nit about nouns.
BE CAREFUL! Use *an* before an *h* that is silent.	It's **an h**our too early. *(Hour sounds like* our.*)*

3 Plural Count Nouns

To form the **plural** of most **count nouns**, add -*s* or -*es*.	one **park** three **parks** one **watch** three **watches**
Some nouns have **irregular** plurals.	one **man** two **men** one **tooth** two **teeth**
Some nouns such as *clothes*, *glasses*, *jeans*, and *scissors* are always plural.	My **jeans** are blue.
BE CAREFUL! Do not put *a* or *an* before plural nouns.	They are friends. **NOT** They are a friends.

4 Proper Nouns

Names of specific people and places are **proper nouns**. Begin these nouns with a capital letter.	**Harlem** is in **New York City**. **Harry Belafonte** is a singer.
BE CAREFUL! Do not put *a* or *an* before proper nouns.	Harry Belafonte was born in Harlem. **NOT** A Harry Belafonte was born in a Harlem.

PRONUNCIATION NOTE

04|02

Plural Noun Endings

When **nouns are plural**, the **ending** can have one of three sounds: /s/, /z/, or /ɪz/.

• /s/	students
• /z/	teachers
• /ɪz/	buses

REFERENCE NOTES

For information on **non-count nouns** and *the* (the definite article), see Unit 26 on page 310.

For a list of **spelling and pronunciation rules for plural nouns**, see Appendices 8 and 10 on page 434.

For a list of **irregular nouns**, see Appendix 9 on page 434.

For a list of **rules of capitalization**, see Appendix 20 on page 439.

EXERCISE 1
DISCOVER THE GRAMMAR

Ⓐ GRAMMAR NOTES 1–4

Read the conversation. Underline all the proper nouns and count nouns.

MIKE: So <u>Doug</u>, who's that with you in the <u>photo</u>?

DOUG: That's me with friends from college.

MIKE: Where are they now?

DOUG: Well, the woman next to me, Jasmine, is in Brazil.

MIKE: Really?

DOUG: Uh-huh. She's a teacher there. And the guy on the left, Bob, is here in New York. He's an accountant.

MIKE: Who's the other woman?

DOUG: That's Amy. She's a street photographer. She always has a camera with her. What a life! She travels all over the world. Last month, she was in India. Before that, she was in Central America. Now her photos are in a show at the library here.

MIKE: I'd love to see them.

DOUG: Them? Or her?

Ⓑ **Look at the conversation in A again. Find these nouns and write them.**

1. One noun that begin with a vowel sound: _____*accountant*_____

2. Three singular nouns that begin with a consonant sound:

   _____ , _____ , _____

3. Two proper nouns: _____ , _____

4. Two plural nouns: _____ , _____

EXERCISE 2 *A* AND *AN*

Ⓐ GRAMMAR NOTE 2 **Write *a* or *an* before each word.**

1. __*a*__ man   5. _____ flower   9. _____ lip

2. _____ hand   6. _____ suit   10. _____ woman

3. _____ hat   7. _____ eye

4. _____ earring   8. _____ ear

B Look at the photo, *Harlem, 1947*. Label the parts of the photo with the words from A.

_____ hat _____

EXERCISE 3 *A, AN*, AND Ø

GRAMMAR NOTES 1–3 Complete the sentences with *a* or *an*. Write Ø (no article) before plural nouns.

1. Henri Cartier-Bresson was __a__ photographer.

2. Cartier-Bresson and Ansel Adams were __Ø__ photographers.

3. Cartier-Bresson was _____ artist, too.

4. All good photographers are _____ artists.

5. Adams was _____ pianist before he was _____ photographer.

6. Adams was also _____ environmentalist.

7. Adams was born in California. Photography began for Adams with _____ trip to Yosemite National Park.

8. Adams said, "It's easy to take _____ photograph, but hard to make _____ masterpiece."

EXERCISE 4 REGULAR AND IRREGULAR PLURAL NOUNS

GRAMMAR NOTE 3 Complete the sentences with the plural form of the nouns in the box. See Appendix 8 (Regular Plural Nouns: Spelling Rules) and Appendix 9 (Irregular Nouns) on page 434 for help.

artist	class	eye	flower	man	person
~~city~~	country	fish	life	museum	watch

1. San Francisco and Los Angeles are _____*cities*_____ in California.

2. Brazil and France are _____ .

3. The Louvre and the Prado are _____ .

4. Seiko and Rolex are kinds of _____ .

5. Your photos of _____ in the water are striking.

6. There are two _____ , a man and a woman, in the photo *Harlem, 1947*.

7. The woman in *Harlem, 1947* has a hat with _____ .

8. Her face is beautiful, especially her _____ .

9. Many _____ and photographers live in New York City.

10. The _____ of famous artists are interesting to read about.

11. I'm taking two photography _____ at The New School in New York.

12. Six _____ and four women are in my "Street Photography" class.

EXERCISE 5 PROPER NOUNS

GRAMMAR NOTE 4 Change small letters to capital letters where necessary. See Appendix 20 (Capitalization and Punctuation Rules) on page 439 for help.

MIKE: Hi, are you ~~amy~~ *Amy* lin?

AMY: Yes, I am.

MIKE: I'm mike cho. I work with Doug.

AMY: Nice to meet you, mike.

MIKE: It's nice to meet you. Your photos are great.

AMY: Thanks. So, mike, are you from phoenix?

MIKE: No, I'm not. I'm from san francisco. I'm here for the Labor Day holiday.

AMY: Oh, san francisco is beautiful. I was there last year.

MIKE: Doug says you travel a lot.

AMY: Yes, I do. I was in india last year, and the year before that I was in almost every country in Central America.

MIKE: That's great.

AMY: Do you travel?

MIKE: When I can. I was in mexico last november during the thanksgiving vacation, and I was in canada with my family for a week last summer.

AMY: Any photos?

MIKE: No. My dad's brother sam is the photographer in our family.

EXERCISE 6 PLURAL NOUN ENDINGS

04|03 **A** PRONUNCIATION NOTE Listen and complete each sentence with the correct word from the box. Then listen again and check the noun ending sounds that you hear.

artists	books	boxes	classes	glasses	~~photos~~	scissors

	/s/	/z/	/ɪz/
1. The ____photos____ are ready.	☐	☑	☐
2. Her art _____ are from 10:00 to 1:00.	☐	☐	☐
3. Be careful. The _____ are sharp.	☐	☐	☐
4. The _____ are full of old photos.	☐	☐	☐
5. The paintings are by different _____ .	☐	☐	☐
6. I need my _____ to see the names of the artists.	☐	☐	☐
7. I have some interesting _____ about African art in that bookcase.	☐	☐	☐

04|03 **B** Listen again and repeat the sentences.

EXERCISE 7
EDITING

GRAMMAR NOTES 1–4

Read the sentences. There are eight mistakes. The first mistake is already corrected. Find and correct seven more.

Matisse and His Doves, 1944

1. Henri Cartier-Bresson's photos are often of famous ~~person~~. *people*

2. This is photo of Henri Matisse.

3. Henri Matisse was great artist.

4. Before Matisse was artist, he was lawyer.

5. Matisse's paintings are in museum all over the world.

6. In this photo, Matisse is in the south of france.

7. We see four bird outside their cages.

Go to MyEnglishLab for more focused practice.

STEP 4   COMMUNICATION PRACTICE

EXERCISE 8   LISTENING

04|04   **A**   Listen to a talk about a famous artist. Then circle the correct answers.

1. Born:	**a.** 1928	**b.** 1958	
2. Place of birth:	**a.** Transylvania	**b.** Pennsylvania	
3. Father's occupation:	**a.** a photographer	**b.** a construction worker	
4. First job after college:	**a.** a photographer	**b.** a commercial artist	
5. Famous things he painted:	**a.** soup cans	**b.** paint cans	
6. Person he painted:	**a.** Jack Kennedy	**b.** Jackie Kennedy	

▶ 04|04 **B** Listen again. Make up the beginnings of three sentences about the artist. Then work with a partner. Say the beginnings of your sentences. Your partner finishes the sentences. Take turns.

EXAMPLE: A: He was a famous...

B: painter and photographer.

B: He was born in...

A: ...

C Work in groups. Close your books. Take turns. Say things about the artist. Continue as long as you can.

EXAMPLE: A: He was a famous painter and photographer.

B: He was born in...

EXERCISE 9 A FEW OF MY FAVORITE THINGS

A PRESENTATION Prepare for your presentation in B. Draw a picture or find photos of places, people, or things you like. Choose pictures that show at least one proper noun, one singular noun, and one plural noun.

B Work in groups. Talk about your pictures. Take turns. When it's your turn to listen, write down your classmates' favorite people, places, and things.

EXAMPLE: This is a photo of my favorite park. It's Yosemite Park in California.

And this is a photo of my good friend. Her name is Margot Stram.

This is a photo of my car.

C Discuss: Do you and your classmates like the same things?

EXERCISE 10 WHAT'S IN YOUR BAG?

A GAME Work in groups. You have ten minutes. Look around the room or find things in your pockets, handbags, and book bags. Try and list one thing for each letter of the alphabet. The group with the most things wins.

EXAMPLE: A: an apple

B: a book

C: a comb

B Look at one other group's things. Can you name everything?

Go to MyEnglishLab for more communication practice.

FROM GRAMMAR TO WRITING

A BEFORE YOU WRITE Read about a photo. Then find a photo of one of your relatives. Complete the chart about your photo.

This is a photo of my grandmother, Chanda Patel. She was born in India in 1935. She's in Los Angeles now. She was an artist. In this photo, she's in a park. There are flowers and trees in the park. My grandmother is old. She is over eighty years old, but I think she's still a striking woman.

	Chanda Patel	**Person in my photo:**
Relative	*grandmother*	
Date and place of birth	*India, 1935*	
Profession	*artist*	
Age of person in photo	*over 80*	
Place of photo	*in a park*	

B WRITE Write a paragraph about your photo. Use the paragraph in A and your chart. Use count nouns and proper nouns. Use capital letters when necessary. See Appendix 20 on page 439 for help.

C CHECK YOUR WORK Read your paragraph. Underline count nouns and proper nouns. Use the Editing Checklist to check your work.

Editing Checklist
Did you . . . ?
☐ use *a* before singular count nouns that begin with consonant sounds
☐ use *an* before singular count nouns that begin with vowel sounds
☐ use Ø before plural count nouns
☐ add *-s* or *-es* to plural count nouns
☐ use a capital letter for proper nouns

D REVISE YOUR WORK Read your paragraph again. Can you improve your writing? Make changes if necessary.

Go to MyEnglishLab for more writing practice.

UNIT 4 REVIEW

Test yourself on the grammar of the unit.

A Complete the sentences. Use *a*, *an*, or Ø (no article).

1. This is _____ photo of my best friend.

2. He is _____ actor.

3. He is _____ from Ireland.

4. His friends are _____ actors, too.

5. They are _____ servers, too.

B Complete the sentences with the words from the box. Use the plural form.

| city | clothes | fish | person | watch |

1. My favorite _____ are Venice and Rio de Janeiro.

2. The two _____ in the photograph show midnight.

3. The woman is wearing _____ from the 1950s.

4. We take photos of the _____ in the sea with our underwater camera.

5. We see three _____ in the photo: a man and two women.

C Add capital letters where necessary.

A: Hi, are you the photographer?

B: Yes, I'm Amy lin.

A: Nice to meet you. I'm ali Mohammed.

B: Are you from london?

A: Yes, I am. I'm here for your thanksgiving Day holiday.

D Correct the paragraph. There are six mistakes.

Melanie Einzig is artist and an photographer. She was born in Minnesota, but lives in New york. Einzig captures moments in time. Her photograph are striking. They are in museum in San francisco, Chicago, and Princeton.

Now check your answers on page 445.

Go to MyEnglishLab to complete the review online.

Descriptive Adjectives
INTERESTING AND UNUSUAL PLACES

STEP 1 GRAMMAR IN CONTEXT

BEFORE YOU READ

Look at the photo of the rock formations. Work with a partner. Answer the questions.

1. What words describe the rock formations?

    beautiful   dangerous   exciting   relaxing   scary   unusual   usual

2. Are there unusual rock formations in your country? Where?

READ

05|01   Read this article about an interesting place.

Cappadocia, a Place of Mystery

Underground cities

This place is like another world, but it is here on Earth. What is this place? It's Cappadocia, in Turkey. Why is it so different? What's so unusual about it? Beautiful underground cities and formations of rock make it a very special place.

    Cappadocia has a long history. Many people lived in the underground cities to be safe from enemies.[1] These cities were big.

---

1 *enemies:* people who want to hurt you

Rock formations

One city, Derinkuyu, had room for more than 30,000 people.

Today only a few people live in cave homes in these cities. But many people from all over the world visit them. From above, Cappadocia looks like another world.

The climate in Cappadocia changes. The weather is comfortable during the long, dry summers, but cold and snowy in the winters. In the late spring and fall, the weather is usually great.

Awesome underground cities, beautiful formations, and an interesting history—these things make Cappadocia a special place to see.

AFTER YOU READ

A VOCABULARY **Complete the sentences with the words from the box.**

climate	comfortable	dry	safe	unusual

1. Be careful. It is not _____ to walk there.

2. Bring water. It is hot and _____ there.

3. My shoes are _____ . I can walk in them for hours.

4. I bought a(n) _____ bowl. It's very different from other bowls.

5. The _____ changes each season.

B COMPREHENSION **Circle the correct words to complete the sentences.**

1. Cappadocia has amazing formations of rock / snow.

2. Underground cities were dangerous / safe places to stay.

3. Cave homes were unusual / usual in Cappadocia long ago.

4. Cappadocia has a short / long history.

5. Cappadocia is dry / wet in the summer.

C DISCUSSION **Work with a partner. Compare your answers in B. Then tell your partner three things about Cappadocia.**

Go to MyEnglishLab for more grammar in context practice.

DESCRIPTIVE ADJECTIVES

Adjective After *Be*		
Noun	*Be*	Adjective
The room	is	**small**.
The rooms	are	

Adjective Before Noun		
	Adjective	Noun
It is a	**small**	room.
They are		rooms.

GRAMMAR NOTES

1 Adjectives: Meaning and Placement

Adjectives describe nouns.	NOUN ADJECTIVE **Cappadocia** is **beautiful**.
Adjectives can come **before** a **noun**.	ADJECTIVE NOUN It's a **big** **room**. NOT It's a ~~room big~~.
Adjectives can also come **after** the verb *be*.	BE ADJECTIVE The room **is** **big**.
When two adjectives come after *be*, we use *and* or *but* to connect them. *And* adds information. *But* shows a contrast or a surprise.	I am hungry **and** tired. He was happy **but** tired.
BE CAREFUL! Do not add -*s* to adjectives. They have the **same form** before singular and plural nouns.	It was a **hot** *summer*. They were **hot** *summers*. NOT They were ~~hots~~ summers.
A **noun** can also describe a noun. Like adjectives, these modifying nouns have the **same form** before singular and plural nouns.	MODIFYING NOUN NOUN Our **hotel** *room* was big. *(singular)* Our **hotel** *rooms* were big. *(plural)*

2 *A* or *an* Before an Adjective

When an adjective comes before a singular count noun, use *a* or *an* before the adjective.	
Use *a* before the adjective if it begins with a **consonant sound**.	It's **a beautiful** place. It's **a modern** hotel.
Use *an* before the adjective if it begins with a **vowel sound**.	It's **an unusual** place. It's **an old** city.

3 Adjective Endings

Some adjectives end in -*ing*, -*ed*, or -*ly*. Don't confuse them with verbs or adverbs.	It's **interesting**. We're **tired**. They're **friendly**.

Go to MyEnglishLab to watch the grammar presentation.

EXERCISE 1   DISCOVER THE GRAMMAR

A GRAMMAR NOTES 1–3   Maria is visiting Turkey. Read her travel blog about her hotel in Cappadocia. Underline the adjectives.

This area is magical. Where am I? I'm at Gamirasu Cave Hotel in the center of Cappadocia. The hotel is in a small, traditional village. It's in a cave. In the past, it was a home. Now it's a hotel. My room is fun. It's old, but has a modern bathroom. The rooms are not expensive. The price of the room includes a delicious breakfast and dinner. The service is good too—the people are helpful and friendly. Also, it's easy to visit all of Cappadocia from the hotel. It was a great choice.

B How does Maria describe each of the following?

1. the village: _____ *small* _____ , _____

2. the bathroom: _____

3. the price of the rooms: _____

4. the breakfast and dinner: _____

5. people: _____ , _____

6. the choice of hotel: _____

EXERCISE 2   PLACEMENT OF ADJECTIVES

GRAMMAR NOTES 1–3   Complete the telephone conversation. Put the words in parentheses in the correct order. Use a capital letter at the start of a sentence.

LISA: Where are you?

BEN: _____ *We're at an outdoor market* _____ in Cappadocia.
                        1. (market / at / we're / outdoor / an)

_____.
              2. (the / awesome / carpets / are)

LISA: Are they for sale?

BEN: Yes, they are. _____.
3. (reasonable / prices / the / are)

LISA: How's the weather?

BEN: _____.
4. (warm / it's / and / sunny)

LISA: You're lucky. _____ here.
5. (cold / windy / and / it's)

How are you and Al?

BEN: _____.
6. (tired / happy / we're / but)

EXERCISE 3 SENTENCES WITH ADJECTIVES

GRAMMAR NOTES 1–3 **Complete the sentences with the words in parentheses. Add the correct form of the verb *be*. Add *a* or *an* if necessary.**

1. We are at Gamirasu Cave Hotel. _____*It is a comfortable hotel*_____.
   (It / comfortable / hotel)

   _____.
   (The rooms / not / expensive)

2. Our guide says, "_____
   (Topdeck / good / restaurant)

   in Cappodacia. _____,
   (the food / delicious)

   and _____."
   (the waiters / friendly / and / helpful)

3. _____.
   (Yesterday / we / at / outdoor / market)

   _____.
   (The vegetables / fresh / and / delicious)

EXERCISE 4 EDITING

GRAMMAR NOTES 1–3 **Read the conversation. There are six mistakes. The first mistake is already corrected. Find and correct five more.**

RITA: Is that a ~~lamp new~~? *new lamp*

TED: Yes, it is. It's from Turkey.

RITA: The colors are beautifuls.

TED: Thanks. I got it at old market in Cappadocia near our hotel.

RITA: Were there many things interesting to buy?

TED: Yes. These bowls colorful are from the market, too.

RITA: The colors unusual. I like them a lot.

TED: Here. This one is for you.

Go to MyEnglishLab for more focused practice.

EXERCISE 5 LISTENING

▶05|02 **A** Listen to the telephone conversation between Sun Hi and her friend Russ. What are they talking about? Circle the correct answer.

a. Russ and Sun Hi's vacation   b. Sun Hi's visit to a national park   c. unusual places

▶05|02 **B** Listen to the conversation again. Complete the sentences. Circle the correct words. Explain your answer to a partner.

1. Sun Hi says Mesa Verde is (awesome) / awful.

2. The homes in the mountains are very cold / old.

3. Spruce Tree House was home to 130 people / 80 people.

4. The hotel is clean / nice.

5. The weather is warm / cold.

6. The park is crowded / not crowded.

▶05|02 **C** Work with a partner. Listen again. Sun Hi uses the words in the box to talk about her vacation. What does she say? Ask questions. Take turns.

awesome	cold	different	reasonable
clean	convenient	huge	unusual

EXAMPLE: A: What's awesome?
          B: Sun Hi says Mesa Verde National Park is awesome. What's clean?
          A: She says . . .

EXERCISE 6 MY FAVORITE PLACE

A Q & A Prepare for a Q & A exercise in B. Work with a partner. Find adjectives on the left that can describe the nouns on the right.

Adjectives			Nouns
cheap	delicious	modern	climate
cold	expensive	safe	food
comfortable	friendly	traditional	people
crowded	hot	unfriendly	shops
dangerous	interesting	unusual	transportation

EXAMPLE: A: Let's see. You can say a cold climate and a hot climate. Anything else?
          B: I think you can also say a comfortable climate.

B Work with a partner. Ask and answer questions about places that you know well. Take turns. Use the nouns and adjectives from the chart in A and your own ideas.

EXAMPLE: A: I know about Mesa Verde.
B: What is it?
A: It's a national park in Colorado.
B: How's the climate?
A: Summers are hot, but winters are cold.
B: Is the food delicious?
A: . . .

EXERCISE 7 POSITIVE OR NEGATIVE?

A WORD PLAY Work in small groups. Complete the chart. Add *a* or *an* and as many adjectives as you can.

A / AN	ADJECTIVE	NOUN
a an	huge unusual	city
a an	big expensive	restaurant

A / AN	ADJECTIVE	NOUN
		hotel
		park

B Write your phrases from A on the board. Then read other groups' phrases and talk about them. Are they positive (good)? Are they negative (bad)? Are they both positive and negative (good and bad)?

POSITIVE (+)	NEGATIVE (−)	BOTH (+ / −)
an interesting city	an expensive city	a huge city

EXAMPLE: A: I think "a huge city" is both good and bad.
B: I agree. A huge city is good when you need a job.
A: But sometimes huge cities are dangerous. That's bad.

Go to MyEnglishLab for more communication practice.

A BEFORE YOU WRITE
Read about Jeju Island. Then complete the chart about an interesting place you know. Tell your partner about your place. Is your place like Jeju Island?

Jeju Island is a beautiful island in South Korea. Many Koreans go to this island on their honeymoon. The people are friendly. The climate is warm and comfortable, but windy. There are awesome beaches, high mountains, and cold, dark caves. One unusual thing to see is the hardworking, older women of Jeju Island. They dive in the water and they, not the men, catch the fish.

LOCATION	Jeju Island, South Korea	My place:
CLIMATE	warm, comfortable, windy	
PLACES TO SEE	awesome beaches high mountains cold, dark caves	
PEOPLE	friendly hardworking, older women divers	

B WRITE Write a paragraph about an interesting place you know. Use the paragraph in A and your chart. Use adjectives.

C CHECK YOUR WORK Read your paragraph. Underline the adjectives. Use the Editing Checklist to check your work.

Editing Checklist
Did you . . . ?
☐ remember not to add -s to adjectives
☐ put an adjective right before a noun, not right after a noun
☐ use a or an before an adjective + count noun
☐ use and or but to connect two adjectives

D REVISE YOUR WORK Read your paragraph again. Can you improve your paragraph? Make changes if necessary.

Go to MyEnglishLab for more writing practice.

UNIT 5 REVIEW

Test yourself on the grammar of the unit.

Ⓐ Complete the sentences. Add *a*, *an*, or Ø (Ø = no article).

1. San Francisco is _____ big city.

2. We like to visit _____ cities.

3. Miami has _____ hot, humid summers.

4. It is _____ interesting place.

5. The Grand Canyon has _____ beautiful rock formations.

Ⓑ Circle the correct words to complete each sentence.

1. We are at a hotel small / a small hotel.

2. The hotel has an interesting garden / a interesting garden.

3. Our hotel room is big and comfortable / a big and comfortable.

4. The people here are kinds and helpful / kind and helpful.

5. It was a great choice / great choice.

Ⓒ Put the words in parentheses in the correct order.

1. (museum / I'm / the / at / new) _____ .

2. (things / interesting / It has) _____ to see.

3. (bowls / unusual / It has) _____ from long ago.

4. (has / It / carpets / beautiful) _____ too.

5. (place / is / The museum / a / great) _____ .

Ⓓ Correct the paragraph. There are five mistakes.

   The Grand Canyon National Park in Arizona is a awesome place to visit. Almost five
million people visit the park every year. It is a park beautiful. The weather is good in the
late spring and summer, but the park crowded is during those months. There are seven
differents places to stay in the park. I like El Tovar. It is a old hotel with a great view.

Now check your answers on page 445.

Go to MyEnglishLab to complete the review online.

6 Prepositions of Place
LOCATIONS

OUTCOMES
- Describe locations with prepositions of place
- Recognize important details in a short article
- Locate places on a map from recorded descriptions
- Give directions to help others find places
- Write a short invitation to a party or an event

STEP 1	GRAMMAR IN CONTEXT

BEFORE YOU READ

Work with a partner. Answer the questions.

1. What's your favorite museum?

2. Where is it?

3. Why do you like it?

READ

▶06|01 **Read this article about the American Museum of Natural History.**

The American Museum of Natural History

Two teens are in front of the four-foot-long (one-meter-long) jaw of a dinosaur. A little boy is next to a 94-foot (29-meter) whale. Three young women are near the Star of India—a very big, blue gem.[1] I'm in a room with butterflies in front of me, in back of me, and above me. Butterflies are everywhere. Where are we? We're all at the American Museum of Natural History. This awesome museum is located in New York City on Central Park West between 77th Street and 81st Street. It's home to an amazing collection.

Do you like to study animals and plants? Are you interested in dinosaurs and butterflies? Do you want to find out more about beautiful gems or the stars in

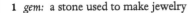

---

1 *gem:* a stone used to make jewelry

the sky? If you do, this museum is for you. It's huge. There are four floors and a lower level. The 94-foot (29-meter) whale and the blue sapphire are on the first floor. The dinosaur skeleton[2] is on the fourth floor. There are free tours and a free app with a GPS. For a special visit, you can spend a night at the museum and sleep under the whale.

So the next time you're in New York City, visit the American Museum of Natural History. Go to AMNH.org and read about the different sections, but choose only one or two parts to see. Save the rest for other visits.

_____

2 *skeleton:* all the bones of a human or animal

AFTER YOU READ

Ⓐ VOCABULARY Complete the sentences with the words from the box.

app	dinosaur	huge	interested	located	tour

1. The museum is _____ on Central Park West across the street from Central Park.

2. Blue whales are _____. Some blue whales are 100 feet (30 meters) long and weigh 200 tons (181 metric tons).

3. She is _____ in the Star of India because she works at a jewelry store.

4. The _____ was one hour. The guide was very good.

5. You can download a(n) _____ for the American Museum of Natural History.

6. The _____ lived between 230 and 65 million years ago.

Ⓑ COMPREHENSION Answer the questions.

1. In what city is the American Museum of Natural History? _____

2. Between what streets is the museum? _____

3. Where is the Star of India? _____

4. Where is the big dinosaur? _____

5. What two things can you find on the first floor? _____

Ⓒ DISCUSSION Work with a partner. Say three false things about the American Museum of Natural History. Your partner corrects you.

Go to MyEnglishLab for more grammar in context practice.

PREPOSITIONS OF PLACE

 The glasses are **between** the book and the watch.

 The glasses are **next to** the newspaper.

 The glasses are **behind** the box.

 The glasses are **under** the table.

 The glasses are **in** his pocket.

 The glasses are **on** the table **near** the window.

 The man is **on the left**. He is **in back of** the woman.

 The man is **on the right**. He is **in front of** the woman.

GRAMMAR NOTES

1 Prepositions of Place

Prepositions of place tell **where something is**. Below are some common **one-word prepositions**.

• *at*	Two students are **at** the door.
• *behind*	Ali is **behind** Olga.
• *between*	Our classroom is **between** room 205 and 209.
• *in*	We're **in** room 207.
• *inside*	Our jackets are **inside** the closet.
• *near*	Our school is **near** the museum.
• *on*	The paintings are **on** the second floor.
• *outside*	My friend is **outside** the museum.
• *over*	The sign **over** the door says, "Exit."
• *under*	A book bag is **under** the bench.

2 Prepositions of Place with Two or More Words

Some prepositions of place have two or more words.

• *across from*	The museum is **across from** a park.
• *in back of*	A garden is **in back of** the art museum.
• *in front of*	A fountain is **in front of** the art museum.
• *next to*	A bookstore is **next to** the art museum.

3 Common Prepositional Phrases

Prepositional phrases have three or more words.

• *on the right*	My father is **on the right**.
• *on the left*	My uncle is **on the left**.
• *in the middle*	I am **in the middle**.
• *in the world*	The Star of India is the biggest sapphire **in the world**.
• *on the corner of*	An art store is **on the corner of** Main Street and Mott Avenue.

4 Prepositions of Place Before *Work, Home*, and *School*

Use *at* before *work*.	I'm **at** work now.
Use *at* or no preposition before *home*.	I'm **at home**. or I'm **home**.
Use *at* or *in* before *school*.	I'm **at school**. or I'm **in school**.
BE CAREFUL! We can say "I'm in school," and "I'm at school," but *in* and *at* can mean something very different. *In* means inside. *At* means at that location.	I'm **in** the car. *(I'm inside the car.)* I'm **at** the car. *(I'm outside, next to the car.)*

5 Prepositions in Addresses

For prepositions in **addresses**, use *in, on,* and *at*.	
Use *in* before a country, a state, a province, or a city.	He's **in** Canada. *(country)* He's **in** British Columbia. *(province)* He's **in** Vancouver. *(city)*
Use *on* before a street, an avenue, a road, or the floor of a building.	My apartment is **on** Tenth *Avenue*. It's **on** the third *floor*.
Use *at* for the number of the building.	We're **at** 78 Main Street.
BE CAREFUL! Use **ordinal numbers** (*first, second, third*) with streets and avenues and the floors of a building. Do not use cardinal numbers (*one, two, three*).	It's on **Seventh** Street. It's on the **fourth** floor. NOT It's on ~~Seven~~ Street. It's on the ~~four~~ floor.
BE CAREFUL! Remember to use *the* before the ordinal number for the floor of a building.	I live **on the** fourth floor. NOT I live ~~on fourth~~ floor.
USAGE NOTE In informal conversation, when we say that a building is on the corner of two streets, we often drop the words *Street* or *Avenue*.	It's on the corner of Main and Fourth.

REFERENCE NOTE

For lists of **ordinal numbers** (*first, second, third,* etc.) and **cardinal numbers** (*one, two, three*), see Appendix 4 on page 432.

Go to MyEnglishLab to watch the grammar presentation.

EXERCISE 1 DISCOVER THE GRAMMAR

GRAMMAR NOTES 1–2, 5 **Read about these museums. Underline the prepositions of place. Then match the descriptions with the photos below.**

_C_ **1.** The National Anthropology Museum of Mexico is <u>in</u> a park in Mexico City. It has things from the Olmec, Maya, and Aztec cultures. Before you enter the museum, you walk under a huge concrete umbrella.

____ **2.** This red brick museum is in Amsterdam, Holland. It's the Rijksmuseum and it's located at Museumstraat 1. In front of the museum, you can see a beautiful canal. The museum has a collection of Dutch and other European art.

____ **3.** The State Hermitage was a palace, but now it is a museum. This green and white section of the museum is on the bank of the Neva River. It is in St. Petersburg in Russia.

____ **4.** The Guggenheim Museum Bilbao is in Bilbao, Spain. The architect was Frank Gehry. The curves of the building catch the light. It is located on the bank of the Nervión River. Inside the museum, there is a huge area with views of Bilbao's water and the hills of the Basque country.

EXERCISE 2 PREPOSITIONS FOR PLACES ON A MAP

GRAMMAR NOTES 1–3, 5 Look at the map. Complete the sentences with the words from the box. You can use some words more than once.

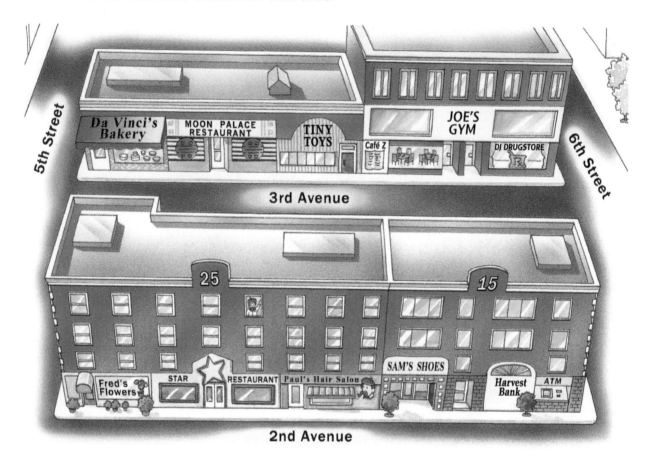

| at | between | next to | on | on the | on the corner of | under |

1. Tiny Toys is _____*on*_____ Third Avenue.

2. Paul's Hair Salon is _____ Sam's Shoes.

3. Da Vinci's Bakery is _____ Third Avenue and Fifth Street.

4. Café Z is _____ DJ Drugstore and Tiny Toys.

5. Paul lives _____ 25 Second Avenue.

6. His apartment is _____ fourth floor.

7. Café Z and DJ Drugstore are _____ Joe's Gym.

8. Fred's Flowers is _____ Second Avenue and Fifth Street.

9. Star Restaurant is _____ Fred's Flowers and Paul's Hair Salon.

10. Harvest Bank is _____ 15 Second Avenue.

EXERCISE 3 MORE PREPOSITIONS OF PLACE

GRAMMAR NOTES 1–5 **Complete the sentences with the words from the box. You can use some words more than once.**

at	between	in	in front of	on

1. My best friend lives in an apartment _____*in*_____ Lakeville.

2. He lives _____ 435 East Water Street.

3. He lives _____ the third floor.

4. His apartment is _____ a library and a bank.

5. The bank is _____ the corner of Lexington Avenue and 77th Street.

6. We need a taxi. . . . Look! There's a taxi _____ that bus.

7. My friend isn't _____ work today.

8. He's _____ home because it's a holiday.

EXERCISE 4 EDITING

GRAMMAR NOTES 1–5 **Read the conversations. There are six mistakes. The first mistake is already corrected. Find and correct five more.**

1. A: Where's the museum?

           on
    B: It's ~~in~~ Five Avenue between Eight and Ninth Streets.

2. A: Excuse me, are the dinosaurs the third floor?

    B: I'm not sure. Ask at the Information Booth.

    A: Where's the Information Booth?

    B: It's in front the stairs.

3. A: Is Jeff at the museum?

    B: No. He's in home right now.

Go to MyEnglishLab for more focused practice.

EXERCISE 5 LISTENING

▶06|02 **A** Look at the world map in Appendix 2 on page 430. Listen to the descriptions. Find each country on the map and write its name.

1. _K o r e a_   4. __ __ __ __ __

2. __ __ __ __ __ __ __   5. __ __ __ __

3. __ __ __ __ __ __ __ __   6. __ __ __ __ __ __ __ __ __

▶06|02 **B** Listen again and check your answers.

C Work with a partner. Look at the world map in Appendix 2 again. Write sentences about a country's location. Use the prepositions *between*, *near*, *next to*, and *in*. Ask your classmates to guess the country.

EXAMPLE: A: This country is between Mexico and Canada. What country is it?
            B: It's the United States.
            A: Right.

EXERCISE 6
IT'S ON THE
SECOND FLOOR

GAME Work in a group. Study the World Art Museum map. Ask and answer questions about places on the map. Try to use as many prepositions as possible in your answers. Take turns.

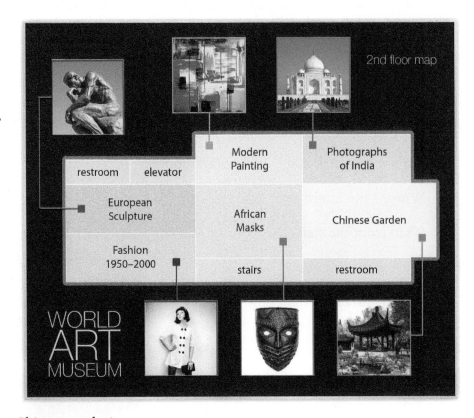

EXAMPLE: A: Where is the Chinese garden?
            B: It's on the second floor.
            C: It's next to a restroom.
            D: It's between a restroom and the Photographs of India.

EXERCISE 7   WHERE IS IT?

A BRAINSTORMING   The class decides on a well-known place in your city. Then work in a group. Use prepositions to describe the location of the place.

EXAMPLE: **Central Park:**

 A: It's between Fifth Avenue and Central Park West.
 B: It's across from the American Museum of Natural History on the West Side.
 C: And it's in Midtown.
 D: It's between 60th Street and 110th Street.

B Write your group's sentences on the board. Compare the sentences of the different groups. Decide which group has the best description and the most correct sentences.

EXAMPLE: A: I think there's a mistake is Group 2's last sentence. The grammar is correct, but the park is not between 60th Street and 110th Street. It's between 59th Street and 110th Street.
 B: Oh, you're right. Thanks.
 A: And I think there's a grammar mistake in . . .

EXERCISE 8
WHERE'S THE BUTTERFLY?

A PICTURE DISCUSSION   Add the things in the box to picture A. Do not show your picture to your partner.

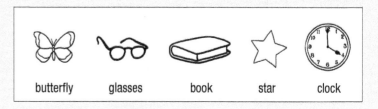

butterfly   glasses   book   star   clock

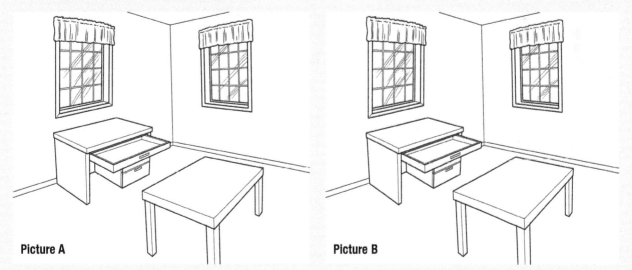

Picture A   Picture B

B Work with a partner. Use prepositions to tell your partner about your picture. Do not show the picture. Your partner draws your picture in picture B. Then compare your pictures.

EXAMPLE: In my picture, the butterfly is under the table. The book is inside the desk. The glasses are on the table. The star is next to the glasses. The clock is on the wall on the right above the desk.

Go to MyEnglishLab for more communication practice.

A BEFORE YOU WRITE
Read George's invitation to his wife's birthday. Then complete the chart with information about a party you are planning.

● ○ ○

GEORGE RAMI shared a message

You're invited to a birthday party for Martha at 12 p.m. on Sunday, June 18 at Bridgeport Café.

Bridgeport Café is at 2 Market Street. It's on the corner of Market and Pine Street. It's across from Pine Park. The party is on the second floor.

Shh! It's a surprise! Hope to see you there!

	George's invitation	Your invitation
Party for	Martha	
Type of party	Birthday	
Given by	George	
Location	Bridgeport Café	
Address	2 Market Street	
Date	Sunday, June 18	
Start time	Noon	

B WRITE Write an invitation to your party. Use George's message in A and your chart to help you. Use prepositions of place.

C CHECK YOUR WORK Read your message. Underline the prepositions. Then use the Editing Checklist to check your work.

Editing Checklist

Did you . . . ?

☐ use *to* after *next*

☐ use *from* after *across*

☐ use *of* after *in front* and *in back*

☐ use *on* before a street

☐ use *at* before a building number

D REVISE Read your message again. Can you improve your writing? Make changes if necessary.

Go to MyEnglishLab for more writing practice.

UNIT 6 REVIEW

Test yourself on the grammar of the unit.

A Look at the picture. Complete the sentences with the words from the box.

| behind | in front of | next to | on | under |

1. The book is _____ the table.

2. The glasses are _____ the table.

3. The cup is _____ the book.

4. The watch is _____ the book.

5. The pencil is _____ the book.

B Complete the sentences. Circle the correct answers.

1. Al's at / on work. His office is on / across the street from the big bank.

2. His apartment is in / at 235 West Second Street. It's on / between the corner of Second and Oak Avenue.

C Look at the picture of a circle, a square, and a triangle. Complete the sentences with the words from the box. You can use some words more than once.

| above | inside | in the | on the | under |

1. The circle is _____ left. The square is _____ middle.

   The triangle is _____ right.

2. The star is _____ the square. The butterfly is _____ the circle.

   The glasses are _____ the triangle.

D Correct the conversation. There are five mistakes.

A: Is Jon on school?

B: No. He's in home.

A: Where does he live?

B: He lives at Oak Street at New City.

A: Does he live in an apartment?

B: Yes. He lives in the third floor.

Now check your answers on page 446.

Go to MyEnglishLab to complete the review online.

Imperatives and the Simple Present

PART **3**

OUTCOMES

- Make offers and suggestions
- Give directions, orders, advice, and requests
- Recognize the advice given in a short article
- Recognize important details in a radio ad
- Discuss what to do and where to go, and make arrangements to meet
- Give advice about everyday problems
- Write an ad for a place to stay

OUTCOMES

- Talk about habits, routines, feelings, and thoughts
- Talk about how often something happens with adverbs of frequency
- Recognize details in a short article about customs
- Recognize details in a conversation about cultural traditions
- Talk about customs and traditions
- Write a paragraph about a holiday or tradition

OUTCOMES

- Ask and answer *yes/no* questions in the simple present
- Answer questions about a questionnaire
- Recognize important details in a conversation
- Complete a questionnaire and discuss results
- Ask and answer questions about objects, interests, likes, and dislikes
- Write an email about yourself

OUTCOMES

- Ask for information, using *wh-* questions in the simple present
- Answer questions about information in a talk show transcript
- Answer questions about details in a conversation
- Talk about dreams and sleep habits
- Ask questions about someone's life and write an interview transcript with the answers

UNIT 7

Imperatives; Suggestions with *Let's, Why don't we . . . ?*

LONG LIFE

OUTCOMES
- Make offers and suggestions
- Give directions, orders, advice, and requests
- Recognize the advice given in a short article
- Recognize important details in a radio ad
- Discuss what to do and where to go, and make arrangements to meet
- Give advice about everyday problems
- Write an ad for a place to stay

STEP 1 GRAMMAR IN CONTEXT

BEFORE YOU READ

Work with a partner. Answer the questions.

1. Who is the oldest person you know? How old is he or she?
2. What do you think is important for a long life?

READ

07|01 **Read this article. Then read the conversation between Joe and Mary.**

Secrets to a Long Life

Yiannis Karimalis was forty years old. He was a bridge painter in the United States. He was sick. His doctor said, "I'm sorry. You have stomach cancer.[1] It is very bad." Yiannis moved back to his hometown on the island of Ikaria in Greece.

Yiannis is over eighty and is still alive today. His doctor is dead.

Many people on the island of Ikaria live long lives. What are their secrets?

1 *cancer:* a serious disease in which cells in the body divide uncontrollably

Scientist Dan Buettner studies the lifestyle[2] of older people in different parts of the world. As a result of his studies in Ikaria, he offers this advice:

- Eat a lot of green vegetables, fresh fruit, olive oil, fish, and Greek honey.
- Drink herbal tea and goat milk.
- Don't worry.
- Take naps.
- Walk. Don't use a car, a bus, or a train.
- Call friends often.
- Pray.

_____

2 *lifestyle:* the way you live

Conversation:

JOE: Interesting article. But I don't have time to nap or think about the food I eat.

MARY: Come on, Joe, these suggestions are easy to follow. Let's try some of them.

JOE: I have a better idea. Let's move to Ikaria!

MARY: Um, why don't we just take a trip to Greece?

JOE: Stop right there. I'm looking up flights to Ikaria.

AFTER YOU READ

Ⓐ VOCABULARY Complete the sentences with the words from the box.

| advice | dead | island | nap | pray | secret |

1. You look very tired. Why don't you take a(n) _____?

2. Don't tell him. It's a(n) _____.

3. The plant is _____. Throw it away.

4. The doctor's _____ to Mark was, "Walk more. Eat less."

5. Some people _____ in a church, mosque, or temple, but you can do it anywhere.

6. Why don't we visit a Greek _____ on our next vacation?

Ⓑ COMPREHENSION What advice does Dan Buettner give in "Secrets of a Long Life"? Read the statements. Check (✓) *True*, *False*, or *No Information*.

	True	False	No Information
1. Don't eat oil.	☐	☐	☐
2. Don't sleep during the day.	☐	☐	☐
3. Don't listen to your doctor.	☐	☐	☐
4. Take walks.	☐	☐	☐
5. Drink juice.	☐	☐	☐

Ⓒ DISCUSSION Work with a partner. Look at the article. Study the advice. Close your book. Tell your partner the secrets of a long life. Take turns.

THE IMPERATIVE

Affirmative Statements	
Base Form of Verb	
Walk	to work.

Negative Statements		
Don't	Base Form of Verb	
Don't	take	a bus.

SUGGESTIONS

Affirmative Statements		
Let's	Base Form of Verb	
Let's	use	olive oil.

Negative Statements			
Let's	Not	Base Form of Verb	
Let's	not	use	butter.

Suggestions for You and Another Person		
Why don't we	Base Form of Verb	
Why don't we	go	on a bike tour?

Suggestions for Another Person		
Why don't you	Base Form of Verb	
Why don't you	get	the cameras?

RESPONSES TO SUGGESTIONS

Agree
That's a good idea. or Good idea.
That sounds good to me. or Sounds good to me.

Disagree
Why don't we . . . instead?
Sorry, I can't. I need to . . .

GRAMMAR NOTES

1 Imperatives: Uses

We use the **imperative** to give **directions**, **orders**, **advice**, **warnings**, and **requests**.

• give directions and instructions	**Turn** right.
• give orders	**Stand** there.
• give advice	**Use** olive oil. **Don't use** butter.
• give warnings	**Be** careful! It's hot.
• make polite requests	Please **call** before noon.

2 Affirmative and Negative Forms

The imperative uses the **base form of the verb**.	**Take** the train.
To make a negative imperative statement, use *don't* + **base form** of the verb.	**Don't worry.** **Don't be** late.

3 The Subject of an Imperative Statement

In an imperative statement, the **subject is always** *you*, but we usually don't say it or write it. The subject can be singular or plural.	Be careful. *(one person)* Be careful. *(two or more people)*

4 *Please* with Imperatives

Use *please* to make orders, warnings, and requests more polite.	**Please stand** there. **Please be** careful.
Please can come **at the beginning** or **the end** of the sentence.	**Please call** before noon. **Call** before noon, **please**.

5 Suggestions with *Let's* and *Let's not*

Use *Let's* or *Let's not* + **base form** for suggestions that include you and another person.	**Let's go.** **Let's not eat** there.

6 Suggestions with *Why don't we . . . ?* and *Why don't you . . . ?*

Use *Why don't we* + **base form** to make a suggestion for you and another person.	**Why don't we go** to the gym?
Use *Why don't you* to make a suggestion or give advice to another person.	**Why don't you look** on the Internet?
IN WRITING Remember to put a question mark (?) at the end of sentences with *Why don't we* and *Why don't you*.	**Why don't we meet** at the gym? **Why don't you drink** herbal tea?

EXERCISE 1   DISCOVER THE GRAMMAR

Ⓐ GRAMMAR NOTES 1–6   **Match each sentence with its purpose.**

_d_   **1.** Take the number 4 bus to the gym.

_____ **2.** Be careful. Don't take more than two pills a day.

_____ **3.** Please don't use your phone in the doctor's office.

_____ **4.** Stop!

_____ **5.** Why don't we get goat milk for a change?

_____ **6.** Why don't you eat honey? It's good for a sore throat.

a. Advice for someone

b. Polite request

c. Warning

~~d.~~ Directions

e. Order

f. Suggestion for you and me

Ⓑ **Read the sentences in A again. Circle three affirmative imperative forms and two negative imperative forms. Underline two suggestions.**

EXERCISE 2   IMPERATIVES AND SUGGESTIONS

GRAMMAR NOTES 1–6   **Complete the conversations. Circle the correct words.**

1. A: Let's to buy / (buy) chicken.

    B: I don't like chicken. And I'm tired of cooking. Why don't we eat / eats out today?

2. A: Please not get / don't get more broccoli. It isn't good.

    B: OK. How about kale?

3. A: Let's no take / not take the train to school. Let's walk. The weather is great.

    B: But it's late. Let's to walk / walk after school.

4. A: Let's call / calls Roberto and invite / to invite him to dinner.

    B: Good idea. What's his number?

5. A: Why don't you take / takes some time off? You look tired.

    B: Don't be worry / worry. I'm fine.

EXERCISE 3   AFFIRMATIVE AND NEGATIVE STATEMENTS

GRAMMAR NOTES 1–6   **Complete the sentences. Use the affirmative or negative imperative forms of the verbs in parentheses.**

1. The bread is still hot. Wait a few minutes. ____*Don't eat*____ it now.
                                                      (eat)

2. It's cold here. Please _____ the window.
                                      (close)

3. It's a secret. Please _____ your brother about my plan.
(tell)

4. For information about Dan Buettner, _____ the Internet.
(check)

5. Let's _____ to the store. It's not far and we need the exercise.
(walk)

6. Let's _____ those doughnuts. They're not very healthy.
(buy)

7. Please _____ me directions to the gym. I want to go there today.
(give)

8. _____ this herbal tea. It's delicious.
(try)

9. _____ a nap now. Help me prepare dinner.
(take)

10. _____ that island in July. The weather is usually awful then.
(visit)

EXERCISE 4 IMPERATIVES FOR DIRECTIONS

Ⓐ GRAMMAR NOTES 1–2 **Joe is giving Mary directions to Olivia's gym. Read their conversation. Then look at the map and put an X on the gym.**

MARY: Excuse me.... Where's Olivia's Gym?

JOE: Um, sure.... The gym is on Second Avenue between 70th and 71st Street. We're on Third Avenue at 73rd Street. Walk down Third Avenue to 71st Street. That's two blocks from here. Turn left at 71st Street. Walk one block to Second Avenue. Then turn right on Second Avenue. It's right there, on your right.

Ⓑ **Look at the map again. You are at the drugstore. Complete the directions to the library.**

Walk down 71st Street to _____

EXERCISE 5 EDITING

GRAMMAR NOTES 1–6 Read the conversation. There are six mistakes. The first mistake is already corrected. Find and correct five more.

JOE: Let's ~~to~~ go to the movies.

MARY: Why we don't go to the park first? It's a beautiful day.

JOE: OK. But first let have lunch. I'm hungry.

MARY: I'm hungry, too. Why don't we have a fruit salad with yogurt and nuts?

JOE: Good idea.

MARY: But you don't use those apples. They're bad. Throws them away.

JOE: OK.

MARY: And why you don't add honey to the yogurt? It's delicious that way.

JOE: You're right. This *is* really good.

Go to MyEnglishLab for more focused practice.

STEP 4   COMMUNICATION PRACTICE

EXERCISE 6 LISTENING

07|02 **A Listen to the ad. What is it for? Circle the correct letter.**

a. a spa   **b.** exercise classes   **c.** healthy meals

07|02 **B Listen again. Complete the chart.**

Name of business	Mia's Health Spot
Kind of class	
Breakfast foods	
Drinks	
Kind of massage	
Number of free weeks	

C Work with a partner. Imagine you are at Mia's Health Spot. Name a time. Your partner makes a suggestion with *Let's* or *Why don't we*. Take turns.

EXAMPLE: A: It's 6:00 a.m.

B: Let's take a yoga class. The yoga class is always fun.

A: Sounds good to me.

B: It's 7:00.

A: Why don't we . . .

EXERCISE 7 GIVE ADVICE

PROBLEM SOLVING Work with a partner. Imagine you have a small problem. For example, you're thirsty, tired, or bored. Tell your partner your problem. Your partner makes a suggestion starting with *Why don't you . . .* Agree or disagree. Tell why. Take turns.

EXAMPLE: A: I'm thirsty.

B: Why don't you have a soda?

A: Soda? That's not healthy.

B: Well, why don't you have some water?

A: OK. That's a good idea.

EXERCISE 8 LET'S WORK OUT

CONVERSATION Work with a partner. You want to do something healthy today. Student A, make a suggestion. Student B, disagree and make another suggestion. Give a reason why. Take turns.

EXAMPLE: A: Let's work out at the gym.

B: Why don't we take a walk instead? I don't want to be indoors.

A: OK. Let's take a walk in Woods Park.

B: Woods Park? Let's not walk there. Let's walk in . . .

EXERCISE 9 PUT YOUR ARMS IN THE AIR!

A PRESENTATION Prepare an exercise routine for your classmates. Use the ideas in the box or your own ideas.

Hop on one foot.	Put your arms in the air.	Touch your toes.
Jump up and down.	Touch your knees.	Wave your arms.

B Lead your class. They follow your instructions.

EXAMPLE: OK, everyone. Put your arms in the air. Good. Now wave your arms like this. No, Lia, not like that, like this. OK. Now . . .

A BEFORE YOU WRITE Read this ad for a hotel on the island of Ikaria. Write the imperative verbs on the lines below. Then compare answers with a partner.

Spiro's
"Hotel for Life"

For a great vacation, come to Spiro's "Hotel for Life" on the beautiful island of Ikaria. Enjoy a comfortable room with an awesome view of the beach. Eat three delicious and healthful meals in our dining room or on your terrace. Swim in our pool. Jog on the beach. Relax in our Jacuzzi. Everything is there for you. Don't delay. Book a room today.

<u>come</u>

B WRITE Write an ad for your own hotel. It can be anywhere in the world, under the water, or in outer space. Use your imagination. Use the imperative verbs in A and your own verbs.

C CHECK YOUR WORK Read your ad. Underline all the imperatives. Then use the Editing Checklist to check your work.

Editing Checklist
Did you . . . ?
☐ use the base form of the verb for the imperative
☐ use *don't* + the base form for the negative imperative

D REVISE Read your ad again. Can you improve your writing? Make changes if necessary.

Go to MyEnglishLab for more writing practice.

UNIT 7 REVIEW

Test yourself on the grammar of the unit.

Ⓐ Complete the sentences. Circle the correct words.

1. Let's get / Let's not get ice cream. It's on sale this week.

2. Why don't we / Let's not invite Bob? He's really nice.

3. Please buy / Don't buy peppers. I don't like them.

4. Let's meet / Let's not meet inside the restaurant. It's cold and windy outside.

5. Touch / Don't touch the wall. The paint is still wet.

Ⓑ Complete the instructions with the imperative forms of the verbs in parentheses. Use the affirmative or negative.

1. _____ comfortable clothes to yoga class. We want you to feel good.
   (wear)

2. _____ heavy clothes. It's warm in the classroom.
   (wear)

3. _____ a mat and water.
   (bring)

4. _____ coffee or soda inside the classroom. You can have those drinks
   (bring)
   after class.

5. Please _____ by check or cash. We don't accept credit cards.
   (pay)

Ⓒ Complete the conversations with *Let's*, *don't we*, or *don't you*.

1. A: _____ go to the gym.   B: Good idea.

2. A: Why _____ take a trip together?   B: OK. Where do you want to go?

3. A: I'm hungry.   B: Why _____ eat a sandwich?

4. A: _____ visit Grandma Millie.   B: That sounds like a great idea.

Ⓓ Correct the sentences. There are six mistakes.

1. Why you don't ask Andrij for help?

2. You look really tired. You take a short nap.

3. Let's to walk to work. Let's not drive.

4. Don't ask Boris to fix the car. Asks Mickey.

5. I'm on a diet, so buy please yogurt. Don't to get sour cream.

Now check your answers on page 446.

Go to MyEnglishLab to complete the review online.   Imperatives; Suggestions with *Let's, Why don't we…?*   **85**

Simple Present: Affirmative and Negative Statements
HOLIDAYS

OUTCOMES
• Talk about habits, routines, feelings, and thoughts
• Talk about how often something happens with adverbs of frequency
• Recognize details in a short article about customs
• Recognize details in a conversation about cultural traditions
• Talk about customs and traditions
• Write a paragraph about a holiday or tradition

STEP 1   GRAMMAR IN CONTEXT

BEFORE YOU READ

Work with a partner. Answer the questions.

1. What is a holiday?

2. Do you like holidays? Do you have a favorite holiday?

READ

▶08|01 Read this article about New Year traditions around the world.

New Year Traditions Around the World

People all around the world observe the New Year. Most people don't work or go to school. They frequently get together with family and friends. In some cultures, the New Year is a serious occasion. In other cultures, it is more festive. Every culture does something to mark the beginning of the year, but the New Year comes at different times in different cultures.

The Chinese New Year is a very important time. It lasts fifteen days. Families gather for a big feast. They often eat special food such as long noodles for a long life and a whole fish for a prosperous[1] year. They watch parades, set off firecrackers, and give children red envelopes with money in them. The envelopes are red because red is a lucky color.

In one European country, every December 31 just before midnight, radios and TV stations play a waltz, and everyone dances at the stroke of midnight. It's the country of Strauss, Mozart, Wiener schnitzel, and Sacher torte. Do you know the country? It's Austria.

---

1 *prosperous:* successful and rich

In a country in South America, people often decorate their homes and wear something yellow for luck and happiness. Sometimes they make a bath of flowers. They also follow a Spanish tradition. They eat twelve grapes at midnight. Can you guess the country? It's Peru.

Why do people always mark the New Year? It's a time to remember the past, look ahead to the future and wish everyone a happy, healthy, and prosperous year.

AFTER YOU READ

A VOCABULARY **Complete the sentences with the words from the box.**

at the stroke of	culture	eve	get together	look ahead	tradition

1. _____ midnight, all over Japan, Buddhist temples ring their bells 108 times.

2. Not every _____ follows the same calendar, so New Year's Day comes at different times of the year.

3. A Cuban New Year _____ is to throw water out the window. People want to wash away bad things from the year before.

4. In the United States, friends often _____ for a party on New Year's Eve.

5. New Year's Day is a time of hope for a better future. People everywhere _____ to the new year.

6. The night before New Year's Day is New Year's _____.

B COMPREHENSION **Match the beginnings of the sentences with the endings.**

_____ 1. People in China eat long noodles

_____ 2. On New Year's Eve, people in Spain often

_____ 3. People see the New Year

_____ 4. People often get together with

_____ 5. On New Year's Eve at midnight, people in Austria

a. family and friends.

b. dance the waltz.

c. as a time to look back and look ahead.

d. for a long life.

e. eat twelve grapes at midnight.

C DISCUSSION **Work with a partner. Compare your answers in B. Then tell your partner three things that you remember from the article "New Year Traditions Around the World."**

EXAMPLE: The Chinese New Year lasts fifteen days. People frequently get together with their family on New Year's Day. In Peru, . . .

Go to MyEnglishLab for more grammar in context practice. Simple Present: Affirmative and Negative Statements **87**

SIMPLE PRESENT: AFFIRMATIVE AND NEGATIVE STATEMENTS

Affirmative Statements

Subject	Verb	
I You* We They	eat like	noodles.
He She It	has	

Negative Statements

Subject	Do not/ Does not	Base Form of Verb	
I You We They	do not don't	eat like have	noodles.
He She It	does not doesn't		

*You can be singular or plural.

ADVERBS AND EXPRESSIONS OF FREQUENCY

Adverbs of Frequency

Subject	Adverb	Verb	
I You We They	usually almost never	cook	on holidays.
He She		cooks	
It		rains.	

Adverbs of Frequency with Be

Subject	Be	Adverb	
I	am	usually almost never	busy.
You We They	are		
He She It	is		

Adverbs of Frequency

always	100%
almost always	↑
frequently	
usually	
often	
sometimes	50%
rarely / seldom	
almost never	↓
never	0%

Expressions of Frequency

Emiko cooks	**every** day. **twice a** week. **three times a** month. **several times a** year. **once in a while**.

GRAMMAR NOTES

1 Simple Present for Things That Happen Again and Again

Use the simple present to talk about **habits**, **regular occurrences**, **customs**, and **routines**.

• habits	She **drinks** tea every morning.
• regular occurrences	They **visit** their parents on most holidays.
• customs	They **dance** the waltz on New Year's Eve.
• routines	He **gets up** at seven.

2 Simple Present for Facts

Use the simple present to express **facts**.	It **rains** a lot in San Francisco.

3 Simple Present for Feelings, Thoughts, and Possessions

Use the simple present to express **feelings**, **thoughts**, and **possessions** such as *love, be, need, want, understand, know,* and *have.*

• feelings	I **love** you.
• thoughts	We **understand** him.
• possessions	She **has** a car.

4 Affirmative Statements

In **affirmative statements**, use the **base form** of the verb for *I, we, you, they,* and **plural nouns**.	**I cook** on New Year's Eve. **They play** cards on New Year's Day. **We wear** traditional clothes on New Year's Day.
Add **-s** or **-es** to the base form of the verb when the subject is *he, she, it,* or a singular noun.	**She dances** the waltz. **Jon watches** TV. **It starts** at 10:00.
BE CAREFUL! *Everyone, everybody, no one, nobody,* and *family* are singular.	**Everyone likes** my mother's cooking. NOT Everyone ~~like~~ my mother's cooking.
The **third-person singular affirmative** forms of *have, do,* and *go* have irregular spelling and pronunciation. • has /**hæz**/ • does /**dʌz**/ • goes /**goʊz**/	 She **has** a new dress for the holiday. He **does** his homework the day before the holiday. He **goes** to his uncle's home on New Year's Eve.

5 Simple Present of the Verb *Be*

The simple present of the verb *be* is irregular. (See Units 1 and 2.)	I **am** tired. He **is** hungry. We **are** tired.
BE CAREFUL! Do not use *be* + another simple present verb after the subject.	I am tired. **or** I feel tired. **NOT** I am ~~feel~~ tired. **NOT** I ~~am~~ feel tired. He is from Italy. **or** He comes from Italy. **NOT** He is ~~comes~~ from Italy. **NOT** He ~~is~~ comes from Italy.

6 Negative Statements

In **negative statements**, use *does not* or *do not* before the base form of the verb.	He **does not work** on New Year's Day. We **do not go** to school on New Year's Day.
USAGE NOTE Use the contractions *doesn't* or *don't* in speaking or in informal writing.	He **doesn't work** on New Year's Day. We **don't go** to school on New Year's Day.
BE CAREFUL! Do not use *no* before the base form of the verb to make a negative statement.	He doesn't work. **NOT** He ~~no~~ work.
BE CAREFUL! When *or* connects verbs in a negative statement, do not repeat *don't* or *doesn't*.	I **don't smoke** or **drink** coffee. **NOT** I don't smoke or ~~don't~~ drink coffee.

7 Adverbs of Frequency and Their Placement

Adverbs of frequency tell **how often** something happens. They include: *always, almost always, frequently, usually, often, sometimes, rarely, seldom, almost never, never*.	
Adverbs of frequency usually come **after the verb** *be*.	That store *is* **usually** open on holidays. It *is* **rarely** closed.
Adverbs of frequency usually come **before other verbs**.	We **often** *go* to the park. We **sometimes** *have* a picnic.
Some adverbs of frequency can go at the start or the end of a sentence.	**Sometimes** we have a picnic. We go there very **often**.
BE CAREFUL! Don't begin or end a sentence with *never, seldom, rarely,* or *always* followed by the subject + verb.	I never cook. I always wash the dishes. **NOT** ~~Never~~ I cook. I wash the dishes ~~always~~.

8 Expressions of Frequency

Expressions of frequency are time markers. They say **how often** something happens.	
Expressions of frequency usually come **at the beginning** or **at the end** of a sentence.	**Every Sunday**, she bakes a cake. She bakes a cake **every Sunday**.

PRONUNCIATION NOTE

Third-Person Singular Verbs

The pronunciation of verbs that end in -*s* is /s/ or /z/. The pronunciation of verbs that end in -*es* is /ɪz/.

• verbs ending in /s/	like**s**	eat**s**	cook**s**	visit**s**
• verbs ending in /z/	play**s**	buy**s**	throw**s**	clean**s**
• verbs ending in /ɪz/	watch**es**	wish**es**	us**es**	exchang**es**

REFERENCE NOTES

For more information on **non-action verbs** such as *like, want, have*, see Unit 17 on page 196.

For **spelling and pronunciation rules** for the **third-person singular** in the **simple present**, see Appendices 13 and 14 on page 436.

For more information on the **present tense of the verb** *be*, see Unit 1 on page 6 and Unit 2 on page 17.

STEP 3   FOCUSED PRACTICE

EXERCISE 1 DISCOVER THE GRAMMAR

GRAMMAR NOTES 1–5, 7–8 **Read the sentences. Circle the simple present verbs. Underline the adverbs and expressions of frequency.**

Songkran (is) the name of the traditional Thai New Year celebration. Every year, people celebrate Songkran in April. On this holiday, Thais throw water at each other. They often use water guns. Sometimes they use containers. Once in a while, they use garden hoses. Thailand is hot and dry, and the water feels good. Gan loves the holiday. He says, "The water feels great, and Songkran is a lot of fun."

EXERCISE 2 AFFIRMATIVE SENTENCES

GRAMMAR NOTES 1–4 **Complete the sentences. Circle the correct answers.**

1. My brother live /(lives)in Sydney, Australia. On New Year's Eve, he always
   watch / watches the New Year celebration at Sydney Harbor. I live in Florida.
   I see / sees the Sydney fireworks on TV in the United States the following day.

2. In the United States, Canada, and the Netherlands, some people jump / jumps
   into a cold lake, sea, or ocean on New Year's Day. My cousin belong / belongs to a
   "polar bear club." He swim / swims in the ocean every New Year's Day. Our family
   think / thinks he's strange.

3. Denmark has / have an unusual New Year tradition. People visit / visits friends at
   midnight on New Year's Eve and throw / throws plates at their door. Popular people in
   Denmark has / have many broken plates at their doorsteps on New Year's Day.

4. In Saudi Arabia, people follow / follows the Muslim lunar calendar. New Year
   come / comes at different times of the year.

EXERCISE 3 NEGATIVE SENTENCES

GRAMMAR NOTE 6 **Complete the sentences. Use the simple present forms of the verbs
in parentheses. Use contractions.**

1. My mother _____*doesn't clean*_____ on New Year's Day. She always cleans the house
   (not / clean)
   before the holiday.

2. On New Year's Day, we open the door and windows. We _____ bad
   (not / want)
   things to stay with us.

3. My brother _____ to bed on New Year's Eve. He stays up all night long.
   (not / go)

4. In my family, the women and girls wear traditional clothes, but the men and boys

   _____ traditional clothes.
   (not / wear)

5. Yael _____ to school on New Year's Day. Relatives visit and the
(not / go)
family enjoys a delicious meal together.

6. We _____ on New Year's Eve or New Year's Day. We prepare for the
(not / work)
holiday on the day of New Year's Eve, and celebrate that night and the whole next day.

EXERCISE 4 ADVERBS OF FREQUENCY

GRAMMAR NOTES 7–8 **Write sentences. Put the words in parentheses in the correct order. Start with a capital letter.**

1. (often / watches / he / parades)

He often watches parades.

2. (goes / he / rarely / football games / to)

_____

3. (a lot / eat / every Thanksgiving Day / we)

_____

4. (my grandparents / visit / I / every holiday)

_____

5. (that store / always / crowded/ is)

_____

6. (we / once in a while / wear / traditional clothes)

_____

EXERCISE 5 THIRD-PERSON SINGULAR VERBS

08|03 PRONUNCIATION NOTE **Underline the verb in each sentence. Then listen to each sentence and check (✓) the sound of the verb ending.**

	/s/	/z/	/ɪz/
1. He <u>cooks</u> for the holidays.	☑	☐	☐
2. He uses a lot of spices.	☐	☐	☐
3. He buys food at the green market.	☐	☐	☐
4. The food costs a lot of money.	☐	☐	☐
5. She knows about different traditions.	☐	☐	☐
6. She watches the fireworks on TV.	☐	☐	☐
7. She misses her family.	☐	☐	☐
8. She thinks about the past.	☐	☐	☐

EXERCISE 6
EDITING

GRAMMAR NOTES 1–7

Correct the paragraph. There are eight mistakes. The first mistake is already corrected. Find and correct seven more.

In the United States, people ~~start usually~~ *usually start* the New Year holiday on New Year's Eve. Many people plans celebrations weeks in advance. My cousin always invite friends to a party. My parents usually goes to a restaurant with friends. Many people watch an event on TV just before midnight. On New Year's Day, people usually am relax from the night before. My brother watches football games on TV, and my sister is go to her friend's home. I sleeps all day long and not do anything.

Go to MyEnglishLab for more focused practice.

STEP 4   COMMUNICATION PRACTICE

EXERCISE 7 LISTENING

08|04 **A** Listen to a conversation about Independence Day celebrations. Then write the name of the country and the date of its Independence Day.

Country	Independence Day	Notes
1. India	August 15th	white, green, orange decorations—colors of flag
2.		
3.		
4.		

08|04 **B** Listen to the conversation again. Take notes about the traditions in the different countries in the chart in A.

C Work with a partner. Talk about the traditions in the four countries.

EXAMPLE: **A:** On Independence Day in India, they decorate everything in white, green, and orange.

B: That's right. White, green, and orange are the colors of the Indian flag.

EXERCISE 8 TRADITION, TRADITION

Ⓐ DISCUSSION Work in a group. Talk about traditions in six countries. One student takes notes.

EXAMPLE: A: In the Netherlands, some people jump in the sea on New Year's Day.
B: That's right. And in India, students celebrate Teacher's Day. The students perform for their teachers and dress like their teachers.
A: How do you know? You're not from India.
B: My friend is from India.
C: In Saudi Arabia, some people don't eat on our New Year. New Year's Day isn't a big occasion.
D: In Poland, we always eat babka on . . .

Ⓑ Tell the class about the traditions.

EXERCISE 9 THAT'S NOT TRUE!

GAME Work in a group. Say three things about different holidays. Two are true and one is false. The other groups guess the false statement.

EXAMPLE: GROUP A: On Labor Day in the United States, most people don't work. On Chinese New Year, children get red envelopes. On Thanksgiving Day, most Americans eat a lot of seafood.
GROUP B: The third sentence is false. Americans eat a lot of *turkey* on Thanksgiving. They don't eat a lot of seafood.

EXERCISE 10 LET'S CELEBRATE!

Ⓐ PRESENTATION Prepare for a presentation. Tell your partner about your favorite holiday. When is it? What do you do on the holiday? Use ideas from the box to tell about the holiday.

clean	don't work	get together with family
cook	eat special food	pray
don't go to school	exchange gifts	wear traditional clothes

EXAMPLE: A: My favorite holiday is Labor Day. I never work on Labor Day. I get together with my family.
B: Oh. My favorite holiday is Thanksgiving. I don't work. I cook a lot of special food, and I eat the food with my family . . .

Ⓑ Give a presentation about your favorite holiday to the class.

EXAMPLE: I'd like to tell you about Labor Day. On Labor Day, people don't work . . .

Go to MyEnglishLab for more communication practice.

FROM GRAMMAR TO WRITING

A BEFORE YOU WRITE Read the information about an Independence Day celebration in the United States. Then choose a holiday that your family celebrates and complete the chart. Work with a partner. Tell your partner about the holiday.

July 4th is Independence Day in the United States. On this holiday, my family usually gets together for a barbecue. My older sister bakes a pie, and my older brother bakes cookies. My aunt doesn't bake anything, but she always helps my mother. They prepare different salads. My father barbecues hamburgers and hot dogs. The holiday is usually fun, but sometimes my brother teases my sister. They act like little children. At the end of the day, we're all tired and full, but happy.

Independence Day		Your holiday:	
Family Member	**What does he or she do?**	**Family Member**	**What does he or she do?**
sister	bakes a pie		
brother	bakes cookies, teases sister		
aunt and mother	prepare salads		
father	barbecues		

B WRITE Write a paragraph about your holiday. Use the paragraph in A and your chart. Use the simple present tense and adverbs of frequency.

C CHECK YOUR WORK Read your paragraph. Underline the simple present and adverbs of frequency. Use the Editing Checklist to check your work.

Editing Checklist

Did you . . . ?
- [ ] add -s or -es to the third-person singular
- [ ] put adverbs of frequency before all verbs except *be*
- [ ] put adverbs of frequency after the verb *be*
- [ ] put expressions of frequency at the start or the end of a sentence

D REVISE YOUR WORK Read your paragraph again. Can you improve your writing? Make changes if necessary.

Go to MyEnglishLab for more writing practice.

UNIT 8 REVIEW

Test yourself on the grammar of the unit.

A Complete the sentences. Circle the correct answers.

1. My father love / loves to celebrate his birthday.

2. He no have / doesn't have brothers, but he has four sisters.

3. He invite / invites all his sisters to our home.

4. We not give / don't give him expensive presents. We give him funny little presents.

5. We have / has a great time.

B Complete the sentences with the correct forms of the words in parentheses. Use the correct word order.

1. Students in India _____ Teacher's Day on September 5.
   (always / celebrate)

2. A student _____ the clothes of a teacher.
   (sometimes / wear)

3. A teacher _____ in the class and pretends to be a student.
   (often / sit)

4. Children _____ in a school performance.
   (usually / dance)

5. Teachers _____ happy on Teacher's Day.
   (usually / be)

C Complete the sentences. Circle the correct answers.

1. Everyone think / thinks about workers on this holiday.

2. Most people don't work / doesn't work on this holiday.

3. In the United States, this holiday come / comes at the end of the summer.

4. The name of this holiday is / are Labor Day.

D Correct the paragraph. There are six mistakes.

Some people don't enjoys holidays and family gatherings. Bill Jones visits usually his wife's sister on holidays. He likes his wife's sister, but he don't like her husband. Mary Brown doesn't like holidays because she lives far from her family. She have a very important job, but she doesn't have close friends. She usually watches movies and wait for the holiday to be over. Always she is happy to return to work.

Now check your answers on page 446.

Go to MyEnglishLab to complete the review online.

Simple Present: Affirmative and Negative Statements   **97**

Simple Present:
Yes/No Questions and
Short Answers
ROOMMATES

OUTCOMES
- Ask and answer *yes/no* questions in the simple present
- Answer questions about a questionnaire
- Recognize important details in a conversation
- Complete a questionnaire and discuss results
- Ask and answer questions about objects, interests, likes, and dislikes
- Write an email about yourself

STEP 1   GRAMMAR IN CONTEXT

BEFORE YOU READ

Work with a partner. Answer the questions.

1. Do you live alone or do you have a roommate?
2. Imagine you are looking for a roommate. What do you want to know about the person?

READ

09|01   Colleges often use questionnaires to help students find the right roommate. Read this roommate questionnaire.

Roommate Questionnaire[1]

	Name: Dan		ame: Jon	
	YES	**NO**	**YES**	**NO**
1. Do you wake up early?	☐	☑	☐	☑
2. Do you stay up late?	☑	☐	☑	☐
3. Are you neat?	☑	☐	☑	☐
4. Does a messy room bother you?	☑	☐	☑	☐
5. Are you quiet?	☐	☑	☑	☐
6. Are you talkative?	☑	☐	☐	☑
7. Are you outgoing?	☑	☐	☐	☑
8. Are you a private person?	☑	☐	☐	☑
9. Are you easygoing?	☐	☑	☑	☐
10. Does noise bother you?	☐	☑	☐	☑
11. Do you listen to loud music?	☑	☐	☑	☐
12. Do you watch a lot of TV?	☑	☐	☑	☐
13. Do you study and listen to music at the same time?	☑	☐	☑	☐
14. Do you study with the TV on?	☑	☐	☑	☐

1 *questionnaire:* a list of questions

AFTER YOU READ

A VOCABULARY **Complete the sentences with the words from the box.**

bother	easygoing	messy	outgoing	private	stay up

1. Is her room always so _____? She needs to put things away.

2. Does that smell _____ you? I feel a little sick from it.

3. Do you usually _____ late? Your lights are always on after midnight.

4. Nothing upsets your brother. Is your sister _____, too?

5. Is your friend's daughter always _____? She wasn't afraid to talk to anyone at the party.

6. My parents don't say much about themselves. Are your parents _____ people, too?

B COMPREHENSION **Read the questions. Choose the correct answers.**

1. Do Dan and Jon wake up late? **a.** Yes, they do. **b.** No, they don't.

2. Are Dan and Jon neat? **a.** Yes, they are. **b.** No, they aren't.

3. Is Dan quiet? **a.** Yes, he is. **b.** No, he isn't.

4. Are Dan and Jon outgoing? **a.** Dan is, but Jon isn't. **b.** Dan isn't, but Jon is.

5. Is Dan a private person? **a.** Yes, he is. **b.** No, he isn't.

6. Is Jon easygoing? **a.** Yes, he is. **b.** No, he isn't.

7. Do Dan and Jon dislike loud music? **a.** Yes, they do. **b.** No, they don't.

8. Does Dan study and listen to music at the same time? **a.** Yes, he does. **b.** No, he doesn't.

C DISCUSSION **Work with a partner. Compare your answers in B. Then discuss: Are Dan and Jon a good match? Give reasons for your answer.**

Go to MyEnglishLab for more grammar in context practice.   Simple Present: *Yes/No* Questions and Short Answers   **99**

SIMPLE PRESENT: *YES/NO* QUESTIONS AND SHORT ANSWERS

Yes/No Questions		
Do/Does	Subject	Base Form of Verb
Do	I you we they	work?
Does	he she it	

Short Answers						
Affirmative				Negative		
Yes,	you I/we you they	do.	No,	you I/we you they	don't.
	he she it	does.		he she it	doesn't.

GRAMMAR NOTES

1 Simple Present: Form of *Yes/No* Questions

For *yes/no* **questions** in the **simple present**, use *do* or *does* before the subject. Use the base form of the verb after the subject.	SUBJECT **Do** you **need** a roommate? **Does** he **have** a roommate?
BE CAREFUL! Do not use *do* or *does* for *yes/no* questions with *be*.	**Are** you from Ecuador? **Is** he from France? NOT ~~Do you be~~ from Ecuador? NOT ~~Does he is~~ from France?

2 Simple Present: Answers to *Yes/No* Questions

We usually use **short answers** in conversation, but we can also use **long answers**.	A: Do you need a roommate? B: **Yes.** or **Yes, I do.** *(short answers)* or B: **Yes, I need a roommate.** *(long answer)*

REFERENCE NOTE

For information on *yes/no* **questions with *be***, see Unit 2 on page 17.

Go to MyEnglishLab to watch the grammar presentation.

EXERCISE 1   DISCOVER THE GRAMMAR

GRAMMAR NOTES 1–2
Read about Dan and Jon. Then match the questions and answers.

In many ways, Dan and Jon are alike. Both Dan and Jon like music and sports, but Dan likes pop music, and Jon likes hip-hop. Both Dan and Jon like basketball, but Jon likes soccer and Dan doesn't. Dan and Jon are both neat. They don't like a messy room. They both like to go to bed late–after midnight. They watch about two hours of TV at night, and they study with the TV on. But in one way Dan and Jon are completely different. Dan is talkative, but Jon is quiet. Dan says, "We're lucky about that. It works out nicely. I talk, he listens." Jon says, "Uh-huh."

_b_	**1.** Do Dan and Jon both like music and sports?	**a.** It doesn't say.
____	**2.** Do Dan and Jon like to go to bed early?	~~**b.**~~ Yes, they do.
____	**3.** Does Dan like pop music?	**c.** Yes, he does.
____	**4.** Is Jon talkative?	**d.** No, they don't.
____	**5.** Do Dan and Jon like movies?	**e.** Yes, they are.
____	**6.** Are Dan and Jon neat?	**f.** No, he isn't.

EXERCISE 2   *YES/NO* QUESTIONS AND SHORT ANSWERS

GRAMMAR NOTES 1–2 Complete the questions with *Do* or *Does* and the verbs in parentheses. Then complete the short answers.

1. (listen)   A: _____*Do*_____ you _____*listen*_____ to music?

B: Yes, _____*we do*_____. **or** Yes, _____*I do*_____.

2. (have)   A: _____ your roommate _____ a TV?

B: No, she _____.

3. (wake up)   A: _____ he _____ early?

B: No, _____.

4. (stay up)   A: _____ they _____ late?

B: Yes, _____.

5. (bother)   A: _____ the TV _____ you?

B: No, _____.

6. (have)   A: _____ your room _____ a big window?

B: Yes, _____.

7. (like)   A: _____ you _____ a cool room?

B: No, _____.

8. (have)   A: _____ the room _____ Wi-Fi?

B: Yes, _____.

9. (go)   A: _____ she _____ to parties all the time?

B: No, _____.

10. (need)   A: _____ we _____ more light?

B: Yes, _____.

11. (sell)   A: _____ they _____ lamps on campus?

B: Yes, _____.

EXERCISE 3 *YES/NO* QUESTIONS WITH *DO* AND *BE*

GRAMMAR NOTES 1–2 Complete the *yes/no* questions with *Do, Does, Am, Is,* or *Are.* Then complete the short answers.

1. A: ___*Am*___ I late?   B: No, ___*you aren't*___.

2. A: ___*Does*___ he come home late?   B: Yes, ___*he does*___.

3. A: _____ you busy?   B: Yes, we ____ ____.

4. A: _____ they have a lot of work?   B: No, _____.

5. A: _____ they roommates?   B: No, _____.

6. A: _____ they live in a dormitory?   B: Yes, _____.

7. A: _____ she your sister?   B: No, _____.

8. A: _____ you live at home?   B: Yes, I _____.

9. A: _____ your roommate play baseball?   B: No, he _____.

10. A: _____ we in the right room?   B: Yes, you _____.

11. A: _____ you friends?   B: Yes, _____.

12. A: _____ you cook well?   B: No, I _____.

EXERCISE 4 *YES/NO* QUESTIONS AND SHORT ANSWERS

GRAMMAR NOTES 1–2 **Complete the conversation. Write questions with the correct forms of the words in parentheses. Then write short answers with *do*, *does*, *don't*, or *doesn't*.**

YURI: So tell me about your new roommate, Edward. ___*Do you like*___ him?
1. (you / like)

SHEN: ___*Yes, I do*___. He's a really nice guy.
2.

YURI: Where is he from? He sounds like a native speaker. _____ from
3. (he / come)

England?

SHEN: _____. He comes from Australia.
4.

YURI: Cool. What's he studying?

SHEN: Music.

YURI: Oh, he's a music major. _____ an instrument?
5. (he / play)

SHEN: Of course. He plays three instruments: violin, cello, and piano.

YURI: Wow. _____ with him?
6. (you / play)

SHEN: _____. I'm not a good musician. But sometimes his cousin plays
7.

with him.

YURI: _____ family close by?
8. (he / have)

SHEN: _____. His uncle, his aunt, three cousins, and his grandmother are
9.

ten minutes away. I was at their home last night.

YURI: Really? _____ them often?
10. (you / see)

SHEN: _____. They invite us for a meal at least once a month. They all
11.

play music, and they're interesting people. His uncle is a

conductor, and his cousin is an opera singer.

YURI: _____ them a small gift when you visit?
12. (you / bring)

SHEN: _____. I'm a poor student.
13.

YURI: Hey, you're not that poor.

EXERCISE 5 EDITING

GRAMMAR NOTES 1–2 Correct the conversations. There are nine mistakes. The first mistake is already corrected. Find and correct eight more.

1. A: Does she ~~goes~~ ^{go} to school?

   B: Yes, she goes.

2. A: Does he needs help?

   B: Yes, he does.

3. A: Do they are like rock music?

   B: Yes, they do.

4. A: Do she live near the university?

   B: Yes, she lives.

5. A: Does he has a roommate?

   B: Yes, he has.

6. A: Are you friends?

   B: Yes, we do.

Go to MyEnglishLab for more focused practice.

STEP 4   COMMUNICATION PRACTICE

EXERCISE 6 LISTENING

09|02 **A** Listen to the conversation. Why is Andrea talking to Valentina Gold?

   a. to find a roommate   b. to work out a problem with her roommate

09|02 **B** Listen to the conversation again and complete the chart with Andrea's answers.

	Andrea	Leyla
Parties		likes parties
Music		likes rock
Sports		plays basketball, soccer, swims
Study habits		studies at night in her room

C Work with a partner. Discuss: Are Andrea and Leyla a good match? Why or why not?

EXAMPLE: A: I think Andrea and Leyla are a bad match because Andrea doesn't like parties, but Leyla likes them.

B: Really? I disagree. I think they're a good match because . . .

EXERCISE 7 COMPARING HABITS AND PERSONALITY

A QUESTIONNAIRE Answer the roommate questionnaire.

Roommate Questionnaire   Name: _____

		YES	NO
1.	Do you wake up early?	☐	☐
2.	Do you stay up late?	☐	☐
3.	Are you neat?	☐	☐
4.	Does a messy room bother you?	☐	☐
5.	Are you quiet?	☐	☐
6.	Are you talkative?	☐	☐
7.	Does noise bother you?	☐	☐
8.	Are you outgoing?	☐	☐
9.	Are you a private person?	☐	☐
10.	Are you easygoing?	☐	☐
11.	Do you listen to loud music?	☐	☐
12.	Do you watch a lot of TV?	☐	☐
13.	Do you study and listen to music at the same time?	☐	☐
14.	Do you study with the TV on?	☐	☐

B Compare your questionnaire answers with your partner. Are you and your partner a good match?

C Work with a partner. Think of one more question for the questionnaire. Ask your partner the question. Then answer it yourself.

EXAMPLE: A: What's your question?

B: My question is, "Do you keep a lot of stuff?"

A: No. I don't like to hold on to things. What about you?

B: I keep a lot of stuff. What's your question?

A: . . .

EXERCISE 8 FIND SOMEONE WHO . . .

A GAME Walk around your classroom. Ask your classmates *yes/no* questions in order to fill out the chart. When a classmate answers "yes," write his or her name in the chart. The first person to complete the chart wins.

EXAMPLE: A: Mattias, do you cook well?
B: Yes, I do. I cook every day.
A: Are you a soccer fan?
B: No, . . .

Find someone who . . .	Name
cooks well	*Mattias*
is a soccer fan	
texts every day	
plays a musical instrument	
is athletic	
is an only child	
has more than three brothers and sisters	
is interested in science	
is interested in business	
has a pet	
listens to the news every day	
is a good dancer	

B Report back to the class.

EXAMPLE: Mattias is a good cook. He isn't a soccer fan . . .

EXERCISE 9 ROOM FOR RENT

ROLE PLAY Work with a partner. You are Student A. You are looking for a room to rent. Your partner, Student B, has a room to rent. Ask your partner questions about the room. Your partner answers your questions and asks you questions about yourself. You can use the ideas in the boxes.

EXAMPLE: A: I have a few questions about the room for rent. First of all, is it near the university?
B: Yes. It's only two blocks away.
A: Good. Does the room have furniture?
B: It has . . .

STUDENT A

a window?
a closet?
a bed? a desk?
Wi-Fi?
a view?

STUDENT B

listen to music?
play an instrument?
have any pets?

Go to MyEnglishLab for more communication practice.

A BEFORE YOU WRITE Read this email to you from a future roommate at an English language school. Work with a partner. What do you want to know about Sammy? Write questions.

● ● ●

Hi,

I'm Sammy Morales from Colombia. I am going to be your roommate. I'm excited about our English language school, but I'm also a little nervous. Maybe you feel the same way.

I'm nineteen years old, and I'm from Fusagasugá, a town near Bogotá, Colombia. I come from a large family. I have five brothers and two sisters. Do you have any brothers and sisters?

I love sports and music. How about you? Do you have a favorite music group? Do you have a favorite sport? Please tell me about yourself.

I look forward to meeting you next month.

All the best,
Sammy

B WRITE Write an email to Sammy. Answer Sammy's questions and ask Sammy your questions from A. Use the simple present.

C CHECK YOUR WORK Read your email. Underline *yes/no* questions in the simple present. Then use the Editing Checklist to check your work.

Editing Checklist
Did you . . . ?
☐ use *do* in simple present *yes/no* questions with *I, you, we,* or *they*
☐ use *does* in simple present *yes/no* questions with *he, she,* or *it*

D REVISE YOUR WORK Read your email again. Can you improve your writing? Make changes if necessary.

UNIT 9 REVIEW

Test yourself on the grammar of the unit.

Ⓐ Complete the sentences with the words from the box.

| Am | Are | Do | Does | Is |

1. _____ you know his brother?

2. _____ his brother messy?

3. _____ he have a lot of friends?

4. _____ they easygoing?

5. _____ I your best friend?

Ⓑ Complete the questions with the correct forms of the words in parentheses.

1. _____ a roommate?
    (you / have)

2. _____ English fluently?
    (his roommate / speak)

3. _____ TV at night?
    (your roommate / watch)

4. _____ talkative?
    (be / your roommate)

5. _____ in the United States?
    (be / your roommate's parents)

Ⓒ Write questions about an apartment. Use the correct forms of the words in parentheses.

1. (be / the neighbors / noisy) _____

2. (the building / have / an elevator) _____

3. (be / the apartment / near buses) _____

4. (the bedroom / have / two closets) _____

5. (be / the bedroom / big) _____

Ⓓ Correct the conversations. There are five mistakes.

1. A: Does he have a big TV in his room? B: Yes, he has.

2. A: Does she needs help? B: No, she don't.

3. A: Do you are friends? B: Yes, we aren't.

Now check your answers on page 446.

Go to MyEnglishLab to complete the review online.

Simple Present:
Wh- Questions
DREAMS

STEP 1   GRAMMAR IN CONTEXT

BEFORE YOU READ

Work with a partner. Answer the questions.

1. Do you dream?

2. Do you remember your dreams?

3. What do you dream about?

READ

▶ 10|01 *Ask the Expert* is a radio talk show. Today Mike Stevens is talking to dream expert Ella Lam. Read their conversation about dreams.

Dreams

MIKE: Good afternoon. I'm Mike Stevens. Welcome to *Ask the Expert*. This afternoon my guest is Ella Lam. She's the author of *Sleep and Dreams*. Thank you for coming.

ELLA: Thanks, Mike. It's great to be here.

MIKE: Ella, we have a lot of questions about dreams. Our first question is from Carolina Gomes. She asks, "Why do we dream?"

ELLA: Actually, nobody really knows why. But I think dreams help us understand our feelings.

MIKE: OK. Our next question is from Jonathan Evans. He asks, "Who dreams? Does everyone dream?"

ELLA: Yes, everyone dreams. And what's more, scientists believe animals dream, too.

MIKE: Wow! That's really interesting. How do we know?

ELLA: Machines show when people or animals dream. But, of course, no one knows what animals dream about.

MIKE: Interesting. OK. Our next question is from Pablo Ortiz. He writes, "People don't remember *all* their dreams. What dreams do they remember?"

ELLA: People remember their unusual dreams. And, unfortunately, they remember their nightmares.

MIKE: Beata Green says, "I have the same dream again and again. What does that mean?"

ELLA: That dream has special meaning for you. You need to think about it.

MIKE: Here's a question from Samuel Diaz. "When do people dream?"

ELLA: They dream during REM or deep sleep. REM means *rapid*[1] *eye movement*.

MIKE: I hear REM sleep is important. Why do we need it?

ELLA: It *is* important. Without it, we can't remember or think clearly.

MIKE: Ron Morgan writes, "Why do I remember my dreams? My roommate doesn't."

ELLA: Well, a University of Iowa professor says, "Creative[2] people remember their dreams."

MIKE: Really? . . . Thank you so much, Ella. We look forward to reading your new book.

---

1 *rapid:* fast
2 *creative:* able to see things in a new way

AFTER YOU READ

A VOCABULARY **Complete the sentences with the words from the box.**

| author | guest | nightmare | remember | unfortunately |

1. Who is the _____ of *Sleep and Dreams*?

2. What is the name of the _____ on tonight's *Ask the Expert*?

3. Do you _____ your dreams?

4. A very bad dream is called a(n) _____.

5. This book about dreams sounds interesting. _____, it's over a thousand pages long, so I don't have time to read it!

B COMPREHENSION **Answer the questions.**

1. Who dreams? _____

2. What do animals dream about? _____

3. Why do people dream? _____

4. What does REM stand for? _____

5. Who remembers dreams? _____

C DISCUSSION **Work with a partner. Compare your answers in B. Give reasons for your answers. Then discuss: What else do you want to know about dreams?**

Go to MyEnglishLab for more grammar in context practice.

SIMPLE PRESENT: *WH-* QUESTIONS; SHORT AND LONG ANSWERS

Wh- Questions

Wh- Word	Do/ Does	Subject	Base Form of Verb
When	do	I	sleep?
Where	do	you	
Why	do	we	
What	do	they	need?
Who	does	she	know?
How	does	it	feel?
How often	does	he	get up?

Answers

Short	Long
From 10:00 p.m. to 5:00 a.m.	You sleep from 10:00 p.m. to 5:00 a.m.
On the futon.	I sleep on the futon.
Because we're tired.	We sleep because we're tired.
Two pillows.	They need two pillows.
My brother.	She knows my brother.
Good.	The blanket feels good.
Three times a night.	He gets up three times a night.

Wh- Questions About the Subject

Wh- Word	Verb	
Who	sleeps	in that bedroom?
Who	sleeps	in this bedroom?

Answers

My brother does.
My parents do.

GRAMMAR NOTES

1 *Wh-* Questions

Wh- **questions** ask for information. They are sometimes called **information questions**.

The form of a *Wh-* question is usually:
Wh- word + *do/does* + subject + base form

WH- WORD	*DO/DOES*	SUBJECT	BASE FORM	
When	do	you	go	to bed?
What	does	he	dream	about?

2 *Wh-* Questions About a Subject

We use *who* to ask about a person who does something (the subject).

Questions about a **subject** follow this form:
Who + **third-person-singular verb**

A: **Who wakes** Felix?
B: **Inez** wakes him. *(Inez = the subject)*

BE CAREFUL! Do not use *do* or *does* with questions about a subject. Do not use the base form of the verb.

Who wakes Feliz?
NOT Who ~~does~~ wakes Felix?
NOT Who ~~do~~ wakes Felix?
NOT Who ~~wake~~ Felix?

3 Who and whom

We use **who** (or **whom**) to ask about a person who is the object of the question.

Questions about an **object** follow this form: **Who(m) + do/does + subject + base form**	A: **Who does Inez wake**? B: Inez wakes **Felix**. *(Felix = the object)*
USAGE NOTE **Whom** can be used instead of **who** in questions about an object, but *whom* is very formal so most people don't use it.	**Who does** Dr. Chen **visit**? **Whom does** Dr. Chen **visit**? *(very formal and not common)*

REFERENCE NOTE

For more information about **who**, **what**, **where**, **when**, and **why**, see Unit 2 on page 17.

Go to MyEnglishLab to watch the grammar presentation.

STEP 3   FOCUSED PRACTICE

EXERCISE 1
DISCOVER THE GRAMMAR

GRAMMAR NOTES 1–2 **Night owls like to stay up late at night. Early birds get up early. Read about a night owl and an early bird. Then match the questions and answers.**

Felix is a night owl. He hates to get up in the morning. On weekends, he goes to bed at 1:00 a.m. and gets up at noon. Unfortunately for Felix, during the week his first class starts at 8:15, and he needs to get up early.

At 7:00 a.m., Felix's alarm rings. He wakes up, but he doesn't get up. He stays in bed and daydreams. At 7:20, his mom comes in. She has a big smile. She says, "Felix, it's time to get up."

Inez is Felix's mother. She's an early bird. She's up at 6:00 a.m. even when she's on vacation. When she wakes Felix up, he says, "Leave me alone. I'm tired."

Finally, at about 7:30, Felix gets up. He jumps out of bed, showers, and gets dressed. At 7:50, he drinks a big glass of juice and runs to the bus stop. The bus comes at 8:00.

_g_ 1. Who hates to get up in the morning?   **a.** On weekends.

____ 2. How does Felix feel in the morning?   **b.** Tired.

____ 3. Who does Inez wake up on school days?   **c.** At 6:00 a.m.

____ 4. Why does Felix run to the bus stop?   **d.** Felix's alarm rings.

____ 5. What does Felix have for breakfast?   **e.** A glass of juice.

____ 6. When does Felix sleep late?   **f.** Because he doesn't want to be late.

____ 7. What happens at 7:00?   **g.** Felix does.

____ 8. When does Inez wake up?   **h.** She wakes Felix up.

EXERCISE 2 WORD ORDER OF *WH-* QUESTIONS

GRAMMAR NOTE 1 Complete the conversations. Read the answers. Then write questions. Put the words in parentheses in the correct order.

1. (do / you / usually get up / When)

   A: *When do you usually get up?*

   B: At 7:00 on weekdays.

2. (Where / come from / your guest / does)

   A: _____

   B: She's from Sydney.

3. (at night / they / How / do / feel)

   A: _____

   B: They're never tired at night. They're night owls.

4. (does / Who / he / dream about)

   A: _____

   B: He dreams about me.

5. (What / she / dream about / does)

   A: _____

   B: Actually, she never remembers her dreams.

6. (wake up / your mother / does / What time)

   A: _____

   B: She wakes up at 6:00 a.m.

EXERCISE 3 *WH-* QUESTIONS ABOUT THE SUBJECT

GRAMMAR NOTES 2–3 Complete the conversations. Read B's answers. Then write A's questions. Use the correct forms of the words in parentheses.

1. (Who / daydream)

   A: *Who daydreams?*

   B: John does.

2. (Who / have / nightmares)

   A: _____

   B: Her brother Sam does.

3. (Who / get up / before 6:00 a.m.)

   A: _____

   B: Grandma Ilene does.

4. (Who / hate / early morning classes)

    A: _____

    B: Bob, Emiko, and Jill do.

5. (Who / need / more than eight hours of sleep)

    A: _____

    B: Feng does.

EXERCISE 4 *WH-* QUESTIONS

GRAMMAR NOTES 1–3 **Read the answers. Then ask questions about the underlined words.**

1. Sabrina daydreams.

    Who *daydreams?* _____

2. Sabrina daydreams during her math class.

    When _____

3. Sabrina daydreams about her boyfriend.

    Who _____

4. Sabrina daydreams during her math class because she doesn't like the class.

    Why _____

5. Sabrina's boyfriend is 3,000 miles away in Alaska.

    Where _____

6. Sabrina feels lonely.

    How _____

7. Sabrina's boyfriend has a good job.

    Who _____

8. Sabrina's boyfriend works for an oil company.

    What _____

EXERCISE 5 *WH-* QUESTIONS: SUBJECT AND OBJECT

GRAMMAR NOTES 2–3 Underline and label the subject (*S*) and object (*O*) in each sentence. Then write one question about the subject and one question about the object. Begin with *who*.

1. My <u>mother</u> calls <u>me</u> every day.
         S   O

    Q: *Who calls you every day?*   Q: *Who does your mother call every day?*

    A: My mother does.   A: My mother calls me.

2. In a dream, Jake meets his boss at a party.

    Q: _____   Q: _____

    A: Jake does.   A: He meets his boss.

3. In a nightmare, two men push Maya.

    Q: _____   Q: _____

    A: Two men do.   A: They push Maya.

4. In my dream, my grandfather visits my friends.

    Q: _____   Q: _____

    A: My grandfather does.   A: My friends.

EXERCISE 6 EDITING

GRAMMAR NOTES 1–3 There are ten mistakes. The first mistake is already corrected. Find and correct nine more.

1. Where do they ~~sleeps~~? *sleep*

2. Why they need two pillows?

3. Who sleep on the sofa?

4. When does she goes to bed?

5. Who wake you?

6. Who does you dream about?

7. How he feels about that?

8. What you dream about?

9. How long does she sleeps at night?

10. Where he sleep?

Go to MyEnglishLab for more focused practice.

EXERCISE 7 LISTENING

⏵10|02 Ⓐ Mia often has the same dream. She tells a doctor about her dream. Listen to their conversation. What is she looking for in the dream?

_____

⏵10|02 Ⓑ Listen again. Answer the questions. Then work with a partner and compare your answers.

1. What important event does Mia have in her dream?   *She has an important test.*_____

2. What does the man in the dream say?   _____

3. What does Dr. Fox think Mia has?   _____

4. What are the two paths Dr. Fox talks about?   _____

5. What does Mia's father want her to study?   _____

EXERCISE 8 SNORING, DREAMING, AND SLEEP

Ⓐ PRESENTATION Prepare for a presentation in B. Answer the questions. Then work with a partner. Ask your partner the questions.

	You	Your Partner
Are you an early bird or a night owl?		
What time do you go to bed?		
What days do you sleep late?		
Does anyone wake you up? If so, who?		
Do you dream? If so, what do you dream about?		
Do you walk or talk in your sleep?		
Do you snore?		
Do you need a lot of sleep? Do you ever have trouble sleeping?		

B Tell the class about your partner's sleep habits. The class asks your partner more questions.

EXAMPLE: A: Ali is a night owl. He usually goes to bed at 2:00 a.m.
          B: Ali, what do you do at night?
          C: I usually read at night.
          D: Are you tired in the morning?
          C: I'm always tired in the morning!

EXERCISE 9 DREAMS

INFORMATION GAP Work with a partner. Student A, follow the instructions below. Student B, follow the instructions on page 445.

STUDENT A

- Student B has a dream again and again. Find out about the dream. Ask Student B the questions below. Write down his or her answers.

  1. Where are you in your dream? _____
  2. Who do you see? _____
  3. Is the person big? Little? _____
  4. Are you big? Little? _____
  5. What does the person say? _____
  6. What do you do? _____

- You have a dream again and again. Read about your dream below. Student B will ask you questions about this dream. Answer Student B's questions.

  You are on an airplane. The pilot comes to you. He says, "I need your help." You go with the pilot. You fly the plane. You land the plane. Everyone claps. You feel good. You wake up.

- **Talk about your dreams. What do they mean?**

Go to MyEnglishLab for more communication practice.

A BEFORE YOU WRITE   Read the interview between Todd Jones and Ella Lam, best-selling author of the book *Sleep and Dreams*. Then work with a partner. Imagine your partner is famous. Ask your partner questions about his or her life. Take notes. Then switch roles.

TODD: How is your life different now that you are famous?

ELLA: People think I'm smarter.

TODD: What do you do in your free time?

ELLA: I travel. I was in South Africa last month, and next month I plan to go to Thailand.

TODD: Where do you live?

ELLA: I live in New York City.

TODD: Do you dream?

ELLA: Yes, I do. And I remember my dreams. Sometimes, I write them down.

TODD: What do you dream about?

ELLA: I dream about horses. I . . .

B WRITE   Write an interview between you and your partner. Use the interview in A and your notes. Use the simple present for all your questions.

C CHECK YOUR WORK   Read your interview. Underline simple present questions. Use the Editing Checklist to check your work.

Editing Checklist
Did you . . . ?
☐ use a *wh-* word + *do/does* + subject + base form for most simple present *wh-* questions
☐ remember NOT to use *do/does* in questions about a subject
☐ remember to use *do/does* in questions about an object

D REVISE YOUR WORK   Read your questions and answers again. Can you improve your writing? Make changes if necessary.

Go to MyEnglishLab for more writing practice.

UNIT 10 REVIEW

Test yourself on the grammar of the unit.

Ⓐ Complete the *wh-* questions with the words from the box.

how	when	where	who	why

1. A: _____ does she snore? B: I don't know why.

2. A: _____ do they get up? B: At about 9:00 or 10:00.

3. A: _____ sleeps in that room? B: Their uncle does.

4. A: _____ do you feel? B: Sleepy.

5. A: _____ do you buy sheets? B: At Bloom's department store.

Ⓑ Write questions with the correct forms of the words in parentheses.

1. (What / you / dream about) _____

2. (What time / your mother / get up) _____

3. (What time / you / go to bed) _____

4. (Where / your brother / sleep) _____

5. (Who / snore / in your family) _____

Ⓒ Read the statement and answers. Then write the questions.

John meets his uncle at the diner on Saturdays.

1. A: _____ B: John does.

2. A: _____ B: His uncle.

3. A: _____ B: At the diner.

4. A: _____ B: On Saturdays.

Ⓓ Correct the questions. There are six mistakes.

1. Where you live?

2. Why he daydreams in class?

3. When does she gets up?

4. How they feel about sleeping pills?

5. Who does you dream about?

6. What time he wake up?

Now check your answers on page 446.

Go to MyEnglishLab to complete the review online.

There Is / There Are;
Possessives

PART 4

OUTCOMES

- Use *there is/are* to introduce people or things
- Use *there is/are* to tell the location of people or things or the time of events
- Recognize details in a short article about a famous place
- Recognize details about a place in a conversation
- Talk about places in your town
- Write a paragraph about a place to shop

OUTCOMES

- Talk about possessions
- Recognize details in a conversation transcript
- Recognize details in a conversation about possessions
- Ask and answer questions about objects and describe them in detail
- Write a paragraph about people in your family

UNIT 11

There is / There are
PLACES TO SHOP

OUTCOMES
• Use *there is / are* to introduce people or things
• Use *there is / are* to tell the location of people or things or the time of events
• Recognize details in a short article about a famous place
• Recognize details about a place in a conversation
• Talk about places in your town
• Write a paragraph about a place to shop

| STEP 1 | GRAMMAR IN CONTEXT |

BEFORE YOU READ

Work with a partner. Discuss the questions.

1. Do you like shopping malls? Why or why not?

2. Where is the nearest mall? Do you go there? Why or why not?

READ

▶11|01 Read this page from a guidebook about the Dubai Mall.

The Dubai Mall

For a wonderful time, join the 750,000 weekly shoppers at the Dubai Mall. There are more than 1,200 stores including "Candylicious," the world's largest candy store. But the mall has a lot more than just the stores. There's a luxury hotel, twenty-two cinema screens, and 120 restaurants and cafés.

Are there things for kids to do? Yes, lots. There's an aquarium, an underground zoo, and an ice rink[1] on the first level. And on the second level, there's the Sega indoor theme park.

What about parking? There are 14,000 parking spaces. And it's easy to find your car. Your parking ticket includes a computer system to help you locate[2] your car.

So make your plans now. There isn't a better place to shop.

---

1 *ice rink:* a place where people can skate on ice
2 *locate:* find

AFTER YOU READ

Ⓐ VOCABULARY Complete the sentences with the words from the box.

| aquarium | including | indoor | join | luxury | parking spaces |

1. He drives a(n) _____ car with leather seats and a great stereo system.

2. There are _____ for only a few cars, so you may need to leave your car at home.

3. There's a(n) _____ garage, so your car stays cool when it is hot outside.

4. There are hundreds of different fish in the _____ .

5. Please _____ us for a tour of the new shopping center.

6. The total bill comes to a thousand dollars _____ tax.

Ⓑ COMPREHENSION Complete the sentences. Circle the correct words.

1. Candylicious is a huge store for sweet / spicy treats.

2. There aren't any restaurants / museums at the Dubai Mall.

3. There are / aren't activities for children at the Dubai Mall.

4. There's a car-locating system / car wash at the Dubai Mall.

5. There's a hotel / an apartment building at the Dubai Mall.

6. Every week, there are more than 7,500 / 750,000 shoppers at the Dubai Mall.

Ⓒ DISCUSSION Work with a partner. Compare your answers in B. Explain why you think your answers are correct. Then answer the question: Would you like to go to the Dubai Mall? Why or why not?

Go to MyEnglishLab for more grammar in context practice.

There is / There are **123**

THERE IS / THERE ARE

Affirmative Statements

There	Be	Subject	Place/Time
There	is	a restaurant	on this level.
		a movie	at 6:30.
There	are	two restaurants	near the entrance.
		shows	at 7:00 and 9:00.

Contractions

there is	→	there's
there is not	→	there isn't
there are not	→	there aren't

Negative Statements

There	Be + not	Subject	Place/Time
There	isn't	a restaurant	on the second level.
There	aren't	any movies	at 8:00.

Yes/No Questions

Be	There	Subject	Place
Is	there	a pizza place	on Second Street?
Are	there	any banks	nearby?

Short Answers

Affirmative		Negative	
Yes,	there is.	No,	there isn't.
	there are.		there aren't.

GRAMMAR NOTES

1 There is / There are

There is and *There are* **introduce** people or things into a conversation or a piece of writing.

We use **there is** to tell about the existence of:	
• a person	**There is** *a salesperson* near the door.
• a thing	**There is** *a shoe store* at the mall.
We use **there are** to tell about the existence of:	
• people	**There are** *two women* in the store.
• things	**There are** *restaurants* on the third level.
USAGE NOTE We often use **there are** to tell about the number of people or things that exist.	There are **14,000** parking spaces at the mall. There are **two** Thai restaurants in that mall.
USAGE NOTE It is very common to use the contraction **there's** with singular nouns. However, we almost never use the contraction **there're** with plural nouns.	**There's** a salesperson near the door. **There are** two women in the store. NOT ~~There're~~ two women in the store.
There in *there is* and *there are* is different from *there* on its own. **There** on its own is an adverb of place. It means "in that place."	**There are** two salespeople **there**.

2 There is/There are for Location or Time

We often use *there is* or *there are* to tell the **location** of people or things or the **time** of events.

• location	There's an aquarium **on the first floor**.
• time	There are concerts **on Friday and Saturday nights**.

3 Negative Forms

In the negative, use *there isn't* and *there aren't*.	**There isn't** a school in the mall.
	There aren't any malls near our home.
USAGE NOTE We don't often use the full forms *there is not* or *there are not*.	

4 Yes/No Questions

Begin *yes/no* questions with *Is there* or *Are there*.	**Is there** a mall nearby?

5 Agreement

When two nouns follow *there is* or *there are*, the verb usually agrees with the **first noun**.	**There's a shoe store** and two hair salons.
	There are two hair salons and a shoe store.

6 There is and It is, He is, and She is; There are and They are

We often use *there is* or *there are* the first time we introduce people or things. We use *he*, *she*, *it*, or *they* to tell more about the people or things.	**There's a Thai restaurant** across the street. *It's* next to the shoe store.
	There's a salesman over there. *He's* next to the cash register.
	There are three little girls in the dress store. *They're* excited about all the beautiful dresses.

REFERENCE NOTE

For more information about *any*, see Unit 27 on page 324.

EXERCISE 1   DISCOVER THE GRAMMAR

Ⓐ GRAMMAR NOTES 1–5 Look at the mall directory. Write *T* (*True*) or *F* (*False*) for each statement.

BURLINGTON MALL DIRECTORY

THIRD LEVEL	House of Kebab	Chinese food	Burgers	Sushi bar	Café	Restrooms
SECOND LEVEL	Women's clothes	Shoe store	Art supply store	Furniture store	Children's clothes	Cosmetics store
FIRST LEVEL	Restrooms	Gift shop	Bookstore	Flower shop	Electronics store	Women's clothes

_T_ **1.** There's a flower shop on the first level.

____ **2.** There's a café on the second level.

____ **3.** There aren't any toy stores.

____ **4.** There are five places to eat.

____ **5.** There isn't a restroom on the second level.

____ **6.** There's a bookstore and an electronics store on the second level.

Ⓑ Look at the mall directory again. Circle the correct answers.

1. A: Are there any office supply stores at the mall?

   B: Yes, there are. / (No, there aren't)

2. A: Are there any jewelry stores at the mall?

   B: Yes, there are. / No, there aren't.

3. A: Is there an amusement park at the mall?

   B: Yes, there is. / No, there isn't.

4. A: Is there an art supply store at the mall?

   B: Yes, there is. / No, there isn't.

EXERCISE 2 *THERE IS / THERE ARE*

GRAMMAR NOTES 1–2 Complete the sentences about the Burlington Mall with *There is* or *There are*.

1. _____*There are*_____ two women's clothes stores at the mall.

2. _____ a good electronics store on the first level.

3. _____ a shoe store next to the art supply store.

4. _____ a lot of places to eat at the mall.

5. _____ restrooms on the first and the third levels.

6. _____ a cosmetics store at the mall.

EXERCISE 3 AFFIRMATIVE AND NEGATIVE STATEMENTS

GRAMMAR NOTES 1–3 Find the incorrect sentences. Rewrite them with the correct word order.

1. There's a mall in the Chinese restaurant. *There's a Chinese restaurant in the mall.*

2. There's a second level on the shoe store. _____

3. There are two women's clothing stores at the mall. _____

4. There's an electronics store on the first level. _____

5. There isn't a mall at the men's clothing store. _____

6. There aren't any classrooms in the desks. _____

EXERCISE 4 AFFIRMATIVE AND NEGATIVE STATEMENTS

A GRAMMAR NOTES 1–3, 6 Complete the conversation. Use *there's, there are, there isn't, there aren't, they're,* or *they aren't*.

AL: This pizza place is awful. _____*There aren't*_____ any tablecloths, and the placemats are dirty.
                                                        1.

KATE: You're right. _____ any napkins either. _____ a busboy here
                                    2.   3.
       somewhere, but I don't see him now.

AL: Well, I need a knife and fork.

KATE: _____ knives and forks on that table. Oh, no. _____ clean.
                    4.   5.

AL: Boy, it's hot in here. _____ even a fan.
                                          6.

KATE: Oh, my gosh! You won't believe this.

AL: What is it?

KATE: Well, _____ a mouse over there, near the wall!
                        7.

AL: What? Ugh, _____ two mice! Let's leave!
                        8.

KATE: What about our food?

AL: Let the mice have it. _____ hungry, too!
                                    9.

○ 11|02 **Ⓑ LISTEN AND CHECK** Listen to the conversation and check your answers in A.

EXERCISE 5 *THERE IS / THERE ARE*, *THERE*, AND *THEY ARE*

Ⓐ GRAMMAR NOTES 1–2, 6 Complete the conversation. Use *there's*, *there are*, *there*, and *they're*.

NICK: How about some Chinese food?

TINA: Well, ___*there's*___ only one Chinese food restaurant nearby. But it's expensive.
              1.
      _____ a lot of other restaurants, though.
              2.

NICK: Today is Sunday. Are they open?

TINA: _____ all open seven days a week.
              3.

NICK: Well, _____ a nice Mexican place over _____.
                    4.   **5.**

TINA: Where?

NICK: Over _____ next to the diner.
                  6.

TINA: I know the place. It's good and not expensive. Let's go.

○ 11|03 **Ⓑ LISTEN AND CHECK** Listen to the conversation and check your answers in A.

EXERCISE 6 *THERE IS / THERE ARE* AND SUBJECT PRONOUNS

GRAMMAR NOTES 1–2, 5–6 Complete the sentences. Use *There's* or *There are* in the first sentence. Use *He's*, *She's*, *It's*, or *They're* in the second sentence.

1. ___*There's*___ a good café over there. ___*It's*___ next to the bookstore.

2. _____ a salesman behind the counter. _____ talking to that woman.

3. _____ a lot of wool sweaters. _____ in the back of the store.

4. _____ a scarf on the floor. _____ your new one, isn't it?

5. _____ some indoor parking spaces over there. _____ near the exit.

6. _____ a small mall on Route 4. _____ next to the amusement park.

7. _____ a lot of people in that line. _____ buying tickets for the movie.

8. _____ a pizza place and two restaurants here. _____ open now.

9. _____ a woman in a blue dress. _____ the owner of the pizza place.

EXERCISE 7 *YES/NO* QUESTIONS AND ANSWERS

GRAMMAR NOTES 1–4, 6 **Look at the calendar. Complete the questions with *Is there* or *Are there*. Then write answers.**

FIND THINGS TO DO *This week*

TODAY	FRIDAY	SATURDAY	SUNDAY
Carmen	**Buyers Flea Market**	*The Misfits*	**Chicago Symphony Orchestra**
Columbia College	4545 West Street	Great Drama with Marilyn Monroe!	*All Beethoven*
Tonight at 8:00	8:00–5:00	Main Street Cinema	Chicago Cultural Center
	Cheap clothing!	4:30, 6:30, 8:30	8:00 p.m.

1. A: _____Is there_____ a performance tonight? What is it?

   B: _____

2. A: _____ any movies or concerts this weekend? When?

   B: _____

3. A: How many showings of the movie _____?

   B: _____

4. A: _____ a flea market? When and where is it?

   B: _____

EXERCISE 8 EDITING

GRAMMAR NOTES 1–6 **Read the sentences about pizza places. There are eight mistakes. The first mistake is already corrected. Find and correct seven more.**

1. Is ~~they~~ *there* a pizza place near you?

2. There not are any pizza places on my street. There is one on the next street and four

   in my town.

3. There be pizza places at almost every mall in the United States. The pizzas come in all

   shapes and sizes.

4. Are traditional pizzas with mushrooms, pepperoni, and broccoli.

5. There is also pizzas with curry, fish, and coconut.

6. In the United States, they are over 70,000 pizza places. There sell lots of pizzas.

7. Pizzas are popular with everyone. There are popular with both young and old people.

Go to MyEnglishLab for more focused practice.

STEP 4   COMMUNICATION PRACTICE

EXERCISE 9 LISTENING

11|04 **A** **Listen to the conversation. Then choose the correct answer to each question.**

1. Where's the mall?
   a. two miles north   **b.** two miles south   **c.** two miles west

2. How are the prices at the mall?
   a. Everything is expensive.   **b.** Everything is inexpensive.   **c.** They vary by store.

3. Is there an Italian restaurant?
   a. Yes, there is.   **b.** No, there isn't.   **c.** Maybe.

4. Where's the food court?
   a. on the second level   **b.** on the third level   **c.** on the ground level

5. Why is there traffic on the drive to the mall?
   a. People are walking   **b.** There's road construction.   **c.** There's an accident.
   in the road.

B **Work with a partner. Use the list below to ask questions about the mall in the listening. Your partner answers them.**

EXAMPLE: A: Is there a department store at the mall?
          B: Yes, there is. There are two department stores.

- a department store
- a movie theater
- places to eat
- parking spaces
- good prices
- a place to buy towels

EXERCISE 10 HOW ARE THEY DIFFERENT?

GAME Work with a partner. Find ten differences between Picture A and Picture B.

EXAMPLE: In Picture A, there's a shoe repair shop between the bakery and the pizza place.
In Picture B, there isn't a shoe repair shop between the bakery and the pizza place. The shoe repair shop is between the pizza place and the flower shop.

Picture A

Picture B

EXERCISE 11 GREAT PLACES TO SHOP

A DISCUSSION Work in groups. Talk about good places to shop in your area or online.

EXAMPLE: A: There's a great place to get running shoes on 3rd Street.
B: Where on 3rd Street?
A: It's between Elm and Oak. It's next to the bank.
C: How are the prices?
A: Not bad.

B Tell the class about four places your group likes to shop. Use *there is* or *there are* in your report.

EXERCISE 12 TIC TAC TOE

GAME Walk around the class. Use the phrases in the boxes to ask your classmates questions. Begin with *Is there* or *Are there any*. If a student answers "yes," write his or her name in the box. The first person to have three names across, down, or diagonally calls out "Tic Tac Toe."

EXAMPLE: ALI: Is there a big mall near your home?
BORIS: Yes, there is. It's on Glendale Avenue. *(Ali writes Boris's name in the box.)*

a big mall near your home[1]	a bakery near your home	shops on your street
a park near your home	two or more credit cards in your purse or pocket	a pet in your home
a pizza place near your home	a bus stop near your home	flowers in your home

---

1 *near your home:* you can walk there in ten minutes or less

Go to MyEnglishLab for more communication practice.

FROM GRAMMAR TO WRITING

A BEFORE YOU WRITE
Read about a store called "Village Gifts." Underline *there's*, *there are*, and *there aren't*. Then take notes in the chart below about a store that you like to shop at and why. Work with a partner. Tell your partner about the place you shop.

There's a small store near my home. It's called "Village Gifts." It's on a street with two other small shops. The owners are a husband and wife. Their gifts include unusual crafts from all over the world. There are some great things to buy—colorful pottery from Mexico, beautiful jewelry from Thailand, traditional rugs from China, and baskets from Jamaica. The owners love the things they sell. There's a story behind every item. That's why I like to shop there. There aren't many shops like that.

My Store

B WRITE Write a paragraph about a place you like to shop. Give reasons why you like to shop there. Use the paragraph in A and your chart. Use *there is* and *there are*.

C CHECK YOUR WORK Read your paragraph in B. Underline *there is* and *there are*. Use the Editing Checklist to check your work.

Editing Checklist
Did you . . . ?
☐ use *there is* for singular nouns and *there are* for plural nouns
☐ check your spelling

D REVISE YOUR WORK Read your paragraph again. Can you improve your writing? Make changes if necessary.

Go to MyEnglishLab for more writing practice.

UNIT 11 **REVIEW**

Test yourself on the grammar of the unit.

Ⓐ Complete the sentences with *There's*, *There are*, *There isn't*, or *There aren't*.

1. _____ any restrooms on this level, but there's one on the next level.

2. _____ a great bakery on Elm Street. It sells delicious cakes and cookies.

3. _____ three Mexican restaurants on West Street. They're all very good.

4. Sorry. _____ a pool in this hotel, but there's a fitness center.

5. _____ a mouse in the corner. Let's get out of here. I don't like mice.

6. _____ two big malls in that town. I often shop in them.

Ⓑ Circle the correct words to complete the *yes/no* questions and short answers.

1. A: Are there / Are they any soda machines in the building?

   B: Yes, there are / they are.

2. A: Is it / Is she the teacher?

   B: Yes, she's / she is.

3. A: Are there / Are they new students?

   B: No, they aren't / she isn't.

4: A: Are there / Is there a men's room on this floor?

   B: No, they aren't / there isn't.

Ⓒ Complete the sentences with *There's*, *There are*, *She's*, *It's*, or *They're*.

1. _____ a new pizza place on Elm Street. _____ next to the post office.

2. _____ a lot of people outside the pizza place. _____ in a long line.

3. _____ a great pizza chef there. _____ funny, and her pizzas are delicious.

Ⓓ Correct the paragraph. There are four mistakes.

Visit the new Shopper's Mall on Route 290. There's over 100 stores. There a movie theater, and they are ten great places to eat. Come early. Every morning at 10:30, there are a free show for children. The mall is three miles from the Tappan Bridge on Route 290.

Check your answers on page 446.

Go to MyEnglishLab to complete the review online.

UNIT

12

Possessive Nouns and Adjectives; Pronouns; Questions with *Whose*

POSSESSIONS

OUTCOMES
• Talk about possessions
• Recognize details in a conversation transcript
• Recognize details in a conversation about possessions
• Ask and answer questions about objects and describe them in detail
• Write a paragraph about people in your family

| STEP 1 | GRAMMAR IN CONTEXT |

BEFORE YOU READ

Work with a partner. Answer the questions.

1. Is your handwriting neat? Is it difficult to read?
2. Look at Michelle and Rick's handwriting. Whose handwriting is neat? Whose is messy?

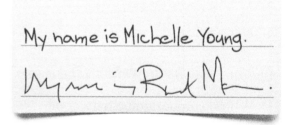

READ

▶12|01   Read this conversation between a teacher and her students.

Whose Composition Is This?

TEACHER: Whose composition is this?

BORIS: Is it a good paper?

TEACHER: It's excellent.

BORIS: It's my composition.

YOLANDA: No, that's not your handwriting. It's Kim's composition. Her name is right there. She's absent today.

TEACHER: Thanks, Yolanda. Whose paper is *this*?

BORIS: Is it a good paper?

TEACHER: It's OK.

BORIS: Then it's mine.

JUAN: It's not yours. It's mine. See, my name is on the back.

TEACHER: You're right, Juan. I recognize your handwriting. Here, Boris. *This* is your composition.

BORIS: Is it a good paper?

TEACHER: It needs some work.

BORIS: I don't think it's mine.

TEACHER: Uh . . . I think it is yours. All the other compositions have a name on them.

AFTER YOU READ

A VOCABULARY Complete the sentences with the words from the box.

| back | composition | excellent | grade | recognize |

1. He has a new hairstyle and is wearing a new suit. It's hard to _____ him.

2. We had to write a _____ about a favorite childhood possession. Mine was about my blue blanket.

3. Are the answers in the _____ of the book?

4. What was your _____ in English? Mine was an A+.

5. Her writing is _____. It is clear, organized, and interesting.

B COMPREHENSION Write short answers to the following questions.

1. Whose composition is very good? _____

2. Who's absent? _____

3. Whose composition has a name on the back? _____

4. Whose composition needs work? _____

C DISCUSSION Work with a partner. Compare your answers in B. Then look at the compositions below. Which composition is Kim's, Juan's, and Boris's? Explain your answers.

1. _____   2. _____   3. _____

Go to MyEnglishLab for more grammar in context practice.

POSSESSIVES; PRONOUNS; QUESTIONS WITH *WHOSE*

Possessive Nouns

Singular Nouns	Plural Nouns
John's last name is Tamez. **Russ's** last name is Stram.	The **girls'** gym is on this floor.
My **mother's** name is Rita. The **woman's** name is Carmen.	My **parents'** car is in the garage. The **women's** restroom is on the first floor.

Subject Pronoun	Possessive Adjective	Possessive Pronoun	
I	**my**	**mine**	That is **my** book. That book is **mine**.
You	**your**	**yours**	Do you have **your** key? Do you have **yours**?
He	**his**	**his**	This is **his** car. This car is **his**.
She	**her**	**hers**	That's **her** house. That house is **hers**.
It	**its**		Look at that bird. **Its** feathers are red and gold.
We	**our**	**ours**	We lost **our** notes. We lost **ours**.
They	**their**	**theirs**	They can't find **their** tickets. They can't find **theirs**.

	Object Pronoun (Singular)
Raul likes	**me**.
	you.
	him.
	her.
	it.

	Object Pronoun (Plural)
Sarah knows	**us**.
	you.
	them.

Questions with *Whose*

Questions	Answers
Whose book report is long?	Carmen**'s**. Carmen**'s** book report is long.
Whose eyes are green?	Igor**'s**. Igor**'s** eyes are green.
Whose compositions are finished?	Yoko**'s** and Kaori**'s**. Yoko**'s** and Kaori**'s** compositions.

GRAMMAR NOTES

1 Possessive Nouns and Possessive Adjectives

Possessive nouns and **possessive adjectives** show that something belongs to someone.

• a possessive noun	This is **Kim's** car. *(the car belongs to Kim)*
• a possessive adjective	It is **her** car.

2 Possessive Nouns

We use **an apostrophe** (') to show possession.	
Add an apostrophe (') + *s* to a **singular noun**.	That's **Juan's** composition.
Add an apostrophe (') to a **plural noun** ending in *-s*.	My **parents'** home is near my home.
Add an apostrophe (') + *s* to an **irregular plural noun**.	The **women's** restroom is on the first floor.
BE CAREFUL! Remember to say or write the *'s* ending on possessive nouns.	That's Maria's book. **NOT** That's ~~Maria~~ book.
BE CAREFUL! A noun + apostrophe (') + *s* may also be a contraction of a noun + *is* in conversation and informal writing.	**Anna's** late. *(= Anna is late.)*

3 Possessive Adjectives

A **noun** follows a possessive adjective.	**His** *sister* is in Busan.
Possessive adjectives replace **possessive nouns**.	A: Where's your *father's* sister? B: **His** sister is in Busan. A: Where's your *mother's* sister? B: **Her** sister is in Seoul.
BE CAREFUL! Possessive adjectives agree with the nouns they replace.	A: Where's your *father's* sister? B: **His** sister is in Busan. **NOT** ~~Her~~ sister is in Busan. *(Sister is feminine, but the possessive adjective agrees with the noun it replaces—father—who is masculine.)*
BE CAREFUL! Do not confuse *its* and *it's*. **Its** is a possessive adjective; *it's = it is*.	This is my turtle. **Its** name is Tubby. **It's** a hot day.

4 Possessive Pronouns

A **possessive pronoun** can replace a **possessive adjective** and **noun**.	This isn't *my umbrella*. **Mine** is blue. *(My umbrella is blue.)*
BE CAREFUL! A noun never follows a possessive pronoun.	This is my hat. This is **mine**. **NOT** This is ~~mine~~ hat.

5 *Whose*

Use **whose** to ask questions about possessions. We often answer questions with *whose* with a possessive noun, a possessive adjective + a noun, or a possessive pronoun.	A: **Whose** car is that? B: It's **Kim's** car. **or** It's **her** car. **or** It's **hers**.
BE CAREFUL! *Who's* sounds like *whose*, but it is short for *Who is*.	**Whose** book is this? **NOT** ~~Who's~~ book is this?

6 Subject Pronouns and Object Pronouns

Remember that all sentences must have **a subject + a verb**. (See Unit 1.)	**Kim works.** *(Kim = subject; works = verb)*
A sentence can also have **a subject + a verb + an object**.	SUBJECT NOUN VERB OBJECT NOUN **Kim** **loves** **Ron.**
We can replace a subject noun with a subject pronoun. We can replace an object noun with an object pronoun.	SUBJECT PRONOUN OBJECT PRONOUN **She** loves **him.** *(She replaces Kim and him replaces Ron)*

REFERENCE NOTES

For more about **irregular plural nouns**, see Appendix 9 on page 434.

Go to MyEnglishLab to watch the grammar presentation.

EXERCISE 1   DISCOVER THE GRAMMAR

GRAMMAR NOTES 1–6 **Read the conversation. Then look at the words in bold and put them into the chart below. The first one in each category is done for you.**

Possessive Nouns	Possessive Pronouns	Possessive Adjectives	Object Pronouns
Marco's	mine	your	it

BEN: Whose book is on the table next to the printer? Is it **Marco's** book?

LI: No, it's **mine**.

BEN: Is that **your** translator, too?

LI: No, it's **Marco's** translator. **Mine** is in **my** backpack. **His** is over there. He always uses **it** in class.

BEN: Where are the workbooks?

LI: I put **them** on the bookshelves over there.

BEN: I always see **you** and Marco together. Are you friends outside of class?

LI: **Marco's** mother and **my** mother are sisters. Marco and I are cousins. We're friends, too.

EXERCISE 2   POSSESSIVE NOUNS

Ⓐ GRAMMAR NOTES 1–3

Read about the Zhang family. Underline the possessive nouns in the reading.

This is the Zhang family. The older man is Lao Zhang. <u>Lao's</u> wife is Feng. They have two daughters, Hua and Mei. Hua's husband is Gang. They have a son, Bao. Mei's husband is Jinsong. They have a daughter, Ting.

B Complete the sentences. Circle the correct answers.

1. Ting's mothers / mother's mother is Ting's grandmother / grandmother's.

2. Hua's sister / sister's daughter is Hua's / Hua niece.

3. Gang's wife / wife's sister is his / her sister-in-law.

4. Bao's uncle / uncle's apartment is in Shanghai.

5. Bao and Ting are cousins / cousin's. Their mothers / mother's are sisters / sister's.

6. Lao Zhang is the families / family's oldest member.

EXERCISE 3 POSSESSIVE ADJECTIVES

GRAMMAR NOTES 1, 3 **Complete the sentences. Use possessive adjectives.**

1. My sister studies in Toronto. _____*Her*_____ school is on Victoria Street.

2. She goes to Edgewood University. She likes _____ classes.

3. Her husband's parents work at the United Nations. _____ jobs are interesting.

   _____ mother is a translator, and _____ father is an interpreter.

4. Right now my brother is in Peru. _____ wife is in Belize, and _____

   children are in the United States with their grandparents.

5. The children have a rabbit. _____ fur is soft.

6. Does your brother like _____ job? Does he meet interesting people?

7. Do you like _____ classes? Are they helpful? Are your classmates friendly?

8. Does your grandmother like _____ new apartment? Is she happy there?

EXERCISE 4 POSSESSIVE PRONOUNS

GRAMMAR NOTES 1, 3–4 **Replace the underlined words with possessive pronouns.**

1. A: Is that your notebook?

   B: No, it's not ~~my notebook~~. It's his notebook. My notebook is in my book bag.
                   mine
                         a.   **b.**   **c.**

2. A: Is this their house?

   B: No. Their house is in back of the library.
             a.

   A: Whose house is this?

   B: It's our house.
         b.

3. A: Are those your sunglasses?

   B: No, they're <u>her sunglasses</u>. <u>My sunglasses</u> are in my bag.
   a. b.

4. A: Is that Jaguar your uncle's car?

   B: No. <u>My uncle's car</u> is the Ford. That's his wife's car. <u>Her car</u> is the Jaguar.
   a. b.

EXERCISE 5 POSSESSIVE ADJECTIVES AND POSSESSIVE PRONOUNS

GRAMMAR NOTES 1, 3–6 **Complete the conversations. Circle the correct answers.**

1. A: I think you have my umbrella.

   B: No. This is (my)/ mine umbrella. <u>You / Yours</u> is over there. It's next to <u>her / hers</u>
   a. b. c.

   electronic dictionary.

2. A: Whose gloves are these? Yours or Julie's?

   B: They're <u>her / hers</u>. <u>My / Mine</u> are wool.
   a. b.

3. A: Where is <u>their / theirs</u> car?
   a.

   B: <u>Their / Theirs</u> car is in the garage.
   b.

   A: Is <u>your / yours</u> there, too?
   c.

   B: No. <u>Our / Ours</u> is on the street.
   d.

EXERCISE 6 SUBJECT AND OBJECT PRONOUNS, POSSESSIVES

GRAMMAR NOTES 1, 3–6 **Complete the sentences. Circle the correct answers.**

1. It's <u>I / my / me / (mine)</u> Please give it to <u>I / my / me / mine</u>.
   a. b.

   <u>I / My / Me / Mine</u> need it.
   c.

2. I don't think <u>he / him / his</u> is on the train. I don't see <u>he / him / his</u>.
   a. b.

3. Our family is from Edmonton. <u>They / Their / Theirs / Them</u> family is from
   a.

   Vancouver, but <u>they / their / theirs / them</u> live in Edmonton now. We live next door
   b.

   to <u>they / their / theirs / them</u>.
   c.

EXERCISE 7 PRONOUNS AND POSSESSIVE ADJECTIVES

GRAMMAR NOTES 3–6 Read and complete the article with the correct subject pronoun, object pronoun, possessive pronoun, or possessive adjective.

International Language Institute
NEWSLETTER

GET TO KNOW NEW STUDENTS AT THE ILI

New Student of the Month

Sandra Gomes

My name is Sandra Gomes. _____ *I* _____ am from São Paulo,
                                        1.

Brazil. _____ am happy to be a student at the International
          2.

Language Institute. _____ is great to learn English and meet
                       3.

people from all over the world. _____ parents and brother
                                  4.

are in Brazil, but _____ sister is here with _____.
                     5.   **6.**

_____ share an apartment together. _____ is nice,
  7.   **8.**

but _____ is far from school. _____ each have a
      9.   **10.**

bedroom. _____ is bigger than _____. That's fine
           11.   **12.**

with _____ because _____ like small spaces.
       13.   **14.**

_____ spend a lot of time together in _____
  15.   **16.**

apartment. That's because _____ both have a TV, a
                            17.

computer, and a lot of friends who visit _____.
                                           18.

EXERCISE 8 SPELLING OF POSSESSIVE NOUNS

▶12|02 GRAMMAR NOTES 2, 6 Listen to the sentences. For each sentence, circle the word you hear.

1. Maria   (Maria's)   Marias

2. Maria   Maria's   Marias

3. Maria   Maria's   Marias

4. partner   partner's   partners

5. partner   partner's   partners

6. partner   partner's   partners

EXERCISE 9 EDITING

GRAMMAR NOTES 1–6 Correct the conversations. There are seven mistakes. The first mistake is already corrected. Find and correct six more.

1. A: Is that ~~you~~ *your* dictionary?

   B: No. It's his dictionary.

   A: Who's?

   B: Dans.

   A: That's not his's. It's Juan's.

2. A: Is Maria sister here?

   B: No, she's not.

   A: Is Maria here?

   B: No, but his brother is.

   A: Where is Maria?

   B: I think she's with his sister.

> Go to MyEnglishLab for more focused practice.

STEP 4   COMMUNICATION PRACTICE

EXERCISE 10 LISTENING

▶12|03 **A** Listen to the conversation. What are Boris and Jasmine talking about? Circle the correct letter.

a. bikes   **b.** baskets   **c.** sales

▶12|03 **B** Listen again. Work with a partner. Write the name of the owner of each bicycle on the lines next to the bicycles. Use the names from the box. Then explain your answers.

| Amy | Johnny |
| Jasmine | Roger and Ted |

1. _Amy_____

2. _____

3. _____

4. _____

C Work with a partner. Take turns. Ask and questions with *whose* about the bikes.

EXAMPLE: A: Whose bike has a basket?

                 B: Amy's bike has a basket.

EXERCISE 11 WHOSE BIRTHDAY IS IN DECEMBER?

A Q & A **Prepare to ask and answer questions with your classmates. Complete the questions with *Whose* or *Who's*.**

1. _____Whose_____ birthday is in December?

2. _____Who's_____ good in art?

3. _____ name means something?

4. _____ a good athlete?

5. _____ eyes aren't dark brown?

6. _____ a good cook?

7. _____ first name has more than eight letters?

8. _____ birthday is in the summer?

9. _____ a good dancer?

10. _____ handwriting is beautiful?

B **Walk around the room. Ask your classmates *yes/no* questions about the things in A. Take notes.**

EXAMPLE: A: Juan, is your birthday in December?
B: No, it's not. Is yours?
A: Yes, it is.

C **Ask your classmates the questions in A. Your classmates look at their notes to find the answer.**

EXAMPLE: A: Whose birthday is in December?
B: Maria's birthday is in December.

EXERCISE 12 WHOSE IS IT?

GAME **Work in a large group. Each student in the group puts something that belongs to him or her in a bag. The group then passes the bag to another group. Students in the second group talk about each object. They guess the owner and give a reason why.**

EXAMPLE: A: OK. This is a keychain. Whose keychain is this?
B: I think it's Boris's keychain. There's a tennis racquet on the keychain, and Boris's passion is tennis.
C: Or Sukana's? She likes tennis, too.
D: It's a big keychain and Sukana has a big bag. Let's go with Sukana.
A: Our group thinks it's Sukana's keychain because the keychain has a tennis racket and Sukana likes tennis.

Go to MyEnglishLab for more communication practice.

FROM GRAMMAR TO WRITING

A BEFORE YOU WRITE Read about a student's family. On a separate piece of paper, draw each member of the family. Work with a partner. Compare your drawings. Then draw a picture of your own family. Tell your partner about each member of your family.

> This is Jorge. He's on the left. Jorge is my sister's husband. He's twenty-five years old and works for a big company. He's a web architect. He enjoys his job. His passion is computers. That's why he has a computer in his hand.
>
> Dahlia is next to Jorge. Dahlia is my sister and Jorge's wife. She's a jewelry designer. She's twenty-two years old. Her passion is art and jewelry. Her T-shirt and her necklace are her designs.
>
> My mom is next to my sister. She's fifty-three years old. She's a kindergarten teacher. She loves music and has a beautiful voice.
>
> My dad is on the right. He has a band. He's the leader. His passion is music, too. He plays a lot of instruments. He's very talented. He's also a great dad.

B WRITE Write about the people in your family. Use the paragraphs in A and your drawings to help you. Use pronouns and possessive adjectives.

C CHECK YOUR WORK Read your description in B. Underline the pronouns and possessive adjectives. Then use the Editing Checklist to check your work.

Editing Checklist
Did you ...?
☐ use an apostrophe with possessive nouns
☐ follow all possessive adjectives with a noun
☐ use correct agreement with possessive adjectives
☐ check your spelling

D REVISE YOUR WORK Read your descriptions of your family again. Can you improve your writing? Make changes if necessary.

UNIT 12 REVIEW

Test yourself on the grammar of the unit.

A Cross out the underlined words. Replace them with *His, Her, Its,* or *Their.*

1. <u>My parents'</u> car is big.

2. <u>My brother's</u> daughter is a history teacher.

3. That bird is injured. <u>That bird's</u> wing is broken.

4. <u>The students'</u> tests are on the teacher's desk.

5. <u>Our aunt's</u> store is on Main Street.

B Complete the conversations. Circle the correct answers.

1. A: You need an umbrella. Take <u>me / mine</u>.

   B: I don't want to use <u>your / yours</u>.

   A: It's OK. I have <u>you / your</u> rain hat.

2. A: <u>Who's / Whose</u> dictionary is on the floor?

   B: It's <u>Ali / Ali's</u>.

C Complete the sentences with *Who's* or *Whose*.

1. _____ test is this?

2. _____ compositions are on the floor?

3. _____ in level 3?

4. _____ family lives in the countryside?

5. _____ the director of your school?

D Correct the conversation. There are five mistakes.

A: Who's bag is that on the floor?

B: I think it's Maria.

A: No. Her bag is on her arm.

B: Well, it's not mine bag. Maybe it's Rita.

A: Rita, is that yours bag?

Now check your answers on page 447.

Go to MyEnglishLab to complete the review online.

Modals: Ability and Permission

PART 5

OUTCOMES
- Express ability in the present and past
- Recognize true and false statements about information in a short article
- Recognize main ideas and details in a conversation about animals
- Discuss abilities of various animals
- Write a paragraph about a pet

OUTCOMES
- Ask, give, and deny permission, using *can* and *may*
- Put items from an article in correct categories
- Recognize important details in a conversation about food allergies
- Talk about rules and regulations
- Ask and answer questions about diets and healthy habits
- Write a note that explains what a person can and cannot eat

Ability: *Can* or *Could*

ANIMALS AND THEIR ABILITIES

OUTCOMES
- Express ability in the present and past
- Recognize true and false statements about information in a short article
- Recognize main ideas and details in a conversation about animals
- Discuss abilities of various animals
- Write a paragraph about a pet

STEP 1   GRAMMAR IN CONTEXT

BEFORE YOU READ

Work with a partner. Answer the questions.

1. Do you have a pet, for example a dog, a cat, or a bird? Do you know someone who has a pet? What kind? What special things can the pet do?

2. Look at the photo. What do you know about parrots?

READ

○13|01 Read this article about an amazing parrot.

A Genius Parrot

Everyone knows parrots can talk. By "talk," we mean they can repeat words. Most parrots can't really express ideas. N'kisi is different. N'kisi is an African grey parrot. He can say almost 1,000 words. He can use basic grammar. He can talk about the present, past, and future. When he doesn't know a form, he can invent one. For example, he used the word "flied," not "flew," for the past tense of the verb "fly."

N'kisi lives in New York City with his owner, Aimee Morgana. He couldn't talk much at first. At first, he could only say a few words. But Aimee was a great teacher, and N'kisi was a good student. Now N'kisi talks to anyone near him.

Donald Broom, a professor of Veterinary Medicine at the University of Cambridge, is not surprised. He says that parrots can think at high levels. In that way, they are like apes and chimpanzees.

Les Rance of the Parrot Society says, "Most African greys are intelligent. They can learn to do easy puzzles. They can say 'good night' when you turn the lights off at night. They can say 'good-bye' when you put a coat on. But N'kisi can do many more things. N'kisi is an amazing bird. He's not just smart. He's a genius."

AFTER YOU READ

A VOCABULARY Complete the sentences with the words from the box. Use the correct form.

genius	intelligent	invent	professor	surprised

1. Monkeys and dolphins are very _____ animals. They can learn many things.

2. Many people are _____ by the abilities of African grey parrots. They can do all sorts of amazing things.

3. Mozart was a(n) _____. He could write great music at the age of six.

4. He's a very good _____. You can learn a lot in his class.

5. We need to _____ a way you can learn languages while you sleep.

B COMPREHENSION Read the statements. Check (✓) *True*, *False*, or *No Information*.

	True	False	No Information
1. N'kisi can say more than 1,100 words.	☐	☐	☐
2. N'kisi can't use basic grammar.	☐	☐	☐
3. N'kisi can talk about the past and the future.	☐	☐	☐
4. N'kisi can understand Italian.	☐	☐	☐
5. Parrots can't think at high levels.	☐	☐	☐
6. N'kisi could only say a few words at first.	☐	☐	☐

C DISCUSSION Work with a partner. Say two things N'kisi can do. Say two things most African grey parrots can do.

Go to MyEnglishLab for more grammar in context practice.

CAN / CAN'T FOR ABILITY AND POSSIBILITY; *COULD* FOR PAST ABILITY

Affirmative Statements

Subject	Can / Could	Base Form of Verb
I You* He We	can could	talk.

* You can be singular or plural.

Negative Statements

Subject	Can't / Couldn't	Base Form of Verb
She It They	can't/cannot couldn't/could not	talk.

Yes / No Questions

Can / Could	Subject	Base Form of Verb
Can	you	understand?
Could		

Short Answers

Affirmative	Negative
Yes, I can.	No, I can't.
Yes, we could.	No, we couldn't.

GRAMMAR NOTES

1 *Can*: Meaning and Form

Can expresses **present ability** or **possibility**. *Can* comes before the verb. The verb is always in the base form.	He **can say** 950 words. *(ability)* We **can teach** your bird to talk. *(possibility)*

2 *Can*: Negative

The **negative** of *can* is *can't*. USAGE NOTE *Cannot* is a form of the negative. It is not very common.	I **can't** understand you. I **cannot** understand you.

3 *Can*: Yes / No Questions and Answers

Change the order of the subject and *can* to turn a statement into a *yes/no* question. Use **short answers** for a *yes/no* question with *can*.	He can speak about the past. Can he speak about the past? Yes, he can.

4 *Could*: Meaning and Forms

Could expresses **past ability**. *Could not* is the full negative form. The more common form is the contraction, *couldn't*.	I **could** run fast in high school. I **could not** drive five years ago. I **couldn't** drive five years ago.

5 *Could: Yes/No* Questions and Answers

Change the order of the subject and *could* to turn a statement into a *yes/no* question.	**You could** speak English last year.⟶⟵**Could you** speak English last year?
Use **short answers** for a *yes/no* question with *could*.	**No, I couldn't.**

PRONUNCIATION NOTE

⏵13|02 **Stress with *Can* and *Can't***

When *can* comes before a base form of the verb, we usually pronounce it /kən/ and stress the verb.	We can **DANCE**.
When *can't* comes before a base form of the verb, we usually pronounce it /kaent/ and stress both *can't* and the verb.	We **CAN'T DANCE**.

Go to MyEnglishLab to watch the grammar presentation.

STEP 3 FOCUSED PRACTICE

EXERCISE 1 DISCOVER THE GRAMMAR

GRAMMAR NOTES 1–2, 4 Read the sentences in columns A and B. Underline *can, can't, could*, and *couldn't*. Circle the base form of the verbs. Then match each sentence in column A with the sentence that follows it in column B.

Column A

_e_ 1. N'kisi can (invent) new words.

____ 2. A camel can live up to six months without water.

____ 3. Cheetahs can go from 0 to 96 km/h in three seconds.

____ 4. At first, N'kisi couldn't say much.

____ 5. Dogs can't talk about their love.

____ 6. The bird couldn't fly south for the winter.

Column B

a. He could only say a few words.

b. They're very fast.

c. It was hurt.

d. They can show their feelings in other ways.

e. He's a smart bird.

g. A human can only go up to five days.

EXERCISE 2 *CAN* AND *CAN'T*

GRAMMAR NOTES 1–2 **Complete the sentences with *can* or *can't* and the verbs in parentheses.**

1. Many parrots _____*can learn*_____ to speak. My parrot _____,
(learn)   (say)
   "You're a genius."

2. My dog _____, but he _____ me my shoes. I'm
(sit)   (bring)
   trying to teach him to bring things to me.

3. My cat _____ mice. He's very good at that. Her cat
(catch)

   _____ mice. He just sits and watches them.
(catch)

4. Her dog _____ Spanish and English. She speaks to her dog in
(understand)
   English, and her husband speaks to the dog in Spanish.

5. Dolphins _____ people in trouble. They are smart and show feelings.
(help)

EXERCISE 3
YES / NO QUESTIONS AND ANSWERS

Ⓐ GRAMMAR NOTE 3
Use *can* and the words in parentheses to write *yes / no* questions. Then guess the answer.

1. (an elephant / swim)   <u>Can an elephant swim? Yes, it can.</u>

2. (elephants / jump)   _____

3. (a bear / climb a tree)   _____

4. (a chimpanzee / use tools)   _____

5. (chimpanzees / invent games)   _____

6. (a penguin / fly)   _____

Ⓑ Check your answers on page 453. Correct any incorrect answers.

EXERCISE 4 PRESENT AND PAST ABILITIES

GRAMMAR NOTES 1, 4–5 **Complete the sentences with *can*, *could*, or *couldn't* and the verbs in parentheses.**

1. Before N'kisi, there was a world famous African grey called Alex. Alex

   _____*could do*_____ many amazing things. He _____ up to six
       a. (do)   **b.** (count)

   things in a group. He _____ colors and materials. Before he died, he
                                   c. (name)

   _____ the sounds of a few letters.
       d. (read)

      Today you _____ about Alex and his trainer, Dr. Irene
                           e. (read)

   Pepperberg, in a book called *Alex and Me*. You _____ Alex in a DVD
                                         f. (see)

   called *Life with Alex*.

2. Some gorillas are smart. Michael was a smart gorilla. He _____ sign
                                         a. (use)

   language. He _____ 600 different gestures. You
                  b. (make)

   _____ about Michael on the Internet.
       c. (learn)

3. I had two dogs. My dog Charlie was a good watchdog, but he _____
                                           a. (do)

   any tricks. My dog Spot was not a good watchdog, but he _____ me
                                         b. (bring)

   my slippers.

EXERCISE 5 STRESS WITH *CAN* AND *CAN'T*

🔊13|03 PRONUNCIATION NOTE **Listen and complete the sentences with *can* or *can't* and the verbs.**

1. A zebra _____*can see*_____ the color blue, but it _____ the
   color orange.

2. You _____ a cow upstairs, but you _____ a
   cow downstairs.

3. Dolphins _____ with their eyes open, but they _____
   on dry land.

4. A pet cat _____ a black bear, but a cat _____ a jaguar.

5. Dogs _____ feelings, but they _____ them.

6. Elephants _____ their trunks to spray water, but they

   _____ .

EXERCISE 6 EDITING

GRAMMAR NOTES 1–6 Read the conversation. There are seven mistakes. The first mistake is already corrected. Find and correct six more. Add *can* to fix one mistake.

MARICEL: Can you <s>coming</s> *come* to my party? It's next Saturday night. You can to meet my new dog.

BELLA: Yes, I'd love to. How I get to your home?

MARICEL: You can to take the train or a taxi.

BELLA: Can you meet me at the train station?

MARICEL: I'm sorry. I can't. I no can drive. Maybe Bob can meets you. He has a car, and he can to drive.

> Go to MyEnglishLab for more focused practice.

| STEP 4 | COMMUNICATION PRACTICE |

EXERCISE 7 LISTENING

▶13|04 **A** Listen to a conversation about dolphins. Check (✓) three things the dolphins in Florida could do.

☐ catch a ball   ☐ paint pictures   ☐ breathe under water

☑ play basketball   ☐ live on land   ☐ talk

▶13|04 **B** Listen again to the conversation. Circle the correct answers.

1. What can all the dolphins at a marine institute in Mississippi do?
   a. play with a piece of paper   b. get fish for a piece of paper

2. What does Kelly do with her paper?
   a. hides it under a rock   b. eats it

3. Why does Kelly tear her piece of paper?
   a. to play a game with her trainer   b. to get more fish from her trainer

C Work with a partner. Ask *yes/no* questions with *can* and *could* about the dolphins in Florida and about Kelly.

EXAMPLES: A: Could the Florida dolphins play basketball?
           B: Yes, they could play basketball.

           A: Can Kelly plan for the future?
           B: Yes, she can.

EXERCISE 8 FACTS ABOUT ANIMALS

A GAME Work in a group. Discuss which animal matches the facts below. Write the letter of your guess on the line next to the statements about the animal.

a. cat

b. frog

c. hippopotamus

d. Spinosaurus

e. ant

f. Dodo Bird

g. crocodile

h. owl

_____ **1.** This animal can't turn its head, but it can see almost 360 degrees because its eyes are on the top and sides of its head.

> EXAMPLE: A: This animal can't turn its head, but it can see almost 360 degrees around itself. What do you think? Is it the owl?
> B: I don't think owls can see all around. I think it's the . . .

_____ **2.** This huge animal spends sixteen hours a day in water. It can make its own sunscreen.

_____ **3.** This animal lived around ninety-five million years ago. Scientists believed this animal could walk on two legs. They also believed it could swim.

_____ **4.** This animal is active at night and can turn its head 270 degrees, but it can't see things close to its eyes.

_____ **5.** This busy little animal can carry many times its weight.

_____ **6.** This animal lived on an island near Madagascar. It was a bird, but it couldn't fly. It was around until about 330 years ago.

_____ **7.** This animal can jump five times its height. It's a very popular pet.

_____ **8.** This animal can swallow stones. It can survive a long time without food. It has very sharp teeth.

B Check your answers on page 453.

Go to MyEnglishLab for more communication practice.

A BEFORE YOU WRITE Read about a student's pet. Then complete the chart with information about your pet or a pet you know about. Work with a partner. Use the chart to tell your partner about the animal.

I have a beautiful parakeet. His feathers are bright green. His name is Chichi. He is two years old. He lives in a cage in my living room. Sometimes he flies around the room. Chichi can sing very beautifully. Chichi couldn't do anything when he was younger. But now he can sit on my finger and eat from my hand. He can't speak, but I'm happy about that. I tell him all my secrets, and he doesn't tell anyone. That's a wonderful quality. I love my Chichi.

	Student's Pet	My Pet
Kind of animal	bird / parakeet	
Description	green feathers	
Name	Chichi	
Age	two years old	
Home	cage	
Abilities	sit on finger / eat from hand	

B WRITE Write a paragraph about a pet. Use the paragraph in A and your chart. Use *can*, *can't*, *could*, or *couldn't*.

C CHECK YOUR WORK Read your paragraph in B. Underline *can*, *can't*, *could*, or *couldn't* and the verb that follows. Use the Editing Checklist to check your work.

Editing Checklist
Did you . . . ?
☐ follow *can*, *can't*, *could*, and *couldn't* with the base form of the verb
☐ use *can* for the present and *could* for the past
☐ check your spelling

D REVISE YOUR WORK Read your paragraph again. Can you improve your writing? Make changes if necessary.

Go to MyEnglishLab for more writing practice.

UNIT 13 REVIEW

Test yourself on the grammar of the unit.

(A) Complete the sentences with *can*, *could*, *can't*, or *couldn't* and the verbs in parentheses.

1. Last year, I _____ much English. Now I _____
           a. (understand)   **b.** (understand)
   a lot more.

2. Jill doesn't exercise these days, so she _____ fast. In high school, she
                                            a. (run)

   was fast. She _____ a mile in seven minutes.
                  b. (run)

3. I _____ five years ago. Now I have a driver's license, and I
          a. (drive)

   _____ well.
      b. (drive)

(B) Complete the questions and answers. Use *can*, *could*, *can't*, or *couldn't*.

1. A: _____ you understand your dreams?

   B: Yes, I _____. They're easy to understand.

2. A: _____ you write reports last year?

   B: No, I _____, but now I can.

3. A: _____ Roger speak Korean?

   B: Yes, he _____. He can speak other languages, too.

(C) Write *yes/no* questions. Put the words in parentheses in the correct order.

1. _____?
                   (your finger / sit / your bird / could / on)

2. _____?
                   (anything / the parrot / say / can)

3. _____?
                   (your shoe / bring you / your dog / could)

4. _____?
                   (the past and the future / talk about / that bird / can)

(D) Correct the conversation. There are four mistakes.

A: Can you to get online?

B: No, I can't. I no could get online last night either.

A: My brother is good with computers. Maybe he can helps. I can to call him after work.

Check your answers on page 447.

Ability: *Can or Could*   **159**

Permission: *Can* or *May*
SPECIAL DIETS

OUTCOMES
- Ask, give, and deny permission, using *can* and *may*
- Put items from an article in correct categories
- Recognize important details in a conversation about food allergies
- Talk about rules and regulations
- Ask and answer questions about diets and healthy habits
- Write a note that explains what a person can and cannot eat

STEP 1	GRAMMAR IN CONTEXT

BEFORE YOU READ

Work with a partner. Answer the questions.

1. Are there any foods that you don't eat? What foods?
2. Why don't you eat them?

READ

▶14|01 Read this article about vegetarians and vegans.

Vegetarians and Vegans

What do Confucius, Leonardo da Vinci, Leo Tolstoy, and Mahatma Gandhi have in common? They were all vegetarians. Vegetarians don't eat meat. But they were not vegans. Vegans don't eat meat, fish, eggs, and dairy products.

Are you thinking, "I could never be a vegan"? Well, there are many nutritious meals you can prepare and eat while following a vegan diet. Here is a menu for one day.

For breakfast, you can have oatmeal with fruit. You can't use regular milk in your cereal, but you can substitute soy milk for regular milk. For lunch, you can have a hummus and avocado sandwich and a salad. Cut up lettuce, carrots, and tomatoes. Add nuts and a dairy-free dressing. If you're thirsty, you can make a fruit smoothie. Put water or soy milk in a blender.[1] Then add bananas and strawberries. For dinner, you can prepare spinach lasagna. You may use tofu instead of cheese and soy milk instead of cream. Then follow any spinach lasagna recipe.

Most of us know why vegetarians don't eat meat—for health reasons, or because they don't want to kill an animal in order to eat it. But why can't vegans eat dairy products or eggs? Vegans say when farmers get milk, they hurt the cows. When farmers get eggs, they hurt the hens. Vegans believe that all animals feel pain, pleasure, and love. So they believe it's wrong to eat animals or do anything to hurt them.

---

1 *blender:* a machine that mixes food to make liquid

AFTER YOU READ

A VOCABULARY Complete the sentences with the words from the box.

| dairy | in common | nutritious | recipe | substitute |

1. Schools are trying to give children _____ lunches. They want children to stay healthy and learn good eating habits.

2. He can't eat anything with milk in it. _____ products upset his stomach.

3. Can I have your mother's _____ for lasagna, or is it a secret?

4. We don't have any sugar at home. We can _____ maple syrup for sugar.

5. My best friend and I love the same sports, music, and movies. We have a lot

_____ .

B COMPREHENSION In the chart below, check the foods that a vegan and a vegetarian can (✓) and can't (✗) eat.

	apple	cheese	chicken	chocolate	eggs	fish	french fries	hamburger	hummus	ice cream	oatmeal	soy milk
Vegan												
Vegetarian												

C DISCUSSION Work with a partner. Compare your answers in B. Explain your answers.

Go to MyEnglishLab for more grammar in context practice.

CAN OR *MAY* FOR PERMISSION

Statements

Subject	Can/Can't May/May not	Base Form of Verb	
You	can can't	use	soy.
He	may may not	eat	eggs.

Yes/No Questions

Can/May	Subject	Base Form of Verb	
Can May	I	have	the recipe?

Answers

Yes, you can. Yes, you may. Sure. Of course. I'm sorry. It's not possible.

GRAMMAR NOTES

1 *Can* and *May*: Meaning and Form

Use *can* or *may* to **give permission**. ("It's OK to …")	
Can and *may* come **before the verb**. The verb is always in the base form.	You **can see** the doctor now. You **may eat** nuts.
When you don't give permission, use *can't* or *may not*.	She **can't** borrow my cookbook. I need it. You **may not** see the doctor without an appointment.
BE CAREFUL! There is no contraction for *may not*.	You **may not** see the doctor without an appointment. **NOT** You ~~mayn't~~ see the doctor without an appointment.
USAGE NOTE *Can* is much more common than *may*. We use *may* in formal situations.	You **can** eat your ice cream now. *(mother to child)* You **may** see the doctor now. *(nurse to patient)*

Use *Can I* or *May I* to **ask for permission**. *May* is more formal than *can*.

• *Can I . . .*	**Can I** come in? *(less formal)*
• *May I . . .*	**May I** come in? *(more formal)*

USAGE NOTE We often answer *yes/no* questions with a short affirmative response or a short apology and a reason.	**Yes, you can.** or **Yes, you may.** *or* **No, I'm sorry. The doctor is not ready for you.**
USAGE NOTE We often use *Can I* or *May I* + *help* to offer help to someone.	**Can I** help you? or **May I** help you?
When we answer, we usually thank someone or say *No thanks* and give a reason.	**Yes, please.** I'm looking for a vegan cookbook. *or* **No thanks.** I don't need anything right now.

Go to MyEnglishLab to watch the grammar presentation.

STEP 3   FOCUSED PRACTICE

EXERCISE 1 DISCOVER THE GRAMMAR

GRAMMAR NOTES 1–2 **Read the conversation between a patient and a nutritionist. Underline *can*, *can't*, *may*, or *may not* and circle the verbs they go with.**

NUTRITIONIST: Can I help you?

PATIENT: Thanks. I have a few questions about the diet you gave me. First of all, can I eat meat?

NUTRITIONIST: Yes, you can, but you can only have boiled, grilled, or baked meat.

PATIENT: What about fried chicken? Can I have it? I love fried chicken.

NUTRITIONIST: Sorry. You may not have any fried food on this diet.

PATIENT: Can I eat nuts?

NUTRITIONIST: Yes, you may. But you can't have too many. And remember, there are a lot of things on this diet that you can eat. You may eat as many green vegetables as you want, and you can drink as much green tea as you want.

PATIENT: That sounds good.

NUTRITIONIST: If you have any more questions, you can call me weekdays between 11:00 and 1:00.

EXERCISE 2 STATEMENTS AND QUESTIONS WITH *CAN* AND *MAY*

Ⓐ GRAMMAR NOTES 1–2 Complete the conversations with *can* or *may* and the verbs from the box.

drive	eat	have	help	keep	look	~~return~~	see	take

Conversation 1 (Can)

DOCTOR: You're doing great.

PATIENT: I feel good too, Dr. Lam. When _____can_____ I _____return_____ to work?
1.

DOCTOR: Next week.

PATIENT: And when _____ I _____?
2.

DOCTOR: Wait another week. Take the train next week.

PATIENT: OK.

DOCTOR: But remember. Watch your diet. Don't eat heavy food and dessert.

PATIENT: _____ I _____ in restaurants?
3.

DOCTOR: Sure. Just watch what you order.

Conversation 2 (May)

RECEPTIONIST: _____ I _____ you?
4.

PATIENT: Thanks. I'd like to make an appointment with Ms. Stein.

RECEPTIONIST: She's free next Tuesday at 10:00. Here are some booklets about nutrition. You

_____ _____ them home and read them.
5.

PATIENT: Thanks. Do you want them back?

RECEPTIONIST: No. You _____ _____ them.
6.

Conversation 3 (Can)

SERVER: Your fish comes with a salad.

BOB: OK. _____ I _____ the dressing on the side?
7.

SERVER: Of course.

BOB: And _____ we _____ the dessert menu?
8.

BOB'S WIFE: Bob, you're on a diet! You can't have dessert.

BOB: But I _____ _____ at the desserts and dream about them.
9.

⏵14|02 Ⓑ LISTEN AND CHECK **Listen to the conversations and check your answers in A.**

EXERCISE 3 ASKING PERMISSION WITH *CAN* AND *MAY*

Ⓐ GRAMMAR NOTES 1–2 Complete the conversation. Write questions with *can* or *may*. Use the information in parentheses.

RECEPTIONIST: (May) _____ *May I help you?*
                                          1. (Do you need my help?)

NURAY: Yes, thanks. I'm Nuray Attaturk. I have an appointment with Dr. Lee for 2:00.

RECEPTIONIST: Hi, Ms. Attaturk. (May) _____
                                          2. (I want to see your health insurance card.)

(After Nuray sees Dr. Lee, he gives her a diet to follow.)

DR. LEE: OK, Nuray. Here's your diet. Any questions?

NURAY: (Can) _____
                        3. (Is it OK to eat snacks?)

DR. LEE: Yes, but you can only have light snacks.

NURAY: (Can) _____
                        4. (Is it OK to have ice cream?)

DR. LEE: No, you can't, but you can have low-fat yogurt instead.

NURAY: (May) _____
                        5. (Is it OK to call you with questions?)

DR. LEE: Certainly. But don't worry. Everything is on these papers. Just read the diet and

           follow the directions. You'll feel better in no time.

NURAY: Thanks, Dr. Lee.

▶14|03 Ⓑ LISTEN AND CHECK **Listen to the conversation and check your answers in A.**

EXERCISE 4 EDITING

GRAMMAR NOTES 1–2 **Correct the conversations. There are six mistakes. The first mistake is already corrected. Find and correct five more.**

1. A: Can we ~~paid~~ later?
                pay

   B: Yes, you can pays half now and half next month.

2. A: May I speaks to the doctor?

   B: I'm sorry. He's with a patient now. Can you calls back later?

3. A: Can I to use salt?

   B: Yes, but not a lot.

4. A: Can I drink coffee or tea?

   B: You may drink tea, but you mayn't drink coffee.

EXERCISE 5 LISTENING

Ⓐ You are going to listen to a conversation between a doctor and his patient, Sandra. Sandra has a food allergy. Before you listen, work with a partner and answer the questions.

1. Do you have any allergies? What are you allergic to?

2. Do you know people who are allergic to any of the following: cats, dogs, strawberries, soy, nuts, or wheat? Who?

3. What can happen to someone with an allergy?

▶14|04 **Ⓑ** Listen to the conversation. Then listen again. Check (✓) the foods that Sandra can't eat.

☐ eggs   ☑ pad thai   ☐ peanuts   ☐ wheat

☐ milk   ☐ peanut butter   ☐ walnuts

Ⓒ Work with a partner. Talk about foods that Sandra's cousin can't eat.

EXAMPLE: A: Well, let's see. It says she can't eat wheat. So I guess she can't eat most kinds of bread.

B: Yes, and she probably can't eat . . .

EXERCISE 6 RULES IN A SCHOOL CAFETERIA

Ⓐ DISCUSSION Work in groups. Prepare for a discussion in B. Make a list of rules for a school cafeteria for children between the ages of six and twelve. Write your list on the board. Use *can* and *can't*.

EXAMPLE: *You can't run in the cafeteria.*
You can bring a sandwich from home.

Ⓑ Read your list to your other groups. Explain your rules.

EXAMPLE: A: You can't run in the cafeteria.

B: Why not?

A: Children can spill their food and make a mess.

EXERCISE 7 YOU CAN'T EAT PRETZELS AND CHIPS

ROLE PLAY Work with a partner. One of you is a patient. The other is a nutritionist. The patient needs a special diet. The nutritionist tells the patient what he or she can and can't eat.

EXAMPLE: A: Hello. How do you feel?
          B: I feel good, but my blood pressure is high and I want to lose some weight. Can you give me a good diet?
          A: Yes, of course. You can eat bread, but you can't eat pretzels and chips. They're very salty.
          B: Can I have . . . ?

EXERCISE 8 PATIENT INFORMATION

INFORMATION GAP Work with a partner. Student A follows the instructions below. Student B will follow the instructions on page 456.

STUDENT A

- Read the information for Dr. Green's patients.

- Student B will ask you questions about this information. Answer Student B's questions. Use *can*, *may*, *can't*, or *may not* to answer the questions.

Green Clinic

PATIENT INFORMATION

Office Hours: Monday, Wednesday, and Friday between 8:00 and 4:00.

Calls: You can call the doctor weekdays between 11:00 and 12:00 at 344-3500.

Please note: Dr. Green does not answer calls evenings or weekends. In an emergency, call 344-3580.

Learn more:
- Attend free lectures on nutrition on the first Monday of every month.
- Join a support group. For more information, email nutrisupport@greenhealth.com.
- See a list of suggested meals at www.greenhealth.com.

Questions? Email Dr. Green at nutridr@greenhealth.com.

Go to MyEnglishLab for more communication practice.

A BEFORE YOU WRITE Work with a partner. Read the note from Ana to Maria and Maria's answer. Then discuss: When someone with a special diet visits you, what do you do?

● ○ ○

Hi Maria,

My son Jorge would love to go to Rosa's pizza party on Saturday, but he can't eat dairy products. Please don't give him anything with milk or cheese in it. I can give him some food that he can eat at the party.

See you on Saturday,

Ana

● ○ ○

Hi Ana,

I'm glad that Jorge can come to the party. I can give him pizza without cheese. My nephew can't eat dairy, either. They can share a cheese-less pizza.

See you Saturday.

Maria

B WRITE You or your son or daughter were invited to a party. You (or your child) would like to go, but can't eat the food. Write a note and then write the answer you would like to get. Use the notes in A and your ideas. Use *can* or *can't*.

C CHECK YOUR WORK Read your paragraph in B. Underline *can* and *can't*. Then use the Editing Checklist to check your work.

Editing Checklist
Did you ...?
☐ use *can* for permission
☐ follow *can* or *can't* with the base form of the verb
☐ check your spelling

D REVISE YOUR WORK Read your paragraph again. Can you improve your writing? Make changes if necessary.

Go to MyEnglishLab for more writing practice.

UNIT 14 REVIEW

Test yourself on the grammar of the unit.

A Complete the paragraph with the correct forms of the words in parentheses.

It's a great diet. You _____ whatever you like. You just
                          1. (may / eat)

_____ a lot. For example, for breakfast you _____
2. (not / can / eat)   **3.** (can / have)

a slice of toast, an egg, and an orange. You can put jelly on the toast, but you

_____ butter. You _____ coffee, tea, or milk.
4. (not / may / use)   **5.** (may / drink)

B Write these questions to a doctor. Use *can* and the words in parentheses.

1. (When / I / return to work) _____

2. (When / I / take a shower) _____

3. (I / go / to the gym) _____

4. (I / ride / my bike) _____

C Ask questions about what students can and cannot do during a test. Put the words
in parentheses in the correct order.

1. (can / eat / during the test / we)   **4.** (can / drink water / we)

_____   _____

2. (a pencil / may / use / I)   **5.** (use / a black pen / I / may)

_____   _____

3. (I / can / during the test / make calls) **6.** (can / a dictionary / we / use)

_____   _____

D Correct the conversation. There are five mistakes.

A: May I sees a menu?   **B:** Sure. Here you go.

A: And can we to have some water?   **B:** I'll be right back with the water. . . . Ready?

A: May I has the chicken?   **B:** Of course. A very good choice.

A: And can you brings me a small salad?   **B:** Certainly. And may I gets you anything else?

Now check your answers on page 447.

Go to MyEnglishLab to complete the review online.   Permission: *Can or May* **169**

Present Progressive

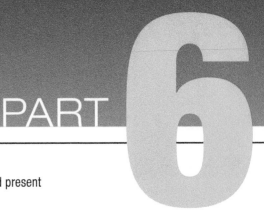

OUTCOMES

- Use the present progressive for events happening now and in the extended present
- Identify details in an online article
- Recognize where people are based on a conversation
- Describe what people are wearing and doing
- Write a paragraph about what is happening now

OUTCOMES

- Ask and answer questions about situations that are happening now
- Answer questions about details in a conversation
- Recognize where people are and what they are doing based on a conversation
- Ask and answer questions about a movie
- Write a conversation that describes what is happening now

OUTCOMES

- Use the simple present and the present progressive
- Describe emotions, experiences, and preferences with non-action verbs
- Recognize details in a short article about technology
- Recognize details of short phone messages
- Discuss reasons for people's actions
- Discuss the ways your prefer to communicate
- Write a description of a picture

Present Progressive: Affirmative and Negative Statements

PEOPLE WATCHING

OUTCOMES
- Use the present progressive for events happening now and in the extended present
- Identify details in an online article
- Recognize where people are based on a conversation
- Describe what people are wearing and doing
- Write a paragraph about what is happening now

STEP 1   GRAMMAR IN CONTEXT

BEFORE YOU READ

Work with a partner. Answer the questions.

1. Do you like to watch people? Why or why not?

2. When you watch people, what questions do you ask yourself about them?

3. Where is a good place to go to observe people? Why?

READ

 Read this article about people watching.

People Watching

You're waiting for a train or a plane, and you're bored. What can you do? You can look at the people around you. I'm at Los Angeles International Airport, and I'm doing that now.

Across from me, I can see two businessmen. They're wearing suits and ties. One man is working on his laptop. The other man is reading a report. Both men are not looking around. They're working hard. They're not traveling for fun. They're traveling for business.

I can also see a mother and her little girl. The little girl is about three years old, and she's sitting on her mother's lap. I'm not certain they're mother and daughter, but I think so. They look alike. They're both wearing jeans. They're having fun. The mother is taking a selfie,[1] and they're both making funny faces.

---

1 *selfie:* a picture you take of yourself

A woman in her thirties is standing in front of the departure and arrival signs. She's wearing a business suit, but she isn't working now. She's talking to someone on the phone. She's smiling. She isn't speaking English. I think she's speaking Korean. Maybe she's talking to her mother. Maybe she's talking to a friend.

It's fun to look at other people. For some people, it's a way to relax. For others, such as writers and artists, it's a way to get ideas.

Writers, artists, photographers, psychologists, and detectives are people watchers. What about you?

AFTER YOU READ

Ⓐ VOCABULARY Complete the sentences with the words from the box.

bored	departure	detective	psychologist	suit

1. The _____ is trying to find the murderer. He's questioning the family and neighbors.

2. Most lawyers and bankers wear a _____ to work.

3. My son is always angry and is having problems at school. A _____ is helping him.

4. We need to check in at the airport two hours before our _____ .

5. Children are rarely _____ on planes. They always have a lot to do and to look at.

Ⓑ COMPREHENSION Complete the sentences. Circle the correct answers.

1. The author of the article is / isn't looking at people at a train station.

2. The businessmen are / aren't resting before their flight.

3. The little girl is / isn't smiling.

4. The woman in her thirties is / isn't enjoying her phone conversation.

5. The woman in her thirties is / isn't speaking English.

Ⓒ DISCUSSION Work with a partner. Look at the reading again. Take turns. Tell your partner three things about the people in the reading.

PRESENT PROGRESSIVE

Affirmative Statements		
Subject	*Be*	Base Form of Verb + *-ing*
I	am	
He		
She	is	
It		relaxing.
We		
You	are	
They		

Negative Statements			
Subject	*Be*	*Not*	Base Form of Verb + *-ing*
I	am		
He			
She	is		
It		not	sleeping.
We			
You	are		
They			

GRAMMAR NOTES

1 **Present Progressive: For This Moment in Time**

Use the present progressive (sometimes called the present continuous) for actions that are or are not happening **at the moment of speaking or writing**.

Past —————————————— **Now** —————————————— Future

They**'re eating.**
They**'re not drinking.**

With this use of the present progressive, we often use these time expressions:

• *now*
• *right now*
• *at the moment*

The machine **isn't working** *now*.
Right now, she**'s resting.**
At the moment, he**'s talking** on the phone.

BE CAREFUL! We don't usually use non-action verbs in the present progressive even for something that is happening now.

I **want** some coffee.
NOT I ~~am wanting~~ some coffee.

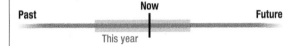

Use the present progressive for actions that are happening **at this time**, but may not be happening at this moment.

Past	Now	Future
	This year	

This year, **he is studying English.**
  (At this moment, he is not studying English.)

With this use of the present progressive, we often use these time expressions:

• *nowadays*

• *these days*

• *this year*

Nowadays, people **are traveling** a lot.

These days, the weather **is changing**.

This year, **we're studying** English.

3 **Present Progressive: Forms**

The present progressive always has a form of *be* + **the verb in the** *-ing* **form**.

Use *am*, *is*, or *are* and the **verb + -ing** to form the present progressive.

I **am watching** people.
He **is reading**.
They **are looking** at their phones.

Put *not* after *am*, *is*, or *are* to form the negative.

I **am not watching** people.
He **is not reading**.
They **are not looking** at their phones.

BE CAREFUL! Do not repeat the verb *be* when the same subject is doing two actions.

They **are singing** and **dancing**.
NOT They are singing and ~~are~~ dancing.

USAGE NOTE Use **contractions** in speaking and informal writing.

She's holding his hand.
I'm texting.
We **aren't** listening.

IN WRITING If a verb ends in a silent *-e*, drop the final *-e* and add *-ing*.

• *close*

• *smile*

• *make*

She's **closing** the window.
He's **smiling** at me.
They're **making** dinner.

REFERENCE NOTES

For more information on **non-action verbs**, see Unit 17 on page 196.

For a list of **non-action verbs**, see Appendix 15 on page 437.

For a list of **spelling rules for the present progressive**, see Appendix 16 on page 437.

Go to MyEnglishLab to watch the grammar presentation.

EXERCISE 1
DISCOVER THE GRAMMAR

Ⓐ GRAMMAR NOTES 1, 3

A student is people watching in her psychology class. Underline all the uses of the present progressive.

I'm in my psychology class. This semester we're studying child psychology. Today's class is almost over. Julia and Maria are closing their books. Our teacher is returning a test. Bob has a smile on his face. He always gets a good grade. Ryan isn't smiling. Maybe his grade is low. Shoko is texting under the table. Jon isn't listening to the teacher. He's thinking about lunch. I can hear his stomach. It's making noises.

Ⓑ Write the base form of the underlined words in A.

1. _____study_____   4. _____   7. _____

2. _____   5. _____   8. _____

3. _____   6. _____

EXERCISE 2   AFFIRMATIVE AND NEGATIVE STATEMENTS

GRAMMAR NOTES 1–3 Complete the sentences with the present progressive forms of the verbs in parentheses.

1. I'm tired of studying. I _*'m taking*_ (take) a break and _____ (look) around.

2. Julie and Maria _____ (play) games, and Bob _____ (text) someone.

3. Shoko and Ryan _____ (do) homework, and Jon _____ (read) the paper.

4. It _____ (rain) outside now. People _____ (use) umbrellas.

5. Some people _____ (stand) at the door. They _____ (wait) for the rain to stop.

6. I _____ (not / do) homework. I'm looking at the people in the library.

7. It _____ (not / snow) now. It _____ (rain).

8. They _____ (not / study) at this moment. They _____ (relax).

9. This semester, Hugo _____ (take) five courses. He _____ (work) hard.

10. This week in psychology class, we _____ (learn) about the behavior of three-year-old children.

EXERCISE 3 AFFIRMATIVE STATEMENTS

GRAMMAR NOTES 1–3 Circle the correct words to complete the email message.

Hi Antonio,

Remember me? I'm Hye Won Paik from Korea. We were together at the English Language
Institute. I 'm work / ('m working) for a Korean cosmetics company now. I'm in Madrid this week
1.
on business, and I stay / 'm staying at the Hotel Ritz. I meeting / 'm meeting with clients from
2.   **3.**
all over Spain. Right now, I sit / 'm sitting in the hotel lobby and watch / watching people.
4.   **5.**
I 'm think / 'm thinking about you, too. Do you remember the fun we had in English class six
6.
years ago? If you're free and in Madrid this week, please write or call.

Your friend from long ago,
Hye Won

EXERCISE 4 AFFIRMATIVE AND NEGATIVE STATEMENTS

GRAMMAR NOTES 1–3 Complete the paragraphs with the present progressive forms of
the verbs in parentheses.

Hye Won is a director of a cosmetics company. This week she _'s traveling_ on
1. (travel)

business. She _____ with clients in Spain.
2. (meet)

It's 8:00 in the evening. Hye Won _____ dinner with a client.
3. (have)

They _____ at Casa Paco, a top restaurant in Madrid. Hye Won and the
4. (eat)

client _____ about business right now. They _____ customs in
5. (not / talk)   **6. (compare)**

Spain and Korea.

On this business trip, Hye Won _____ a week in Madrid and two days
7. (spend)

in London.

Hye Won loves her job and her lifestyle. She says, "I'm glad I'm not married.

I _____ my freedom. I _____ for a husband at the moment.
8. (enjoy)   **9. (not / look)**

Maybe later." Hye Won's parents _____ to worry, but Hye Won is very happy.
10. (begin)

EXERCISE 5
EDITING

GRAMMAR NOTES 1, 3

Correct a student's journal. There are seven mistakes. The first mistake is already corrected. Find and correct six more.

                                      sitting
I'm ~~sit~~ in the park. It's a beautiful day. The leaves changing

color. Today there are a lot of children in the park. They laughing

and are playing. They no are studying. They're lucky. It's hard to

study on a beautiful day.

I trying to study for a test. I'm wait for my classmate, Grace.

We like to work together.

Go to MyEnglishLab for more focused practice.

STEP 4   COMMUNICATION PRACTICE

EXERCISE 6 LISTENING

15|02 **A** **Listen to two telephone conversations. Then find George and Sara in the picture. Write their names next to them.**

B Listen again to the telephone conversations. Complete the sentences. Then check your answers with a partner's.

1. George is _____ in front of Joey's _____ .

2. George is _____ a red _____ and _____ .

3. George is _____ a bag of _____ .

4. Sara is _____ in front of _____ Bank.

5. Ali is _____ in front of _____ _____ .

6. Sara is _____ a black _____ and a gray _____ .

C Work with a partner. Take turns. Describe other people in the picture. Use the present progressive. Your partner points to the person.

EXAMPLE: This man is wearing a navy sports jacket. He's standing next to a woman. They're . . .

EXERCISE 7 WHO'S WEARING WHAT?

A GAME Work in a group. Prepare for the game in B. Look around your class. Who's wearing the following?

a belt	a necklace	a sweater	earrings
a blouse	a ring	a T-shirt	jeans
a button-down shirt	a scarf	a watch	running shoes
a dress	a skirt	boots	sandals

EXAMPLE: A: Soraya is wearing a green sweater.
B: Mohammed is wearing a button-down shirt.

B The class sits in two rows back-to-back. Take turns with the person behind you. Say your name. Can you remember your partner's clothes? Don't look. Tell your partner what he or she is wearing. After you finish, students in one row move to the next seat.

EXAMPLE: A: I'm Mustafa.
B: Hi, Mustafa. I'm Shoko.
A: OK, Shoko, I think you're wearing jeans and a white sweater. Am I correct?
B: That's right. And you're wearing black pants and a black shirt.
A: Actually, my shirt is dark green, not black.

EXERCISE 8 COMPARING PHOTOS

CONVERSATION Work in a group. Ask a classmate from another group to take two photos of your group. In each photo, look or do something different. Look at the two photos and talk about the differences.

EXAMPLE: A: In the first photo, Juan is holding a notebook, but he isn't holding a notebook in the second photo.

B: And in the first photo, Eleni is wearing a watch. She isn't wearing a watch in the second photo. And look, I'm smiling in this photo, but I'm not smiling in that one.

EXERCISE 9 FIND THE DIFFERENCES

GAME Work with a partner. Find ten differences between picture A and picture B. The first pair to find the ten differences wins.

EXAMPLE: In picture A, the two girls are talking and laughing. In picture B, they aren't talking or laughing. They're eating.

Go to MyEnglishLab for more communication practice.

A BEFORE YOU WRITE

A student is looking at people in a school cafeteria. Read her observations. Then look around your classroom, hallway, or school cafeteria. Take notes about two people. Work with a partner. Tell your partner about the people.

I'm in our school cafeteria. It's 12:30 p.m. Two girls are waiting to pay for their food. One girl is tall. The other is not. The tall girl is wearing black pants and a black T-shirt. The other girl is wearing jeans and a red sweater. The tall girl is carrying a tray with yogurt and a salad. The shorter girl is carrying a tray with a sandwich, a salad, an apple, and cookies. She's talking a lot. The other girl is listening. She isn't saying a word. She isn't smiling. I think they're classmates. I don't think they're friends.

	What's the person doing?	What's the person wearing?	What else is happening?
Person #1			
Person #2			

B WRITE Write a paragraph about the people around you. Use the paragraph in A and your chart. Use the present progressive.

C CHECK YOUR WORK Read your paragraph in B. Underline the present progressive verbs. Use the Editing Checklist to check your work.

Editing Checklist

Did you...?

☐ use the present progressive for things that are happening now or nowadays

☐ include a form of *be* + the base form of the verb + -*ing* for the present progressive

☐ check your spelling

D REVISE YOUR WORK Read your paragraph again. Can you improve your writing? Make changes if necessary.

Go to MyEnglishLab for more writing practice.

UNIT 15 REVIEW

Test yourself on the grammar of the unit.

Ⓐ Complete the sentences. Circle the correct answers.

1. I'm not / I no am sleeping.

2. We are prepare / We're preparing for a test.

3. She isn't playing / She no is playing tennis now.

4. They doing / They're doing homework.

5. He is read / He's reading a mystery.

Ⓑ Complete the sentences with the present progressive forms of the verbs from the box.

| carry | drive | listen to | run | stand and talk |

1. A man _____ music on his iPod.

2. Two women _____ on a street corner.

3. Some children _____ to catch their school bus.

4. A young man _____ a red sports car.

5. An older man _____ a bag.

Ⓒ Complete the sentences with the present progressive forms of the verbs in parentheses. Use affirmative or negative forms.

1. John _____ his friend. He _____ him. John says texting is faster.
   a. (text)   b. (call)

2. Lulu is laughing. She _____. She _____ a very funny show.
   a. (cry)   b. (watch)

3. Julie _____ fast. She _____ to win a race.
   a. (swim)   b. (try)

Ⓓ Correct the paragraph. There are four mistakes.

My classmates and I am sitting in a computer lab. One student writing a composition. Two students are check their email. A teacher is helps a student. The other students are reading.

Now check your answers on page 448.

Go to MyEnglishLab to complete the review online.

UNIT

16

Present Progressive:
Yes/No **and**
Wh- **Questions**

MOVIES

OUTCOMES
• Ask and answer questions about situations that are happening now
• Answer questions about details in a conversation
• Recognize where people are and what they are doing based on a conversation
• Ask and answer questions about a movie
• Write a conversation that describes what is happening now

STEP 1 | **GRAMMAR IN CONTEXT**

BEFORE YOU READ

Work with a partner. Answer the questions.

1. What kinds of movies do you like?

   a. action   **c.** comedy   **e.** horror   **g.** other
   b. animation   **d.** drama   **f.** science fiction

2. Look at the picture on the laptop computer. What kind of movie is this? What do you know about this movie?

READ

▶ 16|01   Ann has a cold. Her co-worker Don is calling her on the phone to see how she is. Read their conversation.

A Very Funny Movie

ANN: Hello.

DON: Hi, Ann. How are you feeling today? Any better?

ANN: Uh-huh. I'm coughing less.

DON: Good. Is the fever going down?

ANN: Yes, it is. I'm just resting and watching movies.

DON: Oh? What are you watching?

ANN: *My Big Fat Greek Wedding*.

DON: I remember that movie. It was really funny. What's happening now?

ANN: In this scene, Toula's parents and Ian's parents are meeting for the first time.

DON: Where are you watching it? On your computer?

ANN: Yes.

DON: It's amazing. It's still funny after so many years.

ANN: I know. But, tell me, what's going on at work?

DON: We're working on ten things at the same time.

ANN: Is Mr. Brooks going crazy?[1] Who's doing my work?

DON: Mr. Brooks is impossible, and *I'm* doing your work. But not tomorrow.

ANN: Why? Are you taking the day off?

DON: Yes, I am. I'm catching *your* cold. I guess I need some good movies.

---

1 *going crazy:* feeling upset because there are too many things to do

AFTER YOU READ

(A) VOCABULARY Complete the sentences with the words from the box.

| catching a cold | coughing | fever | scene | still |

1. A: Why are you watching that _____ again?

   B: It's my favorite part of the movie.

2. A: Why are you staying home?

   B: I feel terrible. I think I'm _____ .

3. A: Why is he so hot? Does he have a _____?

   B: Yes, he does.

4. A: Do you _____ like to go to the movies?

   B: Yes, I do. Now the movie theater in my area has big, comfortable chairs.

5. A: He's _____ and sneezing because he's allergic to those flowers.
   He isn't sick.

   B: Oh. Let's put the flowers in another room.

(B) COMPREHENSION Match each question with its answer.

_____ **1.** Why is Ann staying home?   **a.** Yes, she is.

_____ **2.** Is she feeling better today?   **b.** No, Don is.

_____ **3.** What kind of movie is Ann watching?   **c.** He's getting sick.

_____ **4.** What's happening in the movie?   **d.** A comedy.

_____ **5.** Is Mr. Brooks doing Ann's work?   **e.** She has a cold.

_____ **6.** What's happening to Don?   **f.** Toula's and Ian's parents are meeting.

(C) DISCUSSION Work with a partner. Compare your answers. Then look at the reading.
What does Don ask Ann? What does Ann ask Don?

Go to MyEnglishLab for more grammar in context practice.

PRESENT PROGRESSIVE: *YES/NO* QUESTIONS AND *WH-* QUESTIONS

Yes/No Questions

Be	Subject	Base Form of Verb + *-ing*
Am	I	
Are	you	
Is	he she it	resting?
Are	we you they	

Short Answers

Affirmative				Negative		
	you	are.			you're	
	I	am.			I'm	
Yes,	he she it	is.		No,	he's she's it's	not.
	you we they	are.			you're we're they're	

Wh- Questions

Wh- Word	Be	Subject	Base Form of Verb + *-ing*	
Why	is	she	**staying**	home?
What	are	you	**watching?**	
Where		they	**showing**	the movie?

Answers

She's sick.
My Big Fat Greek Wedding.
At the Cineplex.

Wh- Questions About the Subject

Wh- Word	Be	Base Form of Verb + *-ing*	
Who	is	**staying**	home?
What		**happening?**	

Answers

Ann is.
They're singing.

GRAMMAR NOTES

1 Present Progressive: *Yes/No* Questions

Yes/no questions in the present progressive **ask if something is happening now** or nowadays.

To form a *yes/no* question, reverse the subject and the verb *be*.	He is singing. Is he singing?

2 Present Progressive: *Wh-* Questions

Wh- **questions** in the present progressive **ask for information about something happening now** or nowadays.	
Wh- questions in the present progressive begin with a *wh-* word and use *yes/no* **question word order**.	**Where is** he **working**? **What are** they **doing**? **Who are** you **meeting**?
IN WRITING Use *whom* only for very formal written English.	**Whom** is the president meeting?

3 Present Progressive: Questions About the Subject

Questions about the **subject** use **statement word order**—noun + verb. They often begin with *Who* or *What*.	A: **Who is resting?** B: Ann is resting. *(Both the question and the answer have the same word order.)*
When you are forming a question, it is important to know if you are asking about the subject or the object.	
Questions about the **subject** follow this form: *Wh-* **word + *is* + -*ing* form of the verb (+ object)**.	**Who is pushing Maria?** *(The question is about the subject.)*
Questions about the **object** follow this form: *Wh-* **word + form of *be* + subject + -*ing* form of the verb**.	A: **Who are Billy and Pete pushing?** B: Maria. *(The question is about the object—Maria.)*

> Go to MyEnglishLab to watch the grammar presentation.

STEP 3 FOCUSED PRACTICE

EXERCISE 1 DISCOVER THE GRAMMAR

GRAMMAR NOTES 1–3 **Read the questions in the chart. Then answer the questions.**

Column A	Column B	Column C
What's happening now?	How are you feeling today?	Is the fever going down?
What's going on at work?	What are you watching?	Is Mr. Brooks going crazy?
Who's doing my work?	Where are you watching it?	Are you getting sick?

1. Which column has *yes/no* questions? _____

2. Which column has questions about the subject? _____

3. Which column has other *wh-* questions? _____

EXERCISE 2
YES/NO QUESTIONS

A GRAMMAR NOTE 1 Change each statement to a *yes/no* question. Write the question on the line for Speaker A.

1. She is buying the tickets online.

   A: *Is she buying the tickets online?*

   B: _____

2. They are sitting in the first row.

   A: _____

   B: _____

3. They are watching a horror movie.

   A: _____

   B: _____

4. My hat is blocking your view.

   A: _____

   B: _____

5. You are enjoying the movie.

   A: _____

   B: _____

B Write the answer to each question in A. Choose the correct answer from the box below and write the answer on the line for Speaker B.

Yes, I am. Are you?	No, it isn't. I can see the screen.	Yes. It's very scary.
No. They're in the fifth row.	Yes, she is. She always gets tickets online.	

EXERCISE 3 *WH-* QUESTIONS

GRAMMAR NOTE 2 Write questions with the correct forms of the words in parentheses. Use the present progressive.

1. A: (What / you / do?) *What are you doing?*
   B: I'm getting something to eat.

2. A: (What / he / buy?) _____
   B: Popcorn. He always eats popcorn at the movies.

3. A: (Where / they / sit?) _____

    B: In the fifth row in the center.

4. A: (Why / she / put her coat on that seat?) _____

    B: She's saving the seat for her friend.

5. A: (Who / he / wait for?) _____

    B: His roommate. They're meeting in front of the movie theater.

EXERCISE 4
WH- QUESTIONS ABOUT THE SUBJECT

GRAMMAR NOTE 3

The following sentences describe scenes from famous movies. Write questions about the underlined words.

1. <u>Jack and Rose</u> are standing on the top deck of the *Titanic*.

                                                                         (Titanic, 1997, Drama / Romance)

    Who's standing on the top deck of the Titanic? _____

2. <u>Jon and Sara</u> are drinking frozen hot chocolate at Serendipity.

                                                (Serendipity, 2001, Fantasy / Romance)

    _____

3. <u>E.T.</u> is phoning home.

                          (E.T. the Extra-Terrestrial, 1982, Fantasy / Science Fiction)

    _____

4. <u>Elsa</u> is dancing on the ice and singing, "Let It Go."

                                    (Frozen, 2013, Fantasy / Animation)

    _____

5. <u>Michael Corleone</u> is saying, "Keep your friends close, but your enemies closer."

                            (The Godfather: Part II, 1974, Crime / Drama)

    _____

6. Gru and people in the park are exercising to the song, "Happy."

(*Despicable Me 2*, 2013, Animation/Comedy)

_____

7. Dr. Serizawa is saying, "Let them fight."

(*Godzilla*, 2014, Thriller/Action)

_____

EXERCISE 5 *YES/NO* AND *WH-* QUESTIONS

Ⓐ GRAMMAR NOTES 1–2 **Complete Ann and Don's conversation with the correct forms of the words in parentheses. Use the present progressive.**

ANN: Hi, Don. _How are you feeling_ ? _____ ?
　　　　　　　 1. (how / you / feel)　　　　　　　 **2.** (you / feel / any better)

DON: No, I'm not.

ANN: _____ ?
　　　　　　　 3. (you / take / the medicine)

DON: Yes, I am. _____ ?
　　　　　　　　　　 4. (where / you / call from)

ANN: I'm at an Italian restaurant. Don. Listen to this. Meryl Streep is eating here, too.

DON: No kidding! _____ ?
　　　　　　　　　　 5. (who / she / eat / with)

ANN: I think she's with her daughter. I'm not sure.

DON: _____ ?
　　　　　　　 6. (people / ask for her autograph)

ANN: No. Nobody's bothering her, but everyone knows she's here.

DON: Well, when you pass her table, say, "Bon appétit!" Say it the same way she said it in

the movie *Julie and Julia*.

▶16|02 Ⓑ LISTEN AND CHECK **Listen to the conversation and check your answers in A.**

EXERCISE 6 EDITING

GRAMMAR NOTES 1–3 **There are six mistakes. The first mistake is already corrected. Find and correct five more.**

1. A: Excuse me, ~~who~~ who's collecting tickets?

　　 B: He isn't here now. Wait a minute. He'll be right back.

2. A: What you doing?

　　 B: I'm turning off my cell phone.

3. **A:** Is Dad buy popcorn?

 B: Yes, he is.

4. **A:** What taking him so long?

 B: He's waiting in a long line.

5. **A:** Excuse me, is someone sits here?

 B: No, no one sitting here. Have a seat.

Go to MyEnglishLab for more focused practice.

STEP 4   COMMUNICATION PRACTICE

EXERCISE 7 LISTENING

16|03 **A** Listen to the telephone conversation. Answer the questions.

1. Where is Joy?
 a. in Chicago   **b.** in Miami

2. Where is it raining?
 a. in Chicago   **b.** in Miami

3. What are Joy and her family doing today?
 a. They're watching movies.   **b.** They're watching TV.

16|03 **B** Listen again to the telephone conversation. Complete the chart.

Who	Kind of movie	Where / How
Joy's mother	*a comedy*	on her iPad on the balcony at home
	a documentary	
Brian (Joy's son)		at the Cineplex movie theater
	an animated film	
Joy		

© Work with a partner. Look at the chart in B. Take turns. Ask questions about the people, the kinds of movies, and the places they're watching them.

EXAMPLE: A: So, where is Joy's mom watching the movie?
B: On the balcony. What about Joy's husband? Is he watching the documentary on his iPad?

EXERCISE 8 HOME ALONE

ROLE PLAY Student B is watching a movie when Student A calls. Student A asks Student B questions about the movie. Work with a partner. Complete the telephone conversation with your partner. Then switch roles.

A: Hi, _____(name)_____. This is _____(name)_____. Are you busy?

B: Oh, hi, _____(name)_____. I'm watching a movie. Let me turn it off.

A: No. Don't turn it off. What are you watching?

B: _____(name of movie)_____.

A: What's happening?

B: Well, at the moment . . .

EXERCISE 9 CHARADES

GAME Choose an action from the list below. Act it out in front of the class. Classmates raise their hands as soon as they guess the activity. Students get one point for each correct guess.

EXAMPLE: *(Student A performs an action.)*
B: Are you watching a horror movie?
A: No, I'm not.
C: Are you watching a comedy?
A: Yes, I am. *(Student C gets a point.)*

• watch a comedy / a horror movie / an action film

• play soccer / tennis / volleyball

• eat an apple / popcorn / an ice cream / a sandwich / a steak

• ride or drive a car / a bike / a motorcycle / a horse

• play the guitar / the piano / the drums / the saxophone

• Other: _____

Go to MyEnglishLab for more communication practice.

A BEFORE YOU WRITE Work with a partner and have a conversation. Begin the conversation with the dialogue below. Your partner is looking at a movie star. Ask more questions about the star. Take notes on your partner's answers. Then switch roles.

A: Hi, _____(B's name)_____ . It's _____(A's name)_____ .

B: Hi, _____(A's name)_____ . How are you? Why are you calling?

A: Guess who I am looking at right now?

B: Who?

A: _____(name of famous movie star)_____ .

B: You're kidding! What's _____(he or she)_____ doing?

A: Well, _____(he or she)_____ is . . .

B WRITE Write a telephone conversation between you and your partner about a movie star. Use your notes from your conversation in A. Use the present progressive.

C CHECK YOUR WORK Read your telephone conversation. Underline the present progressive verbs. Use the Editing Checklist to check your work.

Editing Checklist
Did you . . . ?
☐ include the verb *be* in all present progressive statements and questions
☐ use correct word order for questions
☐ include a subject in all questions except questions about a subject
☐ check your spelling

D REVISE YOUR WORK Read your questions again. Can you improve your writing? Make changes if necessary.

Go to MyEnglishLab for more writing practice.

UNIT 16 REVIEW

Test yourself on the grammar of the unit.

A Write present progressive *yes/no* questions with the correct forms of the words in parentheses.

1. (you / work) _____

2. (he / buy tickets online) _____

3. (they / watch a mystery) _____

4. (your cousin / enjoy the movie) _____

B Write present progressive *wh-* questions with the correct forms of the words in parentheses.

1. (Where / they / go) _____

2. (What movie / she / watch) _____

3. (Why / Bob / stay home) _____

4. (Who / watch / the children) _____

C Complete the conversations with the correct forms of the words in parentheses. Use the present progressive. Use contractions.

1. A: Why _____ ? _____ a funny movie?
       a. (laugh / the kids)   b. (watch / they)

   B: No, they _____ a game.
        c. (play)

2. A: What _____ ?
       a. (do / you)

   B: I _____ a movie. I _____ to
        b. (make)   c. (plan)
   study film in college.

3. A: What _____ outside?
       a. (happen)

   B: They _____ a movie about our neighborhood.
        b. (make)

D Correct the conversation. There are four mistakes.

A: What you watching?   B: We're watching a detective show.

A: What happening?   B: A boy is missing from his home.

A: The police are looking for him?   B: Yes, they are.

A: Where they looking?   B: Everywhere.

Now check your answers on page 448.

Go to MyEnglishLab to complete the review online.

Simple Present and Present Progressive; Non-Action Verbs

SMARTPHONES

OUTCOMES
- Use the simple present and the present progressive
- Describe emotions, experiences, and preferences with non-action verbs
- Recognize details in a short article about technology
- Recognize details of short phone messages
- Discuss reasons for people's actions
- Discuss the ways your prefer to communicate
- Write a description of a picture

STEP 1   GRAMMAR IN CONTEXT

BEFORE YOU READ

Work with a partner. Answer the questions.

1. How do you use your phone? Circle your answers.

   a. to email
   b. to get directions
   c. to listen to music
   d. to make phone calls
   e. to network with friends
   f. to search the Internet
   g. to take photos
   h. to text

2. What three ways do you use your phone the most?

READ

▶17|01 Read this article about smartphones.

SMARTPHONE MANIA

Smartphones are everywhere. People under twenty[1] don't know a world without them. They come with many features. They come in different colors and sizes. Some smartphones are waterproof and shockproof.[2]

People use their smartphones for a lot more than talking. Xavier uses his phone all the time, but rarely makes phone calls.

He texts and plays games. Right now, he's running late,[3] so he's texting his friend.

It's easy to understand the popularity of these phones. People want to connect with others, and at the same time, they want to be mobile.[4] Smartphones make it possible to do both. Smartphones are big business, and the technology is constantly improving.

---

1 *under twenty:* less than twenty years old
2 *waterproof and shockproof:* don't break when they fall in water and fall on the ground

3 *running late:* not on time
4 *mobile:* able to move around

What about in the future? Nobody knows, but here are the wishes of two people:

Robert says, "I want my phone to teach me a foreign language while I sleep."

Emily says, "I often forget to charge my phone. I want a phone with endless power."

Well, Emily may get her wish a lot sooner than Robert. But, of course, with the speed at which things are changing these days, you never know what the future will bring.

AFTER YOU READ

Ⓐ VOCABULARY Match the words in **bold** with their meanings.

1. I **connect** with Hiro once or twice a week.
   a. dance
   b. make contact

2. That watch is **waterproof**. You can swim with it on.
   a. not hurt by water
   b. dry

3. That new computer comes with a lot of **features**.
   a. parts that do many things
   b. memory

4. He calls her **constantly**. Is he in love?
   a. from time to time
   b. all the time

5. Your work is **improving**.
   a. getting better
   b. getting worse

Ⓑ COMPREHENSION Complete the sentences. Circle the correct answers.

1. Fifteen years ago, almost no one had a _____.
   a. personal computer
   b. cell phone
   c. smartphone

2. Xavier is texting a friend because he is _____.
   a. late
   b. playing a game
   c. tweeting

3. People want to get phone calls, but they don't want to _____.
   a. stay home to get calls
   b. be mobile
   c. make phone calls

4. Emily wants her phone to have _____.
   a. a beeper
   b. power all the time
   c. an alarm

5. Robert wants to learn a language when he is _____.
   a. at school
   b. at work
   c. asleep

Ⓒ DISCUSSION Work with a partner. Compare your answers in B. Then discuss the following question: What is the main reason smartphones are popular?

Go to MyEnglishLab for more grammar in context practice. Simple Present and Present Progressive; Non-Action Verbs **195**

SIMPLE PRESENT AND PRESENT PROGRESSIVE

The Simple Present	The Present Progressive
I **work**.	**I'm working** now.
He **works** on Mondays.	He**'s working** now.
She **doesn't work** with me.	She **isn't working** with him.
They **don't work** with us.	They **aren't working** with us.
Does he **work** with you?	**Is** he **working** with us?
Do you **work** for a phone company?	**Are** you **working** now?

NON-ACTION (STATIVE) VERBS

State of Being	Emotion	Sense/ Appearance	Need/ Preference	Mental Action	Possession	Measurement
be	love hate like dislike	hear see feel taste smell sound look	want need prefer	agree disagree guess understand know remember believe think mean worry	have own belong	cost weigh owe

GRAMMAR NOTES

1 Simple Present

Remember to use the **simple present** to tell or ask about **habits**, **customs**, **routines**, and **facts**. (See Unit 8.)

Past — Now — Future
She shops every Saturday.

I **charge** my phone every evening.
Do you **charge** your phone in the morning?

2 Present Progressive

Remember to use the **present progressive** to tell or ask about an action happening **right now** or **these days**. (See Unit 15.)

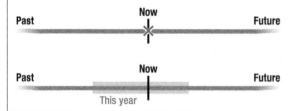

	He**'s checking** email now.
	Is Enrique **checking** email?
	Jon **is teaching** computer science this year.

3 Non-action Verbs

Some verbs do not describe actions. These verbs are called **non-action** or **stative verbs**.

Non-action verbs do the following:

• express emotion	We **like** that computer.
• describe sense or appearance	The music **sounds** relaxing.
• express a need or preference	I **prefer** email.
• describe a thought	Jennifer **knows** you.
• show possession	It **belongs** to me.
• give a measurement	It **costs** two hundred dollars.
• express a state	I **am** tired now.

BE CAREFUL! We usually do not use non-action verbs in the present progressive (*-ing*) form.	I **own** a smartphone. It **costs** a lot.
	NOT I'm owning a smartphone. It's costing a lot.
USAGE NOTE Some non-action verbs can also have an active meaning. When they have an active meaning, they can use the present progressive.	I **have** a new phone. I**'m having** trouble with it.
	I**'m thinking** about my phone. I **think** I need to return it.
	I'm **tasting** the soup. It **tastes** delicious.

REFERENCE NOTES

For a list of **non-action verbs**, see Appendix 15 on page 437.

For more information about the **simple present**, see Unit 8 on page 88, Unit 9 on page 100, and Unit 10 on page 111.

For more information about the **present progressive**, see Unit 15 on page 174 and Unit 16 on page 185.

Go to MyEnglishLab to watch the grammar presentation.

EXERCISE 1
DISCOVER THE GRAMMAR

Ⓐ GRAMMAR NOTES 1–3
Read the paragraph. Circle the simple present verbs. Underline the present progressive verbs.

Ⓑ There are five non-action verbs in A. Find them and write the base form of each verb on the lines below.

_____ *have* _____

_____

_____

_____

EXERCISE 2
SIMPLE PRESENT;
NON-ACTION VERBS;
PRESENT PROGRESSIVE

Ⓐ GRAMMAR NOTES 1–3
Complete the conversation. Use the simple present or present progressive forms of the verbs in parentheses. Use contractions when possible.

Raisa (has) a new phone with a lot of great features. She likes her phone a lot. Her phone keeps her in touch with[1] her friends. Right now, Raisa is texting friends. They are making plans for the evening. She and her friends often text. They don't talk much on the phone. They also connect through social media. Raisa often adds new friends to her social media sites. Sometimes she doesn't know them very well. Raisa's grandmother, Olga, worries about that. Olga doesn't use social media. She prefers to talk on the phone or connect through email.

_____

1 *in touch with:* connected to

ELI: What _____ *are* _____ you _____ *doing* _____?
        1. (do)

MONA: I _____ Instagram. Look! That's Joy Lin from high school. She
        2. (check)

        _____ three kids now. The twins _____ pirate costumes,
        3. (have)   **4.** (wear)

        and the older girl _____ a princess dress. The boy _____
                            5. (wear)   **6.** (look)

        like Joy, doesn't he?

ELIA: Yes, I _____ they all look like Joy.
               7. (think)

MONA: _____ you _____ social media a lot?
        8. (use)

ELI: No, not really. I _____ to text or email friends. I _____
          9. (prefer)   **10.** (believe)

      it's more personal. Also, I _____ about my privacy.
                                            11. (worry)

      _____ you _____ about your privacy?
           12. (worry)

MONA: Sometimes, but I _____ to connect with my friends on social media.
                                   13. (love)

⊙17|02 **B** LISTEN AND CHECK **Listen to the conversation and check your answers in A.**

EXERCISE 3 SIMPLE PRESENT; NON-ACTION VERBS; PRESENT PROGRESSIVE

A GRAMMAR NOTES 1–3 **Complete the conversation. Use the simple present or present progressive forms of the verbs in parentheses. Use contractions when possible.**

JEN: I'm worried about Tim. He ____*isn't doing*____ well in school. He was always a good
                                          1. (not / do)

      student, but this term he _____ games or _____ friends all
                                          2. (play)   **3.** (text)

      the time. I _____ he _____ Spanish. Bob and I
                       4. (think)   **5.** (fail)

      _____ about getting him a Spanish tutor.
             6. (talk)

RAY: What _____ Tim _____?
                  7. (want)

JEN: I _____. Right now, he _____ some new game. He
            8. (not / know)   **9.** (play)

      _____ those computer games. I _____ he
             10. (love)   **11.** (think)

      _____ addicted to them.
             12. (become)

RAY: My friend's daughter was like that. Now she _____ her own company.
                                                              13. (own)

⊙17|03 **B** LISTEN AND CHECK **Listen to the conversation and check your answers in A.**

EXERCISE 4 SIMPLE PRESENT; NON-ACTION VERBS; PRESENT PROGRESSIVE

GRAMMAR NOTES 1–3 Complete the paragraphs with the correct forms of the verbs from the box. Use contractions when possible.

answer	ask	know	look	~~need~~	swim	take	talk	want

Phuong _____*needs*_____ a new phone. He _____ a waterproof phone
                1.   **2.**

because he _____ every day. He _____ for a phone with a good
                 3.   **4.**

camera because he often _____ photos.
                                   5.

Right now, Phuong _____ to a saleswoman. He _____ her a
                                   6.   **7.**

lot of questions. The saleswoman _____ all his questions. She
                                            8.

_____ a lot about phones. She's good at her job.
         9.

EXERCISE 5 EDITING

GRAMMAR NOTES 1–3 Correct the paragraph. There are six mistakes. The first mistake is already corrected. Find and correct five more.

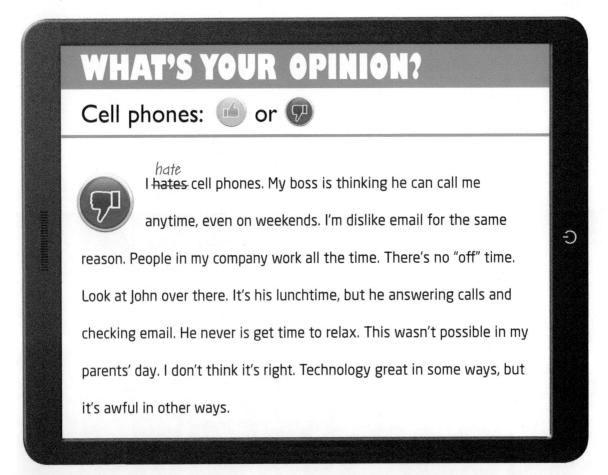

WHAT'S YOUR OPINION?

Cell phones: 👍 or 👎

                                        hate
I ~~hates~~ cell phones. My boss is thinking he can call me anytime, even on weekends. I'm dislike email for the same reason. People in my company work all the time. There's no "off" time. Look at John over there. It's his lunchtime, but he answering calls and checking email. He never is get time to relax. This wasn't possible in my parents' day. I don't think it's right. Technology great in some ways, but it's awful in other ways.

Go to MyEnglishLab for more focused practice.

EXERCISE 6 LISTENING

17|04 **A** Listen to Karina's phone messages. Put a check in the box if the call if is a business call or a call from a family member.

	Business	Family
Message 1	☑	☐
Message 2	☐	☐
Message 3	☐	☐
Message 4	☐	☐

17|04 **B** Listen to the messages again. Draw lines from the caller to his or her relationship to Karina to the reason for the call.

Name of caller	Relationship to Karina	Reason for the call
Bob	aunt	wants advice on smartphones
Lydia	boss	wants a business report
Natalya	daughter	wants Karina's travel plans
Gina	assistant	wants a ride from the station

C Work with a partner. Make guesses about Karina's life.

EXAMPLE: A: I think Karina is a businesswoman. I think she works hard and travels a lot.

B: I agree. I think she is a saleswoman. She has a daughter. I think her daughter is in her teens because she can take the train alone.

EXERCISE 7 CONSIDER THE POSSIBILITIES

PROBLEM SOLVING Work with a partner. Read about things people are doing. Guess why they are doing them.

1. Paul and Ana usually shop at Electronics Plus for their electronics. Today they're shopping at Goodbuys.

   EXAMPLE: A: Paul and Ana are shopping at Goodbuys today because there is a big sale there.

   B: That's one possibility. Maybe they're shopping at Goodbuys because Electronics Plus is closed.

2. Maria usually texts friends. Today she's calling and speaking to them.

3. Shoshana is speaking to someone on the phone. She sounds angry. She has a bill in her hand.

4. Ali usually brings his lunch to work. Today he's eating out.

5. Olivia is smiling. She's reading a text.

6. Joaquin usually wears jeans and a T-shirt in class. Today he's wearing a suit.

7. Rosa and Said are waiting in a very long line. It's raining, but they're laughing. Everyone in the line is between thirteen and twenty-two years old.

8. Uri is talking to someone on the phone. His face is turning red.

EXERCISE 8 PROS AND CONS OF SMARTPHONES

Ⓐ DEBATE Form two groups. Prepare for a debate in B. One group talks about why smartphones are good, and the other group talks about why they are not good. Look at the chart below or use your own ideas.

Why Smartphones Are Good	Why Smartphones Are Not Good
many features	expensive
immediate information	noises
connect anywhere / anytime	you are always available
entertainment / fun	battery dies
	no privacy

Ⓑ Work with the other group. Have a debate about why smartphones are or are not good.

EXAMPLE: A: I think smartphones are great. Everyone in my family has a smartphone, and we do all sorts of things with our phones. My mother emails her friends. My father . . .

B: But those phones are expensive, and the cost is always going up.

EXERCISE 9 TEXTS, CALLS, OR EMAILS?

A DISCUSSION Prepare for a discussion in B. Complete the chart. Make notes about the ways you prefer to communicate or get information and why. Give reasons why.

Which do you prefer?	I prefer...
ebooks or print books	
phone calls or texts or email messages	
smartphones or laptop computers	
electronic planners or paper planners	
news on your computer or news on TV	

B Work in a group. Discuss which forms of communication or media you prefer and why.

EXAMPLE: **A:** Do you like ebooks or print books?

       B: It depends. I read ebooks for fun because they're easy to carry, but I prefer print textbooks. I remember more when I read a print book.

       C: I prefer ebooks to printed books. I don't have space for books.

Go to MyEnglishLab for more communication practice.

A BEFORE YOU WRITE Read about the man in the picture. Then look at the picture of the woman. Make up a story about her. Explain why she's doing the things in the picture. Work with a partner. Tell your partner your story about the woman.

John is on the train. He's going to work. He's reading his mail. He's also having breakfast and listening to music. John is a busy man. He's a vice president of a company. He enjoys his job, but he's busy all the time. He has a wife and three children under four. His family is great, but at home he rarely has time alone. That's why John loves his long train ride to work.

B WRITE Write your story about the woman in A. Use the paragraph in A and your ideas. Use the simple present and the present progressive.

C CHECK YOUR WORK Read your paragraph. Underline the verbs in the simple present and circle the verbs in the present progressive. Then use the Editing Checklist to check your work.

Editing Checklist
Did you...?
☐ add -s or -es to the simple present third-person singular (*he, she, it*)
☐ use *is, am, are* + the base form of the verb and -*ing* for the present progressive
☐ use the simple present for habits, customs, facts, and with non-action verbs
☐ use the present progressive for actions happening now or nowadays

D REVISE YOUR WORK Read your paragraph again. Can you improve your writing? Make changes if necessary.

Go to MyEnglishLab for more writing practice.

UNIT 17 REVIEW

Test yourself on the grammar of the unit.

Ⓐ Complete the sentences with the simple present forms of the verbs in parentheses. Use the affirmative or negative form.

1. They _____ a car.
   (not / own)

2. He _____ to drive.
   (not / like)

3. She _____ a new bike.
   (have)

4. She _____ a lock for it.
   (need)

5. They _____ to buy bikes, too.
   (want)

Ⓑ Complete the paragraph with the simple present or present progressive forms of the verbs in parentheses.

John _____ his new computer now. He _____ the
            1. (use)   2. (surf)
Internet. He _____ about his computer. His computer _____
                  3. (read)   4. (have)
a lot of great features. John _____ to learn how to use all of them.
                                5. (want)

Ⓒ Complete the conversation with the simple present or present progressive forms of the verbs in parentheses.

A: What _____ Tom _____ right now?
            1. (do)

B: He _____ to fix his printer again.
        2. (try)

A: What _____ the problem now?
            3. (be)

B: I _____.
      4. (not / know)

A: I think he _____ a new printer. His printer is very old.
                  5. (need)

Ⓓ Correct the conversations. There are five mistakes.

1. A: Where you calling from?   B: Downtown. I walk along Second Street.

2. A: Is she play tennis at West Park? B: No, she's not. She no like West Park.

3. A: Does he understands Greek?   B: Yes, he does. He was in Greece for a year.

Now check your answers on page 448.

Go to MyEnglishLab to complete the review online.

Simple Present and Present Progressive; Non-Action Verbs **205**

Simple Past

PART 7

OUTCOMES

- Talk about past events, using regular verbs in the simple past
- Recognize details in short messages about travel
- Recognize details in a conversation about a trip
- Discuss past events and experiences
- Write an email about a trip or vacation

OUTCOMES

- Talk about past events with irregular verbs in the simple past
- Put events from a story in a chronological order
- Recognize details in a recorded story
- Tell a story about the past
- Write a short story from your childhood

OUTCOMES

- Ask and answer questions about the past
- Recognize details in a short biography
- Recognize main ideas and details in a conversation about a movie
- Ask questions about movies and plays
- Ask and answer questions about a famous writer
- Write questions and answers about the life of a famous person

OUTCOMES

- Talk about past events, using the simple past
- Understand details in a biography
- Answer questions based on a conversation
- Talk about famous people and past events
- Ask and answer questions about childhood
- Write your life story

Simple Past: Statements with Regular Verbs

TRAVEL

OUTCOMES
- Talk about past events, using regular verbs in the simple past
- Recognize details in short messages about travel
- Recognize details in a conversation about a trip
- Discuss past events and experiences
- Write an email about a trip or vacation

STEP 1   GRAMMAR IN CONTEXT

BEFORE YOU READ

Look at the photos. Answer the questions.

1. Do you recognize these tourist attractions? In which countries are they? (Check answers on page 453.)

2. What popular tourist destinations would you like to visit?

READ

○18|01   Read these messages.

Greetings from Brazil

Hi Dahlia,

You were so right! This city is awesome.

Yesterday morning, Julian and I watched footvolley on Ipanema Beach. The players were great. Then, in the afternoon, we visited Sugarloaf. What a view! In the evening, we enjoyed a delicious meal at a *churrascaria* (a barbecued meat restaurant).

Our flight here was the only bad part of the trip. We didn't land until 1:30 in the morning. Someone from the hotel picked us up, and we arrived at the hotel at about 3:00 a.m.

The people at the hotel are helpful, and our room is beautiful. The weather is great. I didn't need to pack my umbrella or my jacket.

Say hi to everyone at the office.

Love, Karen

Hi Karen,

I'm glad *you're* having such a great time. It's freezing here. Yesterday it snowed all day, and last week it rained.

I stayed late Monday and Tuesday. I prepared everything for the spring conference. Then guess what happened? Mr. Grimes canceled the conference. There was no barbecued meat for me. I dined on sandwiches from the vending machines downstairs.

So enjoy every minute of your vacation.

—I really miss you!

Love, Dahlia

AFTER YOU READ

A VOCABULARY **Complete the sentences with the words from the box.**

| canceled | freezing | land | miss | picked up |

1. Our flight was long. We started off at 9:00 a.m., and we didn't _____ until 3:00 p.m.

2. Bruno _____ five hotel guests and showed them the historic sites in town.

3. She _____ her trip because of the bad storm.

4. It's _____ in this room. The air conditioner was on too high.

5. I love to travel, but I _____ my comfortable bed at home.

B COMPREHENSION **Correct these false statements.**

1. Karen and Julian played footvolley on Ipanema Beach.

2. Karen and Julian enjoyed a delicious dessert at a restaurant.

3. Karen and Julian arrived at the hotel at 3:00 in the afternoon.

4. Mr. Grimes attended the spring conference.

5. Dahlia stayed late on Tuesday and Wednesday.

6. Dahlia dined on sandwiches from the café downstairs.

C DISCUSSION **Work with a partner. Compare your answers in B. Then answer these questions. In which city is Karen? Why is she happy to be there? Why is Dahlia unhappy to be at work?**

THE SIMPLE PAST: STATEMENTS WITH REGULAR VERBS

Affirmative Statements			Negative Statements		
Subject	**Base Form of Verb + -ed**		**Subject**	***Did not***	**Base Form of Verb**
I He She It We You They	landed. arrived. cried.		I He She It We You They	did not didn't	land. arrive. cry.

Past Time Markers		
Yesterday	*Ago*	*Last*
yesterday **yesterday** morning **yesterday** afternoon **yesterday** evening	two days **ago** a week **ago** a month **ago** a year **ago** a couple of days **ago**	**last** night **last** Monday **last** week **last** summer **last** year

GRAMMAR NOTES

1 The Simple Past: Meaning

Use the **simple past** to tell about something that **started and finished at a specific time in the past**.	They **visited** Rio de Janeiro last year.

Past ——————✗————— | Now | ————— Future

We arrived last night.

2 The Simple Past: Forms

There are **three endings** for regular simple past verbs in affirmative statements: *-ed*, *-d*, and *-ied*.

• *-ed*	We landed in Caracas. *(past of* land*)*
• *-d*	I arrived late. *(past of* arrive*)*
• *-ied*	He tried to change his flight. *(past of* try*)*

The verb form **does not change**. It is the same for all subjects.	**I visited** Seoul in 2015. **She visited** Mexico City two years ago. **They visited** Madrid last year. **Karen visited** Rio de Janeiro last month.

3 The Simple Past: Negative Statements

Use *did not* + the base form of the verb in negative statements.	We **did not stay** at a hotel.
USAGE NOTE Use *didn't* for negative statements in **speaking** or **informal writing**.	We **didn't stay** at a hotel.

4 Past Time Markers

We often use the simple past with **past time markers**. These are phrases that tell when something happened in the past.

Some common past time markers are: • *ago* • *last week / month / year* • *yesterday*	She arrived here **two months ago**. I lived in Colombia **last year**. I was in Miami **yesterday**.
Time markers usually come at **the beginning** or **the end** of a sentence.	The plane landed **two hours ago**. **Last night**, we watched a travel show.
BE CAREFUL! Use *ago* after **a length of time**. Do not use *before* + a length of time.	I visited my uncle one month **ago**. NOT I visited my uncle ~~before one month~~.
You can use *yesterday* before *morning*, *afternoon*, and *evening*.	They called us **yesterday evening**. **Yesterday morning**, he went to work.
BE CAREFUL! We say *last night*, not *yesterday night*.	I visited my cousin **last night**. NOT I visited my cousin ~~yesterday night~~.

PRONUNCIATION NOTE

18|02 ### Regular Past Tense Endings

Regular simple past verbs end in three sounds: /**d**/, /**t**/, or /**ɪd**/.

• /d/	He **arrived** late.
• /t/	They **worked** at a hotel.
• /ɪd/	She **waited** for him at the airport.

REFERENCE NOTE

For **simple past spelling** and **pronunciation rules**, see Appendices 17 and 18 on page 438.

EXERCISE 1 DISCOVER THE GRAMMAR

(A) GRAMMAR NOTES 1–4 Look at the sentences. Underline the simple past affirmative verbs. Circle the simple past negative verbs. Then write the base form of each verb.

	Base Form
1. We <u>arrived</u> in Washington, D.C., last Friday.	*arrive*
2. Yesterday afternoon, we walked around the National Zoo.	_____
3. Some friends invited us for dinner last night.	_____
4. Ana baked a cheesecake yesterday morning.	_____
5. The cheesecake didn't look good, but it tasted delicious.	_____ , _____
6. Miguel cooked enchiladas.	_____
7. The enchiladas looked delicious, but they didn't taste good.	_____ , _____
8. We visited Dupont Circle with Ana and Miguel.	_____
9. An hour ago, I called and thanked them for dinner.	_____ , _____

(B) Write the five time markers in the sentences in A.

_____ *last Friday* _____   _____   _____

_____   _____

EXERCISE 2 AFFIRMATIVE STATEMENTS

GRAMMAR NOTES 1–2 Complete the sentences. Use the simple past form of the verbs in the box.

arrive	bake	~~borrow~~	cancel	hurry	visit	walk	watch

1. We _____ *borrowed* _____ a guidebook from our friends.

2. His plane _____ on time.

3. Yesterday she _____ the art museum.

4. He _____ a cake for us. It was terrific.

5. I _____ slowly because I was tired.

6. The airlines _____ many flights because of bad weather.

7. We _____ because we didn't want to miss our connecting flight.

8. Two nights ago, they _____ a movie.

EXERCISE 3 NEGATIVE STATEMENTS

GRAMMAR NOTES 2–3 Underline the verb in the first sentence. Then complete the second sentence with the simple past negative form of the verb.

1. He <u>stayed</u> with friends. He _____ *didn't stay* _____ at a hotel.

2. I wanted coffee. I _____ tea.

3. It rained in the morning. It _____ in the afternoon.

4. She only invited you. She _____ your whole family.

5. He helped you. He _____ me.

6. I watched a movie. I _____ the news.

7. He picked her up from the airport. He _____ her _____ from the train station.

EXERCISE 4 AFFIRMATIVE AND NEGATIVE STATEMENTS

GRAMMAR NOTES 1–3 Complete the travel log with the simple past forms of the verbs in parentheses.

Carlos and I _____ *arrived* _____ in San
1. (arrive)
Francisco last Wednesday night at 9:00.

The next day, it _____, but
2. (rain)
the weather _____ us from
3. (not / stop)
sightseeing. We _____ our
4. (carry)
umbrellas and _____
5. (visit)

Fisherman's Wharf. Then the rain _____, so we _____
6. (stop)   7. (climb)
Telegraph Hill. We _____ around there a bit, and then we
8. (walk)
_____ a bus to Baker Beach. We _____ the sun set next to
9. (board)   10. (watch)
the Golden Gate Bridge, and we _____ to the ocean waves. I was so
11. (listen)
tired. I _____ to stay out any longer. I _____ to go back to
12. (not / want)   13. (want)
our hotel. On the way home, we _____ to have dinner. Chinatown was
14. (decide)
the perfect spot. We _____ a "bird's nest" and red bean soup. It was
15. (order)
delicious. Everything in San Francisco was amazing.

EXERCISE 5 PAST TIME MARKERS

GRAMMAR NOTE 4 Complete the conversations. Use *last*, *ago*, or *yesterday*.

Conversation 1

BEN: Were you away _____*last*_____ week?
1.

SAM: Yes, I was in Mexico City.

BEN: Oh. I was there a couple of months _____.
2.

By the way, Ian called me _____ night. He
3.

wants us to meet for lunch.

Conversation 2

STEVE: Where is Demetrios? I never see him

anymore!

ALLY: I know. He's always traveling. He was in

Montreal _____ weekend. He
1.

was in Prague _____ month.
2.

And two months _____, he
3.

visited his family in Greece.

STEVE: Where is he now?

ALLY: I'm not sure. I called him

_____. I'm waiting for
4.

him to return my call.

EXERCISE 6 SIMPLE PAST AND SIMPLE PRESENT STATEMENTS

GRAMMAR NOTES 1–3 Complete the conversations with the simple past or simple
present forms of the verbs in parentheses.

1. A: When do you usually travel?

   B: We usually _____*travel*_____ in the summer, but last year we _____*traveled*_____ in
   (travel)   (travel)
   the fall.

2. A: Does John like guided tours?

   B: No. He _____ most guided tours, but he _____ the one
   (not / like)   (like)
   yesterday in Chicago.

3. **A:** When does that restaurant open?

    B: It usually _____ at 7:00 a.m., but it _____ until 7:30
                      (open)   (not / open)

        yesterday morning.

4. **A:** Do you travel on business a lot?

    B: No, I don't. I usually _____ on business, but last month I
                                   (not / travel)

        _____ twice on business.
          (travel)

5. **A:** When do you start work?

    B: I usually _____ at 9:00, but I _____ at 8:00 this morning
                  (start)   (start)

        because I was very busy.

6. **A:** Does Jade always take the bus?

    B: She usually _____ a bus or train, but last week she _____
                      (take)   (not / use)

        public transportation. She _____ a car.
                                  (rent)

7. **A:** Where do you have lunch?

    B: I usually _____ something from home, but last Friday was a co-worker's
                  (bring)

        birthday, so five of us _____ a delicious meal at Siam Garden.
                           (enjoy)

EXERCISE 7 REGULAR PAST TENSE ENDINGS

▶18|03 PRONUNCIATION NOTE **Listen to the sentences. Check (✓) the final sound of each verb.**

Last weekend, . . .	/t/	/d/	/ɪd/
1. I watched TV.	✓		
2. I rented a bike.			
3. I listened to music.			
4. I played footvolley.			
5. I visited friends.			
6. I worked.			

EXERCISE 8 EDITING

GRAMMAR NOTES 1–4

Correct the letter. There are six mistakes. The first mistake is already corrected. Find and correct five more.

𝓜

Dear Dahlia,

Paris is unbelievable at night! It's 10 p.m., and I'm writing to you from a café. We arrived
here ~~before two days.~~ *two days ago* My friend Pierre picks me up. We toured the city during the day, and at night we did walked along the River Seine. Today, we dining in Montmartre, and we visited the Louvre Museum. I not like the food in Montmartre, but I did loved the area. I hope all is well with you. Don't work too hard!

Love,
Michelle

Go to MyEnglishLab for more focused practice.

EXERCISE 9 LISTENING

▶18|04 **A** Listen to the conversation. Read the statements. Check (✓) *True* or *False*. Then correct the false statements.

Ryokan

	True	False
1. Marta visited ~~Mexico.~~ *Japan*	☐	☑
2. Marta stayed with friends.	☐	☐
3. Marta stayed at a traditional Japanese inn.	☐	☐
4. Marta rented a car.	☐	☐
5. Marta didn't enjoy her trip.	☐	☐

⊙18|04 **B** Listen again. Complete the sentences with the length of time.

1. Marta was in Japan for _____.

2. Marta stayed in a *ryokan* for _____.

3. Marta visited Kyoto for _____.

4. Marta and her friend talked about Marta's trip for _____.

⊙18|04 **C** Listen again and take notes. Then work with a partner. Look at the list below. What did Marta tell her friend about each of the following?

EXAMPLE: Marta said she stayed with Japanese friends in Tokyo.

- Japanese friends
- a *ryokan*
- Kyoto
- tour guides and shopkeepers
- a car
- public transportation

EXERCISE 10 THE LAST TIME I . . .

CONVERSATION Work with a partner. Use the verbs in the box to ask your partner questions. Begin each question with, "When was the last time you . . ."

cook	play	rent	stay	walk	work
listen to	practice	shop	study	watch	

EXAMPLE: A: When was the last time you cooked pasta?
B: I cooked pasta last week. When was the last time you listened to classical music?

EXERCISE 11 TRUE OR FALSE?

A GAME On a piece of paper, write five things that happened on your last trip. Write four things that are true and one that is not true.

1. *On my last trip, I toured Seattle.*
2. *I rented a car.*
3. *I stayed with friends.*
4. *I visited the Space Needle.*
5. *It rained every day.*

B Work in a group. Take turns reading your sentences. Your classmates guess which one is not true.

EXAMPLE: A: On my last trip, I toured Seattle. I rented a car. I stayed with friends. I visited the Space Needle. It rained every day.
B: I think "I rented a car" is not true. You don't drive!

Go to MyEnglishLab for more communication practice.

A BEFORE YOU WRITE Read Emily's email to Jack. Underline the past tense verbs. Then imagine it's the last day of your trip to an amazing city. Work with a partner. Tell your partner about your trip. Use the underlined verbs or the verbs in the box.

Other Travel Verbs
arrive
enjoy
like
travel
walk
watch

Hi Jack,

Guadalajara is amazing. I landed here four days ago. I stayed at a hotel the first night. Then Hugo invited me to stay with his family.

Yesterday morning, we visited the palace. Then we rented a horse-drawn carriage[1] for an hour to see more of the city. In the afternoon, I shopped for ceramics.[2] Now I can't buy anything else unless I buy another suitcase.

See you soon.

Emily

1 *horse-drawn carriage:* a vehicle pulled by a horse, often for tourists to ride in
2 *ceramics:* pots, plates, and other things made of clay

B WRITE Write an email to a friend about a trip to a city. Use the email in A and your ideas. Use regular verbs in the simple past and past time markers.

C CHECK YOUR WORK Read your email. Underline the past tense verbs. Circle the past tense time markers. Use the Editing Checklist to check your work.

Editing Checklist

Did you . . . ?
- [ ] end regular simple past verbs in *-ed, -d,* or *-ied*
- [ ] place time markers at the beginning or end of a sentence
- [ ] use an amount of time + *ago*
- [ ] use *last* and *yesterday* correctly

D REVISE YOUR WORK Read your email again. Can you improve your writing? Make changes if necessary.

Go to MyEnglishLab for more writing practice.

UNIT 18 REVIEW

Test yourself on the grammar of the unit.

Ⓐ Circle the correct words to complete the sentences.

1. I watch / watched TV last night.

2. We did visit / visited Chile last summer.

3. He picked her up from work an hour ago / before an hour.

4. Last night / A night ago, I stayed home.

5. Our plane didn't land / no landed on time.

Ⓑ Complete the sentences. Use the simple past forms of the verbs in parentheses.

1. I'm helping them now. I _____ them last week, too.
   (help)

2. She's staying with me. Last year, I _____ with her.
   (stay)

3. It snowed during the night, but it _____ in the morning.
   (not / snow)

4. She only asked you. She _____ him.
   (not / ask)

5. We wanted to fly first class. We _____ to fly coach.
   (not / want)

Ⓒ Complete the sentences with the simple past forms of the verbs from the box. Some sentences are affirmative and other sentences are negative.

cancel	enjoy	play	rain	stay

1. My boss _____ the conference. He's trying to save money.

2. She _____ late at work. She needed to get home to her children.

3. It _____, so I didn't need my umbrella.

4. We _____ soccer for three hours. It was a lot of fun.

5. He _____ the movie. It was very boring.

Ⓓ Correct the paragraph. There are five mistakes.

Hello from London. Our friends did invited us here for a week. Yesterday we visit Big

Ben, and we tour Buckingham Palace. This morning, we watch a cricket match. Later we

walked around Piccadilly Circus and are enjoyed coffee and sandwiches at a café.

Now check your answers on page 448.

Go to MyEnglishLab to complete the review online.   Simple Past: Statements with Regular Verbs   **219**

Simple Past: Statements with Irregular Verbs

YOU NEVER KNOW

OUTCOMES
• Talk about past events with irregular verbs in the simple past
• Put events from a story in a chronological order
• Recognize details in a recorded story
• Tell a story about the past
• Write a short story from your childhood

STEP 1 GRAMMAR IN CONTEXT

BEFORE YOU READ

Work with a partner. Answer the questions.

1. What was a surprise in your life?

2. Some people say, "In life, you never know what will happen." What does that mean?

READ

🔊 19|01 Read this Chinese folktale.

You Never Know What Will Happen

A long time ago, there lived a poor Chinese peasant.[1] One day, a beautiful horse appeared on his farm. When the peasant's friends saw the horse they said, "How lucky you are!"

The peasant answered, "You never know what will happen."

Two days later, the horse ran away. The peasant's friends came and said, "What a terrible thing. How unlucky you are! The fine horse ran away."

The peasant didn't get excited. He simply said, "You never know what will happen."

Exactly one week later, the horse returned. And it brought three other horses. When the peasant's friends saw the horses they said, "Oh. You are so lucky. Now you have four horses to help you."

The peasant looked at them and once again said, "You never know what will happen."

The next morning, the peasant's only son was in the field.[2] Suddenly one of the horses ran into him, and the boy fell to the ground. He was badly

---

1 *peasant:* a poor farmer or farm worker
2 *field:* an area of land

hurt. He lost the use of his leg. Indeed, this was terrible, and many people came to the peasant and expressed their sadness for his son's misfortune.[3] But again, the peasant simply said, "You never know what will happen."

A month after the accident, soldiers rode into the village. They shouted, "There is a problem along the border! We are taking every healthy young man to fight." The soldiers took all the other young men in the village, but they didn't take the peasant's son. All the other young men fought in the border war, and they all died. But the peasant's son lived a long and happy life. As his father said, you never know what will happen.

_____

3 *misfortune:* bad luck

AFTER YOU READ

Ⓐ VOCABULARY Complete the sentences with the words from the box.

appeared	border	fought	ran away	rode	unlucky

1. He showed his passport to cross the _____ into Mexico.

2. The story was about a(n) _____ man. Bad things always happened to him.

3. The angry child _____ from home, but his parents found him two hours later.

4. A beautiful red bird _____ on the tree outside my bedroom.

5. She _____ her bicycle to school. She didn't walk or take the bus.

6. The two countries _____ a war over a small piece of land.

Ⓑ COMPREHENSION Number the events in the order they occurred (1 to 6).

_____ A week later, the horse came back with three other horses.

_____ A horse appeared on a peasant's land. Two days later, it ran away.

_____ The next morning, one of the horses ran into the peasant's son and hurt him.

_____ A month later, soldiers rode into the village.

_____ The other young men died. The peasant's son lived a long, happy life.

_____ The soldiers took all the healthy young men to fight, but they didn't take the peasant's son.

Ⓒ DISCUSSION Work with a partner. Compare your answers in B. Then tell the first half of the story in your own words. Your partner tells the second half.

Go to MyEnglishLab for more grammar in context practice. Simple Past: Statements with Irregular Verbs **221**

SIMPLE PAST: STATEMENTS WITH IRREGULAR VERBS

Affirmative Statements		
Subject	Verb	
I You He We	**bought** **rode** **saw**	the horses.

Negative Statements			
Subject	*Did not /* *Didn't*	Base Form of Verb	
I You He We	**did not** **didn't**	**buy** **ride** **see**	the horses.

Be: Affirmative Statements		
Subject	*Was/Were*	
She	**was**	lucky.
They	**were**	unlucky.

Be: Negative Statements		
Subject	*Was not/Were not*	
I	**was not**	home.
We	**were not**	nearby.

Contractions
was not → **wasn't**
were not → **weren't**

GRAMMAR NOTES

1 Irregular Past Verbs

Many **common verbs** are **irregular**. They do not add *-ed* to the base form of the verb.

The past tense of irregular verbs often looks different from the base form of the verb.	
• *bring* → *brought*	He **brought** a friend to school.
• *come* → *came*	She **came** late.
• *eat* → *ate*	He **ate** a big lunch.
• *go* → *went*	They **went** to work.
• *see* → *saw*	We **saw** three beautiful horses.

2 Negative Statements

For **negative statements** in the past, use *did not* + **the base form of the verb** (except for *be*).	They **did not see** him.
USAGE NOTE Use *didn't* for speaking and informal writing.	She **didn't eat** her lunch.

3 Past Tense of *Be*

Remember that the **past tense of** *be* is *was* or *were*. The **negative** is *was not* or *were not*. (See Unit 3.)	I **was** at the library last night. They **were not** home this morning.
USAGE NOTE Use *wasn't* and *weren't* for speaking and informal writing.	It **wasn't** late. They **weren't** in Mexico City.

Use *was* or *were* + *born* to tell when or where people were born.	I **was born** in 1996. They **were born** in Riyadh.

REFERENCE NOTES

For a list of **irregular past forms**, see Appendix 19 on page 439.
For more information about **the past of** *be*, see Unit 3 on page 30.
For more information about **the simple past**, see Unit 18 on page 210 and Unit 20 on page 233.

Go to MyEnglishLab to watch the grammar presentation.

STEP 3 FOCUSED PRACTICE

EXERCISE 1 DISCOVER THE GRAMMAR

A GRAMMAR NOTES 1–3 **Look at the paragraph. Circle the affirmative past tense verbs. Underline** *didn't* + **the base form of the verb.**

I have two brothers. My older brother (was) a great student. He
brought home prizes and won awards. My younger brother felt
bored by school. He didn't study and he didn't do well. My parents
worried about him. Then, in his second year of high school, he had
a great chemistry teacher. He became interested in chemistry. He
began to study hard. He's now a chemistry professor at a university.
So, you never know what will happen.

B **Write the past tense verbs that you circled in A in the chart. Then write the base form of each verb next to it.**

Past	Base Form
was	be

Past	Base Form

EXERCISE 2 SIMPLE PRESENT TO SIMPLE PAST

GRAMMAR NOTES 1–3 Change the verbs in each sentence from the simple present to the simple past.

Ursula Burns

1. In 2014, Forbes ~~calls~~ *called* Ursula Burns the twenty-second most powerful woman in the world.

2. Ursula Burns does not have an easy childhood.

3. Ursula Burns grows up in a poor section of New York City.

4. Ursula's parents are immigrants from Panama.

5. Her father leaves the family.

6. Ursula is a good student.

7. Ursula studies engineering in college.

8. In 1981, she earns a Master's Degree from Columbia University.

9. After college, in 1981, Ursula Burns gets an internship at Xerox.

10. In 2010, Ursula Burns becomes the Chairwoman and CEO of Xerox.

James Earl
Jones

EXERCISE 3
SIMPLE PAST: IRREGULAR VERBS

GRAMMAR NOTES 1–4 Complete the paragraphs with the simple past forms of the verbs in parentheses. Use contractions when possible.

James Earl Jones _____*was born*_____ in Mississippi in
          1. (be born)

1931. At five, his family moved to Michigan. Soon after that,

he _____ to stutter.[1] For many years, he
  2. (begin)

_____ more than a few words. In high school, a
 3. (not / say)

teacher tried to help him. After Jones _____ a
                  4. (write)

poem, this teacher _____ him read it aloud.
          5. (make)

Jones _____ the poem by heart, and he
    6. (know)

1 *stutter:* speak with difficulty because you repeat the first sound in a word

_____ it without stuttering. It _____ his first success at public

7. (say)   **8.** (be)

speaking. Later Jones _____ a scholarship to the University of Michigan. At

9. (get)

first, he studied medicine, but then he changed to theater.

    After college, he _____ to New York. He _____ money so

                    10. (go)   **11.** (not / have)

he _____ all sorts of jobs to pay his bills. After a few years, people

12. (do)

_____ his talent. He _____ a famous and admired actor. Maybe

13. (see)   **14.** (become)

you know his deep, powerful voice. It is the voice of Darth Vader in the *Star Wars* movies

and Mufasa in *The Lion King*.

    Jones _____ the 2008 Screen Actors Life Achievement Award. His life is

             15. (win)

amazing when you think that as a child, speaking _____ his

                                     16. (be)

biggest challenge.

EXERCISE 4   SIMPLE PAST: IRREGULAR AND REGULAR VERBS

GRAMMAR NOTES 1–4   **Complete each paragraph with the simple past forms of the verbs from the box. Use contractions when possible.**

~~be born~~	become	continue	love	major	write

    Joanne Kathleen _____*was born*_____ in England in 1965. As a young child, she

                                   1.

_____ to read and write. At the age of five, she _____ her first

2.   **3.**

book called *Rabbit*, and she _____ to write many stories throughout her

4.

childhood. In college, Joanne _____ in French and then _____ a

                          5.   **6.**

bilingual secretary.

begin	end	go	have	marry	teach

    At twenty-six, she _____ to Portugal. She _____ English

                        7.   **8.**

there. At this time, she _____ working on a story about Harry, a boy with

                         9.

special powers. She met a journalist in Portugal. They _____ and

                                              10.

_____ a daughter in 1993. Unfortunately, the marriage _____

11.   **12.**

in divorce.

J. K. Rowling

not / be	not / have	move	sell	try	not / want

She _____ to Scotland to be near a sister and finish her book. In Scotland,
      13.

her life _____ easy because she _____ much money. She
         14.   **15.**

_____ to sell her book, but the publishers _____ to publish it.
    16.   **17.**

She finally _____ her book to a publisher for about $4,000. Her book became
            18.

a bestseller. Today, her Harry Potter books are famous all over the world, and J. K.

Rowling is a very rich woman.

EXERCISE 5
EDITING

GRAMMAR NOTES 1–4

Correct the sentences. There are eight mistakes. The first mistake is already corrected. Find and correct seven more.

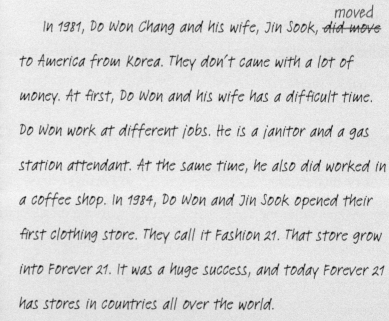

In 1981, Do Won Chang and his wife, Jin Sook, ~~did move~~ *moved*
to America from Korea. They don't came with a lot of
money. At first, Do Won and his wife has a difficult time.
Do Won work at different jobs. He is a janitor and a gas
station attendant. At the same time, he also did worked in
a coffee shop. In 1984, Do Won and Jin Sook opened their
first clothing store. They call it Fashion 21. That store grow
into Forever 21. It was a huge success, and today Forever 21
has stores in countries all over the world.

Go to MyEnglishLab for more focused practice.

EXERCISE 6   LISTENING

19|02   **A**   Listen to Paul's story. Then complete the sentence below.

The story is about a man who is now _____.

a. a father   **b.** a grandfather

19|02   **B**   Listen again. Circle the words that complete the sentence correctly.

1. A grandfather made / (gave) his grandson a beautiful blanket.

2. When the blanket got old, the boy wanted / didn't want to throw it away.

3. The boy's mother made the blanket into a book bag / shopping bag.

4. When the boy tore / lost the bag, his mother bought / made him a pencil case.

5. The boy lost the pencil case. He found it later / never found it.

6. The boy wrote / read a story about his grandfather's gift.

7. Many years later, the boy's son found the gift / story.

C   Work with a partner. Here are four titles for the story. Explain how each title connects to the story. Choose your own title for the story.

1. "My Grandfather's Blanket"

2. "The Many Lives of a Special Gift"

3. "How My Son Learned About My Grandfather"

4. "Lost and Found"

EXERCISE 7 IT WAS A TERRIBLE DAY, BUT THEN . . .

A STORY TELLING **Work with a partner. Tell about a terrible day and a wonderful day. Use *First*, *Then*, and *After that*.**

EXAMPLE: Yesterday was a terrible day. First, I got up late. Then I broke my glasses. After that, I lost an earring.

I had a wonderful day last Monday. First, I saw my grandmother. Then I went to the park. After that, I watched a video.

B **Work in a group. Add a surprise ending to your story in A. Change your wonderful day into a terrible day and your terrible day into a wonderful day. Tell your story to your group.**

EXAMPLE: Yesterday was a terrible day. First, I got up late. Then I broke my glasses. After that, I lost my necklace. I felt terrible because it was my favorite necklace. But then I got a call from my boss. He liked my work and gave me a promotion. So I went out and bought new glasses and a new necklace and I invited a friend to celebrate with me.

EXERCISE 8 A MEMORY GAME

GAME **The whole class sits in a circle. The first student tells one thing he or she did last weekend. The second student tells what the first one did, and then what he or she did. The third student tells what the first and second students did, and what he or she did. Keep playing until everyone has a turn.**

EXAMPLE:

> Last weekend, I went to the movies.

> Last weekend, Ann went to the movies, and I read a book.

> Last weekend, Ann went to the movies. Ava read a book, and I gave a concert.

Go to MyEnglishLab for more communication practice.

A BEFORE YOU WRITE Read this story. Then think about a simple story you know from your childhood. Work with a partner. Tell the story to your partner. Is there a surprise in it?

Solomon was a wise king. He lived about 3,000 years ago.

One day, two women went to King Solomon. One carried a baby and said, "We live nearby and had our babies three days apart. Her baby died in the night, and she changed it for mine. This baby is really mine."

The other woman said, "No! That woman is lying. That's *my* baby."

The two women continued arguing until King Solomon shouted, "Stop!"

He then turned to his guard and said, "Take your sword and divide the baby in two. Give one part to this woman and the other to that one."

The guard pulled out his sword. As he was about to harm the baby, the first woman screamed, "No! Don't do it. Give her the baby. Just don't kill the baby."

King Solomon then said, "Now I know the real mother. Give the baby to the woman who has just spoken."

B WRITE Write the story you talked about in A. Use the simple past tense.

C CHECK YOUR WORK Read your story. Circle all the past tense verbs. Use the Editing Checklist to check your work.

Editing Checklist

Did you . . . ?
- [ ] add *-ed*, *-d*, or *-ied* to form regular simple past verbs
- [ ] use the correct simple past form for irregular verbs
- [ ] use *did not (didn't)* + the base form for negative statements
- [ ] use past time markers at the start or end of a sentence
- [ ] check your spelling

D REVISE Read your story again. Can you improve it? Make changes if necessary. Give your story a title.

Go to MyEnglishLab for more writing practice.

UNIT 19 REVIEW

Test yourself on the grammar of the unit.

Ⓐ Complete the sentences with the simple past forms of the verbs in parentheses.

One day, a fox _____ some grapes. They _____ big and
               1. (see)   **2.** (be)

looked delicious. He tried to reach the grapes, but he couldn't. The fox _____
                                                   3. (be)

very hungry and _____ to get angry. When he still couldn't reach the grapes,
                          4. (begin)

he _____, "I really _____ those grapes."
      5. (say)   **6.** (want)

Ⓑ Complete the sentences. Circle the correct answers.

1. Walt Disney <u>grow up</u> / <u>grew up</u> on a farm with his parents and brothers.

2. He liked cartoons, and he liked to draw. He often <u>draws</u> / <u>drew</u> funny cartoons.

3. He started a company but the business <u>didn't make</u> / <u>didn't made</u> money.

4. He moved to Hollywood and <u>did begin</u> / <u>began</u> a cartoon company.

5. Disney's new company introduced Mickey Mouse. It <u>was</u> / <u>were</u> a huge success.

Ⓒ Complete the sentences with the simple past forms of the verbs from the box. Some sentences are affirmative and other sentences are negative.

leave	lose	run	see	take

1. The concert was terrible. I _____ early.

2. He _____ his keys. He needs to get a new set of keys.

3. We _____ 5 miles (8 kilometers) yesterday. We're practicing for a big race.

4. We _____ him in school. Was he sick?

5. It _____ him a long time to get to school. There was no traffic.

Ⓓ Correct the sentences. There are four mistakes.

The writer William Sidney Porter born in North Carolina in 1862. He wrote under

different names, but he did became best known as O. Henry. His stories were had surprise

endings. O. Henry was a very successful writer, but he spended time in prison.

Now check your answers on page 448.

Go to MyEnglishLab to complete the review online.

Simple Past: Questions
WRITERS

OUTCOMES
• Ask and answer questions about the past
• Recognize details in a short biography
• Recognize main ideas and details in a conversation about a movie
• Ask questions about movies and plays
• Ask and answer questions about a famous writer
• Write questions and answers about the life of a famous person

STEP 1   GRAMMAR IN CONTEXT

BEFORE YOU READ

Work with a partner. Answer the questions.

1. Who are some famous writers from around the world?

2. Who is William Shakespeare? What do you know about him?

READ

▷20|01   Read this magazine article about William Shakespeare.

THE GREAT
William Shakespeare

Who is the greatest writer in the English language? Most scholars[1] say William Shakespeare. He wrote thirty-seven plays and hundreds of poems. He wrote great stories about love, jealousy, pride, and ingratitude.[2] He used language in beautiful and unusual ways. People still see and read his plays today. But many parts of Shakespeare's life are a mystery. There are questions about his birth, his death, his education, and the years when he disappeared.

When was Shakespeare born? He was born in 1564 in Stratford-on-Avon, but we don't know the exact date.

When did Shakespeare die? He died in 1616. Some say he died on April 23, but others say on April 26.

---

1 *scholars:* people who study a subject and know a lot about it
2 *ingratitude:* not feeling thankful for what someone has done for you

How did Shakespeare learn to write so well? Was his education good enough for him to write those plays? He never attended a university.

Did Shakespeare write the plays himself? Did someone help him? Did someone write them for him? In Shakespeare's time, some people did not put their own name on their writing. They used another person's name. Was Shakespeare really the author of the plays?

Finally, there are Shakespeare's lost years. What did Shakespeare do from 1585 to 1592? Did he work? Did he study? Did he travel? Nobody knows.

People continue to ask these questions, but most Shakespeare scholars believe that Shakespeare wrote all the plays and poems himself.

AFTER YOU READ

A VOCABULARY **Complete the sentences with the words from the box.**

exact	jealousy	mystery	plays	pride

1. We can't find that old book. Its location is a _____.

2. When their daughter got her Master's Degree in literature, they looked at her with _____.

3. He left his wife out of _____. He thought she was in love with another man.

4. When I visited London, I saw three _____. The actors were great.

5. What is the _____ number of days she was gone?

B COMPREHENSION **Read the questions. Choose the correct answer.**

1. Where was Shakespeare born?
   a. London   **b.** Stratford-on-Avon   **c.** Oxford

2. When was Shakespeare born?
   a. 1654   **b.** 1564   **c.** 1465

3. When did Shakespeare die?
   a. 1606   **b.** 1516   **c.** 1616

4. Did Shakespeare attend a university?
   a. Yes, he did.   **b.** No, he didn't.   **c.** We don't know.

5. What did Shakespeare do from 1585 to 1592?
   a. He traveled.   **b.** He studied.   **c.** We don't know.

C DISCUSSION **Work with a partner. Compare your answers in B. Then look at the article again. Say two things about Shakespeare's life that are surprising.**

Go to MyEnglishLab for more grammar in context practice.

THE SIMPLE PAST: *YES/NO* AND *WH-* QUESTIONS AND ANSWERS

Yes/No Questions

Did	Subject	Base Form of Verb
Did	I you he she it we they	help?

Short Answers

Affirmative				Negative		
Yes,	you I he she it you they	did.		No,	you I he she it you they	didn't.

Wh- Questions

Wh- Word	Did	Subject	Base Form of Verb
What		I	ask?
Where		you	go?
When	did	he	write?
Why		we	leave?
Who		you	call?
How long		they	stay?

Answers

You asked about his name.
I went to the library. (To the library.)
He wrote at night, after work. (At night, after work.)
We went someplace else.
We called the doctor. (The doctor.)
They stayed for an hour. (For an hour.) (An hour.)

Wh- Questions About the Subject

Wh- Word	Past Form of Verb	
Who	wrote	*Romeo and Juliet?*
What	happened	in *Romeo and Juliet?*

Answers

William Shakespeare did.
Both Romeo and Juliet died.

GRAMMAR NOTES

1 Simple Past *Yes/No* Questions

Yes/no questions in the simple past begin with: ***Did* + subject + base form**	**Did** you **write** the report?
We usually give **short answers** to *yes/no* questions, but we can also give **long answers**.	A: Did you work yesterday? B: **Yes.** or **Yes, I did.** or **Yes, I worked yesterday.** A: Did you study? B: **No.** or **No, I didn't.** or **No, I didn't study.**
Remember that we form questions with **the verb** *be* in a different way. (See Unit 3.)	**Was** Shakespeare an actor? **Were** his plays always popular?

2 Simple Past *Wh-* Questions

| We usually form *wh-* **questions** in the simple past in the following way:

Wh- **word** + *did* + **subject** + **the base form** | **What did** he **write**?
Why did they **go**? |

3 *Wh-* Questions About the Subject

| We form *wh-* **questions about the subject** in the following way:

Who + **past tense of the verb** | A: **Who wrote** *Hamlet*?
B: Shakespeare wrote *Hamlet*.
   (Shakespeare = *the subject*) |
| **BE CAREFUL!** Do not use *did* with questions about a subject. Do not use the base form of the verb. Use the past tense form. | Who **wrote** *Hamlet*?
NOT Who ~~did write~~ *Hamlet*? |

Go to MyEnglishLab to watch the grammar presentation.

STEP 3   FOCUSED PRACTICE

EXERCISE 1 DISCOVER THE GRAMMAR

GRAMMAR NOTES 1–3 **Underline the base forms of the verbs in the questions. Then match the questions and answers. Write the letter of the answer on the line next to the question.**

_d_ 1. Did you <u>see</u> a play last Sunday?

_____ 2. What did you see?

_____ 3. Who directed the play?

_____ 4. Did you enjoy it?

_____ 5. What was it about?

_____ 6. Did you go with a friend?

_____ 7. Who was the lead actor?

_____ 8. Where did they show the play?

a. It was about young lovers.

b. Jonathan Lass was the director.

c. Yes, I did. It was wonderful, but very sad.

~~d.~~ No. I saw a play on Saturday.

e. No, I didn't. I went alone.

f. I saw *Romeo and Juliet*.

g. The performance was outdoors in Lakeville Park.

h. A new actor, Brad Shaw. He was very good as Romeo.

EXERCISE 2 SIMPLE PAST YES/NO QUESTIONS

GRAMMAR NOTE 1 Read the first sentence. Then complete the yes/no question in the simple past. In your question, use the verb from the first sentence.

1. I read all his plays. ___Did___ you ___read___ them, too?

2. We enjoyed the movie. _____ you _____ it, too?

3. The movie had good acting. _____ it _____ a good story?

4. I didn't understand everything. _____ she _____ everything?

5. We didn't like the ending. _____ he _____ the ending?

6. I expected a happy ending. _____ you _____ a happy ending?

7. We saw a review online. _____ they _____ the review online?

8. The review was by Robert Singh. _____ the review good?

EXERCISE 3 SIMPLE PAST SHORT ANSWERS

GRAMMAR NOTE 1 Answer the questions about the great Russian writer Leo Tolstoy. Use the simple past. Write affirmative or negative short answers.

1. A: Did Leo Tolstoy write *War and Peace*?

   B: ___Yes, he did___. He finished it in 1869.

2. A: Did you read *War and Peace* last summer?

   B: _____. I want to read it this summer.

3. A: Did Tolstoy write the book in Russian and French?

   B: _____. He wrote parts of the book in Russian and parts in French.

4. A: Did Tolstoy come from a poor family?

   B: _____. His family was very rich. He was part of the upper class, the aristocracy.

Leo Tolstoy

5. A: Did Tolstoy write about his life?

   B: _____. He kept diaries his whole life. That's why we know so much about him.

6. A: Did he marry?

   B: _____. He married Sofia Behrs.

7. A: Did they have any children?

   B: _____. They had fourteen children.

EXERCISE 4 SIMPLE PAST QUESTIONS

A GRAMMAR NOTES 1–3 Sherryl Woods is a best-selling romance and mystery writer. Read the interview. Complete the questions with the correct forms of the words in parentheses. Use the simple past.

INTERVIEWER: _____ *When did you write* _____ your first book?
                                 1. (When / you / write)

SHERRYL: In 1980. It came out in 1982.

INTERVIEWER: _____ to be a writer?
                              2. (you / always / want)

SHERRYL: No, I didn't. For many years I wanted to be a graphic artist.

INTERVIEWER: _____ always good at writing?
                              3. (be / you)

SHERRYL: Well, my first-grade teacher wrote, "Sherryl is good at everything except making

up stories."

INTERVIEWER: _____ your first-grade teacher?
                              4. (you / like)

SHERRYL: I can't remember.

INTERVIEWER: _____ to write?
                              5. (When / you / start)

SHERRYL: After I graduated from college, I became a journalist.

INTERVIEWER: _____ as a journalist?
                              6. (How long / you / work)

SHERRYL: I worked for newspapers for fourteen years.

INTERVIEWER: _____ writing romance novels?
                              7. (Why / you / start)

SHERRYL: I read one and said, "I can do this, too."

INTERVIEWER: _____ the most?
                              8. (Who / help / you)

SHERRYL: My agent did. She was there for me from the beginning.

INTERVIEWER: _____ when your books became popular?
                              9. (How / you / feel)

SHERRYL: I felt terrific. I remember the first time I saw someone with my book. I said,

"That's my book." The woman looked at me and said, "No, it's not. It's mine." I

said, "No, no, no. It's my book. I wrote it."

▶ 20|02 **B** LISTEN AND CHECK Listen to the interview and check your answers in A.

EXERCISE 5 EDITING

GRAMMAR NOTES 1–3 John Steinbeck was a great American writer. Correct the
questions and answers about him. There are ten mistakes. The first mistake is already
corrected. Find and correct nine more.

Q: When John Steinbeck ~~was~~ _was_ born?

A: He born in 1902.

Q: Where he was born?

A: He was born in Salinas, California.

Q: Where did he studied writing?

A: He studied writing at Stanford

University.

Q: He graduate from Stanford?

A: No, he didn't.

Q: Does he marry?

A: Yes, he did. He married in 1930.

Q: When he published _Tortilla Flat_?

A: In 1936.

Q: What year did _The Grapes of Wrath_ come out?

A: In 1938. It was his best book.

Q: What were it about?

A: It was about a family who lost their farm and became fruit pickers in California.

Q: Did he won many prizes?

A: Yes, he did. He won a Pulitzer Prize and a Nobel Prize in Literature.

Q: When did he died?

A: He died in New York in 1968.

John Steinbeck

Go to MyEnglishLab for more focused practice.

EXERCISE 6   LISTENING

▶20|03   Ⓐ **Listen to the conversation between Jon and Elena. Then read the questions. Circle the correct letter.**

1. What movie did Jon see last night?

     a. *Romeo and Juliet*   **b.** *Shakespeare in Love*

2. Where did the movie take place?

     a. in London   **b.** in Rome

3. When did the movie take place?

     a. in the 1500s   **b.** in the 1600s

4. Who was the main character in the movie?

     a. Romeo   **b.** Shakespeare

▶20|03   Ⓑ **Listen to the conversation again. Take notes. Then work with a partner. Write questions for the following answers.**

1. Q: *What was the movie about?*

     A: Shakespeare's true love.

2. Q: _____

     A: A romantic comedy.

3. Q: _____

     A: Marc Norm and Tom Stoppard.

4. Q: _____

     A: Gwyneth Paltrow and Joseph Fiennes.

5. Q: _____

     A: In 1998.

6. Q: _____

     A: Romeo and Juliet.

7. Q: _____

     A: The families of Romeo and Juliet.

8. Q: _____

     A: The two lovers died in each other's arms.

EXERCISE 7 WHAT WAS THE PLAY ABOUT?

CONVERSATION Work with a partner. Tell your partner about a book or a play that you read or saw. Your partner asks questions about it.

EXAMPLE: A: I saw the play *West Side Story*.
B: What was it about?
A: It was a play about two people who fell in love.
B: When did it take place?
A: In the 1950s.

EXERCISE 8 GARCÍA MÁRQUEZ WAS BORN IN . . .

A Q & A Read about Gabriel García Márquez. Then write four questions about his life.

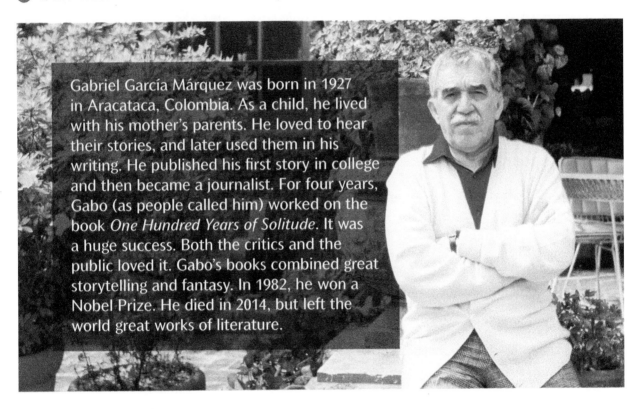

Gabriel García Márquez was born in 1927 in Aracataca, Colombia. As a child, he lived with his mother's parents. He loved to hear their stories, and later used them in his writing. He published his first story in college and then became a journalist. For four years, Gabo (as people called him) worked on the book *One Hundred Years of Solitude*. It was a huge success. Both the critics and the public loved it. Gabo's books combined great storytelling and fantasy. In 1982, he won a Nobel Prize. He died in 2014, but left the world great works of literature.

1. When was Gabriel García Márquez born?

2. _____

3. _____

4. _____

5. _____

B Work with a partner. Your partner closes his or her book. Ask your partner your questions about Gabriel García Márquez. Then close your book and answer your partner's questions.

Go to MyEnglishLab for more communication practice. Simple Past: Questions **239**

A BEFORE YOU WRITE   Mark Twain was a famous American writer. Work with a partner. Look at the information about Mark Twain. Ask your partner questions about his life. Take turns.

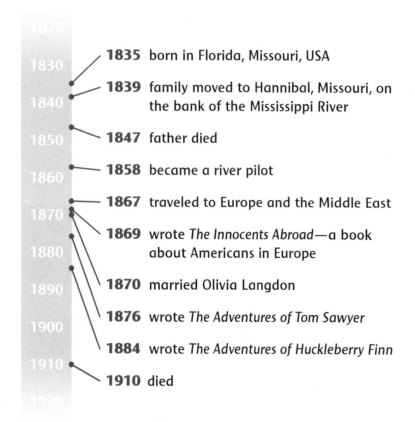

1835 born in Florida, Missouri, USA

1839 family moved to Hannibal, Missouri, on the bank of the Mississippi River

1847 father died

1858 became a river pilot

1867 traveled to Europe and the Middle East

1869 wrote *The Innocents Abroad*—a book about Americans in Europe

1870 married Olivia Langdon

1876 wrote *The Adventures of Tom Sawyer*

1884 wrote *The Adventures of Huckleberry Finn*

1910 died

Mark Twain
(real name Samuel Clemens)
American writer

B WRITE   Write ten questions and answers about the life of Mark Twain. Use the information in A and your discussion. Use *yes/no* and *wh-* questions in the simple past.

C CHECK YOUR WORK   Read your questions and answers. Underline the *yes/no* questions and circle the *wh-* questions. Use the Editing Checklist to check your work.

Editing Checklist

Did you . . . ?

☐ start *yes/no* questions with *did, was,* or *were*

☐ form most *wh-* questions with *wh-* question word + *did* + subject + base form of the verb

☐ use the past tense for questions about the subject

☐ use the correct form with the verb *be*

☐ check your spelling

D REVISE YOUR WORK   Read your questions and answers again. Can you improve your writing? Make changes if necessary.

Go to MyEnglishLab for more writing practice.

UNIT 20 REVIEW

Test yourself on the grammar of the unit.

(A) Write simple past *yes/no* questions with the correct forms of the words in parentheses.

1. _____
   (they / go to the theater)

2. _____
   (we / miss the beginning)

3. _____
   (you / have good seats)

4. _____
   (it / have a good ending)

(B) Write the questions that the underlined words answer.

1. A: _____
   B: Olivia did her homework before dinner.

2. A: _____
   B: John went to Paris last summer.

3. A: _____
   B: Ann helped Claudia with her report.

4. A: _____
   B: Mia and Lily worked for eight hours.

(C) Write questions in the simple past. Put the words in parentheses in the correct order.

1. _____
   (last night / what / see / did / you)

2. _____
   (you / where / see / it / did)

3. _____
   (the show / how long / was)

4. _____
   (you / the performance / did / enjoy)

5. _____
   (who / the star of the show / was)

6. _____
   (you / go out / did / after the show)

(D) Correct the questions. There are six mistakes.

1. Where he did go last night?

2. What saw he?

3. Did he enjoyed it?

4. Who he met?

5. When they left?

6. Who did pay for dinner?

Now check your answers on page 449.

Go to MyEnglishLab to complete the review online.

Simple Past: Review

BIOGRAPHIES

OUTCOMES
• Talk about past events, using the simple past
• Understand details in a biography
• Answer questions based on a conversation
• Talk about famous people and past events
• Ask and answer questions about childhood
• Write your life story

STEP 1   GRAMMAR IN CONTEXT

BEFORE YOU READ

Work with a partner. Answer the questions.

1. Think of people you know. Who can you describe in the following ways? Why?
   a. generous   c. powerful   e. loving
   b. loyal   d. talented   f. smart

2. How do you think people describe you?

READ

21|01   Read this article about a very unusual dog.

A Loyal Friend

Many people say dogs are loving and loyal. For one dog named Hachiko, that description is especially true. He won the hearts of people all over the world because of his love for and loyalty to his master.

Hachiko was an Akita. Akitas are large dogs from Japan. Hachiko was born in 1923. His owner, Ueno, was a professor at Tokyo University. Every morning, Ueno and Hachiko walked to the Shibuya train station together. Every evening, Hachiko met Ueno at the station. This routine continued for a couple of years. One evening, however, Hachiko went to the station, but Ueno didn't get off the train. That day, Ueno was at work when he suddenly had a cerebral hemorrhage[1] and died.

Hachiko didn't know what to do. He looked everywhere for Ueno. He was very sad, and he missed his master a lot. Every day for nine years, he went to the train station and waited for his master's return. After a while, people at the station noticed the dog and began to bring him food. They admired his loyalty. In 1934, they hired a well-known sculptor to build a statue of Hachiko. A year later, in 1935, Hachiko died.

After Hachiko's death, Ueno's students wrote about the amazing dog. In 2004, Lesléa Newman wrote and Machiyo Kodaira illustrated[2] *Hachiko*

---

1 *cerebral hemorrhage:* bleeding in the brain
2 *illustrated:* drew pictures for

Waits. This children's book was based on Hachiko's life. It won many awards. In 2009, Richard Gere starred in a movie based on the book.

These days when people are near the Shibuya train station in Tokyo, they often say, "Let's meet at the statue of Hachiko."

One thing is certain. People will never forget Hachiko.

AFTER YOU READ

A VOCABULARY   Match the words in **bold** with their meanings.

1. I **noticed** that her hands were red.
   a. forgot   b. saw

2. Her **routine** never changes. She gets up, dresses, and goes to Café Z for breakfast every morning.
   a. usual way to do things   b. map

3. The movie **is based on** the book.
   a. comes from ideas in   b. is different from

4. I **admire** his ability in art. He is a very good sculptor.
   a. admit   b. think highly of

5. There is a stone **statue** of our first president in front of the park.
   a. figure that looks like a person   b. painting that looks like a person

B COMPREHENSION   Read the questions. Choose the correct answers.

1. What did Hachiko's master do?
   a. He was a professor.   b. He was a train conductor.

2. When was Hachiko born?
   a. in 1934   b. in 1923

3. Where did Hachiko wait for his master every evening?
   a. at the university   b. at the train station

4. What did Hachiko do after Ueno died?
   a. He waited for Ueno at the train station. b. He looked for Ueno at the university.

5. Why did people admire Hachiko?
   a. He was loyal and patient.   b. He was strong and powerful.

6. What is *Hachiko Waits*?
   a. a book based on Hachiko's life   b. a TV show based on Hachiko's life

C DISCUSSION   Work with a partner. Compare your answers in B.

THE SIMPLE PAST

Affirmative Statements (All Verbs Except *Be*)

Subject	Verb	
I	**stayed**	**home.**
We	**went**	

Affirmative Statements with *Be*

Subject	Verb	
I	**was**	**at home.**
We	**were**	

Negative Statements (All Verbs Except *Be*)

Subject	*Did not* (*Didn't*)	Base Form of Verb	
I	**did not**	**stay**	**with them.**
We	**didn't**	**go**	

Negative Statements with *Be*

Subject	Verb	
I	**was not** **wasn't**	**at work.**
We	**were not** **weren't**	

Yes/No Questions (All Verbs Except *Be*)

Did	Subject	Base Form of Verb
Did	she	**leave?**
	they	

Yes/No Questions with *Be*

Was/Were	Subject	
Was	he	**home last night?**
Were	they	

Wh- Questions (All Verbs Except *Be*)

Wh- Word	*Did*	Subject	Base Form of Verb
When		you	**arrive?**
Where		he	**work?**
How	**did**	it	**begin?**
Why		he	**leave?**
Who(m)		they	**help?**

Wh- Questions with *Be*

Wh- Word	Past Form	Subject	
When	**was**	she	there?
Where		he	from?
How		his	tests?
Why	**were**	you	late?
Who(m)		they	with?

Wh- Questions About the Subject (All Verbs Except *Be*)

Wh- Word	Past Form	
Who	**walked**	to the station?
What	**happened**	to him?
How many people	**waited**	there?

Wh- Questions About the Subject with *Be*

Wh- Word	Past Form	
Who	**was**	his friend?
What		his last name?
How many people	**were**	there?

GRAMMAR NOTES

1 Simple Past Statements

Remember that the simple past has **regular and irregular** verbs. Some of the most common verbs are irregular. (See Units 18 and 19.)	We **liked** the story. *(regular verb)* We **read** the book. *(irregular verb)*
Be, the most common irregular verb, has two forms, *was* and *were*. (See Unit 3.)	He **was** a loyal dog. They **were** sad when he died.

2 Simple Past Negative Statements

Remember to use *didn't* + **the base form** of the verb for negative statements with all verbs except *be*.	I **didn't read** the book. We **didn't see** the movie. He **wasn't** at the train station. They **weren't** happy.

3 Simple Past *Yes/No* Questions

Remember to use *did* + **a subject** + **the base form** of the verb for all *yes/no* questions except questions with the verb *be*. (See Unit 20.)	**Did** he **wait** at the train station? **Did** they **look** for his master?
For the verb *be*, begin with *was or were* + **the subject**. (See Unit 3.)	**Was** he loyal? **Were** they amazed?

4 Simple Past *Wh-* Questions

Remember to use a *wh-* word + *did* + **a subject** + **the base form** of the verb to start most *wh-* questions except questions with the verb *be*.	**Where did** he **wait** for his master? **What did** they **do**? **Where was he** from?
Remember to use a *wh-* word + **the past tense of the verb** for questions about the **subject**.	**Who helped** him? **What happened** next? **Who was** late?

REFERENCE NOTES

For more information about the **past of be**, see Unit 3 on page 30.

For more information about the **simple past** see Unit 18 on page 210, Unit 19 on page 222, and Unit 20 on page 233.

For **pronunciation and spelling rules for the simple past of regular verbs**, see Appendices 17 and 18 on page 438.

For a list of **irregular verbs**, see Appendix 19 on page 439.

EXERCISE 1 DISCOVER THE GRAMMAR

Ⓐ GRAMMAR NOTES 1–4 **Read this conversation about great leaders. Underline sentences (statements and questions) with *be* in the past. Circle other verbs in the past.**

BORIS: Who's the man in the picture?

TEACHER: George Washington. He was the first president of the United States.

BORIS: When was that?

TEACHER: He became the president in 1789.

RODRICA: How long was he president?

TEACHER: For eight years.

RODRICA: Was he a good leader?

TEACHER: Yes. He was very good. And before he became president, he led the army during the American Revolution.

BEKIR: He sounds a lot like Atatürk. Kemal Atatürk was the father of modern Turkey. He was also a great soldier and leader. He gave Turkey many things, including a modern alphabet. Now spelling is easy in Turkish.

TEACHER: Well, George Washington didn't do anything about the English alphabet. Spelling is still hard in English.

EUN YOUNG: King Sejong gave Korea an alphabet. He was one of Korea's greatest leaders.

JOSÉ: In South America, Simón Bolívar led many countries to independence. He didn't change our alphabet, but spelling is not so hard in Spanish.

Ⓑ **Look at the conversation again. Find an example of each of the following in the conversation in A. Write the statement or question on the line.**

1. A simple past statement with *be*: _____

2. A simple past question with *be*: _____

3. A simple past affirmative statement with another verb (not *be*):

_____

4. A simple past negative statement with another verb (not *be*):

_____

EXERCISE 2 AFFIRMATIVE STATEMENTS

GRAMMAR NOTE 1 Complete this paragraph about the man who started eBay. Use the simple past forms of the verbs in parentheses.

Pierre Omidyar _____was born_____ in Paris, France. His
              1. (be / born)

parents _____ from Iran. His mother
        2. (be)

_____ a professor, and his father
3. (be)

_____ medicine. His family _____
4. (practice)   **5.** (move)

to the United States when Omidyar _____ six.
                          6. (turn)

In college, he _____ in computer science. At age twenty-eight, Omidyar
            7. (major)

_____ computer code for a company that he called eBay. The company
8. (write)

_____ extremely successful, and Omidyar _____ a lot of
9. (become)   **10.** (make)

money. In 2004, Omidyar _____ the Omidyar Foundation. In 2005, Omidyar
                11. (start)

and his wife _____ $100 million to the foundation. The money helps poor
         12. (give)

people in developing countries. In 2010, Omidyar _____ forty billionaires.
                            13. (join)

They all _____ to give away at least half of their money before they die.
     14. (promise)

EXERCISE 3 AFFIRMATIVE AND NEGATIVE STATEMENTS

GRAMMAR NOTES 1–2 Complete the sentences with the simple past forms of the verbs in parentheses.

Anne Schreiber _____was_____ a recluse.[1] She never _____. She also
           1. (be)   **2.** (marry)

never _____ close friends. Anne _____ alone in a tiny studio
     3. (have)   **4.** (live)

apartment and _____ the same outfit every day—a black coat and a black
             5. (wear)

hat. For many years, she _____ for the tax department of the U.S.
               6. (work)

government. She _____ an auditor. She _____ sure people paid
         7. (be)   **8.** (make)

their taxes. However, she _____ to pay taxes. She _____ to pay
         9. (not / like)   **10.** (not / like)

for anything.

As a young woman, Anne _____ the suggestions of a brother and
             11. (follow)

_____ all her money in his company. His company _____
12. (invest)   **13.** (go)

---

1 *recluse:* person who chooses to live alone

bankrupt, and she _____ her life savings. She _____ her
                        14. (lose)   15. (not / forgive)

brother. Anne _____ investing again in 1944 when she _____
                    16. (start)   17. (be)

forty-nine years old. This time she _____ her own ideas. By investing well,
                                          18. (use)

she _____ $5,000 into $22,000,000. She _____ better than the
       19. (turn)   20. (do)

biggest businessmen. But she _____ her relatives to know she had so much
                                  21. (not / want)

money because she _____ to give them any of it. And she didn't. Anne
                      22. (not / want)

Schreiber _____ in 1995 at the age of 101. She _____ her
              23. (die)   24. (leave)

money to universities to help poor, bright women get an education.

EXERCISE 4 SIMPLE PAST: QUESTIONS AND ANSWERS

Ⓐ GRAMMAR NOTES 1–4 Read this article about a man with many talents. Then write
wh- questions that the underlined words answer.

When you think of basketball, do you think of Michael Jordan, LeBron James,

Shaquille O'Neal . . . or Dr. James Naismith? Dr. Naismith? Who was he? What did he do

for basketball?

James Naismith was born in Ontario, Canada, in 1861. He was a good athlete and a
                            ‾‾‾‾‾‾‾‾‾‾‾‾‾‾‾‾‾ ‾‾‾‾‾‾‾
                                  1.   2.

good student. He always loved school.
                              ‾‾‾‾‾‾
                                3.

Dr. Naismith earned four degrees, including one in medicine. But his biggest
                       ‾‾‾‾
                        4.

contribution to the world did not come from his work as a medical doctor.

High shool basketball team
from the early 1900's

In the winter of 1891, he worked as a gym instructor in Massachusetts. His students
                    5.
were active and hard to control. He wanted them to play an indoor sport
                     6.
because it was too cold to play outdoors. He invented the game of basketball. It became
                        7.
an instant success in the United States. Soon basketball spread to other countries.
                                                        8.

1. *Where was James Naismith born?*

2. _____

3. _____

4. _____

5. _____

6. _____

7. _____

8. _____

B Write simple past *yes/no* questions about James Naismith. Use the correct forms of the words in parentheses. Then write short answers.

1. (be / he good at sports)

   Q: *Was he good at sports?*

   A: *Yes, he was.*

2. (be / he a good student)

   Q: _____

   A: _____

3. (he / finish college)

   Q: _____

   A: _____

4. (he / become a lawyer)

   Q: _____

   A: _____

5. (he / invent the game of volleyball)

   Q: _____

   A: _____

EXERCISE 5 EDITING

GRAMMAR NOTES 1–4 Correct the questions and
answers about Elizabeth Blackwell. There are eleven
mistakes. The first mistake is already corrected.
Find and correct ten more.

Elizabeth Blackwell

1. Q: Who ^was Elizabeth Blackwell?

   A: She was the first woman physician in

   the United States.

2. Q: Where she was born?

   A: She was born in England.

3. Q: When was she born?

   A: She born in 1821.

4. Q: When she did come to the United States?

   A: She did come to the United States in 1833.

5. Q: Was it hard for her to become a doctor?

   A: Yes, it were. Most medical schools didn't want women.

6. Q: How was her grades in medical school?

   A: She was an outstanding student. Her grades were excellent.

7. Q: When she graduate?

   A: In 1849.

8. Q: What did Dr. Blackwell fight for?

   A: She did fight for the admission of women to medical schools.

9. Q: What did she does in 1869?

   A: She returned to London. She worked and wrote there for many years.

10. Q: When she die?

    A: She died in 1910.

EXERCISE 6 LISTENING

▶21|02 **A** Roger and Carolina are watching a TV quiz show. Listen to their conversation. Then answer the question.

Who could answer all the questions correctly?

a. Roger   **b.** Carolina   **c.** Amy   **d.** Jim

▶21|02 **B** Listen again. Complete the questions and answers in the chart below.

Questions	Answers
1. Who _____painted_____ The Night Watch?	_____Rembrandt_____
2. In what century did he _____?	The _____ century
3. Where was _____?	In _____
4. What is Rembrandt's _____?	Rembrandt _____
5. Who _____ John Lennon _____?	_____
6. What _____ of John Lennon's group?	The _____
7. Where did they _____?	_____, England
8. When _____ their last appearance together?	_____

C Work with a partner and compare your answers in B. Then act out the quiz show together. One of you plays the host and the other the contestant for the first four questions. The other plays the host and the other the contestant for the last four questions.

EXERCISE 7 QUIZ SHOW

A GAME Work in a group. Prepare questions for a quiz show. Write your questions and answers. Use the simple past in each question.

Who wrote One Hundred Years of Solitude? (Answer = Gabriel García Márquez)

B Choose a game host or hostess from your group. Choose classmates from the other groups to be the contestants. Put on a TV quiz show for your class.

EXAMPLE: Welcome, everyone. Our contestants today are Lily Wang from China, Fatima Abadi from Saudi Arabia, and Jorge Mendoza from Argentina. Lily, Fatima, Jorge, are you ready? Raise your hand as soon as you know the answer. OK. Our first question is: Who wrote *One Hundred Years of Solitude*?

EXERCISE 8 WHO INVENTED THE ATM?

INFORMATION GAP Work with a partner. Student A follows the instructions below. Student B follows the instructions on page 457.

Student B follows the instructions on page 457.

STUDENT A

- The chart below is missing some information. Your partner has the same chart with the missing information. Ask your partner questions to find the missing information. Write your partner's answers into your chart.

EXAMPLE: A: Who invented the ATM?
            B: Don Wetzel invented the ATM.
            A: When did he invent it?

Invention	Inventor	Year	Country
ATM	Don Wetzel		
	Frank McNamara, Ralph Schneider		
	Josephine Cochrane		
eyeglasses			
subway			
	Steven Chen, Chad Hurley, Jawed Karim		

- Your partner has a chart that is missing some information. Your chart contains the missing information. Answer your partner's questions so that he or she can write the missing information into his or her chart.

EXAMPLE: B: Who invented the bicycle?
            A: Baron de Sauerbrun.
            B: When did he invent it?

Invention	Inventor	Year	Country
bicycle	Baron de Sauerbrun	1818	Germany
disposable diapers	Marion Donovan	1950	U.S.
paper	Ts'ai Lun	c. 105	China
pencil	Conrad Gessner	1565	Switzerland
thermometer	Galileo	1592	Italy
World Wide Web	Tim Berners-Lee	1989	U.K.

EXERCISE 9 WHAT WERE YOU LIKE AS A CHILD?

A CONVERSATION **Prepare to have a conversation with your classmates about when you were a child. Write notes to answer the questions below.**

1. What did you like to do in your free time?

2. Who did you play with?

3. Who did you admire?

4. Were you athletic?

5. Were you well-behaved?

6. Were you stubborn?

7. Were you talkative?

8. Were you shy?

9. Did you listen to your parents and teachers?

10. Did you watch a lot of TV?

11. Did you like music?

12. Did you like computers?

B **Work in a group. Answer the questions in A and talk about your childhood.**

EXAMPLE: A: When you were a child, were you talkative?

B: Yes. Once my teacher wrote a note to my mother, "Ben never stops talking. He never gives other children a turn." What about you? What were you like? Were you talkative?

C **Tell the class about one of the people in your group. The other groups guess the person.**

EXAMPLE: A: This person was not well-behaved as a child. This person was stubborn and very talkative. This person did not like music, but liked computers.

B: Is it Reza?

A: No, it's Ben.

Go to MyEnglishLab for more communication practice.

FROM GRAMMAR TO WRITING

A **BEFORE YOU WRITE** Read this eighty-year-old man's life story. Then imagine it is the future and you are eighty years old. Answer your partner's questions about your life.

The date today is July 25, 2080, and I'm celebrating my eightieth birthday with my four children, their children, and their children's children. I am a lucky man. I am enjoying a wonderful life. I was born in Warsaw. My family didn't have much money, but we were hard-working. I was the fourth of five children. My father was a house painter. My mother stayed home with the children. After I graduated from high school, I went to the United States. I stayed in the United States and became a computer programmer. In my free time, I made an app. I made a lot of money. Then I lost a lot of money. Then I made much more money. I traveled all over the world. I saw poor people everywhere. Fifteen years ago, I started a foundation and gave money to help poor people. Ten years ago, I helped a young man. Today he is a successful businessman. He and my granddaughter are planning to marry. I am very happy.

Example Questions:

- Where and when were you born?
- Where did you go to school?
- What did you do in your free time?
- What did you become? Why?
- Where did you live?
- Did you marry? Did you have children?
- Did you travel?
- Did you become famous?
- Did you become rich?
- Did you make a difference in the world?
- How is your life today?

B **WRITE** Write your life story. Use the life story in A and your notes. Use the simple past.

C **CHECK YOUR WORK** Read your life story. Underline the past tense verbs. Use the Editing Checklist to check your work.

Editing Checklist
Did you . . . ?
☐ use the simple past of irregular and regular verbs correctly
☐ use the past of *be* correctly
☐ use *did not (didn't)* + base form of the verb for the simple past negative
☐ use *was not, were not (wasn't, weren't)* for the simple past negative of *be*
☐ check your spelling

D **REVISE YOUR WORK** Read your story again. Can you improve your writing? Make changes if necessary.

Go to MyEnglishLab for more writing practice.

UNIT 21 REVIEW

Test yourself on the grammar of the unit.

Ⓐ Complete the sentences with the simple past forms of the verbs in parentheses.

Craig Newmark _____ on December 6, 1952. He _____ in New
$\qquad$ **1.** (be born) $\qquad$ **2.** (grow up)

Jersey. He _____ Morristown High School. He _____ to college
$\qquad$ **3.** (attend) $\qquad$ **4.** (go)

in Ohio. In 1995, he _____ an email list. It _____ a Web-based
$\qquad$ **5.** (start) $\qquad$ **6.** (become)

service in 1996. It _____, and today many people know about Craigslist.
$\qquad$ **7.** (expand)

Ⓑ Write questions with the correct forms of the words in parentheses. Use the
simple past.

1. _____
(when / she / go to college)

2. _____
(who / they / meet)

3. _____
(where / he study)

4. _____
(how long / they live in Canada)

Ⓒ Complete the questions with the simple past forms of *be* or *do*.

1. _____ you late yesterday?

2. _____ they work last night?

3. _____ he at the park with his son?

4. _____ she marry him?

5. _____ he move?

Ⓓ Correct the paragraph. There are four mistakes.

Steve Paul Jobs did start college in 1970, but he no did finish it. In 1976, Jobs and his
friend begin to make their own computers. They worked in Jobs's garage. That was the
beginning of Apple® Computers. Their company become a big success. Apple® changed
the field of computers, and by the age of thirty, Jobs was a multimillionaire.

Now check your answers on page 449.

Go to MyEnglishLab to complete the review online.

The Future

OUTCOMES
- Express future plans, facts, and predictions with *be going to*
- Recognize opinions in letters to the editor
- Understand main ideas and details in a conversation
- Discuss future plans
- Talk about life changes
- Write a letter, expressing an opinion on a topic

OUTCOMES
- Talk about future facts and make predictions and promises with *will*
- Recognize details in an article about the future
- Answer questions about speakers in a conversation
- Make predictions about the future
- Make suggestion and give solutions to everyday problems
- Write a paragraph about life in the future

OUTCOMES
- Express possibility in the present or future
- Recognize details in a weather report
- Recognize details in a conversation about travel plans
- Discuss reasons and possibilities for different situations and events
- Talk about possible plans for the near future
- Write a weather report about a city

OUTCOMES
- Use gerunds and infinitives after certain verbs
- Recognize important details in a magazine article
- Recognize main ideas and details in a short lecture
- Interview classmates about their likes and dislikes; report findings to the class
- Discuss career interests
- Write a paragraph about your career goals

UNIT 22

Be going to for the Future

CITY AND CAMPUS PLANNING

OUTCOMES
- Express future plans, facts, and predictions with *be going to*
- Recognize opinions in letters to the editor
- Understand main ideas and details in a conversation
- Discuss future plans
- Talk about life changes
- Write a letter, expressing an opinion on a topic

STEP 1	GRAMMAR IN CONTEXT

BEFORE YOU READ

Work with a partner. Answer the questions.

1. What's important when people choose a college? Rank the items 1–4 (4 = most important).

   _____ its location (in a big city, in the countryside, etc.)

   _____ its facilities (computer centers, gyms, theaters, etc.)

   _____ its cost (tuition, housing, food, etc.)

   _____ its reputation (what people say about the college)

2. How important is it for colleges to have good sports and fitness programs and facilities?

READ

▶22|01 Read these letters from students to the editor of their online school newspaper.

Why We Go to College

● ● ●

COLUMBUS COLLEGE   LETTERS TO THE EDITOR

TO THE EDITOR:

A week ago, President Clark announced plans for a new fitness center for our college. I love the idea. It's going to give us a chance to exercise and to relax before and after classes. College is not just a time to sit in a library and study. It's a time for us to make our bodies *and* our minds stronger.

When the gym is ready to use, I'm going to go there every day. Yes, we're going to pay for it. There is going to be a tuition increase. But, in my opinion, a gym is going to improve our lives.

Last month, a study showed that students gain 10 pounds (4.54 kilograms) in their first year of college. I'm pretty sure that's not going to happen once we have our new fitness center.

—*Alison Meadows*

TO THE EDITOR:

Last week, President Clark talked about plans for a new fitness center[1] for our college. The center sounds great. It's going to have a beautiful gym, an indoor running track, an Olympic-size pool, a basketball court, exercise machines, and weight-lifting equipment.[2] But this fitness center is going to cost a lot of money.

Where is the money going to come from? You guessed it. Most of the money is going to come from us. Our tuition is going to increase. That's why I'm against the plan.

With a tuition increase, we are going to need to work while we go to school. We're not going to have time to enjoy the fitness center. We're not going to have time to study.

Why is President Clark doing this? He only wants a fitness center because other schools have them. He thinks more students are going to come here if we have a new fitness center. But we're here for a good education, not to go to a gym.

—*Joe Molina*

---

1 *fitness center:* a place to exercise
2 *equipment:* machines

AFTER YOU READ

A VOCABULARY **Match the words in bold with their meanings.**

1. Is the **tuition** the same as it was last year?
   a. the amount of homework   **b.** the amount of money you pay for school

2. Tomorrow the mayor is going to **announce** a plan to close some streets to cars.
   a. tell everyone about   **b.** answer questions about

3. I am **against** the plan to close the street to cars.
   a. not in favor of   **b.** worried about

4. They **increased** the number of students from twenty-two to twenty-five per class.
   a. raised   **b.** changed

5. **In my opinion**, students need a fitness center.
   a. I know   **b.** I think

6. I **gained weight** in my first six months of college because I stopped exercising.
   a. got lighter   **b.** got heavier

B COMPREHENSION Read the following statements. Who said them? Check if you think it was Joe or Alison.

		Joe	Alison
1.	It's going to cost too much money.	☐	☐
2.	It's going to be a great place to relax.	☐	☐
3.	More students are going to need to get a job.	☐	☐
4.	College is not only a place to learn.	☐	☐
5.	We're at college to get an education.	☐	☐

C DISCUSSION Work with a partner. Compare your answers in B. Then give your opinion of the fitness center. Do you think it is going to be good for the college? Why?

Go to MyEnglishLab for more grammar in context practice.

STEP 2 GRAMMAR PRESENTATION

BE GOING TO FOR THE FUTURE

Affirmative Statements

Subject + *Be*	*Going to*	Base Form of Verb	
I'm He's We're You're* They're	going to	study	tonight.
It's		rain	

Negative Statements

Subject + *Be*	*Not*	*Going to*	Base Form of Verb
I'm He's We're You're* They're	not	going to	sleep.
It's			rain.

* *You're* can be either singular or plural.

Yes/No Questions

Be	Subject	*Going to*	Base Form of Verb	
Am	I			
Are	you	going to	drive	tomorrow?
Is	he			

Short Answers

Affirmative	Negative
Yes, you are.	No, you're not.
Yes, I am.	No, I'm not.
Yes, he is.	No, he's not.

Wh- Questions

Wh- Word	*Be*	Subject	*Going to*	Base Form of Verb	
What	is	she		do?	
Where	are	they	going to	go?	
How	am	I		get	there?

Short Answers

Meet her friend.
To the library.
By bus.

Future Time Markers	
today	
tonight	
tomorrow	
this	morning
	afternoon
	evening
tomorrow	morning
	afternoon
	evening
	night
Saturday	night

Future Time Markers with *Next* and *In*		
next	week	
	month	
	year	
	Monday	
	weekend	
in	2020	
	the twenty-second century	
	twenty years	
	two weeks	
	a few days	

GRAMMAR NOTES

1 *Be going to* for the Future: Form

Affirmative statements use a form of *be + going to* + the base form of the verb.	He **is going to start** at 9:00. They **are going to leave** at 8:00.
For questions, put **the subject after a form of the verb** *be* and before *going to*.	**Is he going to** start at 9:00? When **are they going to** leave?
Negative statements use a form of *be + not + going to* + base form of the verb.	He **is not going to start** at 10:00. They **are not going to leave** at 9:00.
Use **contractions of** *be* in speaking and informal writing.	He**'s** going to start at 9:00. They**'re** going to leave at 9:00.
BE CAREFUL! Remember to use a form of *be* before *going to*.	He**'s** going to start at 9:00. NOT He ~~going to start~~ at 9:00.
BE CAREFUL! Remember to use the base form of the verb after *going to*.	He's going to **start** at 9:00. NOT He's going to ~~starts~~ at 9:00.

2 *Be going to* for the Future: Meaning

You can use the *be going to* future to:	
• state **facts about the future**	The water **is going to** boil in five minutes.
• make **predictions** (guesses about the future)	There **is going to be** a hurricane next week.
• talk about **future plans**	I**'m going to become** a teacher.

3 Future Time Markers

The *be going to* future often occurs with **future time markers**.

Some common future time markers are:

• *today, tonight, tomorrow*	We are going to play tennis **tomorrow**.
• *next week, next month, next year*	**Next month**, he's going to open a fitness center.
• *in* + **year**	He's going to retire **in 2029**.

USAGE NOTE Future time markers usually come **at the beginning** or **the end of a sentence**.	They are going to start construction **next week**. **Next week**, they are going to start construction.
USAGE NOTE We use *probably* with *be going to* to say that something is likely, but not definite.	We're **probably going to visit** them tonight.

4 Other Ways of Expressing the Future

There are several other ways to express the future. Two common ones are the **present progressive** and *will* + **the base form of the verb**.

We can use **the present progressive** to talk about future plans.	They **are meeting** tomorrow afternoon. I**'m painting** my room next week.
We usually use a **future time marker** when we use the present progressive for future.	We **are buying** a car *next month*.
We often use these verbs with the present progressive for the future: *go, drive, fly, meet, leave*, and *arrive*.	We**'re going** to the movies tonight. I**'m flying** to California next week.
BE CAREFUL! We do not use the present progressive with non-action verbs.	He**'s going to need** a new car next year. **NOT** He's needing a new car next year.
We can also use *will* + **the base form of the verb** to talk about the future. (See Unit 23.)	We **will buy** a red car.
USAGE NOTE In speaking, *be going to* for the future is more common than *will*.	She **is going to** have her baby soon. *(more common)* She **will** have her baby soon. *(less common)*

PRONUNCIATION NOTE

▶ 22|02   *Going to* and *Gonna*

In speaking, *going to* is usually pronounced "gonna" when it comes before a verb. However, **do not write** "gonna."	We're gonna leave now. *(spoken only)* We're going to leave now. *(written)*

REFERENCE NOTE

For more information about *will* for the future, see Unit 23 on page 274.

Go to MyEnglishLab to watch the grammar presentation.

EXERCISE 1 DISCOVER THE GRAMMAR

A GRAMMAR NOTES 1–4 **Read the sentences. Underline all examples of the subject +**
be going to + **the base form of the verb that follows.**

1. Last week, Mayor Jonas talked about building a sports stadium next year. <u>It's going
   to seat</u> 300,000 people.

2. Next Wednesday, the mayor is giving another speech. She's going to talk about the cost
   of the stadium.

3. They're going to build a garage for the stadium. It's going to have spaces for 5,000 cars.

4. They're going to build stores around the stadium. The stores are going to provide jobs
   for a lot of people.

5. Some people don't want the city to build a new stadium. They're against it because the
   city is going to destroy a historic building when they build the stadium.

B **Look at your answers in A. Circle the one sentence that uses the present progressive
for the future.**

EXERCISE 2 *BE GOING TO* FOR THE FUTURE

GRAMMAR NOTES 1–2 **Two citizens are discussing the mayor's plans to raise money for
the city. Complete the sentences with** *be going to* **and the verbs in parentheses.**

ANN: The city needs money.

WILL: What _____*is*_____ the mayor _____*going to do*_____ about it?
                                                  1. (do)

ANN: He _____ taxes.
                   2. (increase)

WILL: _____ he _____ city workers?
                                      3. (lay off)[1]

ANN: Yes, he is. And he _____ any new police officers or teachers.
                              4. (not / hire)[2]

WILL: That's not good. Crime _____.
                                        5. (probably / increase)

ANN: I agree.

WILL: And children _____ a good education.
                              6. (not / get)

ANN: I _____ a letter to the mayor.
              7. (write)

WILL: What _____ you _____?
                                          8. (say)

---

1 *lay off:* tell a worker to leave the job
2 *hire:* ask someone to work for you

ANN: I _____ him to bring more business to the city.
　　　　　9. (tell)

WILL: How _____ he _____ that?
　　　　　　　　　　　10. (do)

ANN: Tourism. That's the answer.

EXERCISE 3 *WH-* QUESTIONS AND ANSWERS

GRAMMAR NOTES 1–3 **Read the news announcement. Write questions with *be going to*
and the words in parentheses. Then answer the questions. Use short answers.**

**NEW HIGH SCHOOL
ON OAK STREET**

The city plans to start
building a new high school
on Oak Street next March
at a cost of $45 million. The
builder expects to finish the
school in three years. The
school will have space for
3,000 students.

1. (What / city / build)

　A: *What is the city going to build?*

　B: *A new high school.*

2. (Where / it / be)

　A: _____

　B: _____

3. (When / the builders / start)

　A: _____

　B: _____

4. (How much / it / cost)

　A: _____

　B: _____

5. (How long / it / take)

　A: _____

　B: _____

EXERCISE 4 AFFIRMATIVE AND NEGATIVE STATEMENTS

GRAMMAR NOTES 1–2 The West Street Association is against the construction of a new building on West Street. Complete their letter to the editor with affirmative or negative forms of *be going to* and the verbs in parentheses.

West Street
ASSOCIATION

To the Editor:

Jim Lyons wants to build a twenty-story apartment building on West Street. The West Street Association is against the plan. The new building _____*is going to change*_____
                                                                                  1. (change)

the look of West Street. Now all the buildings on West Street are three or four stories high. A

twenty-story building _____ good. The street
                             2. (not / look)

_____ noisy and crowded. School buses
       3. (become)

_____ the street every morning and afternoon.
       4. (block)

Also, the new building _____ spaces for only fifty cars,
                                   5. (have)

but there _____ two hundred apartments. There
                  6. (be)

_____ enough parking spaces for all those cars. Let's stop
       7. (not / be)

construction of Lyons Tower! Let's keep West Street clean and beautiful.

Amy Chen,
President, West Street Association

EXERCISE 5 SIMPLE PAST, SIMPLE PRESENT, *BE GOING TO* FUTURE

GRAMMAR NOTES 1–2 Complete the conversations with the verbs in parentheses. Use the simple past, the simple present, or *be going to* for the future.

Conversation 1

INEZ: _____*Did*_____ you _____*watch*_____ the weather report last night?
                                   1. (watch)

PAUL: Yes. It _____ sunny and warm today and tomorrow.
                      2. (be)

INEZ: Good. There _____ a town meeting outdoors in East Park
                           3. (be)

tomorrow evening. People _____ about the new stadium.
                                  4. (talk)

PAUL: I _____ to go to the meeting, but I can't. I
              5. (want)

_____ to drive my parents to the airport.
       6. (promise)

Conversation 2

DAN: The mayor _____ to close Maple Street to cars. He
        1. (plan)

_____ it a place for people to walk.
      2. (make)

ANNA: How _____ you _____ about it?
                  3. (know)

DAN: The mayor _____ it last night on his weekly radio show.
        4. (announce)

ANNA: I _____ it's a great idea.
      5. (think)

DAN: Well, some storeowners aren't happy. They say they _____
                                                  6. (lose)

business.

ANNA: What else _____ the mayor _____ last night?
                               7. (say)

DAN: In the next five years, he _____ this city into a center for the arts.
                         8. (turn)

ANNA: How _____ he _____ that?
                     9. (do)

DAN: He _____ cheap housing for artists. He
       10. (offer)

_____ a new concert hall, and he _____
      11. (build)   **12.** (put)

artwork in the park.

EXERCISE 6 *GOING TO* AND *GONNA*

22|03   PRONUNCIATION NOTE   **Listen to these sentences. Then listen to each sentence again and write it. Remember not to use "gonna" in writing.**

1. *We're going to go to the meeting.* _____

2. _____

3. _____

4. _____

5. _____

EXERCISE 7
PRESENT PROGRESSIVE FOR THE FUTURE

GRAMMAR NOTE 4 **Look at the mayor's schedule for next Monday and Tuesday. Write questions with the words in parentheses. Use the present progressive for the future. Then answer the questions.**

Schedule

MONDAY, OCTOBER 12

10:00 a.m.	Mayors' Meeting
12:00 p.m.	Lunch with community leaders
4:30 p.m.	Meeting with California Energy Council
7:00 p.m.	Meeting with Police Commissioner Ron Byrd
11:30 p.m.	American Airlines—Flight #41 from Los Angeles to Washington D.C. Dulles Airport

TUESDAY, OCTOBER 13

7:48 a.m.	Arrive Dulles Airport
1:00 p.m.	Madison College—speech
3:00 p.m.	Senior Center Opening
5:00 p.m.	Dinner for police chief—Grand Hotel

1. (Who / the mayor / have lunch with on Monday)

   Q: *Who is the mayor having lunch with on Monday?*

   A: *He's having lunch with community leaders.*

2. (What / he / do / on Monday afternoon)

   Q: _____

   A: _____

3. (Who / he / meet / at 7:00 p.m. on Monday)

   Q: _____

   A: _____

4. (What time / he / fly home from Los Angeles)

   Q: _____

   A: _____

5. (Where / he / speak / in Washington, D.C.)

   Q: _____

   A: _____

6. (When / he / go / to the senior center)

   Q: _____

   A: _____

EXERCISE 8
EDITING

GRAMMAR NOTES 1–4

Correct the newsletter article. There are five mistakes. The first mistake is already corrected. Find and correct four more.

VILLAGE GREEN APARTMENTS

Dear Residents:

Last week, the mayor talked about building a sports stadium in

our neighborhood. I think it's a terrible idea. It's going ^to^ cost taxpayers

millions of dollars. It going to mean traffic jams. Parking is being

difficult, and it's going to bringing noise to the area.

Next Monday at 7:00 p.m., the mayor is goes to answer questions at

the public library. Please come and speak out against the new stadium.

Sincerely,
Dale Ortiz, President, Residents' Association

Go to MyEnglishLab for more focused practice.

STEP 4   COMMUNICATION PRACTICE

EXERCISE 9   LISTENING

▶ 22|04 **A** Listen to a conversation about a new building. Circle the correct answer.

Who is for the new building on West Street?
a. the man   b. the woman   c. both of them

▶ 22|04 **B** Listen again. Write short answers to the following questions.

1. How many stories is the new apartment building going to have? *Twenty*_____

2. How many apartments is the new building going to have? _____

3. What facilities is the building going to have?

   _____

4. What is there going to be on the street level of the apartment building? _____

268   Unit 22

C Work with a partner. Compare your answers in B. Then give two reasons for and two reasons against the new building.

EXAMPLE: A: What do you think is one reason for the building?
B: It's going to help young people. At the moment, they are moving away from the area.

EXERCISE 10 LIFE CHANGES

Q & A Work with a partner. Take turns. Tell about a change that is going to happen in your life or the life of someone you know. For example, tell about a move, a new job, a new school, or a new baby. Your partner asks questions about the change. Then talk about a good and a bad thing about the change.

EXAMPLE: A: My sister is moving away from the city.
B: Why is she going to move?
A: She needs a larger home. She has two children. She's going to have more space, but she and her husband are going to have a long commute to work.

EXERCISE 11 VOTE FOR ME!

A PRESENTATION Your class needs a class president and you want the job. Tell the class four things you are going to do as class president. Explain why.

EXAMPLE: I am going to organize weekly class parties. And I'm going to ask the school to lower tuition. I think the tuition is too high. . . .

B After you hear each talk, ask each candidate for class president about his or her promises.

EXAMPLE: When are we going to have the parties? Where are we going to have them?

VOTE
FOR ME

FOR
CLASS PRESIDENT

Go to MyEnglishLab for more communication practice.

A BEFORE YOU WRITE

Read this letter to the editor. Then work with a partner. Look in the box at three other changes that Columbus College is planning. Discuss why each change is a good or bad idea.

To the Editor:

Last week, our college president spoke about a law to ban cars on campus. I think that's a great idea. The streets are going to be safer for students. The air is going to be cleaner. It's going to be quieter. We're all going to be in better shape. The change is going to make our campus a better place to study, walk, shop, and dine.

Sincerely,
Daniel Rivera

Plans for Columbus College

50% of courses online

No tests, just written reports

No smoking on campus

B WRITE Write a letter to the editor about one of the plans for Columbus College. Use your ideas in A. Write why you are for or against the change, and what the change is going to mean. Use *be going to* for the future.

C CHECK YOUR WORK Read your letter. Underline sentences with *be going to* for the future. Use the Editing Checklist to check your work.

Editing Checklist
Did you . . . ?
☐ use *be going to* + the base form of the verb for the future
☐ use *be* + *not* + *going to* + the base form of the verb for the negative
☐ check your spelling

D REVISE YOUR WORK Read your letter again. Can you improve it? Make changes if necessary.

Go to MyEnglishLab for more writing practice.

UNIT 22 REVIEW

Test yourself on the grammar of the unit.

Ⓐ Complete the sentences with *be going to* and the words in parentheses. Use contractions when possible.

The city _____ a big new park on the waterfront.
             1. (build)

It _____ millions of dollars. It _____
   2. (cost)   **3.** (have)

an amusement park. There _____ a few restaurants.
                              4. (be)

Construction _____ until next summer.
                   5. (not / begin)

Ⓑ Complete the sentences with *be going to* and the words in parentheses. Some sentences are affirmative and some are negative. Use the affirmative or negative form and contractions when possible.

1. Everyone is happy. Taxes _____. No one likes to pay taxes.
                               (increase)

2. It's raining hard. We _____ soccer in the park.
                          (play)

3. John is in the hospital. We _____ him. Do you want to come?
                           (visit)

4. It's Mary's last year. She _____ in December and move away.
                           (retire)

5. I'm tired and it's late. I _____ any more work.
                        (do)

Ⓒ Look at Eun Young's schedule. Write questions with the words in parentheses. Use the present progressive for the future. Write short answers to each question.

> **Eun Young's Schedule**
> Monday: dentist 5:30
> Tuesday: meet Yu Chen at Pappa Pizza 6:30

1. Q: _____   A: _____
   (When / she / go to the dentist)

2. Q: _____   A: _____
   (Where / she / meet / Yu Chen)

3. Q: _____   A: _____
   (she / meet / Yu Chen / on Monday)

Ⓓ Correct the paragraph. There are four mistakes.

This city going to change under our new mayor. People's going to ride bikes, and they're going use public transportation. They're no going to drive big cars. There are probably going to be higher tolls on bridges and more bike paths on the roads.

Now check your answers on page 449.

Go to MyEnglishLab to complete the review online.

Be going to for the Future   **271**

STEP 1   GRAMMAR IN CONTEXT

BEFORE YOU READ

Work with a partner. Answer the questions.

1. Will life in the future be better or worse than it is today?

2. What will be different in the year 2050?

READ

▶ 23|01   Read this magazine article about the future.

THE FUTURE

The World in 2050

Future Science magazine asked scientists to make predictions for the year 2050. What will we eat? How will we look? How will we travel? How long will we live? Here are their predictions.

1 More people will be vegetarians. They won't eat any meat or fish.

2 Robots will cook our meals. We won't spend a lot of time in the kitchen.

3 There will be a cure for the common cold.

4 People will live to be 100 years old on average, and the majority of people will be over sixty.

5 People will be taller and weigh more.

6 People will take memory pills.

7 People will read each other's thoughts.

8 Cars won't run on gas. Cars will run on solar[1] energy.

9 Private planes will be common.

10 Travel to the moon will be common.

11 Scientists will control the weather.

12 Paper money and coins[2] will disappear.

---

1 *solar:* from the sun

2 *coins:* metal money such as quarters or dimes

AFTER YOU READ

A VOCABULARY **Complete the sentences with the words from the box.**

| disappear | majority | memory | robots | spend time |

1. In the future, we will remember more. There will be pills to improve our

_____ .

2. I don't see the moon now. Did the moon _____ behind a cloud?

3. In the future, many people will _____ on the moon. It will be a popular place to visit.

4. I think _____ will do the jobs of many hospital workers.

5. In the future, the _____ of office workers will work from home one or two days a week.

B COMPREHENSION **Look again at the article. Read the questions. Circle the correct answers.**

1. How will people look in the year 2050?

   a. smaller   **b.** shorter   **c.** taller

2. Where will many people travel to?

   a. the moon   **b.** Mars   **c.** the past

3. Which of the following will *not* increase in the future?

   a. the number of vegetarians
   b. the number of people over 100 years old
   c. the number of people who get colds

4. What will be common in 2050?

   a. coins   **b.** private planes   **c.** gas stations

C DISCUSSION **Work with a partner. Compare your answers in B. Then tell your partner which predictions you don't agree with.**

Go to MyEnglishLab for more grammar in context practice.

Will for the Future   **273**

WILL FOR THE FUTURE

Affirmative Statements

Subject	Will / 'll	Base Form of Verb	Time Marker
I			
You			
He			
She	**will** **'ll**	**leave**	tomorrow.
It			
We			
They			

Negative Statements

Subject	Will not/ Won't	Base Form of Verb	Time Marker
I			
You			
He			
She	**will not** **won't**	**leave**	tonight.
It			
We			
They			

Yes/No Questions

Will	Subject	Base Form of Verb	Time Marker
	I		
	you		
	he		
Will	she	**arrive**	tonight?
	it		
	we		
	they		

Short Answers

Affirmative				Negative		
	you				you	
	I				I	
	he				he	
Yes,	she	**will**.	No,		she	**won't**.
	it				it	
	we				we	
	they				they	

GRAMMAR NOTES

1 *Will* for the Future: Form

Use *will* + **the base form of the verb** to talk about things that will take place in the future.

> The class **will begin** on November 2.
> We **will meet** tomorrow at 10:00 a.m.

Use *will* + *not* + **the base form of the verb** to talk about things that will not take place in the future.

> The plane **will not land** at 6:00.
> He **will not be** on time for the meeting.

For questions, put **the subject after *will* and before the base form of the verb**.

> SUBJECT
> **Will classes begin** on November 2?
> SUBJECT
> When **will classes begin**?

BE CAREFUL! Use the base form of the verb after *will*. Remember, the base form is the same for all subjects. It doesn't change form.

> The plane **will arrive** at 6:00 p.m.
> NOT The plane will ~~to arrive~~ at 6:00 p.m.
> NOT The plane will ~~arrives~~ at 6:00 p.m.

2 Contractions

The contraction of *will* is *'ll*. We often use contractions of *will* with **pronouns**.	**We'll be** there before 3:00. **I'll help** you with your suitcases.
The contraction of *will not* is ***won't***.	He **won't be** in school tomorrow. The child **won't eat** carrots.
BE CAREFUL! Do not use contractions in affirmative short answers.	A: Will they be there? B: Yes, they will. NOT Yes, ~~they'll.~~
USAGE NOTE We use contractions of *will* and *won't* in speaking and informal writing.	

3 *Will* for the Future: Meanings

Will has a number of different meanings.

We use *will* to:

• talk about **future facts**	The sun **will rise** at 6:40 a.m. tomorrow morning.
• make **predictions**	In 2050, there **will be** more megacities. In 2050, people **won't catch** colds.
• make a **promise** or **give assurance**	**I'll be** back in five minutes. I **won't do** that again.
• **ask for** or **offer** something	A: **Will** you **help** me? B: Don't worry. **I'll help**.
• **refuse** to do something	I **won't work** after 6 p.m. The child **won't eat** carrots.
USAGE NOTE To say that something is not definite but likely, use *probably* with *will* or *won't*.	People **will probably** take more vacations.
IN WRITING We sometimes use *will* in one sentence and *be going to* in the next sentence.	In 2050, there **will be** more megacities. Those cities **are going to be** very crowded.

Go to MyEnglishLab to watch the grammar presentation.

EXERCISE 1 DISCOVER THE GRAMMAR

GRAMMAR NOTES 1–3 **Read the sentences. Match the sentences with the different meanings of *will* or *won't*.**

_b_ **1.** I won't do it. I think it's wrong.

____ **2.** Will you show me how to use that computer?

____ **3.** I'll be back by 9:00.

____ **4.** There won't be a meeting on February 8.

____ **5.** By 2020, people will fly to the moon for fun.

a. predicts something

~~b.~~ refuses to do something

c. promises to do something

d. asks for something

e. tells about something that is not going to happen

EXERCISE 2 *WILL* FOR THE FUTURE

GRAMMAR NOTES 1–3 **Complete the conversations with *will* or *won't* and the verbs in parentheses. Use the contraction *'ll* after pronouns.**

1. **A:** When ____will____ dinner ____be____ ready?

(be)

    B: Robot Bob says it _____ ready in twenty-two minutes.

(be)

2. **A:** Do you think scientists _____ a cure for the cold?

(find)

    B: Yes, I do. And it _____ great for businesses. People _____

(be)   (miss)

      work so often, and businesses _____ money.

(save)

3. **A:** Dr. Smith, I have a problem. My great grandmother _____ her

(take)

      memory pills. She says they taste bad.

    B: OK. I _____ her some pills that taste like candy. She _____

(give)   (love)

      them.

4. **A:** When do you think we _____ astronauts to the planet Mars?

(send)

    B: No one knows. Right now, we're spending less money on space exploration. So

      it _____ a long time.

(probably / take)

5. **A:** Where _____ the wedding _____?

(take place)

    B: The wedding _____ on the moon.

(be)

    A: And where _____ you _____ for your honeymoon?

(go)

    B: We _____ to Mars.

(probably / go)

EXERCISE 3 *WILL* FOR THE FUTURE

A GRAMMAR NOTES 1–3 **Complete the conversation with *will* or *won't* and the verbs in parentheses. Use the contraction *'ll* after pronouns.**

DAN: So, Laura, when ____will____ you ____finish____ your article about the future?
1. (finish)

LAURA: It _____ ready until 4:00 p.m., but I think you _____ it.
2. (not / be)   3. (like)

DAN: You interviewed Dr. Reicher, right?

LAURA: Yes, I did. He says computers _____ us stay healthy.
4. (help)

DAN: Oh, yeah? How's that?

LAURA: In the future, we _____ computers inside our bodies. They
5. (have)

_____ our blood sugar and blood pressure. We _____ if
6. (check)   7. (know)

we have a problem right away.

DAN: _____ diabetes and heart disease _____?
8. (disappear)

LAURA: No, but people _____ from those diseases so often, and people
9. (not / die)

_____ longer.
10. (probably / live)

DAN: And when _____ this _____?
11. (happen)

LAURA: In about five years, I think.

DAN: Wow.

EXERCISE 4 *WILL* FOR THE FUTURE

GRAMMAR NOTES 1–3 Look at the chart. Write questions about Fogville. Use the words in parentheses and *will* for the future. Then answer the questions.

Predictions for Fogville in 2050

The cost of housing	⬇
The cost of health care	⬇
Taxes	⬇
Crime	➡
The percentage of people under twenty-five	⬆
The percentage of people over sixty-five	➡

Key

Increase = ⬆
Stay the same = ➡
Decrease = ⬇

1. A: <u>Will the cost of housing increase?</u>
   (the cost of housing / increase)
   B: <u>No, it won't. The cost of housing will decrease.</u>

2. A: _____
   (the cost of health care / stay the same)
   B: _____

3. A: _____
   (taxes / stay the same)
   B: _____

4. A: _____
   (crime / go up)
   B: _____

5. A: _____
   (the percentage of people under twenty-five / decrease)
   B: _____

6. A: _____
   (the percentage of people over sixty-five / stay the same)
   B: _____

EXERCISE 5 REVIEW OF PRESENT, PAST, FUTURE

Ⓐ GRAMMAR NOTES 1–3 Complete the conversation with the verbs in parentheses. Use the simple present, the simple past, or the future with *will*. Use contractions when possible.

ELLA: _____Did_____ you _____hear_____ the
1. (hear)
lecture last week?

JAKE: No, what _____ it about?
2. (be)

ELLA: The future. According to Professor Kramer, in

the year 2100, there _____ cities
3. (be)

in the ocean, we _____ trips to
4. (take)

the moon, and we _____ most
5. (learn)

things from computers.

JAKE: By 2100? We _____ all

_____ gone. _____ people
6. (be)

_____ his lecture?
7. (like)

ELLA: Yes, they did. They always do. He

_____ how to make any subject
8. (know)

fascinating.

▶ 23|03 Ⓑ LISTEN AND CHECK **Listen to the conversation and check your answers in A.**

EXERCISE 6 EDITING

GRAMMAR NOTES 1–3 **Correct the conversation. There are six mistakes. The first mistake is already corrected. Find and correct five more.**

A: What does Professor Kramer say about the future of our city?

            will
B: He says there be an increase in the population. Many young people will moves to this

   area. Taxes will increases. The value of homes will also to increase.

A: How about crime? Will it increases?

B: No, it doesn't.

A: Well, it sounds like it will be a great place to live.

Go to MyEnglishLab for more focused practice.

EXERCISE 7 LISTENING

▶23|04 **A** Listen to a conversation between a TV news reporter and two people, Susan Kerins and Jim Morris. Then read the question and circle the correct answer.

Why is the reporter interviewing these two people?

a. They made a lot of money.
b. They won a lot of money.

▶23|04 **B** Listen again. Answer the questions. Check *Susan* or *Jim*.

	Susan	Jim
1. Who will quit work?	☑	☐
2. Who won't quit work?	☐	☐
3. Who will travel?	☐	☐
4. Who will give money to the poor?	☐	☐
5. Who will buy a big house?	☐	☐
6. Who will travel to the moon?	☐	☐
7. Who will probably have angry relatives?	☐	☐

C Work with a partner. Imagine the man (Jim) and the woman (Susan) five years from now. How will their lives be different?

EXAMPLE: A: I think the woman will have new friends.
B: I agree. She's probably going to lose some of her old friends. What about the man?
A: I think . . .

EXERCISE 8 PREDICTIONS FOR 2050

Ⓐ DISCUSSION Work in small groups. Look at the predictions from the article on page 272 again. Do you agree with them? What are your predictions?

1. More people will be vegetarians. They won't eat any meat or fish.

2. Robots will cook our meals. We won't spend a lot of time in the kitchen.

3. There will be a cure for the common cold.

4. People will live to be 100 years old on average, and the majority of people will be over sixty.

5. People will be taller and weigh more.

6. People will take memory pills.

7. People will read each other's thoughts.

8. Cars won't run on gas. Cars will run on solar energy.

9. Private planes will be common.

10. Travel to the moon will be common.

11. Scientists will control the weather.

12. Paper money and coins will disappear.

Ⓑ Tell the class your opinion about four predictions.

EXAMPLE: We all think paper money will disappear. People won't use money or credit cards. They'll use their fingerprints to buy things.

EXERCISE 9 MAKING PREDICTIONS

Ⓐ DISCUSSION Work in small groups. Write predictions for the year 2050 for the areas in the list below.

The environment: The air will be cleaner in 2050. Scientists will solve the problem of air pollution.

- the environment
- health and medicine
- jobs
- sports
- technology

Ⓑ Write one of your group's predictions on the board. Your classmates will tell you if they agree or disagree and give reasons why.

EXAMPLE: I disagree with the prediction that the air will be cleaner in 2050. People will continue to drive cars, build factories, and pollute the air. I think the air will be bad in 2050.

EXERCISE 10 COMPLAINTS AND SUGGESTIONS

(A) PROBLEM SOLVING You are going to tell your classmates about a problem, and they are going to help you solve it. First, write down two complaints. Use *won't* in each complaint.

My boss won't let us keep our phones on at work. I need to have my phone on.
I have young children, and I want the babysitter to reach me in an emergency.

(B) Work in small groups. Tell your complaint to your group. The students in your group will make a suggestion to solve your problem.

EXAMPLE: Why don't you tell your boss that you have young children and need to keep your phone on? I'm sure he'll understand.

EXERCISE 11 DON'T WORRY. I'LL FEED YOUR FISH!

ROLE PLAY Work with a partner. Imagine each situation below. Ask your partner for help. Your partner promises to help.

1. You are going away on business for a week. You are worried about your fish and your plants in your apartment.

   EXAMPLE: A: I'm going to be away all next week. I'm worried about my fish and my plants.
   B: Don't worry about them. I'll feed your fish and water your plants.
   A: Oh, that would be great. Thanks so much. I'll leave the key . . .

2. You are going to take a Spanish class next year. Your partner took the same class last year.

3. You are going to buy a new smartphone. This will be your first smartphone and you are not very good with technology.

4. You need a ride to the airport. Your partner has a car.

5. You're going to move to a small apartment. You need to throw away a lot of things. You can't decide what to throw away.

6. You're going to visit relatives. You need to buy gifts for everyone. You're not good at choosing gifts.

Go to MyEnglishLab for more communication practice.

Ⓐ BEFORE YOU WRITE Read a student's paragraph about travel in the future. Work with a partner. Talk about the topics in the chart and say how life will be different in 2050 in those areas. Use your imagination. Write notes in the chart with your ideas.

In 2050, people will have new ways to travel. First of all, people will have their own wings. They'll use them to fly distances of up to 50 miles (80 kilometers). The wings won't take up much space, and parking won't be a problem. People are also going to have flying cars. These cars will go up to 200 miles an hour (322 kilometers). People will use them to travel from 200 to 400 miles (322 to 644 kilometers). There will be regular planes and jets, and spaceships for trips to other planets. I'll probably live in the countryside and work in the city. My 25-mile (40-kilometer) commute is going to take about six minutes with my flying car. I'll travel to other planets on my vacations.

Education	
Fashion	
Food	
Homes	
Travel	

Ⓑ WRITE Write a paragraph about *one* of the topics in the chart in A. Use *will* for the future. You can also use *be going to* in some sentences to make your writing more interesting.

Ⓒ CHECK YOUR WORK Read your paragraph. Underline *will* + the base form of the verb. Use the Editing Checklist to check your work.

Editing Checklist

Did you use...?

☐ *will* + the base form of the verb for the future

☐ *will not* or *won't* + the base form of the verb for the negative future

☐ future time markers at the beginning or end of a sentence

☐ *will* in some sentences and *be going to* for the future in other sentences

☐ correct spelling

Ⓓ REVISE Read your paragraph again. Can you improve it? Make changes if necessary.

Go to MyEnglishLab for more writing practice.

UNIT 23 REVIEW

Test yourself on the grammar of the unit.

A Circle the correct word to complete the sentences.

1. He doesn't like hats. He <u>will</u> / won't wear them.

2. I have a dentist appointment. I <u>will</u> / won't be at work until noon.

3. He's good with computers. He probably <u>will</u> / won't fix your computer.

4. The sale ends today, but don't worry. There <u>will</u> / won't be another sale next month.

5. I need more time. I <u>will</u> / won't be ready for at least a half an hour.

B Write questions. Put the words in parentheses in the correct order.

1. _____ ?
   (will / to the moon / in twenty years / many people / travel)

2. _____ ?
   (the climate / will / change / in the future)

3. _____ ?
   (eat / people / what / in 2050 / will)

4. _____ ?
   (different / look / people / will / in 2100)

5. _____ ?
   (will / how / people / get around / in the year 2035)

C Write questions with *will*. Use the same verb as the verb in the first sentence.

1. Yesterday was hot. _____ it _____ hot tomorrow, too?

2. Last week, he had a test. _____ he _____ a test next week, too?

3. Last September, there was a storm. _____ there _____ a storm next September, too?

4. Yesterday it rained. _____ it _____ tomorrow, too?

5. He worked late yesterday. _____ he _____ late tomorrow, too?

D Correct the paragraph. There are five mistakes.

I usually bring my lunch to work, but tomorrow I no will bring it because it's my birthday. My co-workers will takes me out to a restaurant. We'll to order a few different dishes, and we'll share them. They'll singing "Happy Birthday," and they'll give me a small gift. I'm sure it will is a lot of fun.

Now check your answers on page 449.

Go to MyEnglishLab to complete the review online.

May or *Might* for Possibility

THE WEATHER

OUTCOMES
- Express possibility in the present or future
- Recognize details in a weather report
- Recognize details in a conversation about travel plans
- Discuss reasons and possibilities for different situations and events
- Talk about possible plans for the near future
- Write a weather report about a city

STEP 1   GRAMMAR IN CONTEXT

BEFORE YOU READ

Answer the questions.

1. How do you find out about the weather?
   - **a.** TV
   - **b.** phone
   - **c.** computer
   - **d.** radio
   - **e.** newspaper
   - **f.** other

2. What kind of weather do you like?

READ

▶ 24|01 **Read this TV weather report and the conversation about it.**

The Weather Forecast

MOTHER: Shh. The weather report is coming on.[1]

ANNOUNCER: It's Sunday, May 15. The time is 9:00 a.m. And now here's the weather forecast with Luis Malina.

LUIS MALINA: Good morning, everyone. If you plan to be outdoors today or Monday, wear a warm jacket and bring an umbrella. The weather will continue to be unseasonable.[2] Today will be cold and windy. And heavy rain will begin tonight or tomorrow. For your morning commute, there may be flooding on the highways. So, if you can, take public transportation. And don't put away those umbrellas too soon because we'll have more rain on Tuesday and Wednesday. By Thursday, the weather may become milder with only a 20 percent chance of showers.[3]

---

1 *coming on:* starting
2 *unseasonable:* unusual for the time of year
3 *chance of showers:* the possibility of short periods of rain

We might even see some sun. But until then, my friends, my best advice is to stay indoors with a good book or movie.

ALEX: I have soccer tomorrow. We might not play.

MOTHER: Don't be too sure. You may still have a game. The meteorologist[4] is often wrong. Remember last Friday? He predicted a beautiful day, but it was awful. And last week, he said we might have a major storm. It turned out to be sunny and dry.

ALEX: Well, I think it will rain tomorrow. Will you watch the game in the rain?

MOTHER: I might. But I just hope you don't play in the rain.

ALEX: Well, I hope we *do*. Remember the last time it rained? We played in the rain, and we won!

---

4 *meteorologist:* weather reporter

AFTER YOU READ

Ⓐ VOCABULARY **Complete the sentences with the words from the box.**

commute	flooding	highways	mild	predicted	storm

1. He lives outside the city. His _____ to work is an hour and a half each way.

2. There is always _____ on that street when it rains. The city needs to fix the problem.

3. The meteorologist _____ beautiful weather for the next three days.

4. There is heavy traffic on all the major _____. Let's wait a couple of hours before we leave.

5. The _____ is getting worse. The wind is causing trees to fall, and all flights are canceled.

6. I want to live someplace where the weather is sunny and _____.

Ⓑ COMPREHENSION **Read the weather forecast again. Circle the correct weather for each day.**

1. Sunday   **a.** sunny and warm   **b.** cold and windy

2. Monday   **a.** light rain   **b.** heavy rain

3. Tuesday   **a.** rainy   **b.** sunny

4. Wednesday   **a.** rainy   **b.** sunny

5. Thursday   **a.** no chance of rain   **b.** a small chance of rain

Ⓒ DISCUSSION **Work with a partner. Compare your answers in B. Then talk about the weather in your area for today and tomorrow.**

MAY OR *MIGHT* FOR POSSIBILITY

Affirmative Statements			
Subject	May/ Might	Base Form of Verb	
I You He She We They	**may might**	**play**	soccer.
It	**may might**	**rain**	tonight.

Negative Statements				
Subject	May/ Might	Not	Base Form of Verb	
I You He She We They	**may might**	**not**	**play**	soccer.
It	**may might**	**not**	**rain**	tonight.

GRAMMAR NOTES

1 *May* and *Might*: Meaning and Form

Use *may* or *might* to express **possibility** in the present or the future.	A: Where's John? B: I don't know. He **may** be on vacation.
Follow *may* or *might* with the **base form** of the verb.	A: What are you going to do this weekend? B: We **might** *go* to a movie.
The **negative** of *may* or *might* is *may not* or *might not*.	We **may not finish** the job. I **might not visit** him this afternoon.
BE CAREFUL! We do not contract *may not* or *might not*.	He may not drive to work. NOT He mayn't drive to work. It might not rain. NOT It mightn't rain.

2 *May, Might, Will*, and *Won't*

Use *may* or *might* to express what is **possible**.	It **may** rain. or It **might** rain.
Use *will probably* to express what is **likely**.	It**'ll probably** rain.
Use *will* to express what is **certain** or **definite**.	It **will** rain.
Use *won't* to express what is **impossible** or certain not to happen.	It **won't** rain.

3 Questions About Future Possibility

Use **will** or **be going to** to **ask questions about future possibility**.	**Will** you go to the party?
You can use *may* or *might* in the answer.	A: **Are** you **going to** wear a raincoat? B: I **might.** **or** I **may.**
BE CAREFUL! Do not use *may* or *might* to ask questions about future possibility.	**Will** you go to the party? NOT ~~May~~ you go to the party? **Are** you **going to** wear a raincoat? NOT ~~Might~~ you wear a raincoat?

4 *I think* and *I'm sure*

You can use *I think* + subject + *might/may/ will/be going to* to express **possibility** or **uncertainty**.	I **think** they **might be** on vacation. I **think** they **will be** back next week.
You can use *I'm sure* + subject + *will/be going to* to express **certainty**.	**I'm sure** they will call.
BE CAREFUL! Do not use *I'm sure* with *may* or *might*.	**I'm sure** they're going to call. NOT I'm sure they ~~might~~ call.

5 *Maybe*

You can also use *maybe* + *will* to express future possibility. *Maybe I will* has a similar meaning to *I might* or *I may*.	**Maybe I'll go** to the party on Saturday. **I may go** to the party on Saturday.

Go to MyEnglishLab to watch the grammar presentation.

STEP 3   FOCUSED PRACTICE

EXERCISE 1 DISCOVER THE GRAMMAR

GRAMMAR NOTES 1–2, 4–5 **Match the sentences. Write the correct letters.**

___d___ **1.** It's definitely going to rain.

_____ **2.** There's an 80 percent chance of rain.

_____ **3.** Maybe it'll rain later.

_____ **4.** There's a 10 percent chance of rain.

_____ **5.** It's definitely not going to rain.

a. It probably won't rain.

b. It'll probably rain.

c. It won't rain.

~~d.~~ I'm sure it's going to rain.

e. It may rain.

EXERCISE 2 AFFIRMATIVE AND NEGATIVE OF *MAY* OR *MIGHT*

GRAMMAR NOTES 1, 4 Complete the conversations with *may* or *might* and the verbs from the box. Use the affirmative or negative form.

be	go	have	leave	need	~~rain~~	take

1. A: Take your umbrella. I think it _____ *might rain* _____ this afternoon.

   B: Really? The forecast was for sun.

2. A: Start dinner without me. It _____ me a long time to get

   home. The rain is causing flooding on the highway.

   B: That's OK. We'll wait.

3. A: Sandy is not doing well in her math class.

   B: She _____ an after-school tutor to help her with math.

4. A: Why are you so worried?

   B: The kids are camping tonight, and the forecast is for unusually cold weather. They

   _____ enough clothes.

5. A: Where's John? The meeting will start in a few minutes.

   B: He _____ late. All flights are delayed because of the wind.

6. A: How are you feeling?

   B: Terrible. I _____ to the concert tonight.

EXERCISE 3
MAY, MIGHT, WILL, AND *WILL PROBABLY*

GRAMMAR NOTES 1–4
Read today's weather forecast. Then circle the correct words to complete the sentences.

Cloudy with periods of rain	High of 50° F (10° Celsius)	Winds SSE at 30 to 40 mph (48 to 64 kph)	60 percent chance of rain

1. It (will be) / won't be a very windy day.

2. It will probably rain / probably won't rain, but it may not rain / won't rain all day.

3. The temperature may reach / probably won't reach 60 degrees.

4. Will they cancel / Might they cancel the ball game for this afternoon?

5. They might cancel / won't cancel the game if the rain is too heavy.

6. I'm sure you will get / might get a text about the game before noon.

EXERCISE 4 *MAYBE, MAY, AND MIGHT*

GRAMMAR NOTES 1, 3, 5 **Change sentences with *maybe* to sentences with *may* or *might*. Cross out the sentence with *maybe*, and write the new sentence on the line.**

1. A: What are you going to do about the concert tonight?

   B: ~~Maybe I'll go.~~ *I may go.* _____ I think my fever is going down.

2. A: Are they going to cancel the barbecue?

   B: Maybe they will. _____ The forecast is for heavy rain.

3. A: Where will you meet if it rains?

   B: Maybe we'll meet at the mall. _____

4. A: Will she bring her baby in the rain?

   B: Maybe she will. _____

EXERCISE 5 EDITING

GRAMMAR NOTES 1–4 **There are six mistakes in the conversations. The first mistake is already corrected. Find and correct five more.**

1. A: Where's Bill?

   B: ~~I'm sure~~ *I think* he might be on vacation in Florida.

2. A: We maybe go to the park today. Do you want to join us?

   B: No, thanks. It's very windy. Why don't you do something indoors?

3. A: May you take the highway?

   B: I may. I'll listen to the traffic report before I decide.

4. A: Are you going to finish your paper on climate change today?

   B: I want to, but I mightn't have enough time.

5. A: What's the weather report?

   B: It's sunny now, but it may to rain this afternoon.

6. A: What's the forecast for tomorrow?

   B: It may rains in the morning, but it will be sunny in the afternoon.

Go to MyEnglishLab for more focused practice.

EXERCISE 6 LISTENING

▶ 24|02 Ⓐ **A couple is taking a trip to Oregon. Listen to their conversation. Check (✓) the activities that the man and woman talk about possibly doing.**

☐ camping   ☐ going to a national park   ☐ skiing

☐ eating at a restaurant   ☐ mountain climbing   ☐ swimming in a lake

▶ 24|02 Ⓑ **Listen again. Circle the correct answers.**

1. How many hats is Jack going to take?
   a. one   **(b.)** two   **c.** three

2. How many books does Jack want to take with him?
   a. one   **b.** two   **c.** three

3. How many sports jackets is Jack packing?
   a. one   **b.** two   **c.** three

4. How are Alison and Jack traveling to Oregon?
   a. by car   **b.** by boat   **c.** by plane

5. How many suitcases is Jack going to take?
   a. one   **b.** two   **c.** three

Ⓒ **Work with a partner. What reason does Jack give for packing the things in the list below? Use *may* or *might* in your answers.**

EXAMPLE: A: So, why does Jack need boots?
                   B: He needs boots because they might go mountain climbing.

- boots   • books
- a raincoat   • a sports jacket
- hats

EXERCISE 7 WHY DO YOU NEED THAT?

CONVERSATION Work with a partner. Take out six things from your pocket, bookbag, or handbag. Explain to your partner why you may need each thing. Use *may* or *might* in your explanation.

EXAMPLE: A: Why do you need a driver's license?

B: I might need to show identification. I don't drive here, but a driver's license is good when you need ID.

EXERCISE 8
THINK OF THE POSSIBILITIES

CRITICAL THINKING Work in small groups. Make guesses about the situation. Use *may* or *might* in your guesses.

1. A six-year-old child is alone on the street. She's crying.

   EXAMPLE: A: She may be lost.

   B: Her mother might be in a car accident.

   C: Maybe her mother just told her that she can't have an ice cream.

2. You see a man lying in the street.

3. You're at your door. You hear noises inside. Because you live alone, you don't understand the situation.

4. Class began fifteen minutes ago and Gina still isn't here. She is always early for class.

5. The supermarket is not usually crowded at this time. Now there are a lot of people in the store, and there aren't many groceries on the shelves.

EXERCISE 9 PLANS FOR TONIGHT

CONVERSATION Work with a partner. Take turns. Ask your partner about his or her plans for tonight. Use *may*, *might*, and *will probably* in your answers. Use the ideas in the list or your own ideas. Explain your answer.

EXAMPLE: A: Are you going to stay home tonight? What are you going to do?

B: I might bake a cake for Rose. It's her birthday tomorrow.

- stay home
- listen to the weather report
- go running

- watch a movie
- study English

- eat out
- cook dinner

Go to MyEnglishLab for more communication practice.

FROM GRAMMAR TO WRITING

Ⓐ BEFORE YOU WRITE Read the weather report. Then write the name of a city and go online and find the weather forecast for the city for today, tomorrow, and the next day. Complete the chart. Work with a partner. Tell your partner the weather forecast for the city.

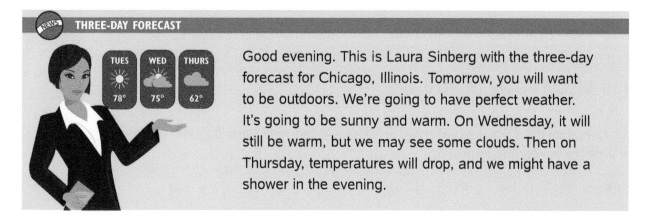

THREE-DAY FORECAST

TUES 78° WED 75° THURS 62°

Good evening. This is Laura Sinberg with the three-day forecast for Chicago, Illinois. Tomorrow, you will want to be outdoors. We're going to have perfect weather. It's going to be sunny and warm. On Wednesday, it will still be warm, but we may see some clouds. Then on Thursday, temperatures will drop, and we might have a shower in the evening.

City:		
Today	**Tomorrow**	**The day after tomorrow**

Ⓑ WRITE Write a weather report for a city. Use the weather report in A and your chart. Use *may* or *might* when possible.

Ⓒ CHECK YOUR WORK Read your weather report. Underline *may* and *might* and the verb that follows. Use the Editing Checklist to check your work.

Editing Checklist

Did you . . . ?

- [ ] use *may* or *might* to express possibility
- [ ] follow *may* and *might* with the base form of the verb
- [ ] use the full form *may not* for the negative
- [ ] check your spelling

Ⓓ REVISE Read your weather report again. Can you improve your writing? Make changes if necessary.

Go to MyEnglishLab for more writing practice.

UNIT 24 REVIEW

Test yourself on the grammar of the unit.

A Complete the sentences. Circle the correct answers.

1. She may <u>to go</u> / <u>go</u> to the library.

2. He may <u>buy</u> / <u>buys</u> a new car.

3. It <u>mightn't</u> / <u>might not</u> rain tonight.

4. They <u>maybe</u> / <u>may</u> return the TV.

5. <u>Will</u> / <u>Might</u> you go to the party?

B Complete the sentences with *may* or *might* and the verbs from the box. Use the affirmative or negative form.

get	need	see	snow	stay

1. Take your boots. It _____ this afternoon.

2. Start dinner without me. I _____ home from work until 10:00 p.m.

3. Karina is upset. The doctor says she _____ surgery.

4. Here's a gift. I _____ you before your birthday.

5. Traffic is heavy now. I _____ here for a while.

C Complete the conversation with *will*, *may*, or *might*.

A: _____ you go to the party?

B: I _____ go. It depends on my boss. He _____ want me to work late that night.

A: When _____ you know?

B: I'm not sure. Maybe my boss _____ tell me on Thursday.

D Correct the sentences. There are five mistakes.

1. He might goes on vacation next week.

2. He may works late tomorrow.

3. They might to visit him tomorrow. Are you free?

4. I might not help him. I might to help her instead.

5. She maybe take a yoga class.

Now check your answers on page 450.

Go to MyEnglishLab to complete the review online.

UNIT 25

Gerunds and Infinitives
CAREERS

OUTCOMES
- Use gerunds and infinitives after certain verbs
- Recognize important details in a magazine article
- Recognize main ideas and details in a short lecture
- Interview classmates about their likes and dislikes; report findings to the class
- Discuss career interests
- Write a paragraph about your career goals

STEP 1 GRAMMAR IN CONTEXT

BEFORE YOU READ

Answer the questions.

1. When you were a child, did anyone ask you: "What do you want to be when you grow up?" How did you answer the question?

2. Do you have a career or a career goal? How did you decide on it?

READ

○25|01 Read this article about choosing the right career.

The Right Career for You

Some people love going to work each morning, but other people hate it. Most of us spend many hours at work, so a career choice is very important.

Bob wants to be a park ranger.[1] He says, "I enjoy being outdoors, and I like talking to people. I'm very interested in plant and animal life."

Rita plans on becoming a chef. She says, "I like working with my hands, and I love to prepare meals. I know it's going to be hard work and long

hours, but I definitely don't want to sit at a desk in an office all day."

Kate hopes to become a high school science teacher. She says, "I enjoy working with teenagers, and I want to have time for myself." Her parents wanted her to become a lawyer, but she doesn't want to work long hours and she doesn't want a lot of stress in her life.

---

1 *park ranger:* a person whose job it is to take care of a park

Here are a few questions to consider before you choose a career:

- What are your talents?[2] What do you enjoy doing? How can your abilities and interests pay you the salary you expect to make?
- How do you like to work? Do you like working with others? Do you prefer working alone?

- How do you handle stress?[3] Do you hate competing? Do you hate meeting deadlines? Do you do well under pressure?
- How much time do you want to spend with family and friends?

These are just a few questions to help you find the right career.

---
2 *talents:* things a person does well

---
3 *handle stress:* act when you have a lot of worries

AFTER YOU READ

A VOCABULARY **Complete the sentences with the words from the box.**

career	chef	competing	deadlines	lawyer	salary

1. My brother enjoys _____ in races. He's fast and usually wins.

2. She hopes to become a _____ and fight for poor people.

3. I enjoy my job, but the _____ is low. I need to find a different job.

4. She doesn't like driving school buses anymore. She wants to change her _____ and become a pilot.

5. He lost his job because his reports were always late. He never met his _____ .

6. She's a _____ at a top restaurant in Paris. Her dishes are famous all over the world.

B COMPREHENSION **Read the sentences. Check the person each sentence is about.**

	Bob	Rita	Kate
1. This person hopes to work with teenagers.	☐	☐	☐
2. This person wants to work with her hands.	☐	☐	☐
3. This person wants to work outdoors.	☐	☐	☐
4. This person expects to work long hours.	☐	☐	☐
5. This person is interested in nature.	☐	☐	☐
6. This person doesn't want to be a lawyer.	☐	☐	☐
7. This person doesn't want a lot of stress at work.	☐	☐	☐

C DISCUSSION **Work with a partner. Look at the article "The Right Career for You" again. Then discuss: What other questions can help you choose the right career?**

Go to MyEnglishLab for more grammar in context practice.

GERUNDS AND INFINITIVES

Subject	Verb	Gerund (Verb + -ing)
I	enjoy	dancing.

Subject	Verb	Infinitive
She	wants	to sing.

Subject	Verb	Infinitive or Gerund
They	like	driving.
		to drive.

Verb + Gerund	Verb + Infinitive	Verb + Infinitive or Gerund
avoid	agree	continue
enjoy	decide	hate
finish	expect	like
keep	hope	love
plan on	intend	prefer
think about	need	try
	plan	
	refuse	
	want	

GRAMMAR NOTES

1 Gerunds

We form the **gerund** with the base form of the **verb + -ing**. The gerund is a **noun** that looks like a verb.	I enjoy **singing**. We finished **studying** at 8:00.
We can use gerunds in different places in a sentence.	
• **after** certain **verbs**	GERUND I enjoy **cooking**.
• as a **subject**	GERUND **Cooking** is fun.
• **after** a **preposition**	GERUND I'm interested in **cooking**.

2 Verb + Gerund

Gerunds can **follow** some **verbs** such as *enjoy*, *finish*, and *avoid*.	He **enjoys studying** science. They **finished cooking** at 6:00 p.m. She **avoids taking** the highway during rush hour.

Remember, the gerund is different from the present progressive (*be* + verb + *-ing*). (See Unit 15.)	I enjoy **working**.
	  (working *is a gerund*)
	I **am working**.
	  (am working *is the present progressive*)

3 Verb + Infinitive

We form the **infinitive** with *to* + **the base form of the verb**. An infinitive can follow verbs such as *want* and *need*.	I want **to work**. She needs **to write** a résumé.
Many of the verbs + infinitive have a **future** meaning.	She **hopes to** become a pilot next year.

4 Verb + Infinitive or Gerund

Some verbs such as *like* and *hate* can come before an **infinitive** or a **gerund**.	I **like writing**. I **like to write**. I **hate working** late. I **hate to work** late.
BE CAREFUL! Do not use a gerund and then an infinitive (or an infinitive and then a gerund) after verbs that can be followed by both forms.	I like **swimming** and **jogging**. **NOT** I like swimming and ~~to jog~~. I like **to swim** and **to jog**. **NOT** I like to swim and ~~jogging~~.

Go to MyEnglishLab to watch the grammar presentation.

STEP 3 FOCUSED PRACTICE

EXERCISE 1 DISCOVER THE GRAMMAR

GRAMMAR NOTES 1–4 Read about the talents and abilities of four young men. Underline the verbs + gerunds. Circle the verbs + infinitives. Then match the men's abilities and talents to their career goals.

___c___ **1.** Joe is good at art. He enjoys coming up with new ideas. He likes to work with others and do creative work.

_____ **2.** Oliver enjoys working with people and wants to help them.

_____ **3.** Lucas hopes to make a lot of money. He is competitive and likes selling things.

_____ **4.** Paul loves to sing, dance, and perform in front of an audience.

_____ **5.** Al likes math and science. He enjoys working with electronics.

a. He wants to work in real estate and sell expensive homes.

b. He plans to become a computer programmer.

~~c.~~ He hopes to be a designer.

d. He intends to become a social worker or a psychologist.

e. He plans on becoming an actor.

EXERCISE 2 GERUNDS

GRAMMAR NOTES 1–2 Complete the sentences. Use the gerund forms of the verbs from the box.

apply	do	go	save	send	~~take~~	work

1. She finished _____*taking*_____ final exams last week.

2. She is thinking about _____ for a part-time job for the summer.

3. She will start _____ out résumés this weekend.

4. She enjoys _____ sales work.

5. She doesn't like _____ with her hands.

6. She avoided _____ out with friends the month before her final exams.

7. She plans on _____ money for a car.

EXERCISE 3 INFINITIVES

GRAMMAR NOTE 3 Complete the sentences. Use the infinitive forms of the verbs from the box.

complete	~~find~~	go	leave	sell	send	spend	work

1. John's looking for a job. He hopes _____*to find*_____ a job in this city.

2. He likes his car. He doesn't want _____ it.

3. He wants _____ time with his friends every weekend. He refuses _____ on weekends.

4. He plans _____ out his résumé[1] to different companies this afternoon.

5. In two years, he intends _____ his job and _____ to business school.

6. He hopes _____ his M.B.A. in four years.

---

1 *résumé:* paper that lists your name, contact information, education, and previous jobs

EXERCISE 4 GERUNDS AND INFINITIVES

GRAMMAR NOTES 1–4 **Complete the sentences with the gerund or the infinitive forms of the verbs in parentheses. In some sentences, you can use a gerund or an infinitive.**

1. He needs _____*to get*_____ a job.
   (get)

2. I like _____ part of a team.
   (be)

3. She prefers _____ at night.
   (work)

4. I prefer _____ in the daytime.
   (work)

5. We avoid _____ between 7:00 and 9:00 a.m.
   (drive)

6. He refused _____ late.
   (stay)

7. They hope _____ in July.
   (move)

8. They finished _____ the report at 7:00 p.m.
   (write)

9. I decided _____ to school.
   (return)

10. She's trying _____ a job with good benefits.
    (find)

11. He likes traveling and _____ presentations.
    (give)

12. She hates to cook and _____.
    (clean)

EXERCISE 5 GERUNDS AND INFINITIVES

Ⓐ GRAMMAR NOTES 1–4 **Complete the conversation. Use the gerund or infinitive forms of the verbs in parentheses.**

ELENA: Do you like _____*acting*_____?
1. (act)

JULIAN: Yes, I do. I really enjoy _____ in front of people.
2. (perform)

ELENA: Is it hard to find work as an actor?

JULIAN: Very hard. Many people want _____ actors. You need
3. (become)

_____ talent, patience, and luck.
4. (have)

ELENA: Do you ever think about _____ careers?
5. (change)

JULIAN: No. I refuse _____ my dream. I keep _____ for parts.
6. (give up)   **7.** (try out)

I think I'm a great actor, and I plan on _____ the world!
8. (show)

◐25|02 Ⓑ LISTEN AND CHECK **Listen to the conversation and check your answers in A.**

EXERCISE 6 GERUNDS AND INFINITIVES

GRAMMAR NOTES 1–4 Complete the sentences. Use the gerund or infinitive forms of the verbs from the box.

get	look	meet	return	study	travel	~~work~~

1. Do you enjoy _____ *working* _____ with children?

2. Do you plan _____ an advanced degree?

3. He expected _____ with the president of the company. Instead, he met with the vice president.

4. He keeps _____ at his watch. I hope he isn't bored.

5. Many people decide _____ law after watching courtroom dramas.

6. Kim is thinking about _____ to school and getting a degree in psychology.

7. Paul intends _____ around the world before he goes to business school.

EXERCISE 7 EDITING

GRAMMAR NOTES 1–4 Correct the letter. There are six mistakes. The first mistake is already corrected. Find and correct five more.

35 Main Street, Apt. 6
New Hope, New Jersey 07675

May 27, 2017

Head Librarian
New Hope Library
7 West Street
New Hope, New Jersey 07675

To Whom It May Concern:

           to
    I want apply for a part-time job at New Hope Library. I am in my senior year of

high school. I expect attend State College next year, and I plan majoring in library

science. I enjoy reading and to work with the public. I'm good at computers, and I

like keep things in order. I've enclosed a résumé. I hope hearing from you soon.

Sincerely,
Joe Reed

EXERCISE 8 LISTENING

▶25|03 **A** Listen to a talk by a designer and complete the sentences. Circle the correct answers.

1. Henry Trinh is a designer for _____.
   a. ABO Designs   **(b.)** XZO Designs   **c.** XYO Designs

2. Trinh is working on a logo for a _____.
   a. shoe company   **b.** cosmetics company   **c.** sports team

3. Trinh tries to keep his designs _____.
   a. modern   **b.** simple   **c.** exciting

4. When people see red, their appetite _____.
   a. decreases   **b.** increases   **c.** stays the same

5. When people see blue, they feel _____.
   a. angry   **b.** sad   **c.** relaxed

▶25|03 **B** Listen again and take notes. Then work with a partner. Look at the list below. Talk about what you learned about each of the topics in the list.

EXAMPLE: A: Trinh loves being a designer.
          B: Yes. And he enjoys creating logos for companies.

- Trinh and his job
- logos
- banks
- men, women, and colors
- designers and teams

EXERCISE 9 FIND SOMEONE WHO...

A GAME Walk around your classroom. Ask your classmates questions to fill out the chart. The first person to complete the chart wins.

EXAMPLE: A: Boris, do you enjoy working with other people?
B: No, I don't. I prefer to work alone.

Find someone who . . .	Name
enjoys working with other people	_____
prefers working alone	_____
wants to make a difference in the world	_____
hopes to be rich	_____
hopes to be famous	_____
wants to work in the arts[1]	_____
hopes to have his or her own business	_____
intends to work with children	_____

1 *the arts:* theater, music, dance, fashion, movies, etc.

B Report back to the class.

EXAMPLE: Ana enjoys working with other people, but Boris prefers working alone.

EXERCISE 10 A GOOD CAREER CHOICE

A DISCUSSION Work with a partner. Tell your partner about your interests. Talk about what you love, like, or hate doing. Talk about some of the topics in the list below.

EXAMPLE: A: Marco, what kind of movies and TV shows do you like?
B: I really like nature shows. How about you?

- movies and TV shows
- free time activities
- sports
- food
- shopping
- children
- travel

B Work in a group. Tell the group about your partner. Discuss possible careers for your partner.

EXAMPLE: Well, Marco enjoys watching TV shows and movies about animals. In his free time, he likes to hike in the woods. He's also a vegetarian. I think he may want to become a biologist or an environmental scientist.

Go to MyEnglishLab for more communication practice.

A BEFORE YOU WRITE Work with a partner. Read a student's paragraph about her career goal. Underline the verbs followed by gerunds and circle the verbs followed by infinitives. Then use the same verbs to tell your partner about your career goals.

I enjoy window shopping and studying the latest fashions. I also love to draw. I hope to combine my two passions and become a fashion designer. I plan to study art and fashion in college this year. I want to get an internship with a design company in the summer. I expect to graduate in four years, and in ten years I intend to have my own fashion design business.

B WRITE Write a paragraph about your future career goals. Use the paragraph in A and your ideas. Use gerunds or infinitives.

C CHECK YOUR WORK Read your paragraph. Underline the gerunds and infinitives. Use the Editing Checklist to check your work.

Editing Checklist

Did you . . . ?

- [ ] use infinitives after verbs such as *want, hope, plan, expect,* etc.
- [ ] use gerunds after verbs such as *avoid, enjoy, plan on,* etc.
- [ ] check your spelling

D REVISE Read your paragraph again. Can you improve your writing? Make changes if necessary.

Go to MyEnglishLab for more writing practice.

UNIT 25 REVIEW

Test yourself on the grammar of the unit.

A Complete the sentences. Circle the correct answers.

1. Do you want to start / starting a business?

2. I hope to sell / selling my business next year.

3. She decided to return / returning to school.

4. She hopes to become / becoming a pilot.

5. She enjoys to fly / flying and to see / seeing the world.

B Complete the sentences with the correct forms of the verbs in parentheses.

1. She doesn't want _____ evenings.
   (work)

2. Her boss refuses _____ her hours.
   (change)

3. She's thinking about _____ her job and _____ back to school.
   (quit)   (go)

4. Her English keeps _____ .
   (improve)

C Write sentences. Put the words in parentheses in the correct order.

1. _____
   (helping / people / she / enjoys)

2. _____
   (to / graduate / in June / expect / we)

3. _____
   (to / trying / study / are / they)

4. _____
   (avoids / and / he / eating / candy / ice cream)

D Correct the paragraph. There are six mistakes.

Carol volunteers at a hospital. She enjoys taking care of patients. Some patients refuse do exercise, but Carol keeps to push them. Carol intends study physical therapy in college. She needs taking a lot of science courses. She expects to goes to college next fall. She hopes get a degree in physical therapy in five years.

Now check your answers on page 450.

Go to MyEnglishLab to complete the review online.

Count/Non-Count Nouns; *Much/Many*; Quantifiers

UNIT 26

Articles with Count and Non-Count Nouns; *Some/Any*
RESTAURANTS AND FOOD

UNIT 27

***How much* and *How many*; Quantifiers**
DESSERTS

UNIT 28

***Too many* and *Too much*; *Enough* + Noun**
THE RIGHT PLACE TO LIVE

OUTCOMES

- Use indefinite and definite articles with nouns
- Use *some* and *any* with count and non-count nouns
- Recognize details in a restaurant review
- Recognize important details in a conversation
- Role play ordering food in a restaurant
- Make recommendations for a restaurant
- Write a review of a place to eat

OUTCOMES

- Ask about quantities of things
- Describe quantities with *a lot*, *a few*, *a little*, *much*, and *many*
- Recognize details in a conversation about food
- List ingredients mentioned in a conversation about a recipe
- Discuss recipes and different kinds of food
- Write a conversation between a shopper and a clerk

OUTCOMES

- Use *too + much/many/few/little* and *not enough* to say there isn't a right amount of something
- Use *enough* to say there is a right amount of something
- Recognize details in an article about two cities
- Compare apartments described in a conversation
- Discuss the pros and cons of living in certain places
- Write a letter about problems in your town or city

Articles with Count and Non-Count Nouns; *Some/Any*

RESTAURANTS AND FOOD

OUTCOMES
• Use indefinite and definite articles with nouns
• Use *some* and *any* with count and non-count nouns
• Recognize details in a restaurant review
• Recognize important details in a conversation
• Role play ordering food in a restaurant
• Make recommendations for a restaurant
• Write a review of a place to eat

STEP 1   GRAMMAR IN CONTEXT

BEFORE YOU READ

Work with a partner. What are the three most important things for you when you choose a restaurant? Check (✓) them.

☐ food you like   ☐ unusual food   ☐ big portions
☐ a lively place   ☐ a quiet place   ☐ a beautiful place
☐ fast service   ☐ polite service   ☐ low prices

READ

26|01 Read these restaurant reviews.

Kassandra's Food Reviews

Al Hambra ✪✪✪✪✪ $$$$$

Spices are the reason people come to Al Hambra. The flavor of ginger, garlic, cumin, and lemon make the chicken in a pot our favorite choice. Another great choice for the main course is the lamb with ginger. There isn't any pork on the menu, but there are some delicious dishes with beef, chicken, or lamb. The portions are small, but the food is tasty. The appetizers are great. We especially like an appetizer called *zaalouk*. This is a salad made of eggplant and tomato. For dessert, we recommend the almond cookies. The restaurant is beautifully decorated and the dishes are beautiful to look at. Al Hambra is small, so be sure to make a reservation in advance.

Note: Al Hambra doesn't have a parking lot and there isn't any parking nearby, so you need to take public transportation. Also, you may need to wait, even with a reservation, but the atmosphere, food, and service are outstanding.

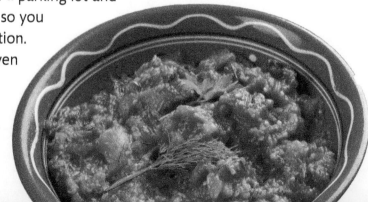

Blue Star Diner ✪✪✪✩✩ 💲💲💲💲💲

Blue Star Diner serves fresh food and huge portions in a comfortable atmosphere. It's not fancy, but the service is fast and the staff is polite. And there are some delicious entrees to choose from. All the fish dishes are good. Entrees come with soup, salad, and dessert. Some desserts are not so good, but the soups are usually tasty, and the salads are fresh. You won't be hungry when you leave the restaurant.

Blue Star Diner never takes reservations, so there is sometimes a long wait. But if you're looking for large portions at reasonable prices, Blue Star is a great choice.

Note: The restaurant is open 24 hours a day, and there's a big parking lot in the back.

AFTER YOU READ

Ⓐ VOCABULARY **Complete the sentences with the words from the box.**

| atmosphere | delicious | main course | menu | reservation | service |

1. The food was _____. We will definitely go back to that restaurant.

2. Everything on the _____ is fresh and tasty. Order whatever you like.

3. I ordered steak for my _____. My friend ordered a pasta dish.

4. All the servers were polite and helpful. The _____ was excellent.

5. The restaurant has soft lights, slow music, and beautiful flowers everywhere. The _____ is romantic.

6. Be sure to make a(n) _____ in advance. That restaurant is always crowded.

Ⓑ COMPREHENSION **Read the sentences about the restaurants. Check the restaurant each sentence describes.**

	Al Hambra	Blue Star Diner
1. You get a lot to eat at this restaurant.	☐	☐
2. This restaurant isn't big.	☐	☐
3. You can't make a reservation.	☐	☐
4. This restaurant never closes.	☐	☐
5. This restaurant doesn't have parking.	☐	☐
6. There aren't any pork chops on the menu.	☐	☐

Ⓒ DISCUSSION **Work with a partner. Compare your answers in B. Then discuss: Which restaurant sounds better to you? Why?**

Go to MyEnglishLab for more grammar in context practice. Articles with Count and Non-Count Nouns; *Some / Any* **309**

ARTICLES WITH COUNT AND NON-COUNT NOUNS; *SOME / ANY*

Count and Non-Count Nouns

Count Nouns	
I bought	a **pear**. **oranges**.

Non-Count Nouns	
I bought	**juice**.

Articles and Nouns

Indefinite Articles		
	Indefinite Article	Singular Count Noun
I bought	**a**	banana.
I didn't buy	**an**	apple.

Definite Article			
	Definite Article	Singular Count Noun	
I bought a banana.	**The**	banana	was delicious.

	Definite Article	Non-Count Noun	
I bought coffee.	**The**	coffee	was strong.

	Definite Article	Plural Count Noun	
He bought oranges.	**The**	oranges	were sweet.

Some / Any + Nouns

	Some / Any	Plural Count Nouns
He owns	**some**	restaurants.
He doesn't own	**any**	cafés.
Does he own	**any**	hotels?

	Some / Any	Non-Count Nouns
Carol wants	**some**	coffee.
Carol doesn't want	**any**	tea.
Does Carol want	**any**	water?

GRAMMAR NOTES

1 Count and Non-Count Nouns

There are **count nouns** and **non-count nouns**.

Nouns such as *apple*, *table*, and *menu* are **count nouns**. We call them count nouns because we **can count** them.	I ate **one pear** and **two apples**.
Nouns such as *milk*, *juice*, and *sugar* are **non-count nouns**. We call them non-count nouns because we **cannot count** them.	We need **milk**, **juice**, and **sugar**.
Some nouns can be both **count** and **non-count** nouns.	He bought three **cakes** for the party. *(count noun)* He ate some **cake**. *(non-count noun)*
USAGE NOTE In informal speaking, some non-count nouns are used as count nouns.	I'd like **two coffees** and **two sodas**. *(= I'd like two cups of coffee and two cans of soda.)*
BE CAREFUL! Do not add *-s* or *-es* to a non-count noun.	I need milk. **NOT** I need ~~milks~~.

2 Indefinite Articles *A, An*

Use *a* or *an* to talk about a person or thing for the first time, or when it is not clear which person or thing you mean.

Use *a* or *an* before a **singular count noun**.	I bought **a *pear*** and **an *apple***.
Remember to use *a* before a **consonant sound**.	A: Do you want **a steak**? B: No. I want **a small** pasta dish.
Remember to use *an* before a **vowel sound**.	A: Did you eat **an appetizer**? B: Yes. I had **an avocado** salad.
BE CAREFUL! Do not put *a*, *an*, or a number before a non-count noun.	I want **rice**. **NOT** I want ~~a~~ rice.

3 Definite Article *The*

Use *the* when it is clear which person or thing you mean.

You can use *the* before singular count nouns, plural nouns, and non-count nouns:

• **singular count nouns**	**The *restaurant*** is open. *(Both the speaker and listener know which restaurant.)*
• **plural nouns**	A: Do you have any napkins? B: Yes. **The *napkins*** are over there. *(the napkins that A asked about)*
• **non-count nouns**	**The *soup*** is delicious.

Use *some* and *any* before **plural count nouns** and **non-count nouns**.

Use *some* with **affirmative statements**.	He wrote **some invitations**. *(plural count noun)* He drank **some juice**. *(non-count noun)*
Use *any* with **negative statements**.	He didn't mail **any invitations**. *(plural count noun)* He didn't drink **any soda**. *(non-count noun)*
We usually use *any* in *yes/no* **questions**.	Did you buy **any** bananas? Did you buy **any** milk?
We can also use *some* in *yes/no* **questions** when we **offer** something or **ask for** something.	Would you like **some** juice? *(an offer)* Can I have **some** more milk? *(a request)*

PRONUNCIATION NOTE

▶ 26|02   **Stress with Indefinite Articles**

The indefinite articles *a* and *an* are usually **unstressed**. They sound like /ə/ and /ən/.	I found **a** new restaurant. It has **an** interesting menu.

REFERENCE NOTES

For more information about **count nouns** and the **indefinite article**, see Unit 4 on page 44.
For **spelling and pronunciation rules for plural nouns**, see Appendices 8 and 10 on page 434.
For a list of **common non-count nouns**, see Appendix 11 on page 435.

Go to MyEnglishLab to watch the grammar presentation.

STEP 3   **FOCUSED PRACTICE**

EXERCISE 1   DISCOVER THE GRAMMAR

GRAMMAR NOTES 1–2, 4   Read the sentences. Underline the noun in each sentence.
Then check (✓) the kind of noun it is.

	Singular Count Noun	Plural Count Noun	Non-Count Noun
1. I made a <u>reservation</u>.	☑	☐	☐
2. I need some information.	☐	☐	☐
3. There's a menu over there.	☐	☐	☐
4. There aren't any spoons.	☐	☐	☐
5. We ate some delicious bread.	☐	☐	☐

	Singular Count Noun	Plural Count Noun	Non-Count Noun
6. We need one more napkin.	☐	☐	☐
7. There was a server there.	☐	☐	☐
8. There's a parking lot in back.	☐	☐	☐
9. Do you want some coffee?	☐	☐	☐
10. There aren't any cookies.	☐	☐	☐
11. There isn't any food left.	☐	☐	☐
12. The people here are very kind.	☐	☐	☐

EXERCISE 2 *A, AN, THE, SOME, ANY*

GRAMMAR NOTES 2–4 **Complete the sentences. Circle the correct answers.**

1. You're in a restaurant. You need a napkin. Your friend sees one and says, _____
   a. "Here's a napkin."   **b.** "Here's the napkin."

2. You ask about a person's job. Someone says, _____
   a. "He's the lawyer."   **b.** "He's a lawyer."

3. It's your child's tenth birthday. You ask her what she wants for her party. She says, _____
   a. "Please bake a cake."   **b.** "Please bake some cake."

4. You're at a restaurant. You say, _____
   a. "Please pass some salts."   **b.** "Please pass the salt."

5. You lost your invitation to a party. You ask your friend, _____
   a. "Where's a party?"   **b.** "Where's the party?"

6. You are in a new neighborhood. You ask, _____
   a. "Are there any good restaurants here?"   **b.** "Are there the good restaurants here?"

7. You're in a restaurant. You say, _____
   a. "I'd like a omelet with spinach and tomato."   **b.** "I'd like an omelet with spinach and tomato."

EXERCISE 3 *A, AN, THE*

GRAMMAR NOTES 2–3 Complete the conversations. Circle the correct answers.

1. A: I made (a) / an reservation for four for tonight.

   B: What time is a / the reservation?

2. A: What's a / the name of a / the restaurant?

   B: It's called Al Hambra. It's a / an Moroccan restaurant.

3. A: Does Al Hambra have a / the website?

   B: Yes, it does. The / A website has photos of the / an dishes they serve.

4. A: How are a / the prices at Al Hambra?

   B: High, but there's a / an early-bird special. It's cheaper from 4 to 6.

5. A: Oh, no! Our table is right next to the / a front door.

   B: Let's move. It's freezing whenever people open a / the door.

6. A: Excuse me, where's a / the restroom?

   B: It's next to a / the kitchen over there.

7. A: The / A view from a / the top of this building is great.

   B: Is there a / an elevator to the top floor?

8. A: Did you like a / the restaurant?

   B: Yes, I did. It was an / the excellent choice.

EXERCISE 4 *A, AN, THE*

Ⓐ GRAMMAR NOTES 2–3 Complete the conversation with *a*, *an*, or *the*.

DAN: Where's ____the____ party?
                    1.

LAURA: At Rectangles Restaurant.

DAN: Are _____ Garcias coming?
                 2.

LAURA: Yes, they are.

DAN: He's _____ chef, right?
                 3.

LAURA: Yes, he is. His wife was _____
                                  4.

       accountant in Spain, but now

       she's _____ chef, too.
              5.

314   Unit 26

DAN: I hope they like _____ food at Rectangles.
6.

LAURA: I'm sure they'll like _____ atmosphere and _____ service. I hope they like
7.   8.

_____ food, too.
9.

DAN: Where do they work?

LAURA: She works at _____ Spanish restaurant, and he works at _____ Italian one.
10.   11.

DAN: Where are their restaurants?

LAURA: _____ Spanish restaurant is in downtown Manhattan. _____ Italian
12.   13.

restaurant is in Queens.

○26|03 **B** LISTEN AND CHECK **Listen to the conversation and check your answers in A.**

EXERCISE 5 *A, AN, THE*

GRAMMAR NOTES 2–3 **Add *a*,
an, or *the* where necessary.**

Kel Warner is *a*͜ college student.

He's English major. He has great

part-time job. He writes for the

school paper. Each week, the

school paper has review of local

restaurant, and Kel writes review.

Kel can take friend to restaurant,

and the school newspaper pays

bill. Kel has wonderful job.

EXERCISE 6 *SOME* AND *ANY*

(A) GRAMMAR NOTE 4 **Complete the conversation with *some* or *any*.**

MAN: Could you bring _____*some*_____ more bread, please?
                                    1.

SERVER: Certainly. . . . Here you go. Anything else?

MAN: _____ water, please. With ice.
                      2.

SERVER: Would you like _____ water, too, ma'am?
                                          3.

WOMAN: No, thanks. I don't want _____ water, but I'd like a glass of ginger ale.
                                                    4.

SERVER: Sure.

WOMAN: Also, could we have _____ more butter?
                                            5.

SERVER: Of course.

MAN: Do you have _____ fish dishes? I don't eat meat, and I don't see _____
                                  6.   **7.**

                fish on the menu.

SERVER: I'm sorry—we don't have fish, but we have _____ delicious vegetarian dishes.
                                                                                  8.

▶ 26|04 **(B)** LISTEN AND CHECK **Listen to the conversation and check your answers in A.**

EXERCISE 7 *SOME* AND *ANY*

GRAMMAR NOTE 4 **Look at the chart about the food in the kitchen of Mario's restaurant. Write sentences with *some* and *any* about the food. Use the nouns in parentheses.**

1. *There are some eggs.*
                          (eggs)
2. *There aren't any tomatoes.*
                          (tomatoes)
3. _____
                          (juice)
4. _____
                          (milk)
5. _____
                          (beef)
6. _____
                          (fish)
7. _____
                          (ice cubes)
8. _____
                          (ice cream)

Food in Mario's Kitchen

eggs	✓
tomatoes	–
Juice	✓
Milk	–
Beef	–
Fish	✓
ice cubes	–
ice cream	✓

EXERCISE 8 STRESS WITH INDEFINITE ARTICLES

▶ 26|05 Ⓐ PRONUNCIATION NOTE **Listen to the sentences. Then listen again and add *a* and/or *an* to each sentence.**

1. I discovered *a* new restaurant on 2nd Street.

2. It has beautiful garden in the back.

3. We sat at table under umbrella.

4. I ate delicious appetizer.

5. It was avocado salad.

6. For the main course, I had eggplant dish.

7. Lily had hamburger.

8. I had apple pie for dessert.

9. Lily had orange sorbet.

▶ 26|05 Ⓑ **Listen again and repeat each sentence.**

EXERCISE 9 EDITING

GRAMMAR NOTES 1–4 **Read the paragraph. There are six mistakes. The first one is already corrected. Find and correct five more.**

My friend Pierre is ^the^ chef at a small French restaurant.

He doesn't have the easy job. He works nights and

weekends in an hot kitchen. A restaurant is always

busy from 6:00 to 9:00 p.m. on weekdays and

from 5:00 p.m. to 11:00 p.m. on Fridays and

Saturdays. Pierre doesn't have some time

to rest. Pierre wants his boss to hire some

more people, but his boss won't do it.

Pierre is looking for the better job.

Go to MyEnglishLab for more focused practice.

EXERCISE 10 LISTENING

▶26|06 **A** Listen to the conversation. Miguel is helping Theresa prepare for a party. Check (✓) the food Miguel buys.

☐ cheese   ☐ ice   ☐ nuts   ☐ soda

☑ chips   ☐ ice cream   ☐ salsa   ☐ tuna

▶26|06 **B** Listen again. Answer the questions.

1. What's the problem? _____

2. Why is Miguel upset? _____

▶26|06 **C** Listen again. Work with a partner. Talk about the food that Miguel buys for the party. Is it the same food you buy for parties? What food do you buy?

EXAMPLE: A: Miguel buys soda. I don't buy any soda for parties. My friends don't drink soda. They drink water or juice.

B: I buy soda, but I never buy . . .

EXERCISE 11 I'D LIKE SOME EGGS

ROLE PLAY Work in groups of three. Two students are customers at a diner. The third student is the server. Look at the breakfast menu. Role-play a conversation about ordering food.

EXAMPLE: A (SERVER):   Good morning. Can I get you some water?

B (CUSTOMER 1): Yes, please.

C (CUSTOMER 2): Yes, but please don't give me any ice.

A (SERVER):   OK. Are you ready to order?

B (CUSTOMER 1): Yes. I'd like . . .

« « BREAKFAST SPECIALS » »

SPECIAL 1 $5.99
Juice: orange, grapefruit, or pineapple
Cereal: hot or cold
Toast or bagel
Coffee or tea

SPECIAL 2 $8.99
Juice: orange, grapefruit, or pineapple
Two eggs served with potatoes or fruit
Toast or bagel
Coffee or tea

SPECIAL 3 $8.99
Juice: orange, grapefruit, or pineapple
Pancakes or waffles
Coffee or tea

EXERCISE 12 A RESTAURANT RECOMMENDATION

A PRESENTATION You are going to talk about a restaurant. First, think about a restaurant you know and like. Take notes in the chart about the restaurant. Use the phrases in the box or your own ideas.

Food: delicious, spicy, bland, simple, rich, salty, sweet
  Any vegetarian choices? Any dairy-free choices?

Service and servers: fast, slow, polite, friendly, helpful

Atmosphere: comfortable, romantic, modern, traditional, noisy, quiet
  Any music?

Cost: inexpensive, reasonable, expensive
  Any discounts?

Location: near public transportation, free parking

Restaurant	
Food	
Service / Servers	
Atmosphere	
Cost	
Location	

B Work in a group. Tell your group about your restaurant. Answer their questions.

EXAMPLE: A: I really like the restaurant Bella Vista.
  B: Where is it?
  A: It's on Main Street. There isn't any free parking, but it's near buses and trains.
  C: What kind of food does it have?
  A: Italian food.
  D: How is . . . ?

Go to MyEnglishLab for more communication practice. Articles with Count and Non-Count Nouns; *Some / Any*

A BEFORE YOU WRITE Read a student's review of a school cafeteria. Then think about a place to eat near your school. It can be a school cafeteria, a restaurant, or a take-out place. Rate the place (★) and the cost ($), and give the address and phone number. Take notes about it in the chart.

✪✪ Fairfax University Cafeteria ⑤

40 Union Square, Middletown, NJ 07748
555-459-0909

You're hungry. You don't have a lot of time or money. Where can you get something to eat? Try the cafeteria at Fairfax University. There aren't any servers because it's a self-service restaurant, but there's never a long wait. Some dishes are not very good, so be careful what you order. The vegetables and spaghetti are overcooked, but there are some delicious sandwiches. So, if you want some quick and cheap food, check out Fairfax University Cafeteria.

Rating scale:

✪✪✪✪ = excellent
✪✪✪ = good
✪✪ = fair
✪ = poor

⑤⑤⑤ = expensive
⑤⑤ = moderate prices
⑤ = inexpensive

Name of Restaurant	
Rating	
Cost	
Food Quality	
Atmosphere	
Service	

B WRITE Write a review of a place to eat near your school. Use the review in A and your chart. Use *a*, *an*, *the*, *some*, and *any* with nouns.

C CHECK YOUR WORK Read your paragraph in B. Underline articles, *some* and *any*, and nouns in your paragraph. Use the Editing Checklist to check your work.

Editing Checklist

Did you...?

☐ use *a* or *an* with singular count nouns, not non-count nouns
☐ use *a* or *an* when it is not clear which person or thing you mean
☐ use *the* when it is clear which person or thing you mean
☐ use *some* with affirmative statements
☐ use *any* with negative statements and questions

D REVISE YOUR WORK Read your paragraph again. Can you improve your writing? Make changes if necessary.

Go to MyEnglishLab for more writing practice.

UNIT 26 REVIEW

Test yourself on the grammar of the unit.

Ⓐ **Complete the sentences. Choose the correct answers.**

1. The baby spilled his milk. I need <u>some</u> / a napkins.

2. Please pass a / <u>the</u> salt.

3. Will you buy <u>a</u> / an avocado for the salad?

4. We didn't find <u>any</u> / some apples at the store.

Ⓑ **Change the sentences to the negative.**

1. We need some glasses. _____

2. I want some help. _____

3. There are some menus on the table. _____

4. He has some free time. _____

Ⓒ **Complete the sentences with *a*, *an*, or *the*.**

We bought Grandpa _____ watch and _____ tie. I hope he liked _____
....1. ....2. ....3.
watch. He didn't like _____ tie. Next year, we'll take him to _____ restaurant. He
..............................4. ....5.
always likes _____ good meal.
..................6.

Ⓓ **Correct the conversations. There are six mistakes.**

1. A: What are you looking for?

   B: I need a stamps. I wrote any letters, and I want to mail them.

2. A: A refrigerator looks empty. There isn't some yogurt.

   B: There aren't an eggs either. We need to go shopping, but we don't have a time

   today. Let's go shopping tomorrow.

Now check your answers on page 450.

Go to MyEnglishLab to complete the review online.

How much and *How many*; Quantifiers

DESSERTS

OUTCOMES
- Ask about quantities of things
- Describe quantities with *a lot, a few, a little, much,* and *many*
- Recognize details in a conversation about food
- List ingredients mentioned in a conversation about a recipe
- Discuss recipes and different kinds of food
- Write a conversation between a shopper and a clerk

STEP 1	GRAMMAR IN CONTEXT

BEFORE YOU READ

Work with a partner. Answer the questions.

1. Do you have a favorite dessert? What is it?

2. Where is it from?

3. What's in it?

READ

⊙ 27|01 **Read this conversation between two students.**

International Desserts

Once a month, students in Robert Fertita's English class bring a dessert from their country. Wasana and Carlos are two students in Robert's class.

WASANA: Carlos, try some of my dessert. It's very popular in Thailand.

CARLOS: OK, thanks, Wasana.

WASANA: How much do you want?

CARLOS: Just a little. That's enough.... Hmm. It's not bad.

WASANA: What do you mean, not bad? It's delicious.

CARLOS: Actually, it *is* pretty good. It's just that color.... I don't usually eat purple rice. What's in it?

WASANA: Well, there's white and black rice, coconut milk, sugar, salt, and mangoes. It's not hard to prepare.

CARLOS: Maybe I'll try to make it. How much rice do you use?

WASANA: A cup of white rice and a cup of black rice. The black rice gives it that dark color.

CARLOS: How much coconut milk?

WASANA: Two cups.

CARLOS: And how many mangoes?

WASANA: Three.

CARLOS: I love mangoes. I have a few in my refrigerator right now. I have an idea. I'll buy the rest of the ingredients and watch you prepare the dessert.

WASANA: OK. But then you have to show me how to make those delicious cookies from Colombia.

CARLOS: You mean the ones with the dulce de leche[1] filling? I can't. I just go to the grocery store and buy them. They sell them all over my neighborhood.

---

1 *dulce de leche:* a dish made with sweetened milk

AFTER YOU READ

Ⓐ VOCABULARY Complete the sentences with the words from the box.

ingredients	in season	neighborhood	prepare	pretty good	taste

1. This lemon chicken has an amazing _____. What's in it?

2. Peaches are not _____ right now, so I bought apples.

3. It takes two hours to _____ that dish.

4. There are two good fruit and vegetable stores in my _____.

5. This cake is _____, but I prefer the pie.

6. Do you know the _____ of this pie? I want to make it.

Ⓑ COMPREHENSION Read the questions. Circle the correct answers.

1. How much of Wasana's dessert does Carlos want to taste?
   a. a lot   **b.** a little

2. How many types of rice does Wasana use in her dessert?
   a. two   **b.** three

3. How much coconut milk does Wasana use?
   a. one cup   **b.** two cups

4. How many mangoes does Wasana use?
   a. two   **b.** three

5. How much time does Carlos spend preparing his dessert?
   a. a little time   **b.** no time

Ⓒ DISCUSSION Work with a partner. Compare your answers in B. Then make three false statements about the conversation. Your partner corrects them.

HOW MUCH AND *HOW MANY*; QUANTIFIERS

Questions with *How Much*		
How much	Non-count Noun	
How much	milk	do you need?

Answers
Quantifier
A lot. (A lot of milk.) **Two quarts.** (Two quarts of milk.) **A carton.** (A carton of milk.) **A glass.** (A glass of milk.) **A cup.** (A cup of milk.) **A little.** (A little milk.) **Not much.** (Not much milk.)

Questions with *How Many*		
How many	Plural Count Noun	
How many	apples	do we need?

Answers
Quantifier
A lot. (A lot of apples.) **One bag.** (One bag of apples.) **Two pounds.** (Two pounds of apples.) **One or two.** (One or two apples.) **A few.** (A few apples.) **Not many.** (Not many apples.)

GRAMMAR NOTES

1   *How much* and *How many*

Use *how much* or *how many* to **ask about the quantity** of something.	
Use *how much* before **non-count nouns**.	**How much *juice*** do you have?
Use *how many* before **count nouns**.	**How many *lemons*** do you need?
USAGE NOTE We don't always repeat the noun after *how much* or *how many* if the listener knows the noun the speaker is talking about.	**How much** does it cost? *(= How much money is it?)* A: I bought cupcakes. B: **How many** did you buy? *(= How many cupcakes did you buy?)*

2 Quantifier: *A lot of*

Use *a lot of* for **large amounts**. You can use *a lot of* in **affirmative statements**, **negative statements**, and **questions**.

Use *a lot of* + **plural count nouns**.	There are **a lot of *nuts*** in the cake. There aren't **a lot of *berries*** in the pie. Are there **a lot of *cookies*** in the kitchen?
You can also use *a lot of* + **non-count nouns**.	There is **a lot of *sugar*** in my tea.
BE CAREFUL! We use *a lot*, not *a lot of*, to answer questions.	A: How many nuts did you eat? B: **A lot.** NOT ~~A lot of.~~

3 Quantifiers: *Much, Many*

Use *much* and *many* for **large amounts**.

Use *much* before **non-count nouns** in negative statements and questions.	There isn't **much *juice***. How **much *milk*** is there?
Use *many* before **plural count nouns** in affirmative statements, negative statements, and questions.	There are **many *oranges*** in the refrigerator. There aren't **many *eggs***. Are there **many *cupcakes***? How **many *apples*** are there?
We can use *Not much* or *Not many* to talk about small amounts when we answer questions with *how much* or *how many*.	A: **How much** milk is left? B: **Not much.** A: **How many** cupcakes did you buy? B: **Not many.**
USAGE NOTE In speaking, we usually use *A lot*, not *Much* or *Many*, to answer questions with *how much* or *how many*.	A: **How much** juice did he drink? B: **A lot.** A: **How many** oranges did he eat? B: **A lot.**
BE CAREFUL! We usually do not use *much* in affirmative statements in conversation and informal writing. We use *a lot of*.	There's **a lot of** milk in the refrigerator. NOT There is ~~much milk~~ in the refrigerator.

4 Quantifiers: *A few, A little*

Use *a few* and *a little* for **small amounts**.

Use *a few* + **count nouns**.	There are **a few *apples*** in the refrigerator.
Use *a little* + **non-count nouns**.	There is **a little *milk*** left.

5 Counting Non-Count Nouns

Use measure words or containers + *of* to count non-count nouns.

A quart, *a liter*, and *a teaspoon* are **measure words**. They give an exact amount.	We need **a quart of milk**. He drank **a liter of water**. Add **2/3 of a cup of sugar**.
A glass and *a box* are **containers**.	I drank **two glasses of lemonade**. We bought **a box of cereal**.

REFERENCE NOTE

For a list of expressions used for **quantifying non-count nouns**, see Appendix 12 on page 435.

Go to MyEnglishLab to watch the grammar presentation.

STEP 3 FOCUSED PRACTICE

EXERCISE 1 DISCOVER THE GRAMMAR

GRAMMAR NOTES 1–4 Underline the noun in each phrase. Then check (✓) the kind of noun it is.

	Singular Count Noun	Plural Count Noun	Non-Count Noun
1. a <u>recipe</u>	✓	☐	☐
2. how much milk	☐	☐	☐
3. how many eggs	☐	☐	☐
4. a lot of raisins	☐	☐	☐
5. a few nuts	☐	☐	☐
6. a little juice	☐	☐	☐
7. an orange	☐	☐	☐

EXERCISE 2 *HOW MUCH*, *HOW MANY*, AND *A LOT*

GRAMMAR NOTES 1–3 Complete the conversations with *How much* or *How many*. Complete the answers with *Not much*, *Not many*, or *A lot*.

1. A: _____How many_____ cookies do you prepare in a week?

   B: _____A lot_____. We bake for everyone at work. We bake a few dozen each week.

2. A: _____ time does it take you to bake that cake?

   B: _____. Only about an hour and a half, including the baking time.

3. A: _____ different kinds of cupcakes do they offer?

   B: _____. There are only two or three choices.

4. A: _____ do they spend on ice cream each week?

   B: _____. They only eat ice cream when friends come over.

5. A: _____ sugar do you use in your muffins?

   B: _____. I don't like muffins that are too sweet.

6. A: _____ eggs did you buy?

   B: _____. Three dozen. I use eggs when I cook, and we all eat eggs
   for breakfast.

7. A: _____ people did you invite?

   B: _____. I invited all my friends and relatives, and I have many friends
   and a big family.

EXERCISE 3 *MANY* AND *MUCH*

GRAMMAR NOTE 3 **Complete the sentences with *many* or *much*.**

If you don't have ___*much*___ time to bake and you're having a party, go to Martha's
                          1.

Bakery. Martha's Bakery has _____ delicious desserts. People from all over the city
                                    2.

go to Martha's Bakery, and _____ restaurants get desserts from Martha's Bakery,
                                 3.

too. There isn't _____ parking near the bakery, so it's best to use public
                      4.

transportation. If you need good bread, they sell _____ different kinds of bread and
                                                          5.

rolls. So, remember: You won't have _____ work or worry if you use Martha's
                                            6.

Bakery for your next party.

EXERCISE 4 *MANY, MUCH,* AND NOUNS

GRAMMAR NOTE 3 **Complete the conversations. Use *many* or *much* and the words from the box.**

choices	information	people	stores	time	~~traffic~~

1. A: How long did it take you to get to the café yesterday?

   B: There wasn't _____ *much traffic* _____, but it still took us a half an hour to get there.

2. A: It was a holiday. Were _____ open?

   B: Yes. A lot of people like to shop on holidays.

3. A: Was your boyfriend with you?

   B: Yes, but he didn't have _____. We got to the café at 8:15, and he had to leave for work at 9:00.

4. A: How _____ were you with?

   B: There were six of us. We went to a café on Elm Street.

5. A: How were the desserts?

   B: Delicious, but there weren't _____. They only had apple pie or chocolate cake.

6. A: What were the ingredients in the apple pie?

   B: I don't know. There wasn't _____ about ingredients on the menu!

EXERCISE 5 *A FEW, A LITTLE, MUCH, MANY,* AND *A LOT OF*

GRAMMAR NOTES 2–4 **Complete the sentences. Circle the correct answers.**

1. We need to get some more apples. We only have (a few)/ a little left.

2. There's a few / a little yogurt in the refrigerator. I didn't finish it all.

3. There's just many / a little milk left. We need to buy more.

4. I want to buy a lot of / much muffins. My grandparents are visiting us, and they love muffins.

5. We don't have many / much cheese. Let's add that to our shopping list.

6. Much / A lot of these rolls are stale. I'll stop at the bakery and buy some fresh ones.

7. Hurry. There isn't many / much time. The store will close in half an hour.

EXERCISE 6 CONTAINERS

A GRAMMAR NOTE 5 **Look at the pictures. Complete the conversation. Circle the correct answers.**

blender

can

jar

pint

container

tablespoon

GRACE: Can you tell me how to make your berry dessert drink?

BRAD: Sure. First, buy a (can) / box of chickpeas, a <u>container / jar</u> of orange juice, a <u>bag / pint</u>
                     1.   **2.**   **3.**
       of fresh strawberries, and a <u>box / jar</u> of honey.
                                      4.

GRACE: And then what do you do?

BRAD: I put the <u>can / box</u> of chickpeas, one and a half <u>cups / bags</u> of orange juice, two
                      5.   **6.**
       <u>cups / cans</u> of strawberries, and two <u>tablespoons / cans</u> of honey in a blender. When
       7.   **8.**
       it's smooth, I add six ice cubes. Then I blend it again. It's delicious!

▶27|02 **B** LISTEN AND CHECK **Listen to the conversation and check your answers in A.**

EXERCISE 7 EDITING

GRAMMAR NOTES 1–5 **Read the conversations. There are seven mistakes. The first mistake is already corrected. Find and correct six more.**

1. A: How ~~much~~ ^{many} cookies are there in the box?

   B: Only one. Mary ate the rest.

2. A: How much soda do we need for the party?

   B: Just a few. We have a lot juice and water.

3. A: How many flour do you need?

   B: Two cups.

4. A: How many egg are there in the cake? And how much sugars?

   B: Four eggs and three cup of sugar.

EXERCISE 8 LISTENING

▶27|03 Ⓐ **Listen to a conversation about a recipe for baklava. Read the statements. Check (✓) *True* or *False*.**

	True	False
1. Laura thinks Murat's baklava tastes good.	☐	☐
2. The recipe is a family secret.	☐	☐
3. Laura will tell Murat about her baklava.	☐	☐

▶27|03 Ⓑ **Listen again. Check (✓) the ingredients in the recipe.**

☐ apple ☐ chopped nuts ☐ cream ☐ phyllo dough ☐ vanilla extract
☑ butter ☐ cinnamon ☐ honey ☐ sugar ☐ water

▶27|03 Ⓒ **Listen again. Take notes on the amount of each ingredient in the baklava. Then ask your partner the amount of each ingredient.**

EXAMPLE: A: How much butter do you need for the baklava?
B: A cup. You need the butter for the pan. How many nuts?

EXERCISE 9 WHAT DO YOU KNOW ABOUT DESSERTS?

Ⓐ GAME **Work in a group. Read the questions. Discuss. Then circle the correct answers.**

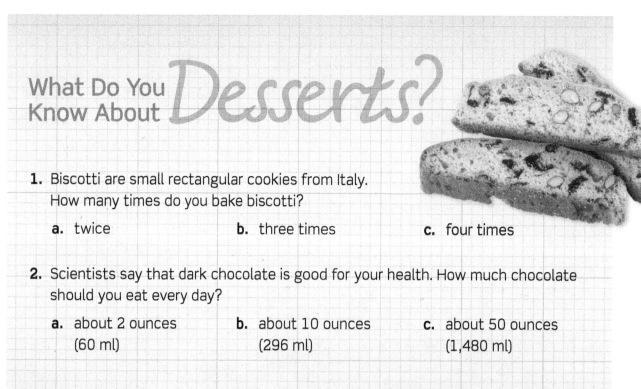

What Do You Know About *Desserts?*

1. Biscotti are small rectangular cookies from Italy. How many times do you bake biscotti?

   a. twice   **b.** three times   **c.** four times

2. Scientists say that dark chocolate is good for your health. How much chocolate should you eat every day?

   a. about 2 ounces (60 ml)   **b.** about 10 ounces (296 ml)   **c.** about 50 ounces (1,480 ml)

3. Chocolate companies make a lot of money. How much is the chocolate industry worth today?

   a. about 100 million dollars

   b. about 10 billion dollars

   c. about 100 billion dollars

4. A lot of chocolate comes from Africa. How much of the world's cocoa comes from Africa?

   a. less than half

   b. about two-thirds

   c. almost all

5. The Brussels Airport is the biggest seller of chocolate in the world. How many pounds of chocolate do vendors sell there every day?

   a. about 500

   b. about 1,000

   c. about 2,000

6. You need milk to make ice cream. How many gallons of milk do you need to make one gallon of ice cream?

   a. two

   b. three

   c. four

7. In the late nineteenth century, cupcake recipes were simple. They used four eggs, three cups of flour, and two cups of sugar. They also used butter. How much butter did they use?

   a. one cup

   b. two cups

   c. five cups

8. The "Black Diamond" is a dessert at a café in Dubai. It consists of a scoop of vanilla ice cream with Italian truffles, Iranian saffron, and gold flakes. How much does this ice cream dessert cost?

   a. $78

   b. $817

   c. $1,718

9. Americans buy a lot of chocolate on Valentine's Day. How many pounds of chocolate do they buy every year on Valentine's Day?

   a. 28 million pounds

   b. 48 million pounds

   c. 58 million pounds

10. There's a World Custard Pie Throwing Championship every year in England. You get 2 points for a hit on the arm. You get 3 points for a hit on the chest. How many points do you get for a hit in the face?

    a. 4 points

    b. 5 points

    c. 6 points

B Check your answers on page 453. The group with the most correct answers wins.

EXERCISE 10 COOKIES AND PIE

INFORMATION GAP Work with a partner. Student A will follow the instructions below. Student B will follow the instructions on page 458.

STUDENT A

- Look at the list of ingredients for chocolate chip cookies. Ask Student B questions to find out how much you need of each ingredient to make chocolate chip cookies. Write the amounts to complete the recipe.

EXAMPLE: A: How much flour do you need for the chocolate chip cookies?
B: Two and half cups.

Chocolate Chip Cookies

7 ounces chocolate chips

_____ flour

_____ teaspoons
baking powder

1 cup chopped walnuts

_____ butter

_____ sugar

_____ brown sugar

_____ eggs

1 teaspoon vanilla extract

- Now look at the list of ingredients for apple pie. Answer Student B's questions about apple pie.

EXAMPLE: B: How much flour do you need for the apple pie crust?
A: Two cups of flour.

Apple Pie

THE CRUST

2 cups flour

1 teaspoon salt

⅔ cup shortening
(= two-thirds of a cup)

5 tablespoons cold water

THE FILLING

⅓ cup sugar
(= a third of a cup)

¼ cup flour
(= one-quarter of a cup)

½ teaspoon ground cinnamon
(= half a teaspoon)

½ teaspoon ground nutmeg

a pinch of salt

8 medium-size apples

2 tablespoons butter

Go to MyEnglishLab for more communication practice.

A BEFORE YOU WRITE Ani, a student, is at a bakery. She's shopping for desserts for a class party. Read her conversation with the baker. Then make a list of desserts for a party for your class. Work with a partner. Tell your partner what you want to buy.

BAKER: May I help you?

ANI: Yes, thank you. I'd like a chocolate cake with chocolate filling.

BAKER: OK. How about this one?

ANI: It looks delicious. How much is it?

BAKER: Twenty-five dollars.

ANI: I'll take it.

BAKER: What else would you like?

ANI: I'd like a few of those red velvet cupcakes. How much are they?

BAKER: Two dollars each. How many would you like?

ANI: Ten, please.

Shopping List

_____

_____

_____

_____

_____

_____

_____

_____

_____

_____

B WRITE Write a conversation at a bakery. Use the conversation in A and your shopping list. Use *how much*, *how many*, and quantifiers.

C CHECK YOUR WORK Read your conversation. Underline *how much* and *how many* and the nouns they refer to. Circle quantifiers. Use the Editing Checklist to check your work.

Editing Checklist
Did you . . . ?
☐ use *how much*, *much*, and *a little* with non-count nouns
☐ use *how many*, *many*, and *a few* with plural count nouns
☐ use *a lot of*, *much*, and *many* for large amounts
☐ use *a little* and *a few* for small amounts

D REVISE YOUR WORK Read your conversation again. Can you improve your writing? Make changes if necessary.

UNIT 27 **REVIEW**

Test yourself on the grammar of the unit.

Ⓐ Complete the sentences with *How many* or *How much*.

1. _____ people went to the party?
2. _____ servers did they have?
3. _____ juice do you need?
4. _____ cups of coffee did he drink?
5. _____ food was left?

Ⓑ Write simple present questions with the words in parentheses. Begin with *How many* or *How much*.

1. _____
   (chocolate / you eat in a week)
2. _____
   (teaspoons of sugar / you take)
3. _____
   (time / you spend online)
4. _____
   (sisters / you have)
5. _____
   (coffee / you drink every day)

Ⓒ Complete the sentences. Circle the correct answers.

1. There isn't much / many food in the refrigerator.
2. There's a lot of / many snow in Alaska.
3. We bought a can / a can of pineapples.
4. He drinks a lot / a lot of tea.
5. We only spent a few / a little money on the party.

Ⓓ Correct the sentences. There are five mistakes.

1. There were only a little people at the meeting.
2. There are a few peach in the refrigerator.
3. How much eggs do you need?
4. How much bottles of juice did they buy?
5. There are not much books in their home.

Now check your answers on page 450.

Go to MyEnglishLab to complete the review online.

UNIT
28

Too many and Too much; Enough + Noun

THE RIGHT PLACE TO LIVE

OUTCOMES
- Use *too* + *much* / *many* / *few* / *little* and *not enough* to say there isn't a right amount of something
- Use *enough* to say there is a right amount of something
- Recognize details in an article about two cities
- Compare apartments described in a conversation
- Discuss the pros and cons of living in certain places
- Write a letter about problems in your town or city

STEP 1   GRAMMAR IN CONTEXT

BEFORE YOU READ

Think about the city you are in. Answer the questions.

1. Does your city or town have any of these problems? If so, check (✓) the problems.

☐ not enough jobs   ☐ too many people   ☐ too much pollution
☐ too few parks   ☐ too much noise   ☐ too much traffic

2. Where would you like to live?

READ

▶ 28|01   Read these student blog posts about two cities.

Dream Locations

Miami Beach, Florida   Some people call my town The American Riviera. Other people say it's the Latin Hollywood. For me, it's a great place to live. We have sunny weather, beautiful beaches, and palm trees. From January to March the sky is blue, and the temperature is in the 70s F (20s C). There are a lot of water activities, the nightlife is great, and it's a very cosmopolitan area.

But it's not perfect. In the summer months, the weather is hot and humid, and storms are common. Public transportation isn't very good. There are too few buses, and there isn't a subway, so there's often too much traffic. In addition, there aren't enough jobs. Unemployment is often high, and salaries are often low.

Some say that in Miami, they pay you in sunshine. But if you have a job, and you like warm weather, beautiful beaches, and a lively nightlife, Miami Beach is a great place to live.

—Jeff Medina

Tromsø, Norway   I find most cities have too much traffic, pollution, and crime. They also have too many people, and not enough trees and animals. That's why I love my town of Tromsø in the country of Norway. Here the air is clean, and you can hike and fish and see the stars at night. There isn't much crime, and there isn't too much traffic. But winters are long, and some people complain because there's too little sunlight. But I'm happy to live here far away from the noise and confusion of big city life.

—Astrid Enberg

AFTER YOU READ

A VOCABULARY **Complete the sentences with the words from the box.**

cosmopolitan	crime	pollution	transportation	unemployment	weather

1. The _____ here is awful. Summers are very hot, and winters are very cold.

2. The _____ from the factories is causing health problems among children in the area.

3. That's a very safe neighborhood. There is almost no _____.

4. This town has good public _____, so you don't need a car.

5. There are people from all over the world in that city. It's a very _____ place.

6. _____ is low here, so he expects to find a good job soon.

B COMPREHENSION **Read the statements. Check (✓) the city the person is describing.**

	Miami Beach	Tromsø
1. There are too many cars on the road.	☐	☐
2. It's a lively place.	☐	☐
3. It's sometimes very cold.	☐	☐
4. It's hot and humid for months.	☐	☐
5. It's a safe place to live.	☐	☐
6. There isn't enough sunlight in winter.	☐	☐

C DISCUSSION **Work with a partner. Compare your answers in B. Discuss: Which city do you prefer? Why?**

Go to MyEnglishLab for more grammar in context practice.

STEP 2 GRAMMAR PRESENTATION

TOO MANY AND *TOO MUCH*, *ENOUGH* + NOUN

Too many/Too few

	Too many/Too few	Plural Count Noun
There are	**too many**	**cars.**
	too few	**parking spaces.**

Too much/Too little

	Too much/Too little	Non-Count Noun
There is	**too much**	**noise.**
	too little	**light.**

***Enough* + Noun**

		Enough	Noun (Plural Count or Non-Count)
We	have	**enough**	**workers.**
	don't have		**money.**

GRAMMAR NOTES

1 *Too many* and *Too few*

Too many and ***too few*** have a **negative** meaning. They come before **plural count nouns**.

Too many means **more than the right amount**.

Too many students registered for the level 2 course.
(There was room for ten students. Fifteen students registered.)

Too few means **less than the right amount**.

Too few students registered for the level 3 course, so they canceled the class.
(Five registered. They needed seven to hold the class.)

2 *Too much* and *Too little*

Too much and ***too little*** have a **negative** meaning. They come before **non-count nouns**.

Too much means **more than the right amount**.

You gave me **too much change.**
(It cost three dollars. I gave you five dollars. You gave me three dollars change.)

Too little means **less than the right amount**.

We had **too little time.**
(We couldn't finish the test.)

BE CAREFUL! *Too much* or *too little* cannot come before an adjective. ***Too*** alone comes before an adjective.

It is **too cold.**
NOT It is too ~~much~~ cold.

Enough has a **positive** meaning. *Not enough* has a **negative** meaning. They come before **plural count nouns** or **non-count nouns**.

Enough means **the amount you need**.	There are **enough eggs**. *(We need six eggs, and we have six eggs.)* There's **enough sugar**. Is there **enough milk**? Are there **enough eggs**?
Not enough means **less than the amount you need**.	There are**n't enough apples**. *(We need three apples, but we only have two apples.)* There is**n't enough milk**.

REFERENCE NOTE

For more information about *too* + **adjective**, see Unit 33 on page 403.

Go to MyEnglishLab to watch the grammar presentation.

STEP 3 FOCUSED PRACTICE

EXERCISE 1 DISCOVER THE GRAMMAR

A GRAMMAR NOTES 1–3 Read about New York City. Underline *too much*, *too many*, *too few*, *too little*, *enough*, and the nouns that follow.

New York City

Many people call New York City the capital of the world. It has a great cultural life and offers a lot of things to do. There are almost <u>too many</u> <u>things</u> to do here. There are job opportunities, good health care, and a very cosmopolitan atmosphere. Some people call it the city that never sleeps.

But housing is very expensive. There are not enough homes for ordinary people. You pay a lot of money to live in an apartment the size of a closet. In addition, there are too few schools, and many schools are overcrowded. Often, there's too much traffic, and too many people work too many hours with too little time for themselves or their families.

Still, this is a city of opportunity, and I'd rather live here with over eight million other New Yorkers than any other place on earth.

B Look at the passage about New York City again. Write the noun that follows each *too* phrase below. Check (✓) the kind of noun it is.

		Non-Count Noun	Plural Count Noun
1. too many	*things*	☐	✓
2. not enough		☐	☐
3. too few		☐	☐
4. too much		☐	☐
5. too many		☐	☐
6. too many		☐	☐
7. too little		☐	☐

EXERCISE 2 *TOO MUCH* AND *TOO MANY*

GRAMMAR NOTES 1–2 Complete the sentences with *too many* or *too much* and the words from the box.

crime	noise	pollution	rats	storms	~~unemployment~~

1. Jobs are hard to find. There's _____ *too much unemployment* _____ in this town.

2. The climate isn't good. There are _____ .

3. The streets aren't safe. There's _____ .

4. It's often hard to breathe the air here. There's _____ .

5. There's _____ in that neighborhood. We can't sleep at night.

6. There are _____ in that area. They should get rid of them.

EXERCISE 3 *TOO LITTLE* AND *TOO FEW*

GRAMMAR NOTES 1–2 Complete the conversations. Circle the correct answers.

1. A: Is the new school open?

   B: No. They had (too little)/ too few time to finish it before the new school year.

2. A: The lines at this supermarket are so long!

   B: I know. They have too little/ too few cashiers. They need to hire more.

3. A: Why do you want to move?

   B: We really like our apartment, but we have too little / too few space. It's not comfortable here for the five of us.

4. A: Why did they cancel the course?

   B: <u>Too little / Too few</u> people registered for it.

5. A: Why do so many young people leave this town?

   B: There are <u>too little / too few</u> things to do here.

6. A: Why is the tree dying?

   B: There was <u>too little / too few</u> rain this spring.

7. A: Is this a good neighborhood for families?

   B: No. There are <u>too little / too few</u> playgrounds for children.

EXERCISE 4 *ENOUGH* AND *NOT ENOUGH*

GRAMMAR NOTE 3 **Complete the conversations. Use *is enough, isn't enough, are enough*, or *aren't enough* and the words from the box.**

bakeries	~~doctors~~	jobs	parks	plumbers	snow	trash cans

1. A: What's the problem?

   B: There _____ *aren't enough doctors* _____ in that hospital. The hospital needs to hire more of them.

2. A: Let's build a snowman, Mommy.

   B: OK, Livi. There _____ . It snowed all night long.

3. A: Look at all the garbage on the sidewalk.

   B: I know. There _____ in this area.

4. A: Why are many people moving away? Is it because they can't find work?

   B: No. There _____ in this area. But the weather is really bad.

5. A: I can't find anyone to fix my sink.

   B: I know. There _____ in this area.

6. A: I think there's going to be a new bakery in that empty store.

   B: That's too bad. There _____ bakeries around here. We really need a good fruit and vegetable market.

7. A: There _____ around here.

   B: I agree. Children need a place to run around and play.

EXERCISE 5 *TOO MUCH, TOO MANY, TOO FEW*, AND *TOO LITTLE*

GRAMMAR NOTES 1–2 **Complete the conversations with *too many, too much, too few,* or *too little*.**

1. A: Why don't you want to move to Rockford?

   B: The climate there is OK, but the health care is terrible. There are _____*too few*_____ doctors and hospitals.

2. A: What's wrong with Middletown?

   B: The climate. It gets _____ rain and humidity. It's wet most of the year.

3. A: How about moving to Newtown?

   B: It's boring. There are _____ things to do there.

4. A: Do you go to that beach?

   B: Not in the summer. There are _____ people at that time of year. It's very crowded.

5. A: Did you buy the house?

   B: No. It had _____ problems.

6. A: Did he get to Miami Beach when he was in Florida for business?

   B: No, he didn't. He had _____ time.

EXERCISE 6 *TOO* AND *ENOUGH*

GRAMMAR NOTES 1–3 **Complete the sentences. Circle the correct answers.**

1. A: Why are there (too few) / enough math teachers in your city?

   B: People with math degrees work for the big companies. The salaries are higher.

2. A: There are not enough / too many cars on the highway today.

   B: You're right. Let's take a different route.

3. A: Is unemployment high in this area?

   B: No. There are too few / enough places to work around here, so most people have jobs.

4. A: Are you going to rent an apartment in this area?

   B: I don't know. I have too little / too much information about this town. I don't want to move before I find out more about the area.

5. A: I don't have too little / enough time to finish my composition. Can I hand it in tomorrow?

   B: Yes, but no later than tomorrow.

EXERCISE 7 EDITING

GRAMMAR NOTES 1–3 Read the conversations. There are six mistakes. The first mistake is already corrected. Find and correct five more.

1. A: What's wrong with that company?

   B: There are too many managers and too ~~little~~ *few* workers.

2. A: Did you buy that apartment?

   B: No. It was too money for too few space.

3. A: Don't go by bus. It will take too many time. Take the train. It's a lot faster.

   B: But the bus is half the price.

4. A: He doesn't take vacations enough. He works seven days a week.

   B: That's not good. Everyone needs a break from work.

5. A: There aren't enough restaurants in my town.

   B: There are too much in my town. There are restaurants everywhere.

> Go to MyEnglishLab for more focused practice.

STEP 4   COMMUNICATION PRACTICE

EXERCISE 8 LISTENING

▶28|02 **A** Ben and Sandy looked at three apartments. Listen to their conversation with a real estate salesperson. Which apartment did they like the most? Circle the correct answer.

a. the first one   **b.** the second one   **c.** the third one

▶28|02 **B** Listen again and complete the chart about the things Ben and Sandy liked and didn't like about the apartments.

	What They Liked	What They Didn't Like
First apartment	*beautiful street*	
Second apartment		
Third apartment		

C Work with a partner. The apartments that Sandy and Ben looked at had some problems. Discuss your own apartment. Does it have any of the same problems?

EXAMPLE: A: My apartment has enough space, but there are too few closets. How about your apartment?

B: My apartment doesn't have enough space. Also, there's too much . . .

EXERCISE 9 THERE ARE TOO FEW PARKING SPACES

A DISCUSSION Work in a small group. Talk about things you don't like in the town or city you are in. Use *too much*, *too many*, *too few*, *too little*, or *(not) enough*. Then write three of your ideas on the board. Write complete sentences.

There are too few parking spaces downtown.

There aren't enough movie theaters in this town.

B Compare your sentences with those of other groups. Talk about ways to change the bad things in your city.

EXAMPLE: A: There are too few parking spaces downtown.

B: That's a problem, but the real problem is the buses and trains. People drive because there aren't enough buses and trains. . . .

EXERCISE 10 THE CITY VERSUS THE SUBURBS

ROLE PLAY Work with a partner. One partner likes living in a big city. The other partner likes living in the suburbs. Act out a conversation about the pros and cons of the two places. Use *too much*, *too many*, *too few*, *too little*, or *(not) enough* in your conversation.

EXAMPLE: A: I like living in the city. I work in the city, and I don't want to drive from the suburbs. It takes too much time.

B: But there are too many people there. It's usually very quiet and beautiful in the suburbs. . . .

A BEFORE YOU WRITE Read this letter to a newspaper. Look at the first chart. Then consider a problem in your area. Answer the questions about your problem in the second chart.

Not Enough Jobs for Young People

Young people are the future of this city, but there are not enough jobs for them here. Too many young people have nothing to do. The city needs to help them find jobs. In the past, the city spent too much money on highways and bridges. It spent too little money on job training. Many young people don't have good workplace skills. The city needs to offer job training and practical skills. The city needs to offer courses in how to write a résumé, do an interview, and get and keep a job. Another problem is that too many young people are getting into trouble. With good jobs, young people will stay out of trouble. It's time to act now.

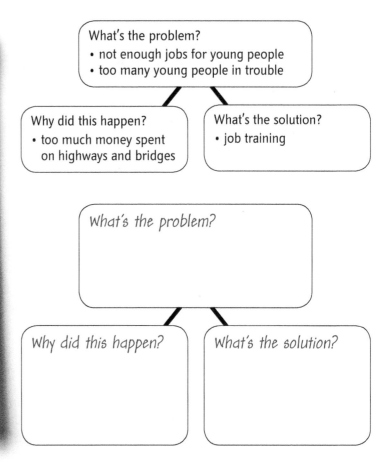

What's the problem?
• not enough jobs for young people
• too many young people in trouble

Why did this happen?
• too much money spent on highways and bridges

What's the solution?
• job training

What's the problem?

Why did this happen?

What's the solution?

B WRITE Write a letter to a newspaper about a problem in your city. Use the letter in A and your chart. Use *too much, too many, too few, too little,* or *(not) enough.*

C CHECK YOUR WORK Read your letter. Underline *too much, too many, too few, too little,* and *(not) enough* in your letter. Use the Editing Checklist to check your work.

Editing Checklist

Did you use...?

☐ *too many* and *too few* before plural count nouns

☐ *too much* and *too little* before non-count nouns

☐ *enough* or *not enough* before plural count nouns or non-count nouns

☐ *too many, too much, too few, too little,* and *not enough* to describe something negative

D REVISE YOUR WORK Read your letter again. Can you improve your writing? Make changes if necessary.

Go to MyEnglishLab for more writing practice.

UNIT 28 REVIEW

Test yourself on the grammar of the unit.

Ⓐ Add *too much* or *too many* to each sentence.

1. The child ate cookies. He has a stomachache.

2. We can't go to the movies today. We have homework.

3. I bought milk. How are we going to finish all of it?

4. There are trucks on that road. Let's take another route.

5. It takes time to get there by bus. Let's take the train.

Ⓑ Complete the sentences with *too much*, *too many*, *too little*, or *too few*.

1. We cooked _____ food. There's a lot left over.

2. Unemployment is high in that area. There are _____ jobs.

3. That town is not safe. There is _____ crime.

4. This area has _____ dishonest politicians.

5. I had _____ time to finish the test. I needed more time.

Ⓒ Complete the sentences with *enough* or *not enough*.

1. The grass is dry this summer. There was _____ rain in the spring.

2. There are _____ buses. If I miss a bus, I have to wait an hour for the next one.

3. We have _____ juice. Don't buy any more.

4. There aren't enough traffic lights on Oak Street, but there are _____ lights on Elm Street.

5. This soup needs something. Maybe there is _____ salt. I'll add some and see.

Ⓓ Correct the paragraph. There are five mistakes.

I want to move. I don't like the climate here. There's too many snow in winter. There are too little nice, sunny days. There's too many air pollution from all the traffic on the streets, and there aren't jobs enough. There also aren't enough park and places for children to play.

Now check your answers on page 451.

Go to MyEnglishLab to complete the review online.

Too many and *Too much*; *Enough* + Noun   **345**

Modals: Advice and Necessity

PART 10

OUTCOMES

- Give or ask for advice
- Recognize cultural customs described in a business article
- Recognize details in a conversation about a business trip
- Discuss business and cultural customs
- Talk about body language and its meaning
- Write a paragraph with advice on how to do business in your country

OUTCOMES

- Say what is necessary with *have to* and *must*, and what is not necessary with *not have to*
- Say what is not allowed with *must not*
- Understand requirements for a history class
- Recognize details in a conversation about college
- Discuss rules in different school settings
- Write a paragraph about school rules

Advice: *Should* and *Had better*

DOS AND DON'TS OF THE BUSINESS WORLD

OUTCOMES
• Give or ask for advice
• Recognize cultural customs described in a business article
• Recognize details in a conversation about a business trip
• Discuss business and cultural customs
• Talk about body language and its meaning
• Write a paragraph with advice on how to do business in your country

STEP 1   GRAMMAR IN CONTEXT

BEFORE YOU READ

Work with a partner. Answer the questions.

1. The people in the photo are shaking hands. When do you shake hands?
2. How do you greet people in your country?
3. A strong handshake is important in the United States. Is it important in other countries?

READ

▶29|01 Read this article about doing business in Chile and Egypt.

Global Business

As an international business person, you should learn the customs[1] of any place you are doing business. You don't want to insult someone because of your inappropriate behavior.[2] Here are a few suggestions for business people headed for Chile or Egypt. Let's start with Chile.

First of all, timing is important. When should you go? Chileans usually take vacations in January and February, so you'd better not plan your business trip at that time.

Next, how should you greet people at business meetings in Chile? You ought to shake hands with everyone. At business receptions, men greet other men with hugs, and women hug and touch cheeks while kissing the air. It shouldn't surprise you to get a hug or kiss from a Chilean.

Finally, when you eat, you should keep your hands on the table. If you're invited to someone's home, you should finish the food on your plate. It shows your appreciation[3] for the meal.

---

1 *customs:* the way people do things because it is traditional
2 *inappropriate behavior:* incorrect way of acting
3 *appreciation:* feeling of being grateful for something

Now let's turn to Egypt. In Egypt, you should not expect to do business on Fridays. It is the Muslim day of rest. Also, throughout the Arab world, people use both the Islamic calendar and the Western calendar. To avoid confusion, you should put two dates on paperwork—the Islamic date and the Western date.

If you're invited for a meal, you should eat with your right hand and leave a little food on your plate. It's a sign that you are full. Also, you'd better not add salt to your food or you might insult the cook.

These are just a few dos and don'ts when doing business in Chile and Egypt. Remember, before you go to another country to do business, read about the culture and remember the saying, "When in Rome, do as the Romans do."[4]

---

4 *When in Rome, do as the Romans do:* When in a foreign country, follow the example of the people there.

AFTER YOU READ

Ⓐ VOCABULARY Complete the sentences with the words from the box.

confusion	headed for	insult	receptions	timing

1. People usually wear suits at Chilean business _____.

2. There was a lot of _____ before Marco arrived and translated for us.

3. Don't give the workers such a low offer. It will _____ them.

4. They're reading about Japanese customs because they're _____ Japan.

5. I think he got the job because his _____ was right. He contacted them when they needed someone.

Ⓑ COMPREHENSION Read the statements. Check (✓) the country in which the statement is true.

	Chile	Egypt
1. It's not a good idea to plan meetings in January or February.	☐	☐
2. You ought to leave some food on your plate.	☐	☐
3. When you eat a meal here, keep your hands on the table.	☐	☐
4. You should not do business on a Friday.	☐	☐
5. You should try not to use your left hand when you eat.	☐	☐
6. It's OK to add salt to your food here.	☐	☐

Ⓒ DISCUSSION Work with a partner. Compare your answers in B. Then discuss: Are the statements in B true for the country you are in now?

Go to MyEnglishLab for more grammar in context practice.

ADVICE: *SHOULD, HAD BETTER*

Should, Shouldn't, and *Ought to*

Affirmative Statements

Subject	*Should / Ought to*	Base Form of Verb
I You He She We They	should ought to	go.
It	should ought to	be there.

Negative Statements

Subject	*Should not*	Base Form of Verb
I You He She We They	should not shouldn't	go.
It	should not shouldn't	be there.

Yes/No Questions

Should	Subject	Base Form of Verb	
Should	we he they	wear	a suit?

Short Answers

Affirmative			Negative		
Yes,	you he they	should.	No,	you he they	shouldn't.

Wh- Questions

Wh- Word	*Should*	Subject	Base Form of Verb
What	should	I	do?
When		we	go?

Had better and *Had better not*

Affirmative Statements

Subject + *Had better*	Base Form of Verb
We **had better** You**'d better**	go.

Negative Statements

Subject + *Had better not*	Base Form of Verb
We **had better not** You**'d better not**	go.

GRAMMAR NOTES

1 Should

Use *should* to **give advice** or talk about what is right or not right to do.	
Use *should* + the **base form** of the verb for **affirmative** statements.	He **should** *bring* them chocolates.
Use *should* + *not* + the **base form** of the verb for **negative** statements.	We **should not bring** roses.
Use negative contractions for speaking and informal writing.	We **shouldn't bring** roses.
You can use *should* to talk about the **present** or the **future**.	You **should** do the report now. *(present)* You **should** turn in the report tomorrow. *(future)*
Change the order of the subject and *should* to turn a statement into a **yes/no question** and most **wh- questions**.	**We should** give them a gift. **Should we** give them chocolate? What **should we** give them?
USAGE NOTE To sound more polite, use *I think* or *maybe* before saying *should*.	**I think** you **should** bring a small gift. **Maybe** we **should** ask him first.
BE CAREFUL! Do not use *to* after *should*.	You **should stand**. NOT You should ~~to~~ stand.
BE CAREFUL! Do not add *-s* to the verb that follows *should*.	He **should stand**. NOT He should ~~stands~~.

2 Ought to

Ought to means the same as *should*, but it is less common.	
Use *to* after *ought*, but not after *should*.	You **ought to read** that book about Chile. It's very helpful.
USAGE NOTE We rarely use *ought to* in **negative** **statements** or **questions**. We use *should* instead.	You **ought not to wear** that color. *(rare)* You **shouldn't wear** that color. *(more common)* **Ought I to wear** a suit? *(rare)* **Should I wear** a suit? *(more common)*

Use **had better** to **give advice**. *Had better* is stronger than *should*. It gives the idea that something bad might happen if you don't follow the advice.

Use **had better** + the **base form** of the verb for **affirmative** statements.	He **had better send** an email message.
Use **had better not** for **negative** statements.	He **had better not forget** his passport.
You can use *had better* to talk about the **present** or the **future**. The *had* in *had better* does not refer to the past.	I **had better** finish my report now. She **had better not** miss her flight tomorrow.
USAGE NOTE We often use *had better* in speaking, not writing. We usually use the short forms *'d better* or *'d better not*.	We**'d better** ask a doctor. You**'d better not** say that.

Go to MyEnglishLab to watch the grammar presentation.

STEP 3   FOCUSED PRACTICE

EXERCISE 1   DISCOVER THE GRAMMAR

A GRAMMAR NOTES 1–3 **Read the questions and answers about using business cards in Japan. Underline *should*, *ought to*, *had better*, and the base form of the verb.**

1. **Q:** When <u>should</u> I <u>present</u> my business card?

   A: Right after you shake hands or bow.

2. **Q:** Should I translate my card into Japanese?

   A: Yes. It's a good idea to have English on one side and Japanese on the other.

3. **Q:** What should I do when I get my colleague's card?

   A: Read it carefully. You ought to remember the information on it.

4. **Q:** Can we do business together before we exchange business cards?

   A: You'd better not do business before you exchange business cards.

Read the statements in A. Check (✓) *True* or *False*.

	True	False
1. You ought to present your business card before you shake hands.	✓	☐
2. You ought to translate your business card into Japanese.	☐	☐
3. You'd better not spend time reading your colleague's business card.	☐	☐
4. You'd better work together before you exchange business cards.	☐	☐

EXERCISE 2 *SHOULD* AND *SHOULDN'T*

GRAMMAR NOTE 1   **Some international students in the United States are comparing customs in different countries. Complete the sentences with *should* or *shouldn't* and the verbs in parentheses.**

1. In some cultures, people can clap hands to call a waiter. You _____*shouldn't do*_____
   (do)
   that here in the United States. I think here you _____ until the
   (wait)
   waiter looks at you.

2. I was in a school cafeteria in the United States. A guy had a cold. He blew his nose at the
   table. In Korea, you _____ your nose at the table. It's
   (blow)
   very impolite.

3. In China, you _____ people. Many people feel uncomfortable
   (touch)
   when others touch them. Here, I notice people touch more often.

4. I think that people in North America don't like silence. Someone is always talking. I guess
   you _____ too quiet here.
   (be)

5. In North America, people often say "We'll have to get together" or
   "I'll see you later." But they don't plan to meet me or see me
   later. In Poland, we don't do that. In my
   opinion, Americans and Canadians

   _____
   (say)
   "I'll see you later" when they really
   want to get together with you.

EXERCISE 3 *OUGHT TO* AND *SHOULDN'T*

GRAMMAR NOTE 2 **Complete the sentences. Complete the sentences with *ought to* or *shouldn't* and a verb from the box.**

become	~~bring~~	forget	invite	send	talk

1. We're going to the Abadis for dinner tomorrow night. We _____*ought to bring*_____ a gift.

2. We _____ to congratulate the Abadis. Their son graduated from law school last week.

3. I'd like to see the Abadis again, but we _____ them for dinner in January. They're going to be away the whole month.

4. Judy Abadi _____ a party planner. She's so good at planning parties.

5. I _____ to the Abadis about doing business in Morocco. I'm going there next month.

6. We had a wonderful time at their home. I _____ a thank-you note.

EXERCISE 4 *YOU'D BETTER* AND *YOU'D BETTER NOT*

GRAMMAR NOTE 3 **Complete the sentences with *'d better* or *'d better not* and the words in parentheses.**

1. In the United States, direct eye contact is a sign of honesty, but in other countries it is a sign of disrespect. You *'d better understand* _____ these differences when you
(understand)
   are meeting with people from different parts of the world.

2. You_____ the bottoms of your feet. In some cultures,
(show)
   it's not polite.

3. You_____ people when you go to China. They might
(hug)
   feel uncomfortable. It's not very common there.

4. You_____ about gift giving in their country. The wrong
(find out)
   gift may cause misunderstanding.

5. When you're at a business meeting in a place you don't know well,
   you_____ bright colors or casual clothes. In some
(wear)
   countries, business people don't like bright colors.

EXERCISE 5 *HAD BETTER* AND *HAD BETTER NOT*

GRAMMAR NOTE 3 **Read the sentences. Then rewrite the sentences with *had better* or *had better not* based on the information.**

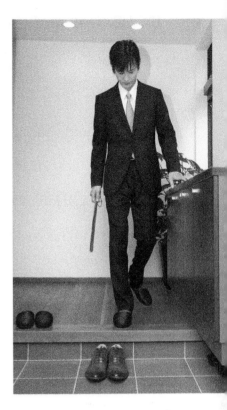

1. Take off your shoes when you visit a person's home in Japan. Japanese people don't wear shoes in their home.

   You had better take off your shoes when you visit a person's

   home in Japan.

2. Be on time when you do business in Germany. Business people in Germany don't like to be late.

   _____

   _____

3. Leave a little food on your plate when you are a dinner guest in China. This shows you like the food.

   _____

   _____

4. Do not touch a person's head in Thailand. The head is the most sacred part of the body.

   _____

5. Don't keep your hands in your pockets in Turkey. It's a sign of disrespect.

   _____

EXERCISE 6 *SHOULD* AND *HAD BETTER*

Ⓐ GRAMMAR NOTES 1, 2 **Add *should* to four more places in the conversations.**

       should
1. A: What I wear?
          ^

   B: You not wear jeans or shorts.

2. A: I think I insulted him.

   B: You apologize.

3. A: They were really helpful. I send them a thank-you note?

   B: That's a good idea.

4. A: I take my shoes off?

   B: Yes, please leave them by the door.

B Add *'d better* to four more places in the conversations.

1. A: I missed the train this morning.
   B: You <u>'d better</u> leave earlier tomorrow.

2. A: You not fly today. There's a bad hurricane and all the flights are late.

   B: Good idea. I'll change my flight and leave tomorrow.

3. A: Can I call John Baker now?

   B: I don't think so. He's on U.S. time. You call him at noon. You won't wake him then.

4. A: Is it OK to pay that bill on Friday?

   B: I don't think so. You pay it today.

5. A: I told John about my birthday. He not forget about it.

   B: John forgets everyone's birthday except his own.

EXERCISE 7 EDITING

GRAMMAR NOTES 1–3 **Read the conversations. There are six mistakes. The first mistake is already corrected. Find and correct five more.**

1. A: When ~~I should~~ *should I* go?

   B: You should to avoid going the last week in December. Many people are away at that time.

2. A: Ought I call people by their first name?

   B: No, you shouldn't. You better call them *Mr.* or *Ms.* and their family name.

3. A: Should he brings a gift?

   B: Yes, he should. I think he bring chocolate. Almost everyone loves chocolate.

Go to MyEnglishLab for more focused practice.

EXERCISE 8 LISTENING

▶29|02 **Ⓐ** Listen to a conversation between Max and his friends Sho and Kaori. Read the questions. Choose the correct answers.

1. Where is Max going?
   a. to China   **b.** to Japan

2. How is he getting there?
   a. by train   **b.** by plane

3. What is his first question about?
   a. traveling in Japan   **b.** paying for things

4. What is his second question about?
   a. greeting people   **b.** business meetings

5. What is his third question about?
   a. shoes   **b.** gifts

6. What does Sho want to do?
   a. be Max's translator   **b.** teach Japanese

▶29|02 **Ⓑ** Listen again. Write the advice to Max from his friends.

1. _____ cash.

2. _____ your shoes before you enter a home.

3. _____ some Japanese.

Ⓒ Work with a partner. Compare the customs in Japan with customs in other countries.

EXAMPLE: In Japan, you should bring cash, but in Germany, you shouldn't bring much cash. You can use a credit card almost everywhere.

EXERCISE 9 GIFT GIVING AROUND THE WORLD

(A) DISCUSSION Work with a partner. Answer the questions about gifts in your culture. Write your answers in your notebook. Then ask your partner the questions.

1. When should you bring a gift?

2. Is the way you wrap a gift important?

3. Should you open a gift right away or should you put it away for later?

4. How and when should you thank a person for a gift?

(B) Work in a group. Talk about gift giving in different cultures. Use your ideas from A.

EXAMPLE: A: In Argentina, you should bring a gift when someone invites you to dinner. The person should open your gift right away.

B: Really? In Colombia, you shouldn't open a gift in front of others.

C: We don't always open gifts right away in Senegal, but gifts aren't so important. In Senegal, you should bring a box of chocolates or French pastries when someone invites you to dinner.

EXERCISE 10 BODY LANGUAGE DOS AND DON'TS

(A) DISCUSSION Work with a partner. Body language is a way people speak without words. Use body language to talk to your partner. Say something with your head, hand, shoulders, arms, eyes, nose, or lips. Does your partner understand you?

(B) Work in a group. Discuss body language that you should or had better not use in different countries.

EXAMPLE: A: In Mexico, women should hold out their hand for a handshake first.

B: It's the same in Germany.

C: In Japan, people should bow when they meet an older person.

A: In Mexico, you'd better not bow. People in Mexico never bow.

Go to MyEnglishLab for more communication practice.

FROM GRAMMAR TO WRITING

A BEFORE YOU WRITE Read about what to call people in the United States. Then work with a partner. Tell your partner about ways of doing business in a culture you know well. Talk about one or more of the topics in the box.

In the United States, you had better be careful about using people's first names when you are doing business. In a business relationship, you should first call people by a title (for example: *Dr.*, *Ms.*, or *Mr.*) and their last names. You should wait for people to tell you to call them by their first names. Some people want to use first names, and others don't. There are no rules.

Managers of companies sometimes tell people to call them by their first names. You shouldn't think this means that you are good friends. It is a part of the culture.

Ways of Doing Business

being on time

eating habits

using business cards

dressing appropriately

tipping

using names and titles

B WRITE Give advice to someone who wants to do business in your country. Use the paragraphs in A and your ideas. Use *should*, *shouldn't*, *had better*, or *had better not*.

C CHECK YOUR WORK Read your paragraph in B. Underline *should*, *shouldn't*, *had better*, and *had better not*. Then use the Editing Checklist to check your work.

Editing Checklist

Did you . . . ?

☐ use *should* and *had better* for advice

☐ follow *should*, *shouldn't*, *had better*, and *had better not* with the base form of the verb

☐ check your spelling

D REVISE YOUR WORK Read your paragraph again. Can you improve your writing? Make changes if necessary.

Go to MyEnglishLab for more writing practice.

UNIT 29 REVIEW

Test yourself on the grammar of the unit.

Ⓐ Complete the sentences. Circle the correct answers.

1. You should to / should read that book.

2. We better / had better call the airline.

3. He shouldn't not / shouldn't wear that outfit for a business meeting.

4. We ought / ought to buy a small gift.

5. I'd better no / I'd better not call her now. She goes to bed early.

Ⓑ Complete the sentences with *had better* or *had better not* and the verb in parentheses.

1. You _____ to pay that bill. You don't want to pay a late fee.
   (forget)

2. She _____ the gift today. The stores will be closed tomorrow.
   (buy)

3. We _____ for them any longer. We'll miss our flight.
   (wait)

4. I _____ by train. The bus is too slow, and I need to be on time.
   (go)

Ⓒ Complete the sentences with *should* or *shouldn't* and a verb from the box.

call	forget	take	work

1. We _____ him to the hospital. He's in a lot of pain.

2. She _____ on that project alone. She needs to get help.

3. I _____ the plumber about that problem. He'll fix it.

4. You _____ your notes. You'll need them for your talk.

Ⓓ Correct the sentences. There are seven mistakes.

1. Where should we meets after work? Ought we go to Rainbow Diner?

2. We better take an umbrella tonight. It's going to rain.

3. Should I to make a reservation for my flight now? I think I outta make it soon.

4. What I should see during my business trip to Uruguay?

5. Should we leaves Brazil tonight or tomorrow?

Now check your answers on page 451.

Go to MyEnglishLab to complete the review online.

Necessity: *Have to* and *Must*

RULES AT SCHOOL

OUTCOMES
• Say what is necessary with *have to* and *must*, and what is not necessary with *not have to*
• Say what is not allowed with *must not*
• Understand requirements for a history class
• Recognize details in a conversation about college
• Discuss rules in different school settings
• Write a paragraph about school rules

STEP 1   GRAMMAR IN CONTEXT

BEFORE YOU READ

Work with a partner. Answer the questions.

1. What do you have to do for your English class? Check (✓) the activities.

   ☐ answer questions in class   ☐ do homework   ☐ wear a uniform

   ☐ do class presentations   ☐ sit in the same seat for each class   ☐ work in groups

2. Are there any school rules you don't like?

READ

▶ 30|01   Read this conversation between Professor Anderson and his students.

The First Day of Class

PROFESSOR: Welcome to American History 102. I'm Rich Anderson. This course covers the period from the American Civil War to the present day.[1] There will be a midterm and a final exam. Your average of the two tests has to be 65 percent or above to pass this course. In addition, there is a term paper.[2] The term paper must be at least ten pages, and you have to include a bibliography.[3] Here's more information about the term paper. . . . Now, are there any questions? . . . Yes?

JONATHAN: When is the term paper due?

PROFESSOR: You have to hand it in by the last day of class. That's December 15. It must not be late. You should hand in an outline by the fourth week of the term. My email address is on the board. You can email the outline to me. You

1 *present day:* today (usually used when talking about history)
2 *term paper:* students' most important written report of the semester
3 *bibliography:* a list of the books and articles used to write a paper

don't have to **give** me a hard copy.[4] However, I would like a hard copy of your paper. Any other questions? . . . Yes?

OLIVIA: Last semester, we **didn't have to buy** a textbook. Is there a textbook for this course?

PROFESSOR: Oh, yes. The textbook is called *American History from the Civil War to Today*.

OLIVIA: Who's the author?

PROFESSOR: I am.

OLIVIA: Do we **have to buy** the book?

PROFESSOR: Only if you don't want to fail the course.

---

4 *hard copy:* printed version

AFTER YOU READ

Ⓐ VOCABULARY **Complete the sentences with the words from the box.**

average	due	fail	midterm	outline	pass

1. To _____ this course, you must hand in a paper and do a group presentation.

2. There will be two tests this semester. The _____ will be on October 15, and the final exam will be December 10.

3. The _____ of 100, 95, 99, and 90 is 96.

4. If I don't study, I will _____ the course.

5. I can't meet you today. My term paper is _____ tomorrow.

6. I wrote a(n) _____ of each chapter to help me study for the test.

Ⓑ COMPREHENSION **Check (✓) what students in Professor Anderson's class have to do and don't have to do.**

	Students have to...	Students don't have to...
1. take a quiz every week	☐	☐
2. take a midterm and final exam	☐	☐
3. give a class presentation	☐	☐
4. hand in an outline	☐	☐
5. read four books for their term paper	☐	☐
6. buy the textbook	☐	☐

Ⓒ DISCUSSION **Work with a partner. Compare your answers in B. Then discuss: Which rules in the chart in B are true for your English class?**

Go to MyEnglishLab for more grammar in context practice.

NECESSITY: HAVE TO AND *MUST*

Have to: Affirmative Statements

Subject	*Have to / Has to*	Base Form of Verb	
I We You They	**have to**	**take**	a history class.
He She	**has to**	**repeat**	the class.
It	**has to**	**be**	three pages long.

Don't have to: Negative Statements

Subject	*Do not / Does not*	*Have to*	Base Form of Verb	
I We You They	**don't**	**have to**	**take**	a history class.
He She	**doesn't**		**repeat**	the class.
It	**doesn't**		**be**	three pages long.

Have to: Yes / No Questions

Do / Does	Subject	*Have to*	Base Form of Verb	
Do	I	**have to**	**study**	tonight?
	you			
	we			
	they			
Does	he			
	she			
	it		**be**	ten pages?

Short Answers

Affirmative				Negative			
	you	**do**.			you	**don't**.	
	I				I		
	you				you		
Yes,	they			No,	they		
	he	**does**.			he	**doesn't**.	
	she				she		
	it				it		

Subject	Must (not)	Base Form of Verb	
I You He She It We They	must must not	park	here.

Past of Have to and Must

Subject	Had to	Base Form of Verb
I You He She It We They	had to didn't have to	work.

GRAMMAR NOTES

1 Have to

Use *have to* + **the base form of the verb** to talk about things that are **necessary**.

Use *have to* for *I*, *you*, *we*, and *they*. Use *has to* for *he*, *she*, and *it*.	I **have to take** a test next week. He **has to pass** the test.
The past of both *have to* and *has to* is **had to**.	Last week, I **had to** take three tests.
BE CAREFUL! *Have to* is different in meaning from the verb *have*.	I have a good history textbook. (= I own the book.) I have to write a term paper. (= I need to write a term paper.)

2 Don't have to

Use *don't have to* + the **base form** of the verb to say that something is **not necessary**. It's not required. There is a choice.

Use *don't have to* for *I*, *you*, *we*, and *they*. Use *doesn't have to* for *he*, *she*, and *it*.	You **don't have to sit** there. *(You can sit in any seat.)* He **doesn't have to work** today. *(It's not required.)*

3 Must

You can also use **must + the base form of the verb** to talk about things that are **necessary**.	
The form of *must* does not change.	You **must pass** the midterm and final exams. She **must take** another test next week.
There is no past tense of *must*. Use **had to** to express something that was necessary in the past.	The children **had to wear** school uniforms last year.
BE CAREFUL! Do not use *to* after *must*.	He **must** write a report. **NOT** He ~~must to~~ write a report.
USAGE NOTE *Must* is less common than *have to* in speaking. In speaking, we usually use *must* to mean that we are almost certain of something.	He passed both tests. He **must** be happy.

4 Must not

Use **must not + the base form** of the verb to say that something is **not allowed**.	You **must not arrive** late for the test. Students **must not talk** during the test.
USAGE NOTE We rarely use *must not* in speaking, except when talking to small children or talking about rules. We use **can't** instead.	You **must not** cross the street here. *(talking to children)* You **can't** cross the street here. *(talking to adults)*

Go to MyEnglishLab to watch the grammar presentation.

STEP 3   FOCUSED PRACTICE

EXERCISE 1   DISCOVER THE GRAMMAR

Ⓐ GRAMMAR NOTES 1–4   Read about La Guardia High School. Underline all forms of *have to*, *don't have to*, *must*, and *can't* and the verbs that follow.

Nicki Minaj, a graduate of La Guardia High School

New York City has a special high school for music, art, dance, and drama. It's called La Guardia High School. The school is free, but students have to pass a test to get in. They also must have good grades. The school usually has about 9,000 applicants a year. It accepts about 650 students. All new students must audition[1] or

---
1 *audition:* give a short performance

show some of their art. Here are some of the requirements for students interested in art:

1. Each student must show the school eight to fifteen pieces of their artwork. The artwork does not have to be a special size, but all art has to be original.² Students can't use photocopies.

2. Each student must complete three drawing exercises. Students have to bring a pencil and their last report card. Students don't have to bring drawing materials. The school has all the necessary drawing supplies for the students.

---

2 *original art:* the actual piece of art, not a copy

Ⓑ Write two more sentences about La Guardia High School with *have* as the main verb.

1. <u>New York City has a special high school for music, art, dance, and drama.</u>

2. _____

3. _____

EXERCISE 2 *HAVE TO* AND *DON'T HAVE TO*

Ⓐ GRAMMAR NOTES 1–2 Complete La Guardia High School's audition requirements for dance. Use *have to* or *don't have to* and the verbs from the box.

attend	~~do~~	perform	return	spend	wear

Many people want to study dance at La Guardia High School. This is what they _____ *have to do* _____. Dance
1.
students _____ two classes: a ballet
2.
dance class and a modern dance class. Students who do well in the

classes _____ to the school for a
3.
second audition. At the second audition, students

_____ on stage for the admissions
4.
committee. Students _____ a lot of
5.
money on new dance outfits for their audition. They just

_____ a leotard and tights when
6.
they dance. There are lockers for their street clothes.

B Complete the audition requirements for music. Use *have to* or *don't have to* and the verbs from the box.

| bring | carry | do | ~~live~~ | play | sing |

LaGuardia High School students

_____ *have to live* _____ in New York City.
           1.

Music majors _____ the
             2.

following things to get into the school. To show their

musical talent, they _____ a
           3.

song, or they _____ an
          4.

instrument. Students _____
             5.

their own violin, flute, guitar, or any other small

instrument to their audition. Of course, they

_____ their piano or drums
         6.

to the school. The school will supply those instruments.

EXERCISE 3 *HAVE*, *HAVE TO*, AND *HAD TO*

GRAMMAR NOTE 1 **Complete the conversation with *have*, *have to*, *had*, or *had to*.**

PING: Would you like to go to the movies this evening?

BORIS: I can't. I _____ *have* _____ a test tomorrow. I _____ study this evening.
                 1.   **2.**

PING: A test, again? You _____ a test last week!
                          3.

BORIS: I know. We _____ a lot of tests. We _____ a test
                        4.   **5.**

        every Thursday.

PING: Wow. So, what do you _____ study tonight?
                            6.

BORIS: Grammar. I _____ review the modals *can*, *could*, *might*, and *must*.
                    7.

PING: Do you _____ memorize rules?
                 8.

BORIS: No. We _____ use the grammar to answer questions. We really
                 9.

        _____ understand it. We also _____ a review quiz after
         10.   **11.**

        every unit.

PING: I feel sorry for you. I don't like tests. Last year, I _____ take a test every
                                                12.

        two weeks, and I was always worried.

EXERCISE 4 *HAVE TO* AND *DON'T HAVE TO*

GRAMMAR NOTES 1–2 **Complete the sentences with *have to*, *has to*, *don't have to*, or *doesn't have to* and the verbs from the box.**

| attend | buy | hand in | pass | pay | say | wear | ~~work~~ |

1. In some classes, you often _____ *have to work* _____ in groups. Teamwork is important.

2. In some high schools, students can wear what they like. They _____ a uniform.

3. In many high schools, students _____ special tests or they can't go on to the next grade.

4. She _____ that book. She can borrow it from the library.

5. She _____ her term paper by December 15.

6. At Hugo's school, students _____ all classes unless they have a doctor's note.

7. My psychology class has many students. I _____ anything in class. I just have to pass the midterm and final exams.

8. Jay goes to a college near his home, so he _____ for room and board.

EXERCISE 5 *MUST* AND *MUST NOT*

GRAMMAR NOTES 3–4 **Read the signs in a school. Explain the rule. Begin with *Students must* or *Students must not*.**

NO SMOKING

SHOW ID

1. *Students must not smoke.* _____

2. _____

NO TEXTING

NO PHONES

3. _____

4. _____

5. _____   **6.** _____

_____   _____

EXERCISE 6 *MUST NOT, CAN'T, DON'T HAVE TO*, AND *DOESN'T HAVE TO*

GRAMMAR NOTES 2, 4 **Complete the sentences. Circle the correct answers.**

1. You (must not) / don't have to enter that room without a mask. There are dangerous chemicals inside.

2. You must not / don't have to sit in a special seat. Any seat is fine.

3. You can't / don't have to talk to anyone during the test. If you do, you will fail the test.

4. She did very well on the last test, so she must not / doesn't have to take this one.

5. You must not / don't have to look at your textbook during the test. It's not allowed.

6. He must not / doesn't have to wear a suit. He can wear pants and a button-down shirt.

7. She can't / doesn't have to bring any food into the testing center. She can eat after the test.

EXERCISE 7 EDITING

GRAMMAR NOTES 1–4 **Read the sentences. There are eight mistakes. The first mistake is already corrected. Find and correct seven more.**

1. We ~~has~~ *have* to learn a lot of new vocabulary words. I can't remember all of them.

2. To learn a new vocabulary word, you must hears it seven times.

3. She don't have to go to school on the weekend.

4. Avi is very smart. He doesn't has to study very much.

5. Our papers are due next week. I have start mine today.

6. We must not do any homework today. Tomorrow is a holiday.

7. You must not to bring any notes with you to the test.

8. You must to bring a photo ID to the testing center.

Go to MyEnglishLab for more focused practice.

EXERCISE 8   LISTENING

▶30|02   **A**   Ali is in his second year of college. He is speaking to an advisor about graduate school. Listen to the conversation. Choose the correct answers.

1. What's an MBA?
   a. a Manager in Business Arts   (**b.**) a Master of Business Administration

2. What is the GMAT?
   a. a test in English and math   **b.** a test in economics and accounting

3. What is Ali's major?
   a. economics   **b.** psychology

▶30|02   **B**   Listen again. Write one thing you have to do to get an MBA. Write one thing you don't have to do.

1. _____

2. _____

C   Work with a partner. Talk about schools you want to attend. Do you have to do any of the things Ali has to do to go to those schools? Talk about the requirements in the box or your own ideas.

get work experience	study psychology
have good grades	take a special test
major in economics	

EXAMPLE: A: I want to go to medical school.
            B: Do you have to get work experience?
            A: No. I have to . . .

EXERCISE 9   STUDENTS DON'T HAVE TO . . .

A   DISCUSSION   Prepare for a discussion in B. Read about two elementary schools.

Sunshine School believes students have to learn to make their own decisions. They have choices. For example, students don't have to take tests. They can write reports and give presentations instead. They don't have to wear uniforms. They can wear anything they like. They can miss a class, and they don't have to show a doctor's note. They can take a family vacation during the school semester, but then they have to give a presentation about it when they return. Students attend school from 9:00 a.m. to 12:00 p.m.

STANDOUT SCHOOL

Standout School believes that the school knows what is good for the children, and children must learn to follow rules. They have to stand when the teacher enters the class. They have to wear a school uniform. At Standout School, students have to take weekly tests. They also have to write reports and give presentations. They can only miss class for a doctor's appointment, and they have to show a note from the doctor when they return. Students have to attend school from 8:00 a.m. to 6:00 p.m.

B Work in small groups. Talk about the two schools in A. What do students have to do in the schools? Which school do you prefer? Why?

EXAMPLE: **A:** In Sunshine School, children don't have to take tests, but in Standout School they have to take a lot of tests. What do you think about that?
B: I don't like tests, so I think Sunshine school is better. What about you?
A: I think Standout School is better. . . .

EXERCISE 10 YOU HAVE TO WEAR A COSTUME ON TUESDAYS

A ROLE PLAY Work with a partner. Role-play a conversation. One of you is an old student. The other is a new student. The new student asks about the rules of the school. The old student makes up some funny or unusual rule.

EXAMPLE: **A:** So, Jobim, are there any rules I need to know about?
B: Oh, yes, Sezar. Remember this. On Tuesdays, you have to wear a costume. You can't wear regular clothes.
A: Really? What kind of costume do we have to wear?
B: Oh, you don't have to wear a special kind of costume. You can be an animal, a superhero, or something else.

B Perform your role play for the class. The class votes on the funniest or most unusual rule.

EXERCISE 11 HOW TO PREVENT CHEATING

A DISCUSSION Work in a group. Think about a school you went to in the past. How did teachers prevent cheating at the school? What did students have to do?

EXAMPLE: **A:** How did teachers prevent cheating at your school?
B: We had to take different tests in the same class. My test was different from my neighbor's test. How about in your school?
A: We had to. . . .

B Make a list of things students have to do at your school to prevent cheating in class. Use your ideas in A. Use *have to* or *must*.

EXAMPLE: At our school, students have to sit in every other seat during tests. Students must . . .

FROM GRAMMAR TO WRITING

A BEFORE YOU WRITE
Read about an elementary school. Then complete the chart about rules in your elementary school or a school you know about. Are the rules good for the children?

Children in Park Ridge Elementary School learn to respect the teachers and take care of the classroom. When the teacher enters the room, children must stand. They say, "Thank you for teaching us." Children have to clean the classroom. They have to wash the desks and clean the boards. In addition, children have to wear a school uniform. Most children like their school uniform. They are proud to wear it.

School Name	
Rule 1	
Rule 2	
Rule 3	
Rule 4	

B WRITE Write a paragraph about the rules of a school you know. Use the paragraph in A and your chart. Use *have to, had to, must, don't have to, didn't have to,* or *must not.*

C CHECK YOUR WORK Read your paragraph in B. Underline all forms of *have to* and *must* and the verb that follows. Then use the Editing Checklist to check your work.

Editing Checklist

Did you...?

- [ ] follow *have to* and *must* with the base form of the verb
- [ ] use *have to* or *must* for rules in the present
- [ ] use *don't have to* and *doesn't have to* for choices in the present
- [ ] use *had to* or *didn't have to* for the past
- [ ] use *must not* or *can't* when something is not allowed
- [ ] check your spelling

D REVISE YOUR WORK Read your paragraph about a school again. Can you improve your writing? Make changes if necessary.

Go to MyEnglishLab for more writing practice.

UNIT 30 REVIEW

Test yourself on the grammar of the unit.

Ⓐ Complete the sentences. Circle the correct answers.

1. You can wear what you want. You <u>must not / don't have to</u> wear a uniform.

2. It's getting late. He <u>have to / has to</u> leave.

3. The law says you <u>must not / must not to</u> drive without a license.

4. She can take the test any day this week. She <u>don't have to / doesn't have to</u> take it today.

5. I <u>have to / must not</u> hand in my term paper tomorrow. I can't go out today.

Ⓑ Complete the sentences with the correct form of *have, have to, don't have to*, or *can't*.

1. You _____ drive without a license. It's illegal.

2. She _____ a lot of homework, and it's all due tomorrow.

3. Do we _____ hand in our paper and study for a test, too?

4. The tickets are good any day this week. We _____ use them today.

5. People _____ wear sneakers when they use the gym.

Ⓒ Complete the sentences with the correct form of *have to* and a verb from the box. Use the present or past.

answer	give	not / bring	read	work

1. He _____ two shifts because two co-workers were out sick.

2. We're busy. We _____ two chapters of our history book.

3. We also _____ questions at the end of each chapter for tomorrow.

4. Last week, we _____ a presentation in front of the entire school.

5. I _____ my laptop to class yesterday. They gave me one to use.

Ⓓ Correct the paragraph. There are five mistakes.

Drew's test starts at 8:10. He must to be in the room at 8:00. He must not came late.

He has to has two pencils. He must brings a photo ID. Cell phones are not allowed in the

room. He doesn't have to bring his cell phone with him.

Now check your answers on page 451.

Go to MyEnglishLab to complete the review online.

Comparisons

OUTCOMES
- Use short and long comparative adjectives
- Understand details in an article that compares two cities
- Recognize details in a conversation about a city
- Talk about similarities and differences between locations and types of transportation
- Write a paragraph comparing two ways of travel

OUTCOMES
- Express how things happen, using adverbs
- Recognize true statements about information in an article
- Recognize details in a presentation
- Use tone of voice to express different feelings
- Describe people's actions, using adverbs
- Write a paragraph about something you do well

OUTCOMES
- Use *too* to say there is more than necessary of something and *enough* to say there is a right amount of something
- Say how two nouns are alike, using *as...as*
- Correct false statements based on an article
- Compare the personalities of two employees discussed in a conversation
- Express opinions about places and things
- Write a paragraph about a place you didn't like

OUTCOMES
- Compare three or more nouns, using superlative adjectives
- Recognize details in a scientific article
- Recognize key information from a quiz show
- Prepare a survey and present results to the class
- Discuss animals and their characteristics
- Write a paragraph about an animal

OUTCOMES
- Use short and long comparative adjectives
- Understand details in an article that compares two cities
- Recognize details in a conversation about a city
- Talk about similarities and differences between locations and types of transportation
- Write a paragraph comparing two ways of travel

STEP 1	GRAMMAR IN CONTEXT

BEFORE YOU READ

Work with a partner. Answer the questions.

1. What's a port? Do you live in a city with a port?

2. Look at the map on page 429. Where is Portland, Maine? Where is Portland, Oregon?

READ

⏵31|01 **Read this article about two U.S. cities called Portland.**

A Tale of Two Portlands

There are two beautiful U.S. cities named Portland. One is in Maine, and the other is in Oregon. Maine is on the East Coast of the United States, while Oregon is on the West Coast. Both Portlands have ports, but Portland, Maine, has an ocean port with beautiful ships, shops, and restaurants. This port is more popular than the Oregon port. Portland, Oregon, at 173 feet (53 meters) above sea level, is higher than Portland, Maine. Both cities are not very big, but they are bigger than any other city in their states. Portland, Maine, has a population of about 66,000. Portland, Oregon, is much larger, with a population of about 620,000.

What's your guess? Which Portland is colder, Portland, Oregon, or Portland, Maine? Did you guess the Portland in Maine? If so, you are correct. Portland, Maine, *is* a lot colder in winter. But both cities have comfortable climates in summer.

Both Portlands offer a nice lifestyle with places to walk, bike ride, and eat. They also have mountains and an ocean nearby. Portland, Oregon, is a city with different neighborhoods with different personalities. It's much more diverse than the other Portland. But Portland,

Portland, Maine

Maine (founded in 1633), is much older than Portland, Oregon (founded in 1845).

You may wonder why the two cities have the same name. There's a reason. Each of the two founders[1] of Portland, Oregon, wanted to name his new city after his hometown. One man came from Boston, Massachusetts. The other came from Portland, Maine. They tossed a coin,[2] and the man from Portland, Maine, won.

Portland, Oregon

1 *founders:* people who started the city
2 *tossed a coin:* threw a coin in the air and guessed the side it would land on

AFTER YOU READ

A VOCABULARY **Complete the sentences with the words from the box.**

| coast | diverse | personalities | population | wonder |

1. We drove along the _____ and took some great photos of the ocean and the rocks.

2. They're talking about going to Maine. I _____ why they chose Maine.

3. My university has a _____ population. Students come from everywhere.

4. My sisters have nice _____. That's why everyone likes them.

5. The _____ of Maine is about 1,330,000 people.

B COMPREHENSION **Answer the questions. Check (✓) the correct Portland.**

	Portland, Maine	Portland, Oregon
1. Which Portland has a bigger population?	☐	☐
2. Which Portland is older?	☐	☐
3. Which Portland has more diverse neighborhoods?	☐	☐
4. Which Portland has warmer winters?	☐	☐

C DISCUSSION **Work with a partner. Compare your answers in B. Then discuss: Which Portland do you prefer? Why?**

Go to MyEnglishLab for more grammar in context practice.

COMPARATIVES

Adjectives

Comparative Forms of Adjectives				
		Comparative Adjective	*Than*	
Portland, Oregon,	is	bigger busier	than	Portland, Maine.
		more crowded		

Comparative Forms of Irregular Adjectives				
		Irregular Comparative Adjective	*Than*	
My map	is	better worse	than	yours.
My new office		farther		my old office.

Yes/No Questions				
		Comparative Adjective	*Than*	
Is	your city	bigger		my city?
Are	the trains	more comfortable	than	the buses?
Is	your phone	better		mine?

Questions with *Which*

Which + Noun			
Which	Noun	Verb	Comparative Adjective
Which	city	is	bigger? more expensive?

Which		
Which	Verb	Comparative Adjective
Which	is	bigger? more expensive?

GRAMMAR NOTES

1 Comparative Adjectives

Use the **comparative** form of adjectives to **compare two people**, **places**, or **things**.

There are **three comparative forms**: • **adjective + -er** • **adjective + -ier** • *more* **+ adjective**	Rhode Island is **smaller** than Maine. I am **busier** than my sister. The train is **more expensive** than the bus.
Use *than* after the comparative adjective. You can **leave out** *than* when the listener knows what you are comparing something to.	I am **older than** my sister. I am **smarter**, too. *(The listener knows I am talking about my sister.)*
We can also use comparative adjectives before **nouns** and **prepositional phrases**. (A prepositional phrase is a preposition + a noun.)	Portland, Oregon, has a **higher** *elevation* than Portland, Maine. Portland, Oregon, is **farther** *from the coast* than Portland, Maine.

2 Short Adjectives

To form the comparative of most **short (one-syllable) adjectives**, add *-er* to the adjective: *long* → *longer*	The Mississippi River is **longer** than the Hudson River.
Add only *-r* if the adjective ends in *e*: *large* → *larger*	Texas is **larger** than Maine.
To form the comparative of adjectives that end in a **consonant + y**, change the *y* to *i* and add *-er*: *busy* → *busier* *easy* → *easier* *heavy* → *heavier*	Dr. Chu is **busier** than Dr. Lee. Level 1 is **easier** than level 2. My desk is **heavier** than my chair.
The adjectives *good*, *bad*, and *far* have **irregular** comparative forms: *good* → *better* *bad* → *worse* *far* → *farther*	My new job is **better** than my old one. The movie was **worse** than the book. The bus stop is **farther** than the train station.
BE CAREFUL! Add *more*, not *-er*, to these short adjectives: *fun* → *more fun* *tired* → *more tired* *bored* → *more bored*	I am **more tired** than you are. **NOT** I am ~~tireder~~ than you are.

3 Longer Adjectives

To form the comparative of most adjectives of **two** or **more syllables**, add *more* before the adjective. *expensive* → *more expensive* *intelligent* → *more intelligent*	The train is **more expensive** than the bus.
Use *less* before a longer adjective to show **the opposite of** *more*.	A car is **more expensive** than a bicycle. A bicycle is **less expensive** than a car.
USAGE NOTE In **formal** English, use the **subject pronoun** after *than*. In **informal** English, you can use the **object pronoun** after *than*.	SUBJECT PRONOUN Steve is younger **than she** is. OBJECT PRONOUN Steve is younger **than her**.
BE CAREFUL! Always compare the same things.	**John's home** is larger than **William's home.** or **John's home** is larger than **William's.** NOT John's home is larger than ~~William~~.
BE CAREFUL! Do not use two comparative forms together.	My bookbag is **larger** than my handbag. NOT My bookbag is ~~more larger~~ than my handbag.

4 *Much* Before Comparative Adjectives

Use *much* before comparative adjectives to make the comparison **stronger**.	Portland, Oregon, is *much* **larger** than Portland, Maine. Portland, Oregon, is *much* **more diverse** than my city.

5 Questions with *Which*

Use *which* + **a noun** to ask about a comparison of two places or things. Use *or* between the places or things you are comparing.	**Which city** is larger, **Tokyo or Seoul**? **Which city** has a larger population, **Moscow or London**?
Use *which* alone when the listener knows what you are comparing.	**Which** is larger? *(The listener knows you are comparing Tokyo and Seoul.)*

REFERENCE NOTE

For information on *(not) as* + **adjective** + *as*, see Unit 33 on page 403.

Go to MyEnglishLab to watch the grammar presentation.

EXERCISE 1 DISCOVER THE GRAMMAR

A **GRAMMAR NOTES 1–5** Read a blog about two cities in Canada. Underline all comparative adjectives.

Amanda's blog

Quebec City, Canada

Vancouver, Canada

Quebec City and Vancouver

Two of my favorite Canadian cities are Quebec City in the east and Vancouver in the west.

Quebec City has the charm of an old historic city. It is a lot <u>older</u> than Vancouver. Vancouver has an old neighborhood, but it's much younger than Quebec City's. Vancouver has a milder climate than Quebec City. People in Vancouver enjoy many beautiful gardens and parks. Stanley Park in Vancouver is bigger than most city parks. People can visit it all year round, but I think it's more fun in the spring or early summer when the flowers are in bloom.

Vancouver has a larger population than Quebec City, and it is growing each year. These days, many film makers work in Vancouver because it is less expensive than cities like Los Angeles and New York.

In Vancouver, most people speak English, while 95 percent of the people in Quebec City speak French. That's because the founders of Quebec were from France, and Quebec still has a European flavor.

Which city is better to visit? I can't say. They're both great places, but in different ways.

B Write the comparative form and the base form of the adjectives you underlined in A.

Base Form	Comparative Form		Base Form	Comparative Form
1. *old*	*older*	5.		
2.		6.		
3.		7.		
4.		8.		

EXERCISE 2 COMPARATIVE ADJECTIVES AND QUESTIONS WITH *WHICH*

GRAMMAR NOTES 1–5 Complete the conversations with the adjectives in parentheses. Use the comparative form. Add *than* when necessary.

1. A: Which city is _____ more expensive _____ to live in, Tokyo or Sydney?
     (expensive)
   B: Tokyo is _____ more expensive than _____ Sydney.
     (expensive)

2. A: Which city is _____ in summer, Bangkok or Seoul?
     (hot)
   B: Bangkok summers are _____ summers in Seoul.
     (hot)

3. A: Which city has a _____ elevation, Bogotá or Mexico City?
     (high)
   B: Bogotá is _____ Mexico City.
     (high)

4. A: Which river is _____, the Nile or the Amazon?
     (long)
   B: The Nile is _____ the Amazon.
     (long)

5. A: Is winter in Quebec City _____ winter in Vancouver?
     (cold)
   B: Yes, it is. Quebec City's winter is _____ Vancouver's.
     (much / cold)

6. A: Is Arizona _____ Pennsylvania?
     (dry)
   B: Yes, it is. It's _____ Pennsylvania.
     (much / dry)

7. A: Are summers _____ winters in Miami?
     (humid)
   B: Yes, they are. Summers are _____ winters in Miami.
     (much / humid)

8. A: Which highway has _____ traffic, West Highway or East Highway?
     (heavy)
   B: West Highway. Traffic on West Highway is always _____ traffic on East Highway.
     (heavy)

9. A: In the past, was the Hudson River _____ it is today?
     (polluted)
   B: Yes, it was. Twenty years ago, it was _____ it is today.
     (much / polluted)

EXERCISE 3 *LESS* AND ADJECTIVES

GRAMMAR NOTE 3 Complete the sentences with *less* and the adjectives in parentheses. Use the comparative form. Add *than* when necessary.

1. Madrid is _____ less expensive than _____ Zürich.
     (expensive)

2. Winter is _____ summer in Houston.
     (humid)

3. Is Kennedy Airport on Tuesday _____ it is on Sunday?
     (crowded)

4. Today the Cuyahoga River in Ohio is _____ it was years ago,
(polluted)
   when it caught fire from the pollution.

5. Is the Eiffel Tower _____ the Egyptian Pyramids?
(popular)

6. Is Maine _____ Oregon?
(diverse)

7. Are airplanes _____ cars?
(dangerous)

8. Are plane rides _____ car rides?
(comfortable)

EXERCISE 4 SENTENCES WITH COMPARATIVE ADJECTIVES

GRAMMAR NOTES 1–3, 5
Look at the chart. Use the
information in the chart
to answer the questions.
Write long answers.

	Middletown	Lakeville
Population	100,000	50,000
Average household income	$85,000	$63,000
Average rent for a two-bedroom apartment	$1,300	$1,000
Cost of a cup of coffee	$2	$1
Percentage unemployed	7%	9%
Number of good hospitals	5	1
Average summer temperature	80°F (26.6°C)	68°F (20°C)

1. Which city is larger (in population)?

   Middletown is larger than Lakeville.

2. Where are salaries higher?

   _____

3. Where are rents lower?

   _____

4. Where is coffee less expensive?

   _____

5. Where is unemployment higher?

   _____

6. Where is medical care better?

   _____

7. Which city is hotter in summer?

   _____

EXERCISE 5 *WHICH* QUESTIONS AND ANSWERS

GRAMMAR NOTES 1–5 Write *which* questions with the words in parentheses. Use the comparative form of the adjectives. Then guess the answers. Write your guesses with long answers with *than*. Check your answers on page 453.

1. (which country / be / large / in size / China or Russia)

   A: *Which country is larger in size, China or Russia?*

   B: *Russia is larger in size than China.*

2. (which river / be / long / the Amazon or the Nile)

   A: _____

   B: _____

3. (which mountain / have / a / high / elevation / Mount Everest or Mount Denali)

   A: _____

   B: _____

4. (which ocean / be / big / the Pacific or the Atlantic)

   A: _____

   B: _____

5. (which city / have / a / high / elevation / La Paz, Bolivia, or Sydney, Australia)

   A: _____

   B: _____

6. (which country / have / a / big / population / Japan or South Korea)

   A: _____

   B: _____

7. (which city / be / expensive / New York or Venice)

   A: _____

   B: _____

EXERCISE 6 COMPARATIVE ADJECTIVES

GRAMMAR NOTES 1–4 Complete the paragraph with the adjectives in parentheses. Use the comparative form.

You are choosing between two cities to live in in California: Los Angeles or Glendale.

You aren't sure which is a _____*better*_____ choice. Los Angeles is a
                         1. (good)

_____ city than Glendale, and it has all the problems of big
      2. (much / big)

cities. Los Angeles is _____ than Glendale, and traffic is
3. (polluted)

_____. The streets of downtown Los Angeles are
4. (bad)

_____ than the streets of Glendale, too.
5. (much / busy)

However, Los Angeles is _____ than Glendale. Los
6. (much / exciting)

Angeles has a great night life. Glendale is _____ at night.
7. (much / quiet)

Both cities have the same great climate. It's hard to compare housing costs. Some parts of

Los Angeles are _____ than Glendale and other parts are
8. (expensive)

_____. However, Los Angeles is close to Glendale, so if you
9. (cheap)

make a mistake, you can always move.

EXERCISE 7 EDITING

GRAMMAR NOTES 1–5 **Read the sentences. There are seven mistakes. The first one is already corrected. Find and correct six more.**

                                     more
1. Our new apartment is much ∧ comfortable than our old apartment.

2. Florida is warm than Maine.

3. Which city is hotter than, New York or San Francisco?

4. A motorcycle is more faster than a bicycle.

5. Traffic at 8:00 a.m. is heavier traffic at 10:00 a.m.

6. The climate in Portland, Oregon, is mild than the climate in Anchorage, Alaska.

7. Drew's apartment is less convenient than his sister.

EXERCISE 8 LISTENING

⏵31|02 Ⓐ Listen to a conversation between two friends. The woman says, "You can thank our mayor." What is the mayor doing to the city?

⏵31|02 Ⓑ Listen again. Complete the sentences. Circle the correct answers.

1. The downtown area is lively / less lively than before.

2. The seats on the buses are more comfortable / less comfortable than they were.

3. It's easier / harder to take the bus.

4. The air is cleaner / dirtier.

5. It's easier / harder to park downtown.

6. West Park is cleaner and safer / dirtier and more dangerous than before.

7. East Park is cleaner and safer / dirtier and more dangerous than before.

Ⓒ Work with a partner. Ask questions comparing Fogville now and before. Use the comparative form of the words in the box.

| clean | dangerous | dirty | easy | hard | lively | safe |

EXAMPLE: A: Is Fogville cleaner than before?
B: Yes, it is. It's cleaner because people don't drop things in the street now. They don't want to pay a fine.

EXERCISE 9 TWO CITIES, TWO TRAIN SYSTEMS

Ⓐ GAME Work in a group. Look at the information about the London Underground and the Moscow Metro. Work together to write as many comparative questions with *which* as you can. Use the comparative forms of the adjectives in the box.

cheap	expensive	fast	long	new	old	short	slow

	LONDON UNDERGROUND	MOSCOW METRO
Year opened	1863	1935
Length of tracks	about 250 miles (400 kilometers)	about 205 miles (330 kilometers)
Number of passengers each day	4 million*	8 million*
Cost of ride in euros	4 euros for shortest distance*	About 0.6 euros*
Speed	20.5 mph (33 km/h)	25.9 mph (41.6 km/h)

*These numbers may vary

Which train system is cheaper, the London Underground or the Moscow Metro?

London Underground

Moscow Metro

Ⓑ The class closes their books. Each group asks another group a comparative question with *which* about the London Underground and the Moscow Metro. You get one point for every correct answer. The group with the most correct answers wins.

EXAMPLE: GROUP A: Which train system is older, the London Underground or the Moscow Metro?
GROUP B: The London Underground is much older. . . .

EXERCISE 10 A TREE-HOUSE IS MORE FUN

(A) DISCUSSION Prepare for a discussion. Work with a partner. Name two unusual things for each category in the chart.

Kinds of homes	a houseboat	a treehouse
Kinds of jobs		
Sports		
Vacation places		
Kinds of food		

(B) Talk about your preferences for each category in A and give reasons why.

EXAMPLE: A: Which is better, a houseboat or a treehouse?
          B: For me, a houseboat is better. A houseboat is more comfortable, and it has a more beautiful view because you can see water.

EXERCISE 11 PEOPLE IN PARIS ARE MORE...

(A) Q & A Prepare for a question-and-answer activity in B. Every student chooses a city he or she knows well and writes the name of the city on the board. (Do *not* choose the city you are in.) Then together make a list of adjectives that describe cities, people, and climates. Write those adjectives on the board.

EXAMPLES: *Cities*   *People*   *Climates*
            clean   friendly   warm
            dangerous   polite   dry
            exciting   relaxed   humid

(B) Work in a group. Write questions comparing the cities on the board to the city you are in. Use the adjectives on the board or choose your own. Ask a comparative question about each city. The student who chose the city answers the question.

EXAMPLE: A: Pierre, did you choose Paris?
          B: Yes, I did.
          A: OK, which city is cleaner, [the city you are in] or Paris?

Go to MyEnglishLab for more communication practice.

A BEFORE YOU WRITE Read about two ways to travel. Then work with a partner. Think of two more ways to travel. Complete the chart. Then compare your two ways to travel.

Ways to Travel

Most cities have buses and trains, but some cities have more unusual ways to travel. In San Francisco, some people travel by trolley. In Venice, people sometimes travel by gondola. Both the trolley and the gondola are more fun than the bus or the train. The gondola is more romantic than the trolley, but the trolley is more exciting, especially when you're traveling down one of San Francisco's steep streets.

Trolley   Gondola

Ways to Travel	Description
trolley	unusual, fun, exciting
gondola	unusual, fun, romantic

B WRITE Write a paragraph comparing two ways of travel. Use the paragraph in A and your chart. Use at least three comparative adjectives.

C CHECK YOUR WORK Read your paragraph in B. Underline the comparative adjectives. Then use the Editing Checklist to check your work.

Editing Checklist

Did you . . . ?
- [ ] add -er to short adjectives to form the comparative
- [ ] use *more* + adjective for longer adjectives
- [ ] use *than* after the comparative adjective
- [ ] check your spelling

D REVISE YOUR WORK Read your paragraph again. Can you improve your writing? Make changes if necessary.

Go to MyEnglishLab for more writing practice.

UNIT 31 REVIEW

Test yourself on the grammar of the unit.

(A) Complete the sentences. Circle the correct answers.

1. She is <u>more</u> / <u>much</u> younger than he is. She is much <u>more tall</u> / <u>taller</u>, too.

2. This singing group is <u>more popular</u> / <u>popular more</u> than the other one.

3. The traffic is <u>more worse</u> / <u>worse</u> now than it was an hour ago.

4. Which city has a <u>better</u> / <u>more good</u> transportation system, Toronto or Vancouver?

5. Is your car more comfortable than your <u>brother</u> / <u>brother's</u>?

(B) Complete the sentences with the correct forms of the adjectives in parentheses. Use _than_.

1. She is seven. Her sister is ten. She is _____ her sister.
   (young)

2. Amy is five feet tall. Joe is six feet tall. Amy is _____ Joe.
   (short)

3. My coat is $199. Her coat is $150. My coat is _____ her coat.
   (expensive)

4. Today is 90°F (32°C). Yesterday was 70°F (21°C). Today is _____
   (hot)
   yesterday.

(C) Look at the chart. Complete the sentences with _less expensive, more expensive, higher, lower._

	New City	Sun City
Bus fare	$2.50	$3.00
Average income	$65,000	$90,000

1. A bus is _____ in New City than in Sun City.

2. A bus is _____ in Sun City than in New City.

3. The average income is _____ in Sun City than in New City.

4. The average income is _____ in New City than in Sun City.

(D) Correct the paragraph. There are six mistakes.

The train is much fast than the bus and the seats are comfortabler. The bus is much more slower than the train, but the views from the bus are more interesting. Which are cheaper, the train or the bus? The bus is much less expensiver, but for me the train is more good because I have very little free time.

Check your answers on page 451.

Go to MyEnglishLab to complete the review online.

Adverbs of Manner
PUBLIC SPEAKING

OUTCOMES
• Express how things happen, using adverbs
• Recognize true statements about information in an article
• Recognize details in a presentation
• Use tone of voice to express different feelings
• Describe people's actions, using adverbs
• Write a paragraph about something you do well

STEP 1   GRAMMAR IN CONTEXT

BEFORE YOU READ

Work with a partner. Answer the questions.

1. When do people have to speak in front of large audiences?

2. How do you usually feel when you give a speech in front of many people?
   a. relaxed   b. a little nervous   c. very nervous

READ

▶ 32|01   Read this article about public speaking.

Public Speaking

Last year, my boss asked me to give a presentation. It was a nightmare. I hate speaking in front of a large group, and I always get nervous. Also, I had to prepare quickly—I had only two days to get ready. The day of the speech came. There were forty people in the room. My manager was there, and my co-workers. I wanted to run out of the room, so I spoke fast, and I didn't look at anyone. Instead I read from my paper. I was afraid to tell a joke. I wanted to sound smart, so I gave too many facts. I used big words and long sentences. People clapped politely, but I knew my speech was awful.

    The next time I gave a speech, I asked a friend for help. She helped me to focus on three ideas, give good examples, and tell jokes. In my next speech,

I spoke slowly and clearly. I thought carefully about everything I wanted to say. I spoke honestly, and I added a few personal examples. I only said things I really believed. I looked at my audience, and I smiled at the right times. This time the applause was long and loud. I connected well with the audience, and I felt good. People gave me their time, and I gave them a speech to remember.

AFTER YOU READ

Ⓐ VOCABULARY Choose the phrase that is closest in meaning to the word in **bold.**

1. The **audience** was interested in every word he said.
   a. people who write about a performance
   b. people who watch a performance

2. When he heard the long **applause**, he felt satisfied.
   a. clapping of hands
   b. stamping of feet

3. Most of his speech was light and funny, but he spoke **seriously** at the end of his talk.
   a. in a way that says something is wrong
   b. in a way that says something is important

4. He told us many **facts** about his country.
   a. true things
   b. opinions he had

5. We laughed at his **jokes**.
   a. funny stories
   b. true stories

6. She **appreciated** my help and thanked me many times.
   a. was nervous about
   b. was grateful for

Ⓑ COMPREHENSION Read the advice. Check (✓) *Yes* if it is from the article. Check *No* if it is not from the article.

	Yes	No
1. Speak quickly.	☐	☐
2. Speak slowly.	☐	☐
3. Use big words.	☐	☐
4. Look at the audience.	☐	☐
5. Use humor.	☐	☐
6. Give personal examples.	☐	☐
7. Have many ideas, not just three or four.	☐	☐
8. Speak briefly.	☐	☐

Ⓒ DISCUSSION Work with a partner. Compare your answers in B. Then discuss: What's the biggest mistake a speaker can make?

Go to MyEnglishLab for more grammar in context practice.

ADVERBS OF MANNER

Subject	Verb	Adverb
He	spoke	well.
		badly.
		clearly.

Subject	Verb		Adverb
She	finished	her speech	quickly.

Adverb Formed with Adjective + -ly		Same Adjective and Adverb Form		Irregular Adverb Form	
Adjective	Adverb	Adjective	Adverb	Adjective	Adverb
bad	badly	early	early	good	well
careful	carefully	fast	fast		
loud	loudly	late	late		
quick	quickly	long	long		
quiet	quietly				
sarcastic	sarcastically				
slow	slowly				

GRAMMAR NOTES

1 Adverbs of Manner

Adverbs of manner **describe action verbs**. They say **how** or **the way something happens**. The adverb often comes at the end of the sentence.	She spoke **slowly**. He walked **fast**.
Most adverbs of manner are formed by **adding -ly** to an adjective.	ADJECTIVE She's a **careful** driver. ADVERB She drives **carefully**.
Some **adverbs** of manner have the **same form as adjectives**: *hard, fast, early*	ADJECTIVE ADVERB She's a **hard** worker. She works **hard**.
Some words that end in -**ly** are **adjectives**, not adverbs: *lively, lovely, ugly, lonely, friendly* These adjectives have no adverb form.	ADJECTIVE She's a **friendly** person. She has a **lonely** job.

2 *Well*: Adverb and Adjective

Well is the **adverb** for the adjective *good*.	ADJECTIVE She's a **good** speaker. ADVERB She speaks **well**.
Well is also an **adjective** that means "in good health."	ADJECTIVE I feel **well**.
USAGE NOTE In very informal speaking, we sometimes say *I'm good* instead of *I'm well*.	A: How are you? B: I'm **good**.

3 Linking Verbs

Linking verbs can connect a subject and an adjective. Linking verbs are followed by **adjectives**.

Here are some common linking verbs:

appear	feel	smell
be	look	sound
become	seem	taste

	LINKING VERB	ADJECTIVE
She	**seems**	**sad**.
It	**sounds**	**beautiful**.

BE CAREFUL! Don't use adverbs after linking verbs.

The grapes **taste good**.
NOT The grapes ~~taste well~~.

Go to MyEnglishLab to watch the grammar presentation.

STEP 3 FOCUSED PRACTICE

EXERCISE 1 DISCOVER THE GRAMMAR

GRAMMAR NOTES 1, 3 **Read the paragraph. Underline the adverbs of manner and the verbs they describe in the paragraph. Then circle the linking verbs and the adjectives that follow them.**

How do you speak well in public? We all know that a public speaker should look good

and make his audience feel comfortable. In addition, a public speaker should remember

three things: to entertain, to instruct, and to inspire. Use humor. It helps your audience

relax. When you instruct, speak briefly. You should also speak clearly. Don't speak too

long. And don't speak too fast. And remember that great speeches inspire and move an

audience. Know your audience and touch their emotions.

EXERCISE 2 ADVERBS OF MANNER

GRAMMAR NOTES 1–2 **Complete each sentence. Change the adjectives in parentheses to adverbs.**

1. The audience listened _____*carefully*_____ .
   (careful)

2. He spoke _____ .
   (quick)

3. Sally writes _____ .
   (good)

4. They speak Spanish _____ .
   (fluent)

5. He spoke _____ .
   (clear)

6. He drove _____ .
   (fast)

7. Did he drive _____ ?
   (dangerous)

8. Did they sing _____ ?
   (bad)

9. The movie began _____ .
   (slow)

10. It rained _____ last night.
    (hard)

11. She woke up _____ .
    (early)

12. He stayed up _____ .
    (late)

EXERCISE 3 LINKING VERBS

GRAMMAR NOTE 3 **Match the beginnings of the sentences with the endings.**

__c__ 1. She looks

____ 2. He looks

____ 3. The soup tastes

____ 4. Her speech was

____ 5. This CD sounds

____ 6. Their home smells

a. awful. I hate heavy metal music.

b. happy. I guess he gave a good talk.

c. sick. Does she have a fever?

d. good. Are they baking cookies?

e. great. People clapped for a long time.

f. terrible. Don't eat it.

EXERCISE 4 ADVERBS OF MANNER AND ADJECTIVES

GRAMMAR NOTES 1–3 **Complete the conversations. Circle the correct answers.**

1. A: How was the debate?

   B: Good. Both sides spoke good / (well).

2. A: How was the food at the reception after the debate?

   B: It tasted bad / badly.

3. A: There were beautiful / beautifully paintings in the room.

   B: Yes. The artist is from Colombia.

4. A: How did Roger do in his last debate?

   B: He didn't do good / well.

5. A: Speak careful / carefully. Everyone is listening to you.

   B: OK.

6. A: How was the talk?

   B: The first part was very slow / slowly, but the second part was better.

7. A: How was Mary's speech?

   B: Not great. She seemed nervous / nervously.

EXERCISE 5 EDITING

GRAMMAR NOTES 1–3 Read the conversations. There are six mistakes. The first mistake is already corrected. Find and correct five more.

1. A: How did he do?

   B: He did ~~good~~. *well*

2. A: Was the food OK?

   B: Everyone loved it. It really tasted well.

3. A: Is Harry a good speaker?

   B: I don't think so. He speaks too slow.

4. A: Did they pass the test?

   B: Yes. They studied hardly and did well.

5. A: Could you hear him?

   B: No, I couldn't. He spoke too soft.

6. A: Do you like this sweater?

   B: No. It looks a little strangely.

Go to MyEnglishLab for more focused practice.

EXERCISE 6 LISTENING

○32|02 **A** Listen to a talk about giving a speech. Complete the sentences.

1. At the start of a speech, you need a good _____.

2. At the end of a speech, you need a good _____.

3. It's a good idea to tell a couple of _____.

○32|02 **B** Listen again. Write the suggestions that the speaker gives.

1. Look _____*directly*_____ at a few people in the audience.

2. Second, speak _____.

3. Dress _____.

4. Speak _____ and use natural _____.

5. Don't read your _____.

6. Don't show a Powerpoint® slide with a lot of _____ on it.

7. Summarize your _____.

8. Thank your audience _____.

C Work with a partner. Talk about the suggestions for giving a speech. Which suggestions in A and B are hard to follow? Which are not difficult? Which suggestions do you like?

EXAMPLE: A: I think it's hard to tell jokes well.
          B: I agree. It's not just the joke, it's how you tell it. It's not hard to . . .

EXERCISE 7 WHAT DO I REALLY MEAN?

ROLE PLAY How we speak gives a different meaning to a sentence. Work with a partner.
Say the following sentences in the ways in the box or choose your own ways. Your
partner guesses how you're talking.

| angrily | decisively | questioningly | sadly | sarcastically |

1. I love English grammar.

   EXAMPLE: A: I love English grammar.
                B: You're speaking sarcastically.
                A: You're right.

2. The speech was great.

3. The movie was wonderful.

4. I love to exercise.

5. It's mine, all mine.

EXERCISE 8 WHAT AM I DOING?

GAME Work in groups. Choose a verb and an adverb from the list. Act it out in front of
your group. They say what you're doing.

Verbs		Adverbs	
dance	sing	badly	quietly
drive	speak	carefully	quickly
eat	walk	nervously	slowly
listen		noisily	

Go to MyEnglishLab for more communication practice.

A BEFORE YOU WRITE Read the essay about babysitting. Work with a partner. Think of something you do well. For example, you may be a good soccer player, a good shopper, or a good cook. Give your partner four suggestions for how to do something.

How to Babysit

I often watch my niece and nephew. They're three and five years old. I enjoy taking care of them. Here are some suggestions for anyone who wants to babysit young children:

- Listen carefully to the children and the parents.
- When something is important, speak seriously, but don't yell.
- When you say you'll do something, do it.
- When children do something really bad, tell them to stop.
- When children do something that's not so bad, don't say anything.
- Before the child or children go to sleep, have them play quietly. Then read to them.

B WRITE Write a paragraph about how to do something. Use the essay in A and your suggestions. Use at least two adverbs of manner.

C CHECK YOUR WORK Read your paragraph in B. Underline the adverbs of manner. Use the Editing Checklist to check your work.

Editing Checklist
Did you . . . ?
☐ place adverbs of manner after the verb
☐ add -ly to adjectives to form most adverbs
☐ use adjectives after linking verbs such as *look*, *seem*, etc.
☐ check your spelling

D REVISE YOUR WORK Read your paragraphs again. Can you improve your writing? Make changes if necessary.

Go to MyEnglishLab for more writing practice.

UNIT 32 **REVIEW**

Test yourself on the grammar of the unit.

Ⓐ Complete the sentences. Change the adjectives in parentheses to adverbs.

1. He drove _____.
   (quick)
2. She spoke _____.
   (fluent)
3. Did he do _____ on the test?
   (good)
4. Walk _____ and look at the beautiful scenery.
   (slow)
5. I spoke _____.
   (clear)

Ⓑ Complete the sentences. Circle the correct answers.

1. Both sides gave good / well arguments.

2. He spoke serious / seriously.

3. She works hard / hardly.

4. He did bad / badly on the last test.

5. I can't understand her because she's talking too quick / quickly.

Ⓒ Complete the sentences with the words from the box.

| briefly | clearly | fast | good | honestly |

   If you want to give a _____ speech, remember these things. Don't speak
                                         1.
for a long time: speak _____. Also, don't swallow your words: speak
                                    2.
_____. Don't speak too _____ because people need time to
          3.   4.
understand your ideas. Speak _____ and say only what you mean.
                                              5.

Ⓓ Correct the conversation. There are five mistakes.

A: Did your speech go good? Did they appreciate your jokes?

B: Well... they laughed polite, but I'm not sure they laughed sincere.

A: It's hard to be funny.

B: I hard worked, and I prepared carefully, but I was nervously.

Now check your answers on page 451.

Go to MyEnglishLab to complete the review online.

33

Adjective + *Enough*; *Too* and *Very*; *As* + Adjective + *As*
COMPLAINTS

OUTCOMES
- Use *too* to say there is more than necessary of something and *enough* to say there is a right amount of something
- Say how two nouns are alike, using *as…as*
- Correct false statements based on an article
- Compare the personalities of two employees discussed in a conversation
- Express opinions about places and things
- Write a paragraph about a place you didn't like

STEP 1   GRAMMAR IN CONTEXT

BEFORE YOU READ

Work with a partner. Answer the questions.

1. What's a complaint?

2. Make a complaint about today's weather, the city you are in, or the building you are in.

READ

▶ 33|01   Read this article about complainers.

Nothing Is Good Enough for Maria

You and your co-workers meet at a restaurant. Maria, one of your co-workers, enters the restaurant and says, "Hey, guys. This place is too noisy, and it's too dark. And the tables aren't big enough." You change restaurants. In the new restaurant, Maria says, "This table is very dirty." You get the menus and Maria says, "The specials here aren't as good as the ones in the other restaurant." Then Maria says, "The seats here are very uncomfortable."

What do you do about complainers? According to psychologist Guy Winch, you should try and understand their point of view. Complainers don't see themselves as complainers. They believe they see things as they really are. Maria feels she's right. In her eyes, the restaurant *is* much too noisy and the table *is* very dirty. Dr. Winch also says, "Don't try and tell the complainer that things aren't as

bad as they think. It's better to try and understand them and say sincerely, 'I see what you mean.'"

Sometimes we find that the complainer causes us to complain. Now we're as bad as the complainer. But is it always bad to complain? Some studies show that complainers live longer than people who don't complain. And complainers point out problems and look for solutions. When we improve a situation, we feel stronger and happier. So, as a complainer, you may live a very long and happy life.

AFTER YOU READ

Ⓐ VOCABULARY **Complete the sentences with the words from the box.**

| according to | in her eyes | point of view | point out | sincerely | solutions |

1. _____ one psychologist, it's sometimes good to complain.

2. I know what you think. Now, I'd like to hear his _____.

3. _____, he can do nothing wrong.

4. I'm not just saying that I will help. I _____ mean it.

5. Ask her. She's good at finding _____ to problems.

6. Did you _____ that a new school will cost a lot of money?

Ⓑ COMPREHENSION **Correct these false statements.**

1. Maria thinks the first restaurant is too quiet and bright.

2. In the second restaurant, Maria says the table is very dark.

3. Guy Winch is a server.

4. One study says complaining is bad for your health.

5. It's always bad to be a complainer.

Ⓒ DISCUSSION **Work with a partner. Compare your answers in B. Discuss: What's good about complaining?**

Go to MyEnglishLab for more grammar in context practice.

ADJECTIVE + *ENOUGH*, *TOO* AND *VERY*, *AS* + ADJECTIVE + *AS*

Adjective + *Enough*

	Adjective	*Enough*
The room is	**big**	**enough**.
It is **not**	**warm**	**enough**.

Too and *Very*

	Too / Very	Adjective	
The coffee is	**too**	**hot**.	Don't drink it.
The coffee is	**very**	**hot**.	It's good.

As + Adjective + *As*

	As	Adjective	*As*	
Jake is		**tall**		his dad.
He isn't	**as**	**heavy**	**as**	his dad.
Is Jake		**tall**		his brother?

GRAMMAR NOTES

1 *Enough*

Enough means as much as necessary, or that you have the **amount you need**.	
You can use *enough* after an **adjective**.	ADJECTIVE He's **old enough**. *(He can drive.)*
Remember that you can also use *enough* before a noun. (See Unit 28.)	NOUN There are **enough chairs**.

2 *Too*

Too means **more than necessary**. It has a negative meaning.	
You can use *too* before an **adjective**.	The room is **too hot**. *(We can't stay.)*
Much too or *way too* makes the meaning **stronger**.	The room is *much* **too hot**.
USAGE NOTE We use *way too* in informal speaking.	The room is *way* **too hot**.
BE CAREFUL! *Too* sounds like *to* and *two*, but the spelling and meaning are different.	Let's go **to** the movies. There are **two** good movies. It's **too** late.

3 Very

Very makes the meaning of an adjective **stronger**.	
Very comes before an **adjective**.	She's **very** talkative.
BE CAREFUL! *Too* and *very* are different. *Too* has a negative meaning, but *very* doesn't.	This soup is **very** hot and delicious. That soup was **too** hot. He burned his tongue.

4 As + Adjective + As

Use *as* + **adjective** + *as* to show how two people, places, or things are alike.	Sally is **as tall as** Paula. *(They're the same height.)*
Use *not as* + **adjective** + *as* to show how two people, places, or things are **not** alike.	Sally is **not as tall as** Mike. *(Mike is taller.)* Paula isn't **as tall as** Mike.
You can also use *as* + **adjective** + *as* to ask questions.	Is Mike **as tall as** his father?

REFERENCE NOTE

For more information on *enough* + **noun**, see Unit 28 on page 337.

Go to MyEnglishLab to watch the grammar presentation.

STEP 3   FOCUSED PRACTICE

EXERCISE 1 DISCOVER THE GRAMMAR

Ⓐ GRAMMAR NOTES 1–4 Read this conversation about a diner that reopened under new management. Underline adjective + *enough*, *too* + adjective, *very* + adjective, and *as* + adjective + *as*.

ALEXI: Where did you eat last night?

RICHARD: At Ellen's Restaurant.

ALEXI: Oh, yeah? I went there last year, and it was <u>very good</u>. How was the food last night?

RICHARD: Well, the soup was very watery, and the coffee wasn't strong enough.

ALEXI: That's terrible.

RICHARD: I had the steak, and it wasn't as tasty as before. Ilene said the chicken was great, but she never complains about anything.

ALEXI: Oh?

RICHARD: They had new menus, and the print was too small. When I got the bill, I found out everything was more expensive than before.

ALEXI: Did they keep the old servers?

RICHARD: No, the servers were new, and they weren't as polite as the old servers.

ALEXI: How was the atmosphere?

RICHARD: Different. The colors were very bright, and the music was very loud.

ALEXI: So, I guess the restaurant was empty.

RICHARD: Actually, it was very crowded.

B Complete the sentences about Ellen's restaurant last night, based on the conversation in A. Match the beginning of each sentence with the ending.

_b_ **1.** The steak	**a.** had too much water in it.
____ **2.** The soup	~~b.~~ was not very tasty.
____ **3.** The coffee	**c.** was louder than it was in the past.
____ **4.** The menu	**d.** had a lot of people.
____ **5.** The servers	**e.** was too weak.
____ **6.** The music	**f.** was hard for Richard to read.
____ **7.** The restaurant	**g.** were less polite than they were in the past.

EXERCISE 2 ADJECTIVE + *ENOUGH*

GRAMMAR NOTE 1 Complete the sentences. Choose an adjective from the box and *enough*.

fast	high	important	loud	old	strong	~~tall~~	warm

1. Can you reach that shelf? I'm not _____*tall enough*_____ .

2. He won't win the race. He isn't _____ .

3. Who can lift the desk? I'm not _____ .

4. We can hear the TV. It's _____ .

5. Ella can't start kindergarten yet.

   She isn't _____ .

6. She didn't get into that college. Her grades

   weren't _____ .

7. You don't have to heat up the soup.

   It's _____ .

8. They left out that part of the speech.

   It wasn't _____ .

EXERCISE 3   *TOO* + ADJECTIVE

GRAMMAR NOTE 2   Underline the adjectives in the sentences. Then add *too* before each adjective.

                        too
1. Homes are <u>expensive</u> in that area. That's why people can't afford to live there.
                ^

2. We don't want to move there. The commute is long. It's two hours to downtown.

3. The train is always crowded. Let's take the bus.

4. That house is small for you. There are six people in your family. How will you manage?

5. The house is big for us. We don't need that much space.

6. I don't like that area. Winters are cold.

7. Don't buy that coffee maker. It's cheap, and it will break.

8. I don't like the summer there. It's humid.

EXERCISE 4   *TOO* OR *VERY*

GRAMMAR NOTES 2–3   Complete the sentences with *too* or *very*.

1. A: Should I wear this black dress for the wedding?

   B: Yes! I think it's ____*very*____ fashionable.

2. A: I love these shoes. They're _____ stylish.

   B: Yes, but the heels are _____ high, and I can't wear them for long.

3. A: Did you get the tickets?

   B: No. We were much _____ late. The concert was sold out last week.

4. A: Can Said go on the roller coaster?

   B: No. He's _____ short. You have to be four feet tall, and he's only three feet six inches.

5. A: Here's your composition. You did a great job. It's _____ well-written.

   B: Thank you.

6. A: Please carry the box inside.

   B: I can't, Mom. It's _____ heavy for me.

7. A: Getting into that school is _____ difficult. Do you think Joe can get in?

   B: No. His grades are much _____ low.

8. A: Are you going to buy the jacket?

   B: Well, it's a good deal, but it doesn't fit. It's way _____ tight in the shoulders.

9. A: Are you ready to go?

   B: No. It's much _____ early. I don't want to be the first to arrive at the party.

10. A: Was the party fun?

   B: We had a _____ good time. We stayed until 2:00 a.m.

EXERCISE 5 *ENOUGH, TOO,* AND *VERY*

Ⓐ GRAMMAR NOTES 1–3 Haley is talking to her aunt about a party. Complete the conversation. Circle the correct words.

AUNT ANNE: So, Haley. How was the party?

HALEY: I had a great time, but there were problems with the place. The air conditioner

didn't work well, so it was (too hot) / hot enough in the room.
        1.

AUNT ANNE: How was the music?

HALEY: Good, but the refreshments were awful. The appetizers were

too salty / salty enough, and the desserts were too sweet / sweet enough. And
        2.   **3.**
there wasn't enough ice, so the drinks weren't too cold / cold enough.
                                                              4.

AUNT ANNE: Too bad.

HALEY: Also, there weren't enough chairs. Most of us had to stand. And the room wasn't

too big / big enough. It was too big / big enough for twenty people, but thirty-five
        5.   **6.**
people came. But I still had a lot of fun.

AUNT ANNE: Your mom sent me a picture of you, and you looked very beautiful / too beautiful.
                                                                          7.
I just wondered about those shoes. Weren't your heels too high / high enough?
                                                                    8.
How could you dance?

HALEY: They were too comfortable / very comfortable, and I danced all night!
                         9.

🔊 33|02 Ⓑ LISTEN AND CHECK Listen to the conversation and check your answers in A.

EXERCISE 6 *TOO, VERY, ENOUGH, AS...AS*

GRAMMAR NOTES 1–4 **Complete the sentences. Use the adjectives in parentheses and** *too, very, enough,* **or** *as...as.*

1. Mr. Jones isn't _____ *as old as* _____ he looks.
   (old)

2. The music was much _____. It hurt my ears, so we left before the
   (loud)
   end of the concert.

3. The food wasn't _____ for Bob. He likes very spicy food.
   (spicy)

4. That painting is _____. I want to hang it up in my living room.
   (beautiful)

5. That electrician is way _____ expensive. Let's find someone
   (expensive)
   less expensive.

6. Your mother's kitchen _____ my mother's kitchen. They both like to
   (clean)
   clean a lot!

7. Boots are _____ and warm. You should get a pair.
   (fashionable)

8. I understood a lot, but not everything in the movie. My French isn't

   _____ .
   (good)

9. My new shoes look good, but they aren't _____ my old shoes.
   (comfortable)

EXERCISE 7 *AS...AS*

Ⓐ GRAMMAR NOTE 4 **Complete the conversation. Use** *as...as* **and the correct forms of
the words in parentheses. Use contractions where possible.**

LYNN: Jeff got a great job offer in Lakeville, but I don't want to move.

BINA: Why not?

LYNN: Well, the schools in Lakeville _____ *aren't as good as* _____ the schools here
                                    1. (be / not / good)
      in Middletown.

BINA: But you don't have children.

LYNN: We may one day. And in Lakeville, the shopping _____
                                                    2. (be / not / convenient)
      it is here.

BINA: Shopping in Lakeville is just _____ shopping here.
                                  3. (convenient)
      Sometimes I even go there to shop.

LYNN: Well, the parks _____ they are in Middletown, and the
       4. (be / not / beautiful)

people _____ the people here.
       5. (be / not / friendly)

BINA: The people in Lakeville are just _____ the people here.
       6. (friendly)

Three of my co-workers live in Lakeville, and they're great. . . . How can you say that

people there aren't friendly? What's the real reason you don't want to move?

LYNN: Well . . . my family. Everyone is here. I feel bad because Jeff really wants to take the job,

but I just don't want to move away from them.

⏵33|03 **Ⓑ LISTEN AND CHECK** Listen to the conversation and check your answers in A.

EXERCISE 8 EDITING

GRAMMAR NOTES 1–4 **Read the sentences. There are six mistakes. The first mistake is
already corrected. Find and correct five more.**

1. My family's apartment isn't ~~enough big~~ *big enough* for

   four people.

2. My history course isn't as interesting than my

   computer course.

3. I can't vote. I'm to young. You have to be eighteen

   years old, and I'm only sixteen.

4. It's too way cold. We can't go swimming outdoors.

5. Is my brother enough old? Can he really join the

   army? He's eighteen.

6. I'm as taller as my father.

EXERCISE 9 LISTENING

▶ 33|04 **A** Listen to the conversation. Two managers are talking about two young employees, Colin and Maria. Complete the sentence. Choose the correct answer.

The managers _____ .

a. are planning to promote Maria and Colin

b. promoted Maria, but didn't promote Colin

▶ 33|04 **B** Listen again. Then complete the sentences. Circle the correct answers.

1. Maria is "reliable" means _____ .
   (**a.**) she does what she says she will do
   b. she usually says nice things to others

2. "Colin is too critical" means _____ .
   a. Colin complains about other people's work when it is bad
   b. Colin complains about other people's work when it is bad *and* when it is good

3. "She'll bring out the best in others" means _____ .
   a. she'll take people to nice places
   b. she'll help people do a better job

4. "She's a team player" means _____ .
   a. she'll be loyal to the company and help her co-workers
   b. she'll join a company sports team

C Work with a partner. Study the meaning of the words in the box. Then take turns asking questions about Colin and Maria. Use *as . . . as* and the adjectives in the list.

critical: always saying something is bad or wrong
enthusiastic: showing interest and excitement about something
helpful: wanting to help
punctual: being on time
reliable: being a person who does what they say they will do
smart: intelligent

EXAMPLE: A: Is Maria as critical as Colin?
        B: No. Colin is too critical, and Maria isn't critical.

EXERCISE 10 DON'T EVER GO THERE!

A ROLE PLAY **Prepare to do role plays. Choose one of the following topics and take notes about it. Use** *too* **or** *enough* **for your reasons.**

- a place you don't like and three reasons why
- a sports event, movie, or concert you didn't like and three reasons why

I don't like Lakeville Amusement Park.

Reasons:
1. *Park: too crowded*
2. *Lines: too long*
3. *Rides: not long enough*

B **Work with a partner. Do a role play on the topic you chose in A. Use your notes. Then switch roles.**

EXAMPLE: A: Don't ever go to Lakeville Amusement Park.
      B: Really? Why not?
      A: I was there last Saturday, and it was awful. First of all, it was way too crowded. And the lines were too long for the good rides.
      B: Anything else?
      A: Yes! The rides weren't long enough. After we finally got on a ride, it was over in two minutes.
      B: I won't ever go there!

EXERCISE 11 THAT'S WAY TOO EXPENSIVE!

PROBLEM SOLVING Work in a group. Look at the chart. Then discuss why each gift is or isn't good for the person. Use *too*, *enough*, or *as...as* in your discussion.

EXAMPLE: A: I think a pen is too cheap for a favorite uncle on his fortieth birthday.
B: I agree. But it's not just too cheap. It isn't special enough for a fortieth birthday. I think...

Person	Occasion	Gift	Amount
favorite uncle	his fortieth birthday	a pen	$5.00
rich boss	dinner at his home	a digital watch	$1,000.00
best friend	marriage	a dishwasher	$400.00
grandmother	her seventieth birthday	a good camera	$300.00
nine-year-old nephew	birthday	a bottle of cologne	$50.00

EXERCISE 12 IT'S TOO COLD

Ⓐ CONVERSATION Work in small groups. Use the ideas in the box to make suggestions about what to do tomorrow. Talk about what, when, and where.

EXAMPLE: A: Let's go bird watching in West Park tomorrow at noon.
B: Let's have a picnic at Spring Lake next Saturday morning.

go bird watching
go bungee jumping
go to a movie
go to a museum
go to a restaurant
have a picnic
study together

Ⓑ Work with other groups. Listen to a group's suggestion. Reject it. Use *too* + adjective, *very* + adjective, adjective + *enough*, or *as...as* in your response.

EXAMPLE: A: Let's go bird watching in West Park tomorrow at noon.
B: No, let's not do that. It's too cold.
C: West Park is too far from here.
D: West Park isn't as pretty as East Park.

Go to MyEnglishLab for more communication practice.

FROM GRAMMAR TO WRITING

A BEFORE YOU READ
Read about a terrible shoe store. Then think about a store you didn't like. Complete the chart with your complaints. Then work with a partner. Tell your partner about the store.

I went to the new shoe store on Main Street last week. It was awful. The shoes were in boxes, and you could help yourself, but the boxes in my size were too high. When I asked for help, the salesperson was very rude. When I finally tried on a pair of shoes, the left shoe wasn't big enough, and the right shoe was too big. That's because they had two different sizes in the box. In addition, the air conditioner didn't work, so it was too hot. Finally, the prices weren't as low as they advertised. So, if you need shoes, don't shop at Joe's Shoe Store on Main Street.

Name of Store	
Complaint 1	
Complaint 2	
Complaint 3	
Complaint 4	

B WRITE Write a paragraph about a store you don't like. Use the paragraph in A and your chart. Use *too*, *very*, *as . . . as*, or *enough* in your writing.

C CHECK YOUR WORK Read your paragraph in B. Underline the use of *too*, *very*, *as . . . as*, and *enough*. Then use the Editing Checklist to check your work.

Editing Checklist
Did you use . . . ?
☐ adjective + *enough* to say that something is the right amount
☐ *very* + an adjective to make the meaning of an adjective stronger
☐ *too* + an adjective for a negative meaning
☐ *(not) as* + adjective + *as* to show how things are or are not alike

D REVISE YOUR WORK Read your paragraph again. Can you improve your writing? Make changes if necessary.

UNIT 33 **REVIEW**

Test yourself on the grammar of the unit.

Ⓐ Complete the sentences. Circle the correct answers.

1. Is that car big enough / enough big?

2. His car is not as fast as / than mine.

3. He can't get a driver's license. He's very / too young.

4. He's not too / as young as he looks.

5. I'm very / too happy. My son graduated from college last week.

Ⓑ Complete the sentences. Use *enough*, *too*, or *very* and the words from the box.

busy	fast	good	late	short	warm

1. The water isn't _____ for swimming.

2. We got to the party much _____, so we didn't get any cake.

3. I don't like my haircut. My hair is _____.

4. She runs slowly, so she isn't _____ to be on the track team.

5. He looks _____ in his new sweater. I'm glad I got it for him.

Ⓒ Complete the sentences with *as ... as* or *not as ... as* and the adjectives in parentheses.

1. I'm heavier than my father. I'm _____.
                                                              (thin)

2. My new coat is less expensive than my old one. My old coat is _____.
                                                                                           (cheap)

3. I am the same height as my brother. I'm _____.
                                                                       (tall)

4. I'm the same age as my cousin. My cousin is _____.
                                                                       (old)

Ⓓ Correct the paragraph. There are six mistakes.

This year, the party wasn't good as last year. The music was very much loud. It was

hard to dance because the room was too way hot. I like to dance, so I felt too bad about

that. Also, the drinks weren't enough cold, and the food wasn't tasty as last year.

Now check your answers on page 452.

Go to MyEnglishLab to complete the review online.

UNIT
34

The Superlative
ANIMALS AROUND THE WORLD

OUTCOMES
- Compare three or more nouns, using superlative adjectives
- Recognize details in a scientific article
- Recognize key information from a quiz show
- Prepare a survey and present results to the class
- Discuss animals and their characteristics
- Write a paragraph about an animal

STEP 1 GRAMMAR IN CONTEXT

BEFORE YOU READ

Work with a partner. Look at the photo. Answer the questions.

1. What do you know about penguins?

2. Do you like penguins? Why or why not?

Macaroni Penguins

READ

34|01 Read this article about penguins.

The Penguin

The penguin is one of the easiest birds to recognize. Penguins have black backs and white bellies.[1] They look fat. They stand upright, and they walk like ducks. Unlike other birds, most penguins can't fly, but they can swim very fast.

In 1519, Spanish explorers under Ferdinand Magellan saw penguins when they sailed around South America. They thought this bird was one of the strangest birds in the world. To them, the penguins looked like another strange bird, the Great Auk of Greenland and Iceland. The Great Auk was a large black and white bird that did not fly. The Spanish word for Great Auk is *pinguis*, which means "fat." And that's how penguins got their name.

---

1 *bellies:* stomachs

The Superlative   **415**

There are seventeen kinds of penguins. They all live below the equator, but they don't only live in very cold climates. Some, like the Little Blue Penguins (sometimes called Fairy Penguins), live in warmer climates. The Little Blue Penguins are the smallest of all. They are a little over a foot (30.5 centimeters) tall. They got their name because of their blue feathers. These penguins live in the warm waters off southern Australia and New Zealand.

The largest penguins are the Emperor Penguins. They are almost four feet (about 1.2 meters) tall and weigh from 70 to almost 90 pounds (about 32 to 41 kilograms). They live on the ice around the Antarctic continent. This is the coldest climate on earth.

Of the seventeen different species of penguins, the Macaroni Penguins have the biggest population, while the Galapagos Penguins have the smallest. In fact, some scientists worry that the Galapagos Penguins may become extinct.

People say penguins are the cutest, the funniest, and the most loved birds. They also say they're the most formal. Do you know why? It's because they look as if they're wearing tuxedos.[2]

---

2 *tuxedos:* formal suits worn at weddings or other very formal occasions

Blue (Fairy) Penguin   **Great Auk**   **Emperor Penguin**

AFTER YOU READ

A VOCABULARY **Complete the sentences with the words from the box.**

centimeters	inches	pounds
extinct	kilogram	species

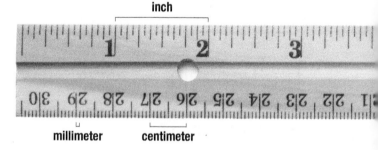

inch

millimeter   centimeter

1. My son grew six _____ in the last three years. That's half a foot.

2. One thousand millimeters is the same as 100 _____ .

3. In the United States, people usually measure their weight in _____ .

4. One _____ is the same as 2.2 pounds.

5. There are seventeen different _____ of penguins.

6. Some scientists worry that global warming may cause penguins to become _____ .

B COMPREHENSION Match the birds with the descriptions.

_____ 1. Galapagos Penguins

_____ 2. Little Blue Penguins

_____ 3. Emperor Penguins

_____ 4. Great Auks

_____ 5. Macaroni Penguins

a. The biggest penguins

b. The smallest population of penguins

c. The smallest penguins

d. The largest population of penguins

e. Birds that lived in Greenland and Iceland

C DISCUSSION Work with a partner. Compare your answers in B. Then discuss: What was the most interesting fact you learned about penguins?

Go to MyEnglishLab for more grammar in context practice.

STEP 2	GRAMMAR PRESENTATION

SUPERLATIVE FORMS OF ADJECTIVES

Superlative Forms of Adjectives			
		Superlative Adjective	
The Emperor Penguin	is	**the biggest**	of all the penguins.
That photo		**the funniest**	of all.
That program		**the most interesting**	one on TV.

Superlative Forms of Irregular Adjectives			
		Superlative Adjective	
This	is	**the best**	photo of all.
We	had	**the worst**	weather on Saturday.
Her home	is	**the farthest**	from school.

GRAMMAR NOTES

1 Superlative Adjectives

Use the **superlative** form of adjectives to compare **three or more people, places, or things**.

There are three superlative forms:
- *the* + adjective + *-est*
- *the* + adjective + *-iest*
- *the most* + adjective

The cheetah is **the fastest** animal on earth.

The penguin is **the funniest** bird in the zoo.

The bird section was **the most interesting** part of the zoo.

2 Short Adjectives

To form the superlative of **short** (one-syllable) **adjectives**, add *the* before the adjective and *-est* to the adjective.	
fast → *the fastest*	The cheetah is **the fastest** animal on earth.
long → *the longest*	
If the adjective ends in *-e*, add *-st*.	
large → *the largest*	Alaska is **the largest** state in the United States.
To form the superlative of short **adjectives that end in -y**, add *the* before the adjective, then drop the **-y** and add *-iest* to the adjective.	
funny → *the funniest*	The penguin is **the funniest** bird in the zoo.
The adjectives *good*, *bad*, and *far* have **irregular** comparative and superlative forms.	
good → *better* → *the best*	Early morning is **the best** time for bird watching.
bad → *worse* → *the worst*	Sunday afternoon is **the worst** time to visit the zoo.
far → *farther* → *the farthest*	The Birdhouse is **the farthest** section from the entrance.

3 Longer Adjectives

To form the superlative of **long** adjectives, add *the most* before the **adjective**.	
interesting → *the most interesting*	The bird section was **the most interesting** part of the zoo.
dangerous → *the most dangerous*	
BE CAREFUL! Do not use *-est* and *most* together.	It is **the tallest** animal.
	NOT It is the ~~most tallest~~ animal.
	It is **the most interesting** show.
	NOT It is the ~~most interestingest~~ show.

4 Superlative + Prepositional Phrase

After the superlative, we often use **a prepositional phrase** to identify the group we are talking about.	The giraffe is **the tallest** animal *in the zoo*. The rhinoceros beetle is **the strongest** *of the animals*.

5 One of + Superlative + Plural Noun

One of often comes before a superlative adjective.	It is **one of the largest animals** in the world. It is **one of the most intelligent animals** of all.
BE CAREFUL! The noun that follows *one of* + the superlative is always **plural**.	The greyhound is one of the fastest **dogs**. NOT The greyhound is one of the fastest ~~dog~~.

Go to MyEnglishLab to watch the grammar presentation.

EXERCISE 1 DISCOVER THE GRAMMAR

A GRAMMAR NOTES 1–5 Underline the superlative in each sentence.

1. The cockroach is probably <u>the most unpopular</u> insect in the world.

2. Cockroaches live everywhere, even in the cleanest kitchens.

3. The world's heaviest cockroach is the Australian Giant Burrowing Cockroach.

4. The best way to kill a cockroach is with boric acid.

5. One of the most famous cockroaches is in a story by Franz Kafka. In it, a man turns into a cockroach.

B Write the superlative forms of the adjectives from A and their base forms.

Adjective	Superlative form
1. *unpopular*	*the most unpopular*
2.	
3.	
4.	
5.	

EXERCISE 2 SUPERLATIVE ADJECTIVES

GRAMMAR NOTES 1–3 Complete the sentences with the words in parentheses. Use the superlative form of the adjective. Then guess the name of the animal that each sentence describes. Choose from the animals in the box. Check your answers on page 453.

the African elephant	the giraffe	the Macaroni Penguin
~~the blue whale~~	the hummingbird	the sailfish

1. It is ___*the biggest*___ animal in the world. = _The blue whale_
(big)

2. It is _____ land animal. = _____
(large)

3. It is _____ animal. = _____
(tall)

4. It is _____ bird. = _____
(small)

5. It is _____ fish. = _____
(fast)

6. It is _____ of all the penguins. = _____
(colorful)

EXERCISE 3 SUPERLATIVE ADJECTIVES

GRAMMAR NOTES 1–3 Complete the paragraphs with facts about snakes and jellyfish. Use the superlative form of the adjectives in parentheses.

King Cobra

Do you know which country has

_____ *the highest* _____ percentage of deadly
1. (high)

snakes? It's Australia. But it doesn't really worry

Australians, because only three people die of snake bites

in Australia each year. The country with

_____ number of deadly snake
2. (large)

bites is India. In India, the _____
3. (scary)

snake is the king cobra. It mainly lives in the rain forests

and plains. _____ snake in the
4. (small)

world is the threadsnake. It is about 3.9 inches (10

centimeters) long. _____ snake
5. (long)

in the world is the python. Scientists say it can grow up

to about 20 feet (6.09 meters).

One of _____ species on
6. (old)

earth is the jellyfish. We believe jellyfish were around

more than 650 million years ago. They are one of

_____ sea creatures, too. There
7. (frightening)

are over 2,000 different kinds of jellyfish. Some are

tiny, and others are huge. _____
8. (long)

jellyfish are about 120 feet (36.5 meters).

_____ jellyfish are the box
9. (deadly)

jellyfish. They live in the waters off Australia.

Jellyfish

EXERCISE 4 *ONE OF* + SUPERLATIVE

GRAMMAR NOTES 1–3, 5 **Complete the conversations with *one of* and the words in parentheses. Use the superlative form of the adjectives and plural form of the nouns.**

Peacock

1. A: I think the peacock is

   <u>   one of the prettiest birds   </u>
   (pretty / bird)

   in the world.

   B: I agree.

2. A: I'm going to be in San Diego. Is the San Diego Zoo a good place to go?

   B: I think so. It's _____ in the United States.
   (popular / zoo)

3. A: Can an octopus open a jar?

   B: Yes, it can. It's _____ in the sea.
   (smart / animal)

4. A: Are there any good nature shows on TV?

   B: Yes. _____ is on at 8:00 p.m. tonight.
   (good / nature show)

5. A: Are you laughing at that monkey?

   B: Yes. He's _____ in the zoo.
   (funny / animal)

6. A: My son loves to look at dinosaurs. Where can you see dinosaur bones?

   B: The Museum of Natural History in New York City has

   _____ of dinosaur bones in the world.
   (good / collection)

EXERCISE 5 COMPARATIVE AND SUPERLATIVE

GRAMMAR NOTE 1 **Complete the sentences with the adjectives in parentheses. Use the comparative or superlative form.**

1. African elephants are different from Asian elephants. Asian elephants have

   <u>   smaller   </u> ears and _____ tusks than African
   (small)   (short)

   elephants. The African elephants are _____ and
   (large)

   _____ than Asian elephants.
   (tall)

2. Bear's milk is _____ than human milk, but seal milk is
   (rich)

   _____ of all milk from animals. Seal milk is 60 percent fat.
   (rich)

3. _____ snake in the world is the Barbados threadsnake. It reaches
   (small)

   just slightly less than 4 inches (10.16 centimeters) in length.

4. _____ snakes in the world are the anaconda and the python.
   (large)

   They are similar in many ways, but the python lays eggs and the anaconda doesn't.

5. Most female snakes are _____ than male snakes.
   (large)

6. A snake's body temperature is about the same as the temperature outside. When the

   temperature warms up, snakes are _____, and when it gets
   (active)

   _____ outside, they are less active.
   (cold)

7. Many people think the great white shark is _____ of all sharks
   (dangerous)

   to humans. Studies show that it's not true. Great white sharks mostly attack when they

   confuse humans with seals or sea lions.

EXERCISE 6 EDITING

GRAMMAR NOTES 1–5 **Read the sentences. There are seven mistakes. The first mistake
is already corrected. Find and correct six more.**

1. The Berlin Zoological Garden is the ~~most old~~ *oldest* zoo in Germany. It opened in 1844.

2. It is one of the most popular zoo in the world.

3. The zoo has biggest collection of different species in the world.

4. The zoo is very crowded Sunday afternoons. That is the most bad time to visit.

5. The pandas are the popularest animals in the Berlin Zoological Garden.

6. The Birdhouse is one the most modern bird houses in Europe.

7. The most good time to visit the zoo is in the spring or the fall.

Go to MyEnglishLab for more focused practice.

EXERCISE 7 LISTENING

○34|02   **A** Listen to a quiz show about animals. Read the questions. Choose the correct answers.

1. The first question asks, "Which land animal has the longest gestation period?"
   A gestation period is _____ .
   a. the time the baby is inside its mother   **b.** the time the baby learns to walk

2. The second question asks, "Which animal is _____?"
   a. the fattest   **b.** the fastest

3. The third question asks, "Which animal is _____?"
   a. the loudest   **b.** the proudest

4. The last question asks, "Which animal is _____?"
   a. the smallest   **b.** the deadliest

○34|02   **B** Listen again. What were the answers to the four questions in the quiz show? Choose from the words in the box.

ant	cheetah	cow	horse	monkey	peacock
bear	cockroach	elephant	lion	mosquito	tiger

Question 1: the Asian _____

Question 2: the _____

Question 3: the howler _____

Question 4: the _____

C Work with a partner. Say two statements about animals using the superlative. Your partner decides if they are true or false. Take turns.

EXAMPLE: A: The Asian elephant is the loudest land animal.
          B: That's not true. The howler monkey
             is the loudest land animal.

EXERCISE 8 THE MOST BEAUTIFUL ANIMALS

Ⓐ SURVEY Prepare questions for a survey in B. Use the superlative and the words in the box.

| beautiful / animal | good / pet | interesting / animal | smart / animal |

What's the most beautiful animal?

Ⓑ Ask four classmates to answer your questions in A. Then ask each student a reason why he or she thinks so.

Question	Student 1	Student 2	Student 3	Student 4
1. What's the most beautiful animal?				

EXAMPLE: A: Florian, what's the most beautiful animal?
  B: The peacock.
  A: Why?
  B: I think it's the most beautiful animal because it has the most colorful feathers.

Ⓒ Report results to the class.

EXAMPLE: Florian thinks that the peacock is the most beautiful animal because it has the most colorful feathers.

EXERCISE 9 PROBLEM ANIMALS

DISCUSSION Work in a group. Talk about animals or insects that are problems for humans—for example, cockroaches, ants, mice, raccoons, squirrels, deer, or bears.

1. What animals cause the biggest problems in your area? Why?

2. What's the best way to handle the problem?

EXAMPLE: A: I think one of the biggest problems around here is bears.

B: Bears? I disagree. There are a lot of bears, and they are big and scary, but they rarely bother people. I think that raccoons are our worst problem. Last summer, a raccoon climbed in my attic and made a home there. It was hard to get rid of her.

EXERCISE 10 ANIMALS FROM A TO Z

A COMPARISON Prepare to compare animals in B. Work in a group. Try to write the name of one animal for each letter of the alphabet. Then write the animals on the board.

EXAMPLES: A = ant
B = bear
C = . . .

B Work in a group. Choose three animals. Use the adjectives in the box to make superlative statements about the animals. Then report to the class.

| beautiful | big | dangerous | fast | intelligent | loud |

EXAMPLE: OK, so we compared the ant, the bear, and the cockroach. The bear is the biggest of the three animals. We think the bear is the most dangerous to humans. We think the bear is the most beautiful, but none are really beautiful.

Go to MyEnglishLab for more communication practice.

A BEFORE YOU WRITE   Read about a student's visit to a zoo. Then work with a partner. Tell your partner about a visit to a zoo or a time you looked carefully at animals.

Last August I visited the Bronx Zoo. This zoo is one of the best zoos in the world. It covers 265 acres and is home to over 6,000 animals. I enjoyed the Butterfly Zone and the World of Birds, but the most interesting part was the Congo Gorilla Forest. I saw a rain forest and a lot of gorillas. The funniest gorilla acted like a person. The people laughed a lot. I laughed, too. Then someone said, "He's acting like you!"

B WRITE   Write a paragraph about a time you looked at animals carefully. Use the paragraph in A and your ideas. Use two examples of the superlative.

C CHECK YOUR WORK   Read your paragraph in B. Underline examples of the superlative. Use the Editing Checklist to check your work.

Editing Checklist

Did you . . . ?

☐ use superlative adjectives to compare three or more people, places, or things

☐ form the superlative by adding *the* before an adjective and adding *-est* to the adjective for short adjectives

☐ form the superlative by adding *the most* before longer adjectives

☐ use *one of* + the superlative form + a plural noun

☐ check your spelling

D REVISE YOUR WORK   Read your paragraph again. Can you improve your writing? Make changes if necessary.

Go to MyEnglishLab for more writing practice.

UNIT 34 REVIEW

Test yourself on the grammar of the unit.

Ⓐ Complete the sentences. Use the superlative form of the adjectives in parentheses.

1. Who was _____ monkey in the cage?
   (funny)

2. What is the name of _____ whale?
   (big)

3. What is _____ nature show on TV?
   (good)

4. _____ sharks in the world are not _____.
   (large)   (dangerous)

Ⓑ Complete the sentences. Circle the correct answers.

1. It's 101°F (38.3°C). It's the most hottest / the hottest day of the year.

2. She's 112 years old. She's the older woman / the oldest woman in town.

3. The day after Thanksgiving is a busiest / the busiest shopping day of the year.

4. It was the best interesting / the most interesting show on TV last month.

5. The tiger is the popularist / the most popular animal at the zoo.

Ⓒ Complete the sentences. Use the superlative form of the adjective and the plural form of the noun.

1. The dolphin is one of _____ in the world.
   (intelligent / animal)

2. The parrot is one of _____ in the world.
   (colorful / bird)

3. He has one of _____ in the stadium.
   (bad / seat)

4. It was one of _____ of the year.
   (long / day)

Ⓓ Correct the conversation. There are six mistakes.

A: What's hardest part of your job here at the zoo?

B: The difficultest part for me is telling people not to bother or feed the animals.

A: And which animal is the most smart?

B: Bill the gorilla. He's one of funniest and smartest animal. He's also one of

   the interesting. And I think he's of the cutest, too!

Now check your answers on page 452.

Go to MyEnglishLab to complete the review online.

Appendices

Anchorage · Juneau ⊛
Alaska

Yukon Territory
⊛ Whitehorse
Northwest Territories
Yellowknife ⊛
Nunavut
Iqaluit ⊛

Newfoundland
St. John's ⊛
Newfoundland
Gulf of
St. Lawrence
Charlottetown
Prince
Edward
Island
New
Brunswick
Fredericton ⊛
Maine
Halifax ⊛
Nova Scotia

British
Columbia
Alberta
Edmonton ⊛
Saskatchewan
Banff ·
Saskatoon ·
Manitoba
Québec

Victoria ⊛ · Vancouver
Seattle ·
⊛ Olympia
Lake
Winnipeg
Regina ⊛
Winnipeg ⊛
Ontario
Québec
City
Concord, ·
New Hampshire
Montpelier, ⊛
Vermont
Montreal ⊛
Maine
Augusta
⊛

Portland ·
⊛ Salem
Corvallis ·
Washington
Helena
⊛
Missouri River
North Dakota
Bismarck ⊛
Minnesota
Lake Superior
Michigan
Lake Huron
Lake Ontario
Ottawa ⊛
Toronto ·
Lake Erie
Portland ·
Boston,
Massachusetts
Oregon
Boise ⊛
Idaho
Montana
Wyoming
St. Paul ⊛
Minneapolis ·
Pierre ⊛
South Dakota
Wisconsin
Madison ⊛
Milwaukee ·
Lansing ⊛
Lake Michigan
Detroit ·
Albany ⊛
New York
New
York
Providence,
Rhode Island
Pennsylvania
Hartford,
Connecticut

Sacramento ⊛ · Carson City
San Francisco ·
California
Nevada
Las
Vegas ·
Great
Salt Lake
Salt Lake City ⊛
Utah
Cheyenne ⊛
Denver ⊛
Colorado
Nebraska
Lincoln ⊛
Iowa
Des Moines ⊛
Missouri River
Chicago ·
Illinois
Springfield ⊛
Indianapolis ⊛
Indiana
Ohio
Columbus ⊛
West
Virginia
Harrisburg ⊛
Philadelphia ·
Trenton,
New Jersey
Dover,
Delaware
Annapolis,
Maryland
Richmond ⊛
Virginia
Washington, D.C.

Los Angeles ·
San Diego ·
Grand Canyon ·
Arizona
Phoenix ⊛
Santa Fe ⊛
New Mexico
Kansas
Topeka ⊛
Kansas City ·
Jefferson City ⊛
Missouri
Kentucky
Frankfort ⊛
Charleston ⊛
Nashville ⊛
Tennessee
Memphis ·
Appalachian Mountains
Raleigh ⊛
North Carolina
Columbia ⊛
South
Carolina
Atlanta ⊛
Rocky Mountains

Pacific
Ocean
El Paso ·
Texas
Oklahoma
Oklahoma City ⊛
Little Rock ⊛
Arkansas
Mississippi River
Alabama
Montgomery ⊛
Mississippi
Jackson ⊛
Georgia
Atlantic
Ocean

Honolulu ·
Hawaii
Rio Grande
San Antonio ·
Austin ⊛
Houston ·
Dallas ·
Louisiana
Baton
Rouge ⊛
New Orleans ·
Tallahassee ⊛
Florida
Orlando ·
Miami ·
Gulf of Mexico

N
W E
S

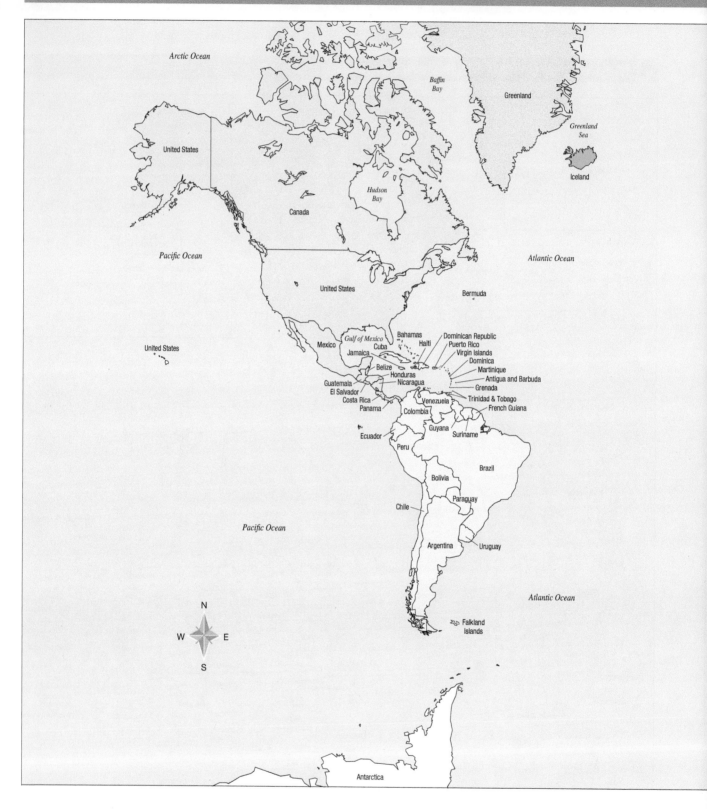

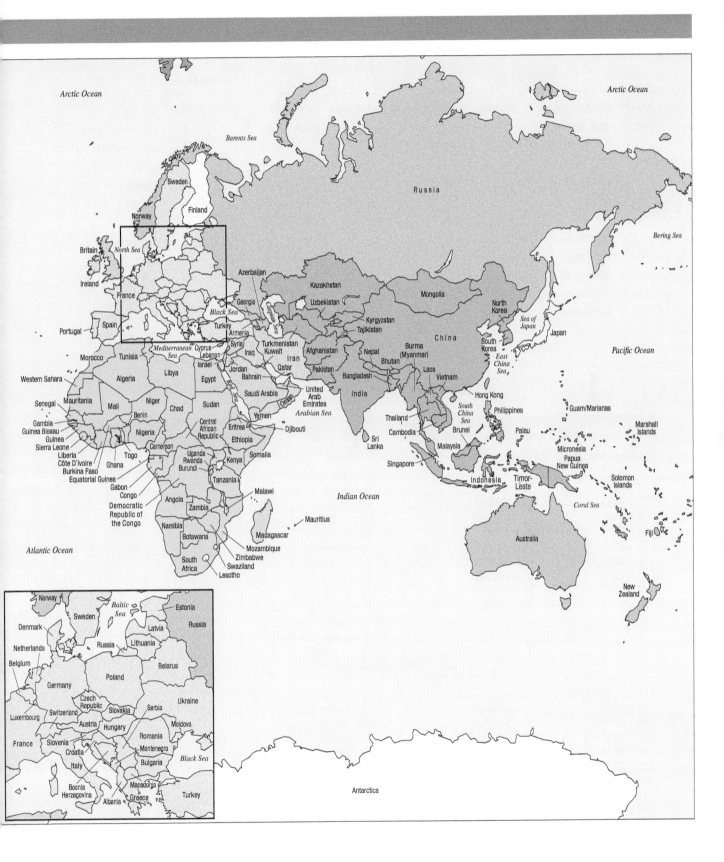

Arctic Ocean

Barents Sea

Sweden

Norway

Finland

Britain

North Sea

Ireland

France

Azerbaijan

Black Sea

Georgia

Turkey

Armenia

Portugal

Spain

Cyprus

Syria

Lebanon

Israel

Iraq

Jordan

Bahrain

Kuwait

Qatar

Mediterranean Sea

Morocco

Tunisia

Libya

Egypt

Western Sahara

Algeria

Saudi Arabia

Senegal

Mauritania

Mali

Niger

Chad

Sudan

Gambia

Benin

Yemen

Guinea Bissau

Nigeria

Eritrea

Guinea

Sierra Leone

Central African Republic

Liberia

Togo

Ethiopia

Côte D'ivoire

Ghana

Cameroon

Djibouti

Burkina Faso

Uganda

Somalia

Equatorial Guinea

Rwanda

Kenya

Gabon

Burundi

Congo

Tanzania

Democratic Republic of the Congo

Angola

Zambia

Malawi

Namibia

Botswana

Madagascar

Mauritius

Mozambique

South Africa

Zimbabwe

Swaziland

Lesotho

Atlantic Ocean

Russia

Bering Sea

Kazakhstan

Mongolia

North Korea

Uzbekistan

Kyrgyzstan

Tajikistan

Turkmenistan

Afghanistan

Nepal

Bhutan

China

South Korea

Japan

Sea of Japan

Pacific Ocean

Iran

Pakistan

Burma (Myanmar)

Laos

East China Sea

Bangladesh

Hong Kong

United Arab Emirates

Oman

India

Vietnam

Arabian Sea

Thailand

Cambodia

South China Sea

Brunei

Guam/Marianas

Sri Lanka

Malaysia

Philippines

Palau

Marshall Islands

Singapore

Indonesia

Micronesia

Papua New Guinea

Timor-Leste

Solomon Islands

Indian Ocean

Coral Sea

Fiji

Australia

New Zealand

Antarctica

Norway

Baltic Sea

Estonia

Sweden

Russia

Denmark

Latvia

Netherlands

Russia

Lithuania

Belgium

Belarus

Luxembourg

Germany

Poland

Czech Republic

Switzerland

Slovakia

Serbia

Ukraine

Austria

Hungary

Moldova

France

Slovenia

Romania

Croatia

Montenegro

Black Sea

Italy

Bulgaria

Bosnia Herzegovina

Macedonia

Albania

Greece

Turkey

3 Pronunciation Table

A|01 These are the pronunciation symbols used in this text. Listen to the pronunciation of the key words.

VOWELS				CONSONANTS			
SYMBOL	KEY WORD	SYMBOL	KEY WORD	SYMBOL	KEY WORD	SYMBOL	KEY WORD
i	beat, feed	ə	banana, among	p	pack, happy	z	zip, please, goes
ɪ	bit, did	ɚ	shirt, murder	b	back, rubber	ʃ	ship, machine, station,
eɪ	date, paid	aɪ	bite, cry, buy, eye	t	tie		special, discussion
ɛ	bet, bed	aʊ	about, how	d	die	ʒ	measure
æ	bat, bad	ɔɪ	voice, boy	k	came, key, quick	h	hot, who
ɑ	box, odd, father	ɪr	ear, beer	g	game, guest	m	men
ɔ	bought, dog	ɛr	bare	tʃ	church, nature, watch	n	sun, know
oʊ	boat, road	ɑr	bar	ʤ	judge, general, major	ŋ	sung, ringing
ʊ	book, good	ɔr	door	f	fan, photograph	w	wet, white
u	boot, food, student	ʊr	tour	v	van	l	light, long
ʌ	but, mud, mother			θ	thing, breath	r	right, wrong
				ð	then, breathe	y	yes, use, music
				s	sip, city, psychology	t̬	butter, bottle

4 Numbers

CARDINAL NUMBERS

1 = one	11 = eleven	21 = twenty-one
2 = two	12 = twelve	30 = thirty
3 = three	13 = thirteen	40 = forty
4 = four	14 = fourteen	50 = fifty
5 = five	15 = fifteen	60 = sixty
6 = six	16 = sixteen	70 = seventy
7 = seven	17 = seventeen	80 = eighty
8 = eight	18 = eighteen	90 = ninety
9 = nine	19 = nineteen	100 = one hundred
10 = ten	20 = twenty	101 = one hundred and one
		200 = two hundred
		1,000 = one thousand
		1,000,000 = one million
		1,000,000,000 = one billion

ORDINAL NUMBERS

1st = first	11th = eleventh	21st = twenty-first
2nd = second	12th = twelfth	30th = thirtieth
3rd = third	13th = thirteenth	40th = fortieth
4th = fourth	14th = fourteenth	50th = fiftieth
5th = fifth	15th = fifteenth	60th = sixtieth
6th = sixth	16th = sixteenth	70th = seventieth
7th = seventh	17th = seventeenth	80th = eightieth
8th = eighth	18th = eighteenth	90th = ninetieth
9th = ninth	19th = nineteenth	100th = one hundredth
10th = tenth	20th = twentieth	101st = one hundred and first
		200th = two hundredth
		1,000th = one thousandth
		1,000,000th = one millionth
		1,000,000,000th = one billionth

5 Days, Months, and Seasons

DAYS OF THE WEEK

Weekdays	Weekend
Monday	Saturday
Tuesday	Sunday
Wednesday	
Thursday	
Friday	

MONTHS OF THE YEAR

Month	Abbreviation	Month	Abbreviation
January	Jan.	July	Jul.
February	Feb.	August	Aug.
March	Mar.	September	Sept.
April	Apr.	October	Oct.
May	May	November	Nov.
June	Jun.	December	Dec.

SEASONS

Spring
Summer
Autumn or Fall
Winter

6 Titles

Mr. (Mister) /mɪstər/   unmarried or married man
Ms. /mɪz/   unmarried or married woman
Miss /mɪs/   unmarried woman
Mrs. /mɪsɪz/   married woman
Dr. (Doctor) /dɑktər/   doctor (medical doctor or Ph.D.)

7 Time

It's one o'clock.
(It's 1:00.)

It's five after one.
(It's 1:05.)

It's one-ten.
It's ten after one.
(It's 1:10.)

It's one-fifteen.
It's a quarter after one.
(It's 1:15.)

It's one twenty-five.
It's twenty-five after one.
(It's 1:25.)

It's one-thirty.
It's half past one.
(It's 1:30.)

It's one forty-five.
It's a quarter to two.
(It's 1:45.)

It's one-fifty.
It's ten to two.
(It's 1:50.)

1 You can ask and give the time in this way:

A: **What time is it?**
B: It's one **o'clock**.

2 We often write time with numbers.

It's one o'clock. = It's **1:00**.
It's two-twenty. = It's **2:20**.

3 We use the abbreviation **a.m.** for times from midnight to noon.
It's 10:00 **a.m.**

We use the abbreviation **p.m.** for times from noon to midnight.
It's 10:00 **p.m.**

4 When people say 12:00 a.m., they mean midnight. When people say 12:00 p.m., they mean noon.

8 Regular Plural Nouns: Spelling Rules

1 Add **-s** to most nouns.

book	book**s**
table	table**s**
cup	cup**s**

2 Add **-es** to nouns that end in **-ch**, **-s**, **-sh**, or **-x**.

watch	watch**es**
bus	bus**es**
dish	dish**es**
box	box**es**

3 Add **-s** to nouns that end in **vowel + y**.

day	day**s**
key	key**s**

4 Change the **y** to **i** and add **-es** to nouns that end in **consonant + y**.

baby	bab**ies**
city	cit**ies**
strawberry	strawberr**ies**

5 Add **-s** to nouns that end in **vowel + o**.

radio	radio**s**
video	video**s**
zoo	zoo**s**

6 Add **-es** to nouns that end in **consonant + o**.

potato	potato**es**
tomato	tomato**es**

EXCEPTIONS:

kilo	kilo**s**
photo	photo**s**
piano	piano**s**

9 Irregular Plural Nouns

SINGULAR	PLURAL
half	halves
knife	knives
leaf	leaves
life	lives
shelf	shelves
wife	wives

SINGULAR	PLURAL
child	children
foot	feet
man	men
mouse	mice
person	people
tooth	teeth
woman	women

SINGULAR	PLURAL
clothes	clothes
deer	deer
fish	fish
pants	pants
scissors	scissors
sheep	sheep

10 Plural Nouns: Pronunciation Rules

1 The **final sounds** for regular plural nouns are /s/, /z/, and /ɪz/.

boots	boys	horses

2 The plural is pronounced /s/ **after the voiceless sounds** /p/, /t/, /k/, /f/, and /θ/.

cups	cuffs
hats	myths
works	

3 The plural is pronounced /z/ **after the voiced sounds** /b/, /d/, /g/, /v/, /m/, /n/, /ŋ/, /l/, /r/, and /ð/.

crabs	doves	rings
cards	drums	girls
rugs	fans	stores

4 The plural **s** is pronounced /z/ **after all vowel sounds**.

day	days
toe	toes

5 The plural **s** is pronounced /ɪz/ **after the sounds** /s/, /z/, /ʃ/, /tʃ/, and /dʒ/. (This adds another syllable to the word.)

races	churches
causes	judges
dishes	

11 Non-Count Nouns

Non-count nouns are singular.

ACTIVITIES
baseball
biking
football
golf
hiking
running
soccer
swimming
tennis

CITY PROBLEMS
crime
pollution

FOOD AND DRINKS
bread
broccoli
butter
cake
cheese
chicken
chocolate
coffee
corn
fat
fish
flour
fruit
ice cream

juice
lettuce
meat
milk
pasta
pizza
salad
soda
soup
spaghetti
spinach
tea
water
yogurt

IDEAS AND FEELINGS
friendship
happiness
love

GASES
air
oxygen
smoke

MATERIALS
clay
cotton
glass
gold
leather
paper
silk
silver
wood
wool

SCHOOL SUBJECTS
art
English
geography
history
mathematics
music
photography
psychology
science

VERY SMALL THINGS
cereal
corn
dust
pepper
rice
salt
sand
sugar

WEATHER
fog
ice
rain
snow
wind

NAMES OF CATEGORIES

clothing	(BUT: coats, hats, shoes ...)
equipment	(BUT: computers, phones ...)
food	(BUT: bananas, eggs ...)
furniture	(BUT: beds, chairs, lamps ...)
homework	(BUT: assignments, problems ...)
jewelry	(BUT: earrings, necklaces ...)
mail	(BUT: letters, packages ...)
money	(BUT: dollars, euros, pounds ...)
time	(BUT: minutes, months ...)
work	(BUT: jobs, projects ...)

OTHER
Some non-count nouns don't fit into any list.
You must memorize these non-count nouns.

advice
garbage/trash
help
information
news

12 Quantifying Non-Count Nouns

a bottle of (milk, soda, ketchup)
a bowl of (cereal, soup, rice)
a can of (soda, beans, tuna fish)
a cup of (hot chocolate, coffee, tea)
a foot of (snow, water)
a gallon of (juice, gas, paint)

a head of (lettuce)
a loaf of (bread)
an inch of (snow, rain)
a pair of (pants, gloves)
a piece of (paper, cake, pie)
a pint of (ice cream, cream)

a quart of (milk)
a roll of (toilet paper, paper towels)
a slice of (toast, cheese, meat)
a tablespoon of (flour, sugar, baking soda)
a teaspoon of (sugar, salt, pepper)
a tube of (toothpaste, glue)

13 The Simple Present: Spelling Rules

1 Add *-s* for most verbs.

work	work**s**
buy	buy**s**
ride	ride**s**
return	return**s**

2 Add *-es* for verbs that end in *-ch*, *-s*, *-sh*, *-x*, or *-z*.

watch	watch**es**
pass	pass**es**
rush	rush**es**
relax	relax**es**
buzz	buzz**es**

3 Change the *y* to *i* and add *-es* when the base form ends in **consonant + y**.

study	stud**ies**
hurry	hurr**ies**
dry	dr**ies**

4 Do not change the *y* when the base form ends in **vowel + y**. Add *-s*.

play	play**s**
enjoy	enjoy**s**

5 A few verbs have **irregular forms**.

be	**is**
do	**does**
go	**goes**
have	**has**

14 The Simple Present: Pronunciation Rules

1 The third-person singular in the simple present always ends in the letter *-s*. There are three different pronunciations for the final sound of the third-person singular.

/s/	/z/	/ɪz/
talk**s**	love**s**	dance**s**

2 The final sound is pronounced /s/ after the voiceless sounds /p/, /t/, /k/, and /f/.

top	top**s**
get	get**s**
take	take**s**
laugh	laugh**s**

3 The final sound is pronounced /z/ after the voiced sounds /b/, /d/, /g/, /v/, /m/, /n/, /ŋ/, /l/, /r/, and /ð/.

describe	describe**s**
spend	spend**s**
hug	hug**s**
live	live**s**
seem	seem**s**
remain	remain**s**
sing	sing**s**
tell	tell**s**
lower	lower**s**
bathe	bathe**s**

4 The final sound is pronounced /z/ after all **vowel sounds**.

agree	agree**s**
try	tr**ies**
stay	stay**s**
know	know**s**

5 The final sound is pronounced /ɪz/ after the sounds /s/, /z/, /ʃ/, /ʒ/, /tʃ/, and /dʒ/. /ɪz/ adds a syllable to the verb.

miss	mi**sses**
freeze	free**zes**
rush	ru**shes**
massage	massa**ges**
watch	wat**ches**
judge	jud**ges**

6 *Do* and *say* have a change in vowel sound.

do /du/	does /dʌz/
say /seɪ/	says /sɛz/

15 Non-Action Verbs

STATE OF BEING	EMOTIONS	MENTAL STATES	POSSESSION AND RELATIONSHIP	SENSES	WANTS AND PREFERENCES
be	dislike	agree	belong	feel	need
	hate	believe	cost	hear	prefer
	like	disagree	have	look	want
	love	guess	owe	see	
	miss	know	own	smell	
		remember		sound	
		think		taste	
		understand			

16 The Present Progressive: Spelling Rules

1 Add *-ing* to the base form of the verb.

read	read**ing**
stand	stand**ing**

2 If the verb ends in a **silent -e**, drop the final *-e* and add *-ing*.

leave	leav**ing**
take	tak**ing**

3 In **one-syllable** verbs, if the last three letters are consonant-vowel-consonant (CVC), double the last consonant and add *-ing*.

```
C V C
↓ ↓ ↓
s i t      sit**ting**
```

```
C V C
↓ ↓ ↓
p l a n    plan**ning**
```

EXCEPTION: Do not double the last consonant in verbs that end in *-w*, *-x*, or *-y*.

sew	sew**ing**
fix	fix**ing**
play	play**ing**

4 In verbs of **two or more syllables** that end in consonant-vowel-consonant, double the last consonant only if the last syllable is stressed.

admít	admit**ting**	*(The last syllable is stressed.)*
whísper	whisper**ing**	*(The last syllable is not stressed, so don't double the -r.)*

5 If the verb ends in *-ie*, change the *ie* to *y* before adding *-ing*.

die	**dying**
lie	**lying**

Stress
' shows main stress.

17 The Simple Past: Spelling Rules

1 If the verb ends in a **consonant**, add *-ed*.

return	return**ed**
help	help**ed**

2 If the verb ends in *-e*, add *-d*.

live	live**d**
create	create**d**
die	die**d**

3 In **one-syllable** verbs, if the last three letters are consonant-vowel-consonant (CVC), double the last consonant and add *-ed*.

```
C V C
↓ ↓ ↓
h o p      hop**ped**
```

```
C V C
↓ ↓ ↓
g r a b    grab**bed**
```

EXCEPTION: Do not double the last consonant in **one-syllable** verbs that end in *-w*, *-x*, or *-y*.

bow	bow**ed**
mix	mix**ed**
play	play**ed**

4 In verbs of **two or more syllables** that end in consonant-vowel-consonant, double the last consonant only if the last syllable is stressed.

prefér	prefer**red**	*(The last syllable is stressed.)*
vísit	visit**ed**	*(The last syllable is not stressed, so don't double the -t.)*

5 If the verb ends in **consonant + y**, change the *y* to *i* and add *-ed*.

worry	worr**ied**
carry	carr**ied**

6 If the verb ends in **vowel + y**, add *-ed*. (Do not change the *y* to *i*.)

play	play**ed**
annoy	annoy**ed**

EXCEPTIONS:

lay	la**id**
pay	pa**id**
say	sa**id**

18 The Simple Past: Pronunciation Rules

1 The regular simple past always ends in the letter *-d*. There are three different pronunciations for the final sound of the regular simple past.

/t/	/d/	/ɪd/
rac**ed**	liv**ed**	attend**ed**

2 The final sound is pronounced /t/ after the voiceless sounds /p/, /k/, /f/, /s/, /ʃ/, and /tʃ/.

hop	hop**ped**
work	wor**ked**
laugh	laug**hed**
address	addre**ssed**
publish	publi**shed**
watch	wat**ched**

3 The final sound is pronounced /d/ after the voiced sounds /b/, /g/, /v/, /z/, /ʒ/, /dʒ/, /m/, /n/, /ŋ/, /l/, /r/, and /ð/.

rub	ru**bbed**	rhyme	rhy**med**
hug	hu**gged**	return	retur**ned**
live	liv**ed**	bang	ban**ged**
surprise	surpri**sed**	enroll	enro**lled**
massage	massa**ged**	appear	appea**red**
change	chan**ged**	bathe	bat**hed**

4 The final sound is pronounced /d/ after all **vowel sounds**.

agree	agr**eed**
die	di**ed**
play	play**ed**
enjoy	enj**oyed**
snow	sn**owed**

5 The final sound is pronounced /ɪd/ after /t/ and /d/. /ɪd/ adds a syllable to the verb.

start	start**ed**
decide	deci**ded**

19 Irregular Past Tense Verbs

BASE FORM	PAST FORM	BASE FORM	PAST FORM	BASE FORM	PAST FORM	BASE FORM	PAST FORM
become	became	feel	felt	leave	left	sit	sat
begin	began	fight	fought	lend	lent	sleep	slept
bite	bit	find	found	lose	lost	speak	spoke
blow	blew	fly	flew	make	made	spend	spent
break	broke	forget	forgot	meet	met	stand	stood
bring	brought	get	got	pay	paid	steal	stole
build	built	give	gave	put	put	swim	swam
buy	bought	go	went	quit	quit	take	took
catch	caught	grow	grew	read*	read*	teach	taught
choose	chose	hang	hung	ride	rode	tear	tore
come	came	have	had	ring	rang	tell	told
cost	cost	hear	heard	run	ran	think	thought
do	did	hide	hid	say	said	throw	threw
draw	drew	hit	hit	see	saw	understand	understood
drink	drank	hold	held	send	sent	wake	woke
drive	drove	hurt	hurt	shake	shook	wear	wore
eat	ate	keep	kept	shoot	shot	win	won
fall	fell	know	knew	shut	shut	write	wrote
feed	fed	lead	led	sing	sang		

*Pronounce the base form /rid/. Pronounce the past form /rɛd/.

20 Capitalization and Punctuation Rules

	USE FOR . . .	EXAMPLES
capital letter	• the pronoun *I*	My friend and **I** are on vacation.
	• proper nouns	**Ali** is from Turkey.
	• the first word of a sentence	**They** live in Spain.
apostrophe (')	• possessive nouns	Is that **Marta's** coat?
	• contractions	**That's** not hers. **It's** mine.
comma (,)	• after items in a list	He bought apples, pears, oranges, and bananas.
	• to connect two sentences with *and* or *but*	They watched TV, and she played video games.
	• after the name of a person you are writing to	Dear John,
exclamation point (!)	• at the end of a sentence to show surprise or a strong feeling	You're here! That's great! Stop! A car is coming!
period (.)	• at the end of a statement	Today is Wednesday.
	• after abbreviations	The party is on Nov. 3.
question mark (?)	• at the end of a question	What day is today?

Glossary of Grammar Terms

action verb A verb that describes an action. It can be used in the progressive.

> Sachiko **is planning** a big party.

adjective A word that describes (or modifies) a noun or pronoun.

> That's a **great** idea.

adverb A word that describes (or modifies) an action verb, an adverb, an adjective, or a sentence.

> She drives **slowly**.

adverb of frequency A word that tells the frequency of something.

> We **usually** eat lunch at noon.

adverb of manner A word that describes a verb. It usually answers the question *how*.

> She speaks **clearly**.

affirmative statement A sentence that does not use a negative verb form (*not*).

> **I have a car.**

apostrophe A punctuation mark used to show possession and to write a short form (contraction).

> He**'**s in my father**'**s car.

base form The form of the verb without any ending such as *-ing*, *-ed*, or *-s*. It is the same as the infinitive without *to*.

> Arnold will **come** at 8:00. We should **eat** then.

be going to future A verb form used to make predictions, express general facts in the future, or talk about definite plans that were made before now.

> Mei-Ling says it**'s going to be** cold, so she**'s going to take** a coat.

capital letter The big form of a letter of the alphabet. Sentences start with a capital letter.

> **A, B, C**, etc.

comma Punctuation used to separate single things in a list or parts of a sentence.

> We went to a restaurant**,** and we ate chicken**,** potatoes**,** and broccoli.

common noun A noun for a person, an animal, a place, or a thing. It is not capitalized.

> The **man** got a **book** at the **library**.

comparative form An adjective or adverb ending in *-er* or following *more*. It is used in comparing two things.

> My sister is **older** and **more intelligent** than my brother.
> But he studies **harder** and **more carefully**.

consonant The letters *b, c, d, f, g, h, j, k, l, m, n, p, q, r, s, t, v, w, x, y, z*.

contraction A short form of two words. An apostrophe (') replaces the missing letter.

> **It is** late and **I am** tired. **I should not** stay up so late.
> **It's** late and **I'm** tired. **I shouldn't** stay up so late.

count noun A noun you can count. It usually has a singular and a plural form.

> In the **park**, there was a **man** with two **children** and a **dog**.

definite article *The*; makes a noun specific.

> We saw a movie. **The** movie starred Sean Penn.

demonstrative adjective An adjective used to identify the noun that follows.

> **This** man is resting, but **those** men are busy.

demonstrative pronoun A pronoun used in place of a demonstrative adjective and the noun that follows.

> **This** is our classroom, and **these** are my students.

direct object A noun or pronoun used to receive the action of a verb.

> She sold a **car**. He bought **it**.

exclamation point A punctuation mark (!) used at the end of a statement. It shows strong emotion.

> Help**!** Call the police**!**

formal language Language we usually use in business settings, academic settings, and with people we don't know.

> **Good morning, ladies** and **gentlemen. May** we begin?

gerund The -*ing* form of a verb. It is used as a noun.

> **Skiing** is fun, but we also enjoy **swimming**.

imperative A sentence used to give an instruction, a direction, a command, or a suggestion. It uses the base form of the verb. The subject (*you*) is not a part of the sentence.

> **Turn** right at the corner. **Drive** to the end of the street. **Stop!**

indefinite article *A* and *an*; used before singular, nonspecific non-count nouns.

> Jaime brought **a** sandwich and **an** apple for lunch.

infinitive *To* + the base form of a verb.

> **To travel** is my dream. I want **to see** the world.

informal language The language we usually use with family and friends, in email messages, and in other informal settings.

> **Hey, Doug, what's up?**

inseparable phrasal verb A phrasal verb that cannot have an object between the verb and the particle.

> She **ran into** John.

irregular verb A verb that does not form the simple past by adding -*d* or -*ed*.

> They **ate** a fancy meal last night. The boss **came** to dinner.

modal A word that comes before the main verb. Modals can express ability, possibility, obligation, and necessity.

> You **can** come early, but you **mustn't** be late, and you **should** wear a tie.

negative statement A statement with a negative verb form.

> He **didn't study**. He **wasn't** ready for the test.

non-action verb A verb that does not describe an action. It can describe an emotion, a state, a sense, or a mental thought. We usually don't use non-action verbs in the progressive.

> I **like** that actor. He **is** very famous, and I **believe** he won an Oscar.

non-count noun A noun we usually do not count. We don't put *a*, *an*, or a number before a non-count noun.

> All you'll need is **rice, water, salt,** and **butter.**

noun A word that refers to a person, animal, place, thing, or idea.

> **Paula** has a **friend** at the **library**. She gave me a **book** about **birds**.

noun modifier A noun that describes another noun.

> Samantha is a **chemistry** professor. She loves **spy** movies.

noun phrase A phrase formed by a noun and words that describe (modify) it.

> It was **a dark brown leather jacket**.

object A noun or pronoun following an action verb. It receives the action of the verb.

> I sent **a letter**. He read **it**.

object pronoun A pronoun following a verb or a preposition.

> We asked **him** to show the photos to **them**.

period A punctuation mark (.) used at the end of a statement.

> I'd like you to call on Saturday**.** We need to talk**.**

phrasal verb A two-part (or three-part) verb that combines a verb and a preposition or particle (for example, *on* or *up*). The meaning of the parts together is often different from the meaning of the verb alone.

> We **put on** our gloves and **picked up** our umbrellas.

phrase A group of words that can form a grammatical unit.

> She lost **a red hat**. He found it **under the table**.

plural The form that means more than one.

> **We** sat in **our chairs** reading **our books**.

possessive An adjective, noun, or pronoun that shows possession.

> **Her** book is in **John's** car. **Mine** is at the office.

preposition A small word that goes before a noun or pronoun object. A preposition often shows time or place.

> Maria saw it **on** the table **at** two o'clock.

prepositional phrase A phrase that consists of a preposition followed by a noun or a noun phrase.

> Chong-Dae saw it **under the black wooden table.**

present progressive A verb form that shows an action happening now or planned for the future.

> I**'m working** hard now, but I**'m taking** a vacation soon.

pronoun A word that replaces a noun or a noun phrase. There are subject pronouns, object pronouns, possessive pronouns, and demonstrative pronouns.

> **He** is a friend—I know **him** well. **This** is his coat; **mine** is black.

proper noun The actual name of a person, place, or thing. A proper noun begins with a capital letter.

> **Tom** is living in **New York**. He is studying **Russian** at **Columbia University**.

quantifier A word or phrase that comes before a noun and expresses an amount of that noun.

> Jeannette used **a little** sugar, **some** flour, **four** eggs, and **a liter of** milk.

question mark A punctuation mark (?) used at the end of a question.

> Where are you going**?** When will you be back**?**

quotation marks Punctuation marks ("...") used before and after the actual words a person says.

> I said, **"Where are you going?"** and **"When will you be back?"**

regular verb A verb that forms the simple past by adding -*d* or -*ed*.

> We **lived** in France. My mother **visited** us there.

sentence A group of words with a subject and a verb.

> **We opened the window.**
> **Did they paint the house?**

separable phrasal verb A phrasal verb that can have an object between the verb and the particle.

> She **put on** her coat. She **put** it **on** before he **put** his coat **on**.

simple past A verb form used to show a completed action or idea in the past.

> The plane **landed** at 9:00. We **caught** a bus to the hotel.

simple present A verb form used to show habitual actions or states, general facts, or conditions that are true now.

> Kemal **loves** to ski, and it **snows** a lot in his area, so he**'s** very happy.

singular The form that means only one.

> I put on my **hat** and **coat** and closed the **door**.

small letter The small form of a letter of the alphabet. We use small letters for most words except for proper nouns and the word that starts a sentence.

> **a**, **b**, **c**, etc.

subject The person, place, or thing that a sentence is about.

> **The children** ate at the mall.

subject pronoun A pronoun used to replace a subject noun.

> Irene works hard. **She** loves her work.

superlative form An adjective or adverb ending in -*est* or following *most*. It is used in comparing three or more things.

> We climbed the **highest** mountain by the **most dangerous** route.
> She drives the **fastest** and the **most carelessly** of all the drivers.

syllable A group of letters with one vowel sound. Words are made up of one or more syllables.

> One syllable—**win**
> Two syllables—**ta ble**
> Three syllables—**im por tant**

verb A word used to describe an action, a fact, or a state.

> He **drives** to work now. He **has** a new car, and he **is** a careful driver.

vowel The letters *a*, *e*, *i*, *o*, or *u*, and sometimes *y*.

wh- question A question that asks for information. It begins with *what, when, where, why, which, who, whose,* or *how*.

> **What**'s your name?
> **Where** are you from?
> **How** do you feel?

will future A verb form used to make predictions, to talk about facts in the future, to make promises, to offer something, or to state a decision to do something at the time of speaking.

> It **will** probably rain, so I**'ll take** an umbrella. I**'ll give** you my extra one.

yes/no question A question that has a *yes* or a *no* answer.

> **Did you arrive on time?** Yes, I did.
> **Are you from Uruguay?** No, I'm not.
> **Can you swim well?** Yes, I can.

Unit Review Answer Key

UNIT 1

A 1. are   3. am   5. are
2. is   4. is

B 1. 'm   3. 're   5. 're
2. 's   4. 's

C 1. He's not or He isn't   3. We're not or We aren't
2. They're   4. She's

D   My father and mother are from India, but they're in Canada now. My parents are doctors. My father a [*is*] sports doctor, and my mother ~~she~~ is a family doctor. My parents and I love sports. My father ~~are~~ [*is*] a soccer fan, and my mother a [*is*] baseball fan. I'm a soccer fan. My father and I ~~am~~ [*are*] fans of Lionel Messi and Nuno Gomes. My sister ~~no is~~ [*isn't* or *is not*] good at sports. She's not a sports fan. She loves movies.

UNIT 2

A 1. Where's   4. Are
2. How's   5. Is
3. What's

B 1. I am
2. it isn't or it is not
3. they aren't or they are not
4. we are
5. you're not or you aren't or you are not

C 1. What's today's date? or What is today's date?
2. Where's the men's room? or Where is the men's room?
3. Why's he absent? or Why is he absent?
4. When's your first class? or When is your first class?
5. Who's your teacher? or Who is your teacher?

D 1. ~~She~~ [*Is*] she your teacher?
2. What your [*'s* or *is*] name?
3. Where your [*'s* or *is*] class?
4. ~~Is~~ [*Are*] Bob and Molly good friends?
5. Why you [*are*] late?

UNIT 3

A 1. was   3. Were   5. Was
2. was   4. were

B 1. c   2. b   3. d   4. a

C 1. was   3. Were   5. were   7. was
2. was   4. was   6. wasn't

D   John ~~is~~ [*was*] at a job interview yesterday. It ~~were~~ [*was*] for a job at a bank. The questions ~~no were~~ [*weren't* or *were not*] easy, but John's answers were good. He was happy. It a [*was*] good day for John.

UNIT 4

A 1. a   3. Ø   5. Ø
2. an   4. Ø

B 1. cities   4. fish
2. watches   5. people
3. clothes

C A: Hi, are you the photographer?
B: Yes, I'm Amy Lin.
A: Nice to meet you. I'm Ali Mohammed.
B: Are you from London?
A: Yes, I am. I'm here for your Thanksgiving Day holiday.

D   Melanie Einzig is artist [*an*] and ~~an~~ [*a*] photographer. She was born in Minnesota, but lives in New ~~york~~ [*York*]. Einzig captures moments in time. Her ~~photograph~~ [*photographs*] are striking. They are in ~~museum~~ [*museums*] in San ~~francisco~~ [*Francisco*], Chicago, and Princeton.

UNIT 5

A 1. a   3. Ø   5. Ø
2. Ø   4. an

B 1. a small hotel   4. kind and helpful
2. an interesting garden   5. a great choice
3. big and comfortable

C 1. I'm at the new museum
2. It has interesting things
3. It has unusual bowls
4. It has beautiful carpets
5. The museum is a great place

D The Grand Canyon National Park in Arizona is ~~a~~ *an* awesome place to visit. Almost five million people visit the park every year. It is a ~~park beautiful~~ *beautiful park*. The weather is good in the late spring and summer, but the park ~~crowded is~~ *is crowded* during those months. There are seven ~~differents~~ *different* places to stay in the park. I like El Tovar. It is ~~a~~ *an* old hotel with a great view.

UNIT 6

A
1. on
2. under
3. behind
4. next to
5. in front of

B
1. at / across
2. at / on

C
1. on the / in the / on the
2. inside / above / under

D
A: Is Jon ~~on~~ *at* school?
B: No. He's ~~in~~ *at* home.
A: Where does he live?
B: He lives ~~at~~ *on* Oak Street ~~at~~ *in* New City.
A: Does he live in an apartment?
B: Yes. He lives ~~in~~ *on* the third floor.

UNIT 7

A
1. Let's get
2. Why don't we
3. Don't buy
4. Let's meet
5. Don't touch

B
1. Wear
2. Don't wear
3. Bring
4. Don't bring
5. pay

C
1. Let's
2. don't we
3. don't you
4. Let's

D
1. Why ~~you~~ don't *you* ask Andrij for help?
2. You look really tired. ~~You take~~ *Take* a short nap.
3. Let's ~~to~~ walk to work. Let's not drive.
4. Don't ask Boris to fix the car. ~~Asks~~ *Ask* Mickey.
5. I'm on a diet, so buy ~~please~~ *please* yogurt. Don't ~~to~~ get sour cream.

UNIT 8

A
1. loves
2. doesn't have
3. invites
4. don't give
5. have

B
1. always celebrate
2. sometimes wears
3. often sits
4. usually dance
5. are usually

C
1. thinks
2. don't work
3. comes
4. is

D Some people don't ~~enjoys~~ *enjoy* holidays and family gatherings. Bill Jones ~~visits usually~~ *usually visits* his wife's sister on holidays. He likes his wife's sister, but he ~~don't~~ *doesn't* like her husband. Mary Brown doesn't like holidays because she lives far from her family. She ~~have~~ *has* a very important job, but she doesn't have close friends. She usually watches movies and ~~wait~~ *waits* for the holiday to be over. ~~Always she is~~ *She is always* happy to return to work.

UNIT 9

A
1. Do
2. Is
3. Does
4. Are
5. Am

B
1. Do you have
2. Does his roommate speak
3. Does your roommate watch
4. Is your roommate
5. Are your roommate's parents

C
1. Are the neighbors noisy?
2. Does the building have an elevator?
3. Is the apartment near buses?
4. Does the bedroom have two closets?
5. Is the bedroom big?

D
1. A: Does he have a big TV in his room?
   B: Yes, he ~~has~~ *does*.
2. A: Does she ~~needs~~ *need* help?
   B: No, she ~~don't~~ *doesn't*.
3. A: ~~Do you are~~ *Are* you friends?
   B: Yes, we ~~aren't~~ *are*. or ~~Yes~~ *No*, we aren't.

UNIT 10

A
1. Why
2. When
3. Who
4. How
5. Where

B
1. What do you dream about?
2. What time does your mother get up?
3. What time do you go to bed?
4. Where does your brother sleep?
5. Who snores in your family?

C 1. Who meets his uncle at the diner on Saturdays?
2. Who does John meet at the diner on Saturdays?
3. Where does John meet his uncle on Saturdays?
4. When does John meet his uncle at the diner?

D 1. Where *do* you live?
2. Why ~~he daydreams~~ *does he daydream* in class?
3. When does she ~~gets~~ *get* up?
4. How *do* they feel about sleeping pills?
5. Who ~~does~~ *do* you dream about?
6. What time *does* he wake up?

UNIT 11

A 1. There aren't
2. There's
3. There are
4. There isn't
5. There's
6. There are

B 1. A: Are there
   B: there are
2. A: Is she
   B: she is
3. A: Are they
   B: they aren't
4. A: Is there
   B: there isn't

C 1. There's / It's
2. There are / They're
3. There's / She's

D Visit the new Shopper's Mall on Route 290. There's *are* over 100 stores. There *is* a movie theater, and ~~they~~ *there* are ten great places to eat. Come early. Every morning at 10:30, there ~~are~~ *is* a free show for children. The mall is three miles from the Tappan Bridge on Route 290.

UNIT 12

A 1. ~~My parents'~~ *Their*
2. ~~My brother's~~ *His*
3. ~~That bird's~~ *Its*
4. ~~The students'~~ *Their*
5. ~~Our aunt's~~ *Her*

B 1. A: mine
   B: yours
   A: your
2. A: Whose
   B: Ali's

C 1. Whose
2. Whose
3. Who's
4. Whose
5. Who's

D A: ~~Who's~~ *Whose* bag is that on the floor?
   B: I think it's ~~Maria~~ *Maria's*.
   A: No. Her bag is on her arm.
   B: Well, it's not ~~mine~~ *my* bag. Maybe it's ~~Rita~~ *Rita's*.
   A: Rita, is that ~~yours~~ *your* bag?

UNIT 13

A 1. a. couldn't understand
      b. can understand
2. a. can't run
   b. could run
3. a. couldn't drive
   b. can drive

B 1. A: Can
   B: can
2. A: Could
   B: couldn't
3. A: Can
   B: can

C 1. Could your bird sit on your finger?
2. Can the parrot say anything?
3. Could your dog bring you your shoe?
4. Can that bird talk about the past and the future?

D A: Can you ~~to~~ get online?
   B: No, I can't. I ~~no could~~ *couldn't* get online last night either.
   A: My brother is good with computers. Maybe he can ~~helps~~ *help*. I can ~~to~~ call him after work.

UNIT 14

A 1. may eat
2. can't eat
3. can have
4. may not use
5. may drink

B 1. When can I return to work?
2. When can I take a shower?
3. When can I go to the gym?
4. When can I ride my bike?

C 1. Can we eat during the test?
2. May I use a pencil?
3. Can I make calls during the test?
4. Can we drink water?
5. May I use a black pen?
6. Can we use a dictionary?

D A: May I ~~sees~~ *see* a menu?
   B: Sure. Here you go.
   A: And can we ~~to~~ have some water?
   B: I'll be right back with the water.... Ready?
   A: Yes. May I ~~has~~ *have* the chicken?
   B: Of course. A very good choice.
   A: And can you ~~brings~~ *bring* me a small salad?
   B: Certainly. And may I ~~gets~~ *get* you anything else?

A
1. I'm not
2. We're preparing
3. She isn't playing
4. They're doing
5. He's reading

B
1. is listening to
2. are standing and talking
3. are running
4. is driving
5. is carrying

C
1. a. is texting
   b. isn't calling or 's not calling
2. a. isn't crying ('s not crying)
   b. 's watching or is watching
3. a. 's swimming or is swimming
   b. 's trying

D
My classmates and I ~~am~~ *are* sitting in a computer lab. One student *is* writing a composition. Two students are ~~check~~ *checking* their email. A teacher is ~~helps~~ *helping* a student. The other students are reading.

A
1. Are you working?
2. Is he buying tickets online?
3. Are they watching a mystery?
4. Is your cousin enjoying the movie?

B
1. Where are they going?
2. What movie is she watching?
3. Why is Bob staying home?
4. Who's watching the children?

C
1. a. are the kids laughing
   b. Are they watching
   c. 're playing
2. a. are you doing
   b. 'm making
   c. 'm planning
3. a. 's happening
   b. 're making

D
A: What *are* you watching?

B: We're watching a detective show.

A: What *'s* happening?

B: A boy is missing from home.

A: ~~The police are~~ *Are the police* looking for him?

B: Yes, they are.

A: Where *are* they looking?

B: Everywhere.

A
1. don't own
2. doesn't like
3. has
4. needs
5. want

B
1. is using
2. is surfing or 's surfing
3. is reading or 's reading
4. has
5. wants

C
1. is, doing
2. is trying or 's trying
3. is
4. don't know
5. needs

D
1. A: Where *are* you calling from?

   B: Downtown. I ~~walk~~ *'m walking* along Second Street.

2. A: Is she ~~play~~ *playing* tennis at West Park?

   B: No, she's not. She ~~no like~~ *doesn't like* West Park.

3. A: Does he ~~understands~~ *understand* Greek?

   B: Yes, he does. He was in Greece for a year.

A
1. watched
2. visited
3. an hour ago
4. Last night
5. didn't land

B
1. helped
2. stayed
3. didn't snow
4. didn't ask
5. didn't want

C
1. canceled
2. didn't stay
3. didn't rain
4. played
5. didn't enjoy

D
Hello from London. Our friends ~~did invited~~ *invited* us here for a week. Yesterday we ~~visit~~ *visited* Big Ben, and we ~~tour~~ *toured* Buckingham Palace. This morning, we ~~watch~~ *watched* a cricket match. Later, we walked around Piccadilly Circus and ~~are~~ enjoyed coffee and sandwiches at a small nearby café.

A
1. saw
2. were
3. was
4. began
5. said
6. wanted

B
1. grew up
2. drew
3. didn't make
4. began
5. was

C
1. left
2. lost
3. ran
4. didn't see
5. didn't take

D
The writer William Sidney Porter ^was born in North Carolina in 1862. He wrote under different names, but he ~~did~~ became best known as O. Henry. His stories ~~were~~ had surprise endings. O. Henry was a very successful writer, but he ~~spended~~ *spent* time in prison.

UNIT 20

A
1. Did they go to the theater?
2. Did we miss the beginning?
3. Did you have good seats?
4. Did it have a good ending?

B
1. When did Olivia do her homework?
2. Where did John go last summer?
3. Who helped Claudia with her report?
4. How long did Mia and Lily work?

C
1. What play did you see last night?
2. Where did you see it?
3. How long was the show?
4. Did you enjoy the performance?
5. Who was the star of the show?
6. Did you go out after the show?

D
1. Where ~~he did~~ *did he go* last night?
2. What ~~saw he~~ *did he see*?
3. Did he ~~enjoyed~~ *enjoy* it?
4. Who ~~he met~~ *did he meet* or *met him*?
5. When ~~they left~~ *did they leave*?
6. Who ~~did pay~~ *paid* for dinner?

UNIT 21

A
1. was born
2. grew up
3. attended
4. went
5. started
6. became
7. expanded

B
1. When did she go to college?
2. Who did they meet?
3. Where did he study?
4. How long did they live in Canada?

C
1. Were
2. Did
3. Was
4. Did
5. Did

D
Steve Paul Jobs ~~did start~~ *started* college in 1970, but he ~~no did~~ *didn't* or *did not* finish it. In In 1976, Jobs and his friend ~~begin~~ *began* to make their own computers. They worked in Jobs' garage. That was the beginning of Apple® Computers. Their company ~~become~~ *became* a big success. Apple® changed the field of computers, and by the age of thirty, Jobs was a multimillionaire.

UNIT 22

A
1. is going to build
2. 's going to cost
3. 's going to have
4. are going to be
5. is not going to begin

B
1. are not going to increase
2. 're not going to play or aren't going to play
3. 're going to visit him
4. 's going to retire
5. 'm not going to do

C
1. Q: When is she going to the dentist?
   A: On Monday at 5:30.
2. Q: Where is she meeting Yu Chen?
   A: At Pappa Pizza.
3. Q: Is she meeting Yu Chen on Monday?
   A: No, she isn't.

D
This city ^*is* going to change under our new mayor. People~~'s~~ *are* going to ride bikes, and they're going *to* use public transportation. ~~They're no~~ *They're not* or *They aren't* going to drive big cars. There are probably going to be higher tolls on bridges and more bike paths on the roads.

UNIT 23

A
1. won't
2. won't
3. will
4. will
5. won't

B
1. Will many people travel to the moon in twenty years?
2. Will the climate change in the future?
3. What will people eat in 2050?
4. Will people look different in 2100?
5. How will people get around in the year 2035?

C
1. Will…be
2. Will…have
3. Will…be
4. Will…rain
5. Will…work

D   I usually bring my lunch to work, but tomorrow

I ~~no will~~ bring it because it's my birthday. My
   won't

co-workers will ~~takes~~ me out to a restaurant. We'll
           take

~~to~~ order a few different dishes, and we'll share them.

They'll ~~singing~~ "Happy Birthday," and they'll give me
     sing

a small gift. I'm sure it will ~~is~~ a lot of fun.
             be

UNIT 24

A **1.** go   **4.** may
     2. buy   **5.** Will
     3. might not

B **1.** may snow **or** might snow
     2. may not get **or** might not get
     3. may need **or** might need
     4. may not see **or** might not see
     5. may stay **or** might stay

C **1.** Will   **4.** will
     2. may   **5.** will
     3. might **or** may

D **1.** He might ~~goes~~ on vacation next week.
               go
     2. He may ~~works~~ late tomorrow.
             work
     3. They might ~~to~~ visit him tomorrow. Are you free?
     4. I might not help him. I might ~~to~~ help her instead.
     5. She ~~maybe~~ take a yoga class.
         may **or** *might*

UNIT 25

A **1.** to start   **4.** to become
     2. to sell   **5.** flying / seeing
     3. to return

B **1.** to work   **3.** quitting / going
     2. to change   **4.** improving

C **1.** She enjoys helping people.
     2. We expect to graduate in June.
     3. They are trying to study.
     4. He avoids eating candy and ice cream. **or** He avoids
         eating ice cream and candy.

D   Carol volunteers at a hospital. She enjoys taking

care of patients. Some patients refuse ^*to*^ do exercise,

but Carol keeps ~~to push~~ them. Carol intends ^study
         pushing   *to*

physical therapy in college. She needs ~~taking~~ a lot of
                       to take^

science courses. She expects to ~~goes~~ to college next
                  go

fall. She hopes ^get a degree in physical therapy in
          to

five years.

UNIT 26

A **1.** some   **2.** the   **3.** an   **4.** any

B **1.** We don't need any glasses.
     2. I don't want any help.
     3. There aren't any menus on the table.
     4. He doesn't have any free time.

C **1.** a   **3.** the   **5.** a
     2. a   **4.** the   **6.** a

D **1.** **A:** What are you looking for?
                   some   *some*
         B: I need ~~a~~ stamps. I wrote ~~any~~ letters, and I want

           to mail them.
           The   *any*
     2. **A:** ~~A~~ refrigerator looks empty. There isn't ~~some~~

           yogurt.
                        any
         B: There aren't ~~an~~ eggs either. We need to go
                        time **or** *any time*
           shopping, but I don't have ~~a time~~ today. Let's go

           shopping tomorrow.

UNIT 27

A **1.** How many   **4.** How many
     2. How many   **5.** How much
     3. How much

B **1.** How much chocolate do you eat in a week?
     2. How many teaspoons of sugar do you take?
     3. How much time do you spend online?
     4. How many sisters do you have?
     5. How much coffee do you drink every day?

C **1.** much   **4.** a lot of
     2. a lot of   **5.** a little
     3. a can of

D **1.** There were only a ~~little~~ people at the meeting.
                   few
     2. There are a few ~~peach~~ in the refrigerator.
                peaches
     3. How ~~many~~ milk do you need?
           much
     4. How ~~much~~ bottles of juice did they buy?
           many
     5. There are not ~~much~~ books in their home.
              many

A 1. The child ate *too many* cookies.
2. We have *too much* homework.
3. I bought *too much* milk.
4. There are *too many* trucks on that road.
5. It takes *too much* time to get there by bus.

B 1. too much
2. too few
3. too much
4. too many
5. too little

C 1. not enough
2. not enough
3. enough
4. enough
5. not enough

D I want to move. I don't like the climate here. There's too ~~many~~ *much* snow in winter. There are too ~~little~~ *few* nice, sunny days. There's too ~~many~~ *much* air pollution from all the traffic on the streets, and there aren't ~~jobs enough~~ *enough jobs*. There also aren't enough ~~park~~ *parks* and places for children to play.

UNIT 29

A 1. should
2. had better
3. shouldn't
4. ought to
5. I'd better not

B 1. had better not forget
2. had better buy
3. had better not wait
4. had better go

C 1. should take
2. shouldn't work
3. should call
4. shouldn't forget

D 1. Where should we ~~meets~~ *meet* after work? ~~Ought~~ *Should* we go to the Rainbow Diner?
2. We *'d or had* better take an umbrella tonight. It's going to rain.
3. Should I ~~to~~ make a reservation for my flight now? I think I ~~outta~~ *ought to* make it soon.
4. What ~~I should~~ *should I* see during my business trip to Uruguay?
5. Should we ~~leaves~~ *leave* Brazil tonight or tomorrow?

UNIT 30

A 1. don't have to
2. has to
3. must not
4. doesn't have to
5. have to

B 1. can't
2. has
3. have to
4. don't have to
5. have to

C 1. had to work
2. have to read
3. have to answer
4. had to give
5. didn't have to bring

D Drew's test starts at 8:10. He must ~~to~~ be in the room at 8:00. He must not ~~came~~ *come* late. He ~~have to has~~ *has to have* two pencils. He must ~~brings~~ *bring* a photo ID. Cell phones are not allowed in the room. He ~~doesn't have to~~ *must not or can't* bring his cell phone with him.

UNIT 31

A 1. much, taller
2. more popular
3. worse
4. better
5. brother's

B 1. younger than
2. shorter than
3. more expensive than
4. hotter than

C 1. less expensive
2. more expensive
3. higher
4. lower

D The train is much ~~fast~~ *faster* than the bus and the seats are ~~comfortabler~~ *more comfortable*. The bus is much ~~more~~ *slower* than the train, but the views from the bus are more interesting. Which ~~are~~ *is* cheaper, the train or the bus? The bus is much less ~~expensiver~~ *expensive*, but for me the train is ~~more good~~ *better* because I'm a busy student with very little free time.

UNIT 32

A 1. quickly
2. fluently
3. well
4. slowly
5. clearly

B 1. good
2. seriously
3. hard
4. badly
5. quickly

C 1. good
2. briefly
3. clearly
4. fast
5. honestly

D A: Did your speech go ~~good~~ *well*? Did they appreciate

your jokes?

B: Well…they laughed ~~polite~~ *politely*, but I'm not sure they
laughed ~~sincere~~ *sincerely*.

A: It's hard to be funny.

B: I ~~hard~~ worked *hard*, and I prepared carefully, but I
was ~~nervously~~ *nervous*.

UNIT 33

A 1. big enough
2. as
3. too
4. as
5. very

B 1. warm enough
2. too late
3. too short
4. fast enough
5. very good

C 1. not as thin as my father **or** not as thin as he is
2. not as cheap as my new one **or** not as cheap as my new coat
3. as tall as my brother **or** as tall as he is
4. as old as I am **or** as old as me

D This year, the party wasn't *as* good as last year. The

music was very ~~much~~ loud. It was hard to dance
because the room was ~~too way~~ *way too* hot. I like to dance,
so I felt ~~too~~ *very* bad about that. Also, the drinks weren't
~~enough cold~~ *cold enough*, and the food wasn't *as* tasty as last year.

UNIT 34

A 1. the funniest
2. the biggest
3. the best
4. The largest / the most dangerous

B 1. the hottest
2. the oldest
3. the busiest
4. the most interesting
5. the most popular

C 1. the most intelligent animals
2. the most colorful birds
3. the worst seats
4. the longest days

D A: What's *the* hardest part of your job here at the zoo?

B: The ~~difficultest~~ *most difficult* part for me is telling people not to

bother or feed the animals.

A: And which animal is the ~~most smart~~ *smartest*?

B: Bill the gorilla. He's one of *the* funniest and smartest
~~animal~~ *animals*. He's also one of the *most* interesting. And I

think he's one of the cutest, too!

Unit Review Answer Key

Key to Exercises with Guessed Answers

UNIT 13

EXERCISE 3

2. Can elephants jump?   No, they can't.
3. Can a bear climb a tree?   Yes, it can.
4. Can a chimpanzee use tools?   Yes, it can.
5. Can chimpanzees invent games?   Yes, they can.
6. Can a penguin fly?   No, it can't.

EXERCISE 8

1. b   3. d   5. e   7. a
2. c   4. h   6. f   8. g

UNIT 18

BEFORE YOU READ

1. The Eiffel Tower, Paris, France
   The Great Wall of China, Beijing, China
   Machu Picchu, Peru

UNIT 27

EXERCISE 9

1. a   4. b   7. a   10. c
2. a   5. c   8. b
3. c   6. b   9. c

UNIT 31

EXERCISE 5

2. A: Which river is longer, the Amazon or the Nile?
   B: The Nile is longer than the Amazon.
3. A: Which mountain has a higher elevation, Mount Everest or Mount Denali?
   B: Mount Everest has a higher elevation than Mount Denali. or Mount Everest is higher than Mount Denali.
4. A: Which ocean is bigger, the Atlantic or the Pacific?
   B: The Pacific Ocean is bigger than the Atlantic Ocean.
5. A: Which city has a higher elevation, La Paz, Bolivia or Sydney, Australia?
   B: La Paz, Bolivia has a higher elevation than Sydney, Australia. or La Paz, Bolivia is higher than Sydney, Australia.
6. A: Which country has a bigger population, Japan or South Korea?
   B: Japan has a bigger population than South Korea. or Japan's population is bigger than South Korea's. or Japan's population is bigger than South Korea's is.
7. A: Which city is more expensive, New York or Venice?
   B: New York is more expensive than Venice.

UNIT 34

EXERCISE 2

2. the elephant   5. the sailfish
3. the giraffe   6. the Macaroni Penguin
4. the hummingbird

Information Gaps, Student B

EXERCISE 9 DREAMS

INFORMATION GAP Work with a partner. Student B, follow the instructions below.
Student A, follow the instructions on page 117.

STUDENT B

- You have a dream again and again. Read about your dream below. Student A will ask you questions about this dream. Answer Student A's questions.

    You are in the third grade. You see your third-grade teacher. Your teacher is very big. You are small. Your teacher says, "Your schoolwork is great. You are my favorite student." You smile. Then you laugh. Then you wake up.

- Student A has a dream again and again. Find out about the dream. Ask Student A the questions below. Write down his or her answers.

    1. Where are you in your dream? _____

    2. What do you do? _____

    3. Who comes to you? _____

    4. How do you feel? _____

    5. What does he say? _____

    6. What happens? _____

- Talk about your dreams. What do they mean?

EXERCISE 8 PATIENT INFORMATION

INFORMATION GAP Work with a partner. Student B follows the instructions below.
Student A will follow the instructions on page 167.

STUDENT B

- Student A has information about Dr. Green's Clinic. Ask Student A the questions below to get the information.

- Listen carefully to Student A's answers. Write down the answers.

  1. When can I see the doctor?

  _____

  2. When can I call her?

  _____

  3. Can I contact her by email?

  _____

  4. What can I do in an emergency?

  _____

  5. Are there any free lectures on nutrition?

  _____

  6. Can I join a support group?

  _____

  7. How can I get good meal suggestions?

  _____

EXERCISE 8 WHO INVENTED THE ATM?

INFORMATION GAP Work with a partner. Student B follows the instructions below.
Student A follows the instructions on page 252.

STUDENT B

- Your partner has a chart that is missing some information. Your chart contains the missing information. Answer your partner's questions, so that he or she can write the missing information into his or her chart.

EXAMPLE: A: Who invented the ATM?
B: Don Wetzel invented the ATM.
A: When did he invent it?

Invention	Inventor	Year	Country
ATM	Don Wetzel	1968	United States
credit card	Frank McNamara, Ralph Schneider	1950	United States
dishwasher	Josephine Cochrane	1886	United States
eyeglasses	Salvino D'Armate, Alessandro della Spina	1280	Italy
subway	Sir John Fowler	1863	United Kingdom
YouTube	Steven Chen, Chad Hurley, Jawed Karim	2005	United States

- The chart below is missing some information. Your partner has a chart that contains your missing information. Ask your partner questions to find the missing information. Write your partner's answers into your chart.

EXAMPLE: B: Who invented the bicycle?
A: Baron de Sauerbrun.
B: When did he invent it?

Invention	Inventor	Year	Country
bicycle	Baron de Sauerbrun		
	Marion Donovan		
paper			
	Conrad Gessner		
thermometer			
World Wide Web			

EXERCISE 10 COOKIES AND PIE

INFORMATION GAP Work with a partner. Student B will follow the instructions below. Student A will follow the instructions on page 332.

STUDENT B

- Look at the list of ingredients for chocolate chip cookies. Answer Student A's questions about them.

  EXAMPLE: A: How much flour do you need for the chocolate chip cookies?
  B: Two and a half cups.

Chocolate Chip Cookies

7 ounces of chocolate chips

2½ cups flour
    (= two and a half cups)

3 teaspoons baking powder

1 cup chopped walnuts

1 cup butter

¾ cup sugar
    (= three-quarters of a cup)

¾ cup brown sugar

2 eggs

1 teaspoon vanilla extract

- Now look at the recipe for apple pie. Ask your partner questions to find out how much you need of each ingredient to make apple pie. Write the amounts to complete the recipe.

  EXAMPLE: B: How much flour do you need for the apple pie crust?
  A: Two cups of flour.

Apple Pie

THE CRUST

_____ flour

1 teaspoon salt

⅔ cup shortening
    (= two-thirds of a cup)

_____ cold water

THE FILLING

_____ sugar

_____ flour

½ teaspoon ground cinnamon

½ teaspoon ground nutmeg

a pinch of salt

_____ medium-size apples

_____ butter

Index

This index is for the full and split editions. All entries are in the full book. Entries for Volume A of the split edition are in black. Entries for Volume B are in blue.

Credits *Continued from page xxix*

(bottom right) Alona_s/Fotolia; **369:** (top left) Arcady/Fotolia, (top right) Ambassador806/Fotolia; **370:** nezezon/Fotolia; **371:** Fredy Sujono/Fotolia; **372:** (background) picsfive/Fotolia; **374–375:** doethion/Fotolia; **376:** sean pavone/123RF; **377:** Rigucci/Shutterstock; **381:** (left) merrvas/Fotolia, (right) Dan Breckwoldt/Shutterstock; **385:** (left) Bart Everett/Shutterstock, (right) trekandphoto/Fotolia; **386:** andreykr/Fotolia; **387:** (left) dglavinova/Fotolia, (right) Dmitry Sitin/Fotolia; **388:** TTstudio/Fotolia; **389:** (center) holbox/Shutterstock, (right) Sergii Figurnyi/Fotolia; **391:** R. Gino Santa Maria/Shutterstock; **395:** kasto/Fotolia; **397:** Photographee.eu/Fotolia; **398:** (top) Africa Studio/Fotolia, (bottom) Comaniciu Dan/Shutterstock; **399:** (background) paladin1212/Fotolia; **401:** pathdoc/Fotolia; **405:** Elnur/Shutterstock; **406:** Elnur/Fotolia; **409:** sebra/Fotolia; **411:** txakel/Fotolia; **412:** (top to bottom) prapann/Fotolia, Adeus Buhai/Fotolia, Piotr Pawinski/Fotolia, Murat BAYSAN/Fotolia, bright/Fotolia; **413:** (background) Scisetti Alfio/Fotolia; **415:** mzphoto11/Fotolia; **416:** (center left) Olga Khoroshunova/Fotolia, (center) DK Images, (center right) Elena Shchipkova/123RF, (bottom) Mega Pixel/Shutterstock; **420:** (top left) Eric Isselée/Fotolia, (bottom right) Leysan/Fotolia; **421:** Eric Isselee /123RF; **423:** tristan tan/Shutterstock; **425:** J. Bicking/Shutterstock; **426:** Eric Isselee/Shutterstock; **455:** Mayrum/Fotolia; **458:** (background) B.Melo/Fotolia, (center left) LeNi/Shutterstock, (bottom left) Denise Kappa/Shutterstock

ILLUSTRATION CREDITS

Steve Attoe – pages 180, 204
ElectraGraphics, Inc. – pages (top) 73, 112
Suzanne Mogensen – page 65
Dusan Petricic – page 131
Dave Sullivan – page 101
Gary Torrisi – pages 19, 68, 71, (bottom) 73, 81, 109, 136, 144, 178, 203